"Likely to remain the definitive work for years to come, a biography as industriously researched as it is beautifully and sensitively written—a riveting chronicle." —London *Time Out*

"Spoto has produced an excellent biography. He stays close to his sources, eschews psychological claptrap and idle speculation and is sympathetic without seeming sycophantic. His insights add appreciably to an understanding of Williams's plays and vividly depict the underworld of the playwright's inspiration." —*The Yorkshire Post*

"Spoto shapes a lifetime of obsession, suffering and creative genius into a fast-paced, tightly woven chronicle." —*Library Journal*

"By all known criteria this is an outstanding biography. The author's delicate craftsmanship and impeccable research combine to produce a series of portraits from youth to an age at which Rembrandt so excelled in another medium. An excellent book." —London *Catholic Herald*

"Spoto's warmth and humanity as a biographer seem much greater than that of his subject. This biography is altogether a superior job." —*Sydney Morning Herald*

"The first serious Williams biography since the playwright's death." —*The New York Times Book Review*

"It is to Spoto whom we must turn for dispassionate and reliable analysis of Williams's life and work." —*The Washington Post*

"A landmark biography, rich and sensitive." —*Book Week*

"Spoto tells the story with candor and dignity—his book is yet another example of the kindness of strangers." —*London Times Higher Education Supplement*

"I admire the book's thoroughness: Spoto never loses sight of Williams' genius, and never lets his knowledge of the man's failures lead to condescension." —Edmund White, *The New Republic*

"Spoto's moving and sensitive portrait reveals multiple links between the man and his works." —*Publishers Weekly*

"Remarkable and impressive, a book set in the context of both the times and of Williams's plays." —BBC Book Reviews

"Spoto approaches the subject with a blend of honest reverence for the body of work, a strong knack for the telling detail, and more than a little fascination of the bad times after the talent has failed." —*Atlanta Journal and Constitution*

"Possibly the best biography of an American playwright since Louis Sheaffer's two-volume study of O'Neill. Most accurate, and a full portrait told gently and justly." —*The Los Angeles Times*

"America's greatest playwright has been well served. Spoto has brought a rare dignity to some of the most difficult material imaginable. I stand in awe of his achievement." —Susan Brownmiller

"Surely required reading for all who want to understand the plays." —*Cleveland Plain Dealer*

THE KINDNESS
OF STRANGERS

for Marilyn

with good thoughts,

Donald Spoto

THE KINDNESS OF STRANGERS

The Life of Tennessee Williams

BY

DONALD SPOTO

DA CAPO PRESS • NEW YORK

Library of Congress Cataloging-in-Publication Data

Spoto, Donald, 1941–
   The kindness of strangers: the life of Tennessee Williams / by Donald
Spoto.—1st Da Capo ed.
      p.   cm.
   Originally published: Boston: Little, Brown, 1985.
   Includes bibliographical references and index.
   ISBN 0-306-80805-6 (alk. paper)
   1. Williams, Tennessee, 1911–1983—Biography. 2. Dramatists, American—
20th century—Biography. I. Title.
PS3545.I5365Z836 1997
812′.54—dc21   97-8428
[B]   CIP

First Da Capo Press edition 1997

This Da Capo Press paperback edition of *The Kindness of
Strangers* is an unabridged republication, with minor
emendations, of the edition published in Boston in 1985.
It is reprinted by arrangement with the author.

Published by Da Capo Press, Inc.
A Subsidiary of Plenum Publishing Corporation
233 Spring Street, New York, N.Y. 10013

Manufactured in the United States of America

Designed by Robert G. Lowe

for Irene

"Look, here is some water!
What is to stop me being baptized?"

— *The Acts of the Apostles*

Fame is a bee.
It has a song —
It has a sting —
Ah, too, it has a wing.

— Emily Dickinson

Contents

Acknowledgments

MY LITANY of saints includes many whose kindness and generous assistance facilitated the various stages of my research.

At the University of Texas at Austin, where very large portions of the Tennessee Williams papers and the files of Audrey Wood are catalogued at the Humanities Research Center, I was given gracious help over a considerable period of time by the endlessly cheerful efficiency of Ken Craven. Cathy Henderson, Ellen Dunlap, Pat Fox and Barbara McCandless also came to my aid during various visits to the University.

Gary L. Smith, director of admissions and registrar at the University of Missouri–Columbia, enabled me to find important material and the record of Williams's attendance there. His colleagues, Julie Still in the Rare Books Room and Larry D. Clark in the drama department, were equally helpful in locating relevant data.

At the University of Iowa, Julia Mears arranged for me to obtain Williams's records.

Daniel C. Patri, at the Billy Rose Theatre Collection of the Lincoln Center Library for the Performing Arts, New York, directed me to important materials — among them, the Cheryl Crawford papers and the correspondence between Williams and Brooks Atkinson.

The director of personnel at the International Shoe Company, St. Louis, is Paul E. Nagel; he helped me to untangle employment records and to fix important times in Tennessee Williams's life in the 1930s.

Robert Knutsen, in Special Collections at the University of Southern California's Doheny Library, made it easy for me to work in the Warner Brothers files on films based on Williams plays. And at Metro-Goldwyn-Mayer, Herbert Nusbaum offered his usual friendly welcome and cleared time and space for me to study Williams's period at M-G-M.

Walter Kerr kindly allowed me to quote from his letters to Tennessee Williams and made several perceptive additional remarks.

At New Directions Books, James Laughlin directed me to Griselda

Ohannesian, who opened the Williams files and enabled me to follow the history of the plays' published versions.

Harry Rasky and Patrice Brun, at the Canadian Broadcasting Corporation, made it possible for me to see Mr. Rasky's documentary film celebrating Williams's life and career.

The Goodman Theatre, Chicago, was important to Williams in his late career. I am grateful to Gregory Mosher, Steve Scott, Ann Cusack and Susan Padveen for welcoming me to their offices, for providing a complete record of their Williams productions and correspondence, and for an extremely cordial encouragement.

At Florida Keys Community College, I was warmly received by William Seeker, president; Hal Massey, provost; Maria J. Soule, librarian; and Linda Jones, director of public relations.

Pat Castro and Jody Rodriguez, at the Monroe County Court House, Key West, helped me to locate important files and records.

Personal interviews provided an incalculably rich field of material. First and most important in this regard was Dakin Williams, my subject's brother, who shared important family memories, facts, anecdotes and impressions, and who generously assigned me permission to quote from the letters, journals and other writings of his mother, Edwina Dakin Williams.

Meade Roberts, who collaborated on two major screenplays based on works by Tennessee Williams, and who knew him and his social and professional circle during very important years, was an incomparably generous guide all through the preparation of this book. His memory is as keen as his literary sensibility, and he not only gave me firsthand accounts of important events and dates — he also guided me to other people and places I might otherwise have missed. I owe him my gratitude for much that is special material here.

Jill Krementz, one of the artists who has raised photography from a craft to an art, generously opened her collection of Tennessee Williams photographs to me. Her generosity, her enthusiasm, and her creative contributions grace the cover and the inserts of this book.

Invaluable information, reminiscences and reflections were offered by these generous people who knew and worked with Tennessee Williams, and to them I am very grateful indeed: Eve Adamson, Richard Alfieri, Craig Anderson and Elena Azuola, Robert Anderson, Eloise Sheldon Armen, Bonnie Sue Arp, Don Bachardy, Hermione Baddeley, Marji Bank, Bill Barnes, Barbara Baxley, Paul Bigelow, Fritz Bultman, Sandy

Campbell, Jay Leo Colt, Elsworth and Virginia Conkle, Ellis Conkle, Frank Corsaro, Cheryl Crawford, Olive Deering, Anthony Dexter, Mitch Douglas, Mildred Dunnock, Margaret Foresman, Robert Fox, Muriel Bultman Francis, Lucy Freeman, Mary Garrett, Bill Glavin, David Gregory, Thomas Griffin, Chuck Ingebritsen, Christopher Isherwood, Burl Ives, Scott Jaeck, Elia Kazan, Steven Kunes, the Rev. Joseph LeRoy, S.J., Tony Lincoln, Joseph Losey, Elmer Lower, Charles McDaniel, Joseph L. Mankiewicz, Theodore Mann, Anne Meacham, Taylor Mead, Sylvia Miles, Paul Morrissey, Gregory Mosher, Johnny Nicholson, Frederick Nicklaus, Carlo and Mirella Panarello, Lester Persky, Gene Persson, Wendell Phillips, Les Podewell, Sheldon Posnock, Irving Rapper, Donovan Rhynsburger, Pancho Rodriguez, Ned Rorem, Alfred Ryder, Marian Seldes, Gloria Hope Sher, Edwin Sherin, Sylvia Sidney, Stephen Silverman, Jane Smith, Maureen Stapleton, Rachel Stephens, Vassilis Voglis, George Whitmore and Donald Windham.

A variety of assistances, information and cooperation was also forthcoming from Catherine Arnott, Victoria Bacon, Lansing Bailey, John Baisi and Norman Schneider and the staff at Copy-Line, Inc., Stephen Banker, Eric Bentley, David Blum, Andreas Brown, Hume Cronyn, Joseph H. Fulton, Harold Gefsky, Richard A. Holmes, Judith Katz, Richard L. Kennedy, Ernest Lehman, Lyle Leverich, Elaine Lorillard, David and Helen Loth, Robert M. Luck, Michael Mattil, Patrick Merla, Colleen Mohyde, Julie Haydon Nathan, Gerald Pinciss, Sidney Porcelain, Cynthia Reed, A. L. Rowse, Murray Sargent, Renee Schwartz, Alan Shapiro, Sam Staggs, Mike Steen, Jane Sylvester, Piero Taverna, Samuel Taylor, Adrian and Andrea Turner and Gore Vidal.

In New Orleans, I was welcomed to Loyola University by the Rev. Ernest Ferlita, S.J., who helped me find several important contacts. In the same city, W. Kenneth Holditch and Cynthia Ratcliffe guided me, with their superb knowledge as scholarly guides, through the French Quarter. Kate Schweppe Moldawer was helpful in Key West. And in St. Louis Greg Young offered considerable assistance on several occasions.

Tennessee Williams's first New York production was offered by the legendary Drama Workshop at the New School for Social Research. By a happy coincidence, that has been my academic home-base since 1975, and the encouragement and affectionate collegiality I receive there is a great boon in my life. Dean Allen Austill redeems the pristine meaning of his title: he is a perceptive administrator, a patient colleague and a good friend. Lewis Falb, who guides the humanities division at the New

School, displayed constant, cheerful interest in the day-to-day growth of the manuscript. And among my students, a number helped me to track down arcane materials, rare books and articles and miscellanea: Sylvia Brown, Diane Churchill, Jane Conlon, Leonard Feigenblatt, Chris Fleetwood, Louise Fox, John Freitas, Arthur Green, Emily Harrow, Wendy Kafka, Elizabeth Kenney, Abby Kessler, Sheila Knapp, Richard Longmore, Raul Martinez, Renee McMichael, Diane Outciral, Margot E. Quinn, Anthony Sacramone, Kelley Shields, John Sirabella, Vicki Stamm, Lauren Stevens, Allen Thompson, Patricia Weber and Patricia Wilkes.

My literary agent, Elaine Markson, is not only a devoted representative — she is also a loyal friend. To her and to her associates, Geri Thoma, Raymond Bongiovanni and Elizabeth Kohen, I owe thanks for as much warm support as professional expertise. And in London, there is Deborah Rogers, who looks after my professional interests in Great Britain with similar acuity and affection. Just as I am grateful to Elaine for my happy union with Little, Brown and Company, so much I acknowledge Deborah for introducing me to The Bodley Head and editor Maureen Rissik.

James T. Caroscio, M.D., who is a gifted physician and an attentive friend, supplied important information on the history and chemistry of drugs and drug therapy. Jerry Bradley has helped me, all through my writing, to keep in order many practical aspects of daily life. And John Darretta again showed his loyal and devoted friendship — not least of all in his discussions with me about some fine points of literary history.

Irene Mahoney (to whom I dedicate this book) is a cherished friend for over thirty-five years, and Ned Mullaney for over twenty-five. No words can express my gratitude for their constancy and their love; they do my life more good than they know.

And how to thank William Phillips? I am of all writers the most fortunate in having so fine an editor at Little, Brown and Company. There are important points in this book that owe their sharper focus to his counsel and their final shaping to his intelligence, sensitivity and perception. As if that were not enough to be grateful for, I am also blessed with his friendship and confidence. As that fact and these pages of acknowledgments disclose, life is very rich indeed.

D.S.

New York
June 28, 1984

Preface

TENNESSEE WILLIAMS first entered my life in the spring of 1956, when I was a high school student in New Rochelle, New York. Our drama club had just finished a boisterous production of George M. Cohan's comic mystery *Seven Keys to Baldpate,* and my performance as a politician of questionable morality had sealed my decision to become an actor. The director then held auditions for the coming autumn production. He had settled on *The Glass Menagerie,* and I won the role of Tom — who, we were told, was really Tennessee Williams himself. With all the passionate eagerness of a fifteen-year-old, I enrolled in Saturday morning acting classes at the American Academy of Dramatic Arts in New York.

By the time school resumed in September, I had memorized the role, only to learn that the drama coach had departed to pursue a career in politics and the production of *The Glass Menagerie* was canceled by the principal. But also by this time, I had discovered the strange and tender world of Tennessee Williams and his work, and I was following news of the theatre religiously.

During the next several years, Williams was discussed more and more as a shocking writer of difficult and severe plays: *Cat on a Hot Tin Roof* had been controversial enough (with its implications of homosexuality and impotence), but it was followed by *Orpheus Descending* (which dealt with sexual exploitation and ended in violence), *Suddenly Last Summer* (which added cannibalism to all those earlier motifs) and then *Sweet Bird of Youth* (which seemed to continue the horrors, with the characters' drug and sex addictions, venereal disease and castration). Tennessee Williams and his work were always newsworthy, and it seemed that not a month passed without an article or interview in magazines and papers about the playwright and his social and professional world. We heard a great deal about Williams, but we learned very little, for interviews were restricted to safe topics and always subject to the heavy censorship requirements and the prevalent fractious moralism of the 1950s.

All that changed in the following years, by which time I had prudently become more realistic about my theatrical ambitions and had developed other interests. In the 1960s and 1970s, my enthusiasm for his work persisted, even as his career was in an odd, dark eclipse. But he was still a news item; indeed, if his plays were no longer considered to have the same wild alchemy of the sordid and the sensitive, he now did. He replaced his work as the talk of the town, or at least of the television talk show. When his *Memoirs* were published in 1975 (and a selection of his letters to his old friend Donald Windham soon after), the trend of attention to sensational aspects of his life continued. What had been unmentionable in the 1950s — that Williams was homosexual — was by 1970 all that many people (and sometimes even he) considered interesting. This corresponded to a new climate of curiosity and tolerance (if not exactly a warm acceptance) about the varieties of sexual preference in America.

But the basic problem persisted. Whereas earlier we read a great deal about Williams but learned little partly because of *silence* on private matters, in the 1970s we read and heard a great deal about Williams but learned little because of *emphasis* on private matters. *Memoirs* provided a neat smoke screen, for the details of social and sexual life were really not intimate: they did not disclose the person. To state that one is heterosexual (or not) provides no information on the depth or quality of life, after all — we know nothing, from such an admission, about whether one kicks the cat, is loyal to friends, pays taxes, is concerned for the poor, is capable of fidelity and devotion, or reflects on the wonder and mystery of the human condition. *Memoirs,* I had discovered at once, told us very little indeed about Tennessee Williams's deepest life, the logic of his work, and the place of that work in his hierarchy of values.

By the time of his death, in February 1983, I had gathered substantial material. Those supervising the disposition of his estate told me that there would be no decision on an authorized biography — news which neither disappointed nor deterred me, since the freedom available to an unrestricted writer had already become clear during my writing of Alfred Hitchcock's life. And so I undertook this book.

My research took me from the places he lived to the people he knew, from the theatres and studios where he worked to the vast depositories of his letters and papers at the University of Texas at Austin. I soon learned the astonishing inaccuracies of fact, the misrepresentations Williams was responsible for, the egregious omissions of important events and people in his public statements and published disclosures. Great dramatist that he was, he seemed unable to resist the temptation to alter the facts, the chronology, the characters in his own life — to give them, in the recounting, more color or a neater structure than reality provided.

Scores of interviews and months of study in private and public collections of journals, letters and collections of theatre material began to reveal clearer contours of the man's life and character. Elia Kazan, who directed four of his plays, was on the mark when he said to me, "Tennessee's life is in his work." That is not too schematic a summary of the remarkable cross-hatching of art and life which emerges in a consideration of Williams, and it helps to explain the lack of congruence between *his* accounts of his life and the dimensions of reality. What Williams wrote of his friend and fellow playwright William Inge can be said of himself: his life and career and search comprised "a drama as fine and admirable as any of the ones he has given, one after another."

Tennessee Williams's creative legacy is perhaps far vaster than many of his admirers realize: a complete catalog would have to include more than twenty-five full-length plays, more than forty short plays, a dozen produced (and unproduced) screenplays and an opera libretto. These have been translated into at least twenty-seven languages, including Tamil, Welsh, Marathi and Hindi. In addition, there are two novels, a novella, more than sixty short stories, more than one hundred poems, an autobiography, a published volume of letters, introductions to plays and books by others, and occasional pieces and reviews. He gave new meaning to the word prolific.

He also provided scholars, students and journalists with a rich field to explore. In his bibliographical handbook (*The Critical Reputation of Tennessee Williams: a reference guide,* Boston: G. K. Hall, 1983), John S. McCann lists more than 2500 articles on Williams published (mostly in the United States) between 1939 and 1981. And Drewey Wayne Gunn (in *Tennessee Williams: A Bibliography,* Metuchen: The Scarecrow Press, 1980) catalogs over fifty theses and dissertations, four hundred critical articles and books, eighty interviews and thirty-three volumes of collected reviews of Williams's work. I have consulted most of this material; little of it deals with his life, but anything that suggests leads or correspondences had to be pursued.

* * *

The story of Tennessee Williams's life, I think, reveals him as a man more disturbing, more dramatic, richer and more wonderful than any character he ever created. His sensitivities and sympathies were broad, his experience of loneliness and loss made him responsive to others' lives. And he succeeded, remarkably often, in translating those sympathies and cries of emotional solidarity with the wounded into the stuff of great art — *The Glass Menagerie, Summer and Smoke, A Streetcar Named Desire, Cat on a Hot Tin Roof, Suddenly Last Summer, The Night of the Iguana.*

There is something mysterious about the chemistry of that creativity. He was subject to periods of clinical depression but not to philosophical or spiritual inquiry. He was capable of extreme acts of generosity to friends and lovers, and then he could suddenly retreat from everyone into a private, self-absorbed world, from which he might emerge asking others to respond to his various needs. His life was a sine curve of actions and attitudes that at their worst inevitably hurt him more than anyone, and that at their best delighted and enriched others more than himself. He depended not only on the loyalty and commitment of others in order to pass his days with some order and affection, and to enable him to work; he also seemed to rely on frequent excursions to the frontiers of illness, madness and what (in *The Night of the Iguana*) he called "the unlighted sides" of human nature.

His connections with his art, with his life, and with other people were both loving and selfish, involved and coolly detached, tender and brutal; in other words, he was a human being. The paradox resulted in a body of writing that often succeeded better than he did. His work is a series of variations on the great emotional cycles of his own tortured life. The biographer cannot judge the final truth in his subject's soul, he can only assess the meanings that subject seems to have discerned in life. "I hope that I have been able to contribute an understanding about people," Tennessee Williams said not long before his death. No teller of his difficult life could aim higher.

A Note on the Published Plays of Tennessee Williams:

There are substantial differences between variant versions of plays by Tennessee Williams. The so-called acting versions, published mostly by Dramatists Play Service, often contain major alterations from the original play *as performed,* and from the versions he wished to represent him in bound book form — published by New Directions. For the sake of consistency, my citations are drawn from *The Theatre of Tennessee Williams,* the seven-volume New Directions set (1971–1981) which the playwright intended to represent a more or less final record of his plays, at least until he might, later, have another look and make some emendations on notepaper at home. As recently as four months before his death, he was rewriting scenes from twenty-year-old plays.

Chapter One

IN THE SHADOW
OF THE CHURCH
(1911–1928)

I've literally grown up right in the very
shadow of the Episcopal church. At Pass
Christian and Natchez, Biloxi, Gulfport, Port
Gibson, Columbus and Glorious Hill!

— Miss Collins, in *Portrait of a Madonna*

COLUMBUS, a town in eastern Mississippi and the seat of Lowndes County, lies on the Tombigbee River. Originally settled with the unlikely name of Possum Town in 1817, it was noted chiefly for cotton trading, and boats heavy with bales crowded its dock for decades. During the Civil War it was a fiercely Confederate stronghold, and in fact the first observance of Confederate Decoration Day was held in Columbus in 1866. Much of the town was spared the destruction of the war and its aftermath, and by the turn of the twentieth century many antebellum homes stood unchanged. In 1884, Mississippi State College for Women — the first state-supported university for women in America — enrolled its first students on a former Columbus estate.

In the early 1900s, life in the town conformed to the characteristics, principles and practices of Southern social philosophy. Although the majority of the population was black and legally free from slavery, the tradition of white supremacy prevailed: the country-gentry ideal flourished under families of mostly English, Irish and northern European ancestry. Town life still seemed more rural than urban; the pace was unhurried; the belief in a fixed, divinely ordained social order was taken for granted, as were stability, a complex system of manners and etiquette, the art of hospitality and a highly developed sense of the genteel life — to these may be added all the quaint customs of refinement and delicacy familiar to readers and moviegoers over the last several decades. Jealous of its traditions and deeply nostalgic for the values of the Christian home, Southern towns like Columbus distrusted Northern intellectuals and politicians, and the people were proud of the Confederate tradition of bravery and independence. The Northern ideals of progress, material advancement, the mingling of diverse cultures, freedom and mobility — these were held suspect in a way of life that invested considerable energy and talent in sustaining the values of a cherished and (it was thought) gentler era.

Just as the extreme forms of politeness and courtesy were the daily, external signs of moral righteousness, so was local social life arranged round the front parlor, the school, the church hall. Neighbors and even friends regularly prefixed "Miss" or "Master" to others' first names in ordinary conversation. Training in manners and the social graces, in the proper gestures, the correct posture and gait, the way a lady held a wrist-fan, the way a gentleman bowed at the waist, the colors of everyday dress: all were measurements of life. Crudeness was reason for social ostracism, and the imitation of Victorian manners paralleled the importation of Victorian furniture. Georgian mansions also reflected the South's luxuriant, sometimes opulent idolization of Old World gentility and the veneration of style and charm. And although the permanence of this life was questioned by a few before World War I, the enduring power of the Southern-Victorian morality was considered as fixed as the stars. Not sternly ascetical (like the New England Puritan), this ethic nevertheless encouraged an almost impossible and highly theatrical prudery. In the North there had been a tradition of simplicity, industriousness, sensual denial; but in the South (as far back as the time of the great New England orators and long afterward) manner *was* morality. To the description of that moral code — its history and influence, its shifts and its upheavals — Mississippi writers as different as William Faulkner, Eudora Welty and Tennessee Williams often dedicated themselves. Great artists that they became — as their talents transcended parochialism — they nevertheless mixed the colors of their literary vision from the same social palette. And the life they described, like the life they first knew, was one of a strange paradox: prudery and delicacy coexisted with a languid, florid indulgence in the sweetness of detail.

In 1905, Reverend Walter Edwin Dakin became pastor of St. Paul's Episcopal Church in Columbus. That year, the town listed no more than four thousand in its census (virtually none of them Jewish or Roman Catholic), and the minister's social charm, his elegant manner and his serious, hardworking wife and lovely twenty-one-year-old daughter favorably impressed the parish and the entire community. Reverend Dakin (born in Ohio in 1857) came from a family that had left Wales in the 1600s and settled in the Midwest. He had been a Quaker and a teacher before deciding to study for the Episcopalian ministry. This branch of American Protestantism he apparently selected because the bishopric — to which he always aspired but which eluded him — held a promise of glamour and grandeur. From the time of his ordination, in 1895, to his appointment at St. Paul's, Columbus, ten years later, Reverend Dakin — restless, always eager for a pleasanter town and a more comfortable rectory — had moved with his family more than half a dozen times. His taste for luxury remained unsatisfied.

His wife, the former Rosina Otte (called Rose from childhood), had a very different personality. The daughter of German immigrants, she had been born in Buffalo, New York. Her parents then moved west, where, like her future husband, she too had been raised in the simplicity of rural Ohio towns. Her strict upbringing had been reinforced by several years at a Catholic boarding school in Youngstown, where the Ursuline nuns confirmed her in the virtues of thrift, self-denial, piety and humility. She almost became a Catholic herself before the irresistible and handsome Walter Dakin sealed several years of friendship with a wedding ring. In 1884, after they had been married several years, their only child, Edwina Estelle, was born at the Otte home in Marysville, Ohio.

While her husband completed his education and won a teacher's license in the late 1880s, Rose Dakin kept their home, helped with his research and sustained with remarkable grace his compulsive moves. Pampered and indulged by her father, Edwina flourished in the towns of Ohio and Tennessee and Mississippi to which they moved, while her mother worked harder than ever to supplement the family income. Eventually Mrs. Dakin took in laundry and sewing and gave piano lessons so that her husband could complete his studies for the ministry and so that her daughter would not be denied treats.

By the time Edwina was ready for high school, in 1897, the Dakins had returned for a time to Ohio, and she attended the Harcourt Place Seminary, Gambier, a school for wealthier young ladies to which she was admitted on scholarship. The studies were not burdensome, the social life was busy, and the minister's attractive daughter sang in the school chorus, danced at musicales and local parties, and enjoyed every advantage her father's status, her mother's hard work and her own winsome charm bestowed. She had a score of male admirers from Kenyon College — they were termed "gentlemen callers" in the early 1900s — and from the local military academy and the theological school. "I was rarely required," she later admitted about her early life, "to do anything I did not want to do."

With Reverend Dakin's constant uprooting of his wife and daughter to accept one improved position after another, it was natural that Edwina's social life also lacked stability. Between 1901 and 1905, while they went from Ohio to Tennessee to various towns in Mississippi (Port Gibson, Natchez, Vicksburg), she recorded in her diaries no less than forty-five young men for whom she harbored some romantic feelings. At Gambier, she was all aflutter over Richard Lodge before shifting her attention to H. G. Fitzgerald, then to Louis Simon, Arthur Aubrey, Rowland Balfour and John McKim. "I danced with a lot of men," she noted plainly after one party.

In Tennessee, there were many more whose names she recorded along with brief commentaries ("Mr. Frederick Statt has grown to be *very* good-looking!"); and in Mississippi she wrote of her special attraction to Messrs. Huston, Gorman, Martin, Devoe, Henry, Billie, Waller, Morrison, Davidson, Connor and Bagby. Two young men (memorialized simply as Warren and Harry) outdid themselves in sending her little lyrics. She knew them only casually, it seems, but their poems were pasted in her scrapbooks and bordered with brief notations about their suitability as gentlemen callers. By the time she was twenty, she was expert in all the social arts and none of the domestic, and her beauty and a fine singing voice might have enabled her to fulfill what she wrote in her diary was her "secret ambition, to become an actress, a musical comedy star." But for a respectable young lady in the early years of this century that was not a reasonable hope; her participation always remained on the level of amateur theatricals. Her greatest performance was perhaps that of the archetypal "Southern belle," a role the Ohio-born Edwina played so well that it finally became her life; with a convert's fervor, she more than adapted to her Southern homes and habits — she virtually erased from her speech and manner anything that was not appropriate to the Southern Victorian maiden.

By autumn of 1905 the Dakins were involved in all the church and civic activities of Columbus, and at once Edwina — now an eligible twenty-one — attracted attention. "I remember watching her," a neighbor wrote years later, "as her skirts flounced about her ankles, thinking to myself that as soon as I was eighteen I would have long skirts too. She never knew me, but she was the minister's daughter and known to many that she did not know." The local newspaper recorded that "Miss Dakin will be quite an acquisition to our younger social set." Just so, for at once a tornado of attention swept round her:

"Mr. Lide called in the afternoon," she wrote in her diary. "We went to the ice cream parlour, returning in time to see Mr. Harris, Mr. Peyton and Mr. Hardy, who made an engagement to take me to the dance. After

they all left, Mr. Carr and myself went for a drive." Her mother, meanwhile, worked twenty-hour days, giving herself to every parish, school
and community club that sought her time and energy. She continued to
offer music lessons as well, for her husband's compensation was only one
hundred dollars a month. He had social prestige, influence, respect —
even admiration from the people of Columbus, who appreciated that this
Northerner had studied theology at the University of the South, at
Sewance, Tennessee, and the hint of a drawl modified his accent.

   In early 1906, when she was appearing in an amateur production of
The Mikado in Columbus, a friend introduced Edwina Dakin to Cornelius Coffin Williams. Known to friends and co-workers as "C.C.," he had
come to town from Memphis, where he worked for the telephone company in what might later be termed a paralegal capacity. She called him
Cornelius from that day forward.
   Cornelius Williams had attended for one year the University of Tennessee's law school, but voluntary service in the Spanish-American War
intervened. Demobilized as an officer, he did not resume his former plans
but took a position with the Cumberland Telephone Company, and
when he met Miss Edwina he had come to Columbus to plead a case. The
evening he saw *The Mikado* began an eighteen-month courtship, sometimes interrupted for many weeks. At such times, Edwina entertained
other young men in the rectory parlor. Unwilling to curtail her social life
and well aware that most of her friends were already married (if not also
mothers) by the age of twenty-one, she continued the kind of acceptable
social behavior that coexisted with intense sexual prudery. Relations between the sexes were rarely more than innocent flirtations; sensual indulgence meant an extra lemonade after a late dance, or ice cream on a warm
evening, or strolling without white gloves in August. Each era finds its
own pleasures.
   Although the Dakins saw little of Cornelius Williams at first, he
seemed to be an acceptable serious suitor for their daughter, for he was
from a Tennessee family with a first-rate pedigree. Five years older than
Edwina (and therefore, they presumed, more mature), he had been born
in 1879 in Knoxville. His father, Thomas Lanier Williams, traced his ancestry back to French Huguenots, to musicians at the English courts, and
to politicians and soldiers in North Carolina and Tennessee. His mother,
Isabel Coffin, was descended from Virginia settlers, Tennessee statesmen,
and at least one poet: her uncle was Tristram Coffin, who is linked to the

development of Nantucket Island. While her husband's family listed Tennessee senators, hers boasted at least three governors. Before Cornelius's birth, Isabel and Thomas Lanier Williams had two daughters, Ella and Isabel. Then, in 1884, when the boy was five, his mother died. Cornelius and Isabel (always called Belle) were raised in the quietly rigid Rogersville Synodical College, a Tennessee seminary the boy found overwhelmingly oppressive. After attending a series of boarding schools where he earned a reputation as a hell-raiser, given to card-playing, fighting, boisterous high spirits and (from a remarkably early age) drinking home brew he and buddies filched from neighbors. The pedigree was still there but — perhaps because his youth lacked precisely the decencies of family life — the polish was not.

Nevertheless, Cornelius at twenty-seven — after military service and responsible employment — presented a handsome, courtly air when he called in 1906 and 1907 in Columbus, and when he asked for Edwina's hand, the Reverend nodded approval. "Many men have said I love you," Edwina wrote in her diary on June 1, 1907, "but only three said Will you marry me. I will marry one next Monday. Finis. Goodbye." And with this curious adieu to her maidenhood, she exchanged vows with the Tennessee telephone man in a quiet ceremony in her father's church on June 2. They departed at once for Gulfport.

The details of the early married life of Cornelius and Edwina Dakin Williams, to 1909, may perhaps never be entirely clear, but this much is certain: pregnant with their first child, Edwina fled her husband and returned to the rectory in Columbus. Apparently it was not only work that kept Cornelius in the southern part of Mississippi: the memories of the Tennessee seminary he had lived in as a boy were so unpleasant that he refused to live in another clerical shadow. He visited regularly, however — a few days each month — and when Edwina gave birth to a girl on November 17, 1909, they agreed on a name: she was called Rose Isabel, after both their mothers. Soon afterward, he returned to his job with the telephone company, traveling up and down the state on their behalf, and Edwina remained — permanently, it seemed — with her parents. To no one's surprise, Grandmother Dakin added nursemaid duties to her busy schedule, and Edwina quickly resumed an active social life. When an imminent visit by Cornelius was announced, she was indifferent. The marriage between the rowdy traveler and the pampered Southern belle had clearly been a terrible mistake.

After one of his longer visits to Columbus, however, Edwina received two pieces of news: a letter from her husband, that he was now selling men's shoes and clothing along the Delta; and a note from her physician, confirming her suspicions that she was expecting another child. During the late fall of 1910, Cornelius's visits to Columbus became markedly less pleasant, for he returned to the rectory several evenings drunk and incoherent, and there was talk of card games in bawdy houses at the edge of town. The Dakins pretended to take no notice. Their daughter was embarrassed, angry and sometimes frightened.

On Palm Sunday — March 26, 1911 — Edwina Dakin Williams was preparing to attend services in her father's church when she collapsed in her bedroom and was rushed to a little clinic nearby. A few hours later, she gave birth to a boy, whom the Reverend soon christened Thomas Lanier Williams (after the child's paternal grandfather, who had died in 1908). Tommy Williams insisted on "Tom" by the time he was ten. A few old friends (or new ones, under special circumstances) called him Tom even after 1939, when the first story published under the name Tennessee Williams appeared.

Almost immediately after her return to the rectory on South Second Street in Columbus, Edwina engaged a black servant to help care for her two children and to see to the shopping and cooking. The young woman's name was Ozzie, and for several years she went wherever the Dakins, their daughter and grandchildren went. Ozzie tried, unsuccessfully, to teach Miss Edwina to cook, but the only item her aristocratic mistress learned was angel food cake. By this time, the Dakins noticed, their daughter — perhaps to offset the rumors of her husband's misconduct — began to affect a somewhat grand, slightly imperious manner. She was also a nonstop talker who allowed no more than a second of silence in any gathering.

By the end of 1913, Reverend Dakin — eager to be on the move again, anxious for a slightly better position in a more prestigious community — had secured a pastorate in Nashville, Tennessee, at the Church of the Advent. They remained there almost two years, when they moved to a church in Canton, Mississippi. That was the Reverend's shortest tenure, however, and by Christmas 1915 they settled in western Mississippi — in Clarksdale, a pleasant town where the family thrived and even Cornelius's swaggering visits seemed tolerable. In the heart of the Delta, on the Sunflower River, Clarksdale was an agricultural processing and distribution center near the spot where, tradition has it, De Soto discovered the Mississippi River. Life here was a stencil of gracious living in the Old South.

In early 1916, Rose was six and Tommy almost five, and they had known few companions except for one another. "She was an ideal playmate," Tennessee Williams said many years later. "She was very charming, very beautiful. She had an incredible imagination. We were so close to each other, we had no need of others." The psychological affinity between brother and sister became so intense, in fact, that when Rose had a cold, or tonsillitis, or mumps, Tommy was convinced he, too, was ill. The two were called "the couple" by Ozzie, as they caught lightning bugs during summer evenings and wandered through the neighborhood and the town's parks alone for hours. "I was a gentle little boy who liked to play with girls," Williams said, and no girl was ever more important to him, then or later, than his sister, Rose.

Their mother, meanwhile, enjoyed the privileges to which Reverend Dakin's status entitled her: deference, prestige, social invitations. Because of Ozzie, Edwina was released from most household duties, and although she was committed to parish club activities, she devoted part of each day to Rose and Tommy. She noticed, from his earliest years, that her son had unusual powers of concentration: "Other children would pick a flower, then carelessly throw it away," she wrote later, "but Tom would stand peering into the heart of the flower as though trying to discover the secret of its life." He paid attention, too, when she read stories and plays, when she sang hymns, recited English and Scottish ballads she had learned in school, and acted out tall tales, the wild adventures of folk heroes like Paul Bunyan, Davy Crockett, Annie Oakley, and Johnny Appleseed.

There were other stories for the children, too. Reverend and Mrs. Dakin knew the Bible stories, and the children heard them at church and at home. The holy men of antiquity, from Moses to Paul, were presented as crusading message-bearers; Jesus was a refuge and a healer; angels guarded sleeping children. Dogma was minimized, comfort maximized. Again unlike the New England Puritans, religion was not so much a challenge as it was a caress. It was a nice thing for nice people, but it had its place and was not permitted too wide a field of activity. God and Country were the enduring realities, to be sure, but President Wilson they could see.

If the Dakins provided uplifting stories, Ozzie was a dramatic competitor. She not only sang spirituals, hymns and African lullabies to Rose and Tommy, she also regaled them with the rich store of black and In-

dian folklore — much of it free invention at every telling, all of it colorful, some of it violent. Ghosts and gremlins were summoned up before
them, and she was convinced there was the same degree of "de debbil" in
everyone as there was of salt in sweat. Ozzie's warnings about demons
and damnation were a neat counterpoint to the majestic sweep of the
hymnal and the Book of Common Prayer. Along with chicken pies and
cornbread, Ozzie fed the children wonderfully spun tales about this
world and the other. Edwina, puzzled when Tommy remained digging in
the backyard for several hours one day, laughed when he said that he was
"diggin' to de debbil."

Life in Clarksdale was not unrealistically happy, however, and there
were the usual childhood ailments. Measles, chicken pox, a slight case of
fever, a skin infection alternately kept Rose out of school. Then, by 1917,
when she was ready to attend, Tom fell prey to a round of illnesses that
kept him out of first grade. Most frightening was a bout of diphtheria
that was followed by a severe kidney infection. He was confined to bed
for so long that his muscles were weakened, and by the time he seemed
well enough to go out he was unable to walk more than a few steps. As
late as his seventh birthday, in 1918, he could not sustain the pace of
other, more active, children. His earlier term at a nursery school had been
disastrous in any case: when his mother left the schoolroom he threw a
tantrum that was very nearly a fit, and the teacher, alarmed, insisted that
Edwina remain for several weeks.

But other children's chatter, and the teacher's stories, could not engage
Tommy Williams's attention for very long. His grandparents' Bible
stories, Ozzie's fables and folklore, even Edwina's ballads, were far more
dramatic. At night, when his mother came to his room, she often heard
bits and pieces of stories he was making up, alone and aloud, in the room
he shared with his sister.

"It was around this time that I began to invent private, solitary amusements," he told an interviewer years later. The games and the stories
lengthened during his illnesses, and during the long period of recuperation when he could not walk. Edwina then ministered to him night and
day. "She never let him forget that she saved his life," according to Lucy
Freeman, a writer who worked with Edwina on her memoirs later. "It
was probably the first great dramatic performance he saw, her rendition
of his childhood illnesses and her nursing duties." By this time — late
1917 — Ozzie had departed, leaving a legacy of folklore and an unwit-
ting endorsement of the prevailing class system.

Even when he recovered from his long confinement, Tom found that the fundamentally happy life of the minister's family occasionally knew the dreadful as well as the delicate. The cloistered atmosphere of the rectory was balanced by a wave of terrible viruses that took the lives of dozens of parishioners. "I got a more intimate view of human problems that year," Tennessee Williams said later. "I remember my grandfather's visits to deathbeds."

"Grandfather was quite a character in Mississippi during those early years," according to the Williams's third child, Walter Dakin, who was born in 1919. "He was a very selfish person, very self-important and very much a social snob. He wouldn't associate with Baptists, for example, or with Methodists, or with people who came from a denomination that didn't have bishops. He was so lordly that when people got to know him they often called him the Bish — 'here comes the Bish!' But he was wonderful to have around in a social situation, because he was such an extrovert. His taste for life's luxuries was checked by Grandmother's frugality. She was more reserved, more serious — maybe because of her German upbringing. And she was a natural aristocrat. Mother told me that whenever Tom thought he was misbehaving as a child, he would ask, 'What would Grand think of this?' The possibility of her displeasure would haunt him. She was his conscience and his angel, and she sewed up money in letters and gift packages for him all his life."*

There was not a great deal of money for the household in Clarksdale, but there was a fine rectory with spacious rooms, a bright, friendly town full of flowers and parks and polite, deferential neighbors. "They had more than money," as Tennessee Williams's younger brother said later. "They had the status of being the minister's family. Tom's life was gentle and genteel, and Rose was the little princess, the minister's granddaughter, the apple of everyone's eye. They were like a royal family, even though they weren't obviously rich."

On young Tommy Williams, however, no influence was stronger than his mother's. She was a beautiful, strong-willed, socially ambitious woman who observed every prescription of Southern etiquette and charm. Aristocratic manners were equated with profound virtue; delicacy of diction and a studied poise had almost religious significance; hard work was a man's solemn duty. And sex (when it was mentioned at all, which was about as often as a July snowfall in Mississippi) was a man's

* Rose Dakin (always called "Grand" by the Williams family) is celebrated in two of Tennessee Williams's most deeply felt short stories, "The Angel in the Alcove" and "Grand."

mysterious reward and a woman's grim obligation: such was God's inscrutable plan for filling the earth.

In early summer 1918, Edwina Williams returned to the rectory in Clarksdale one evening and quietly told her mother that she was pregnant a third time. The news might have been received more happily if it had not coincided with another imminent change in her life. Cornelius had won a managerial position with the Friedman-Shelby branch of the International Shoe Company, based in St. Louis. They were to move at once, for now he anticipated a more stable family life, and he intended to be a father to the new baby in the day-to-day routines that he had missed when Rose and Tom were toddlers. The Dakins encouraged the move, although Edwina doubted the depth of Cornelius's abilities to live up to his promises. She knew he was a private drinker, an open gambler, and a covert womanizer.

And so in July the rector's daughter and her husband and their two children took a frightfully hot train journey north to St. Louis. From the moment of their arrival, the relocation had a devastating effect on the children, whose gentle, ordered parochial life was at once replaced by a cruder, noisier industrial atmosphere ill-suited both to Miss Edwina's social aspirations and to her children's physical frailty. Where Mississippi life had been colorful and close to nature, St. Louis seemed at first merely crowded and coarse; where the warmer attitudes of the Delta softened life and speech, St. Louis seemed all hectic business.

"The changes must have been shocking for them," reflected the biographer and social historian David Loth, who was born and raised in St. Louis during the same years. "Although it was originally a French fur-trading post and a major trading port before the development of Kansas City, it had a busy factory life, a rapidly expanding intellectual life, and a cosmopolitan spirit that the more insulated Southerner would have found disorienting. There was a pronounced German spirit to St. Louis, also — there were at least two German-language daily newspapers for the benefit of the German immigrant population, and Joseph Pulitzer began as a reporter for one of them.

"But it was also, by the time of World War I, the fourth largest city in America, after New York, Chicago and Philadelphia, and it had a population of about 600,000 people — many of whom worked in factories. Cornelius Williams undoubtedly found a managerial position here because of the sudden expansion of St. Louis as a great shoemaking center. Most of us knew someone who worked in the shoe factories or warehouses."

But the industrial importance of St. Louis and its urban mix and sprawl did not make much difference to nine-year-old Rose and seven-year-old Tom. All they remembered was that they were mocked because of their Southern accents and refined manners, although Loth doubts this could have been a virulent or even frequent mockery. "If they were social outcasts because of their accent, it might have been because of the part of town they inhabited. Most St. Louisans were cosmopolitan enough not to take exception to a deep Southern drawl. In certain fringe areas there may have been less tolerance, of course — and children can be inordinately cruel about these things; it's a way of forming their little exclusive groups. Downtown, however, everyone mingled easily."

In one important way, of course, St. Louis resembled Mississippi: there was total segregation between whites and blacks, and that segregation had its focus and its emphasis in the school system. "Half of Missouri had fought for the Confederacy," Loth added, "and the grandchildren of Confederate soldiers weren't allowed to forget it."

The mixture of modernity with ancient prejudice and ethnic diversity was oddly juxtaposed with a first-rate educational system. "We had the best city school system in the midwest," according to Loth, "and by several years of national ratings it was considered one of the best school systems in all America. High school teachers quite regularly had doctorate degrees from the best universities in the country."

In addition, the increase of recreational facilities in the 1920s owed a great deal to Dwight Davis, the commissioner of public works. He is most remembered for his place in the history of tennis, for it was he who gave his name to the famous Cup. It was his civic-mindedness that developed the parks and recreational areas and public baths serving rich and poor alike. Soon Tom Williams would escape to Forest Park or Creve Coeur Lake for a quiet refuge; like famous natives of St. Louis — Sally Benson, Emily Hahn, T. S. Eliot, Sara Teasdale — he later remembered whole days in the delicious greenery of Forest Park.

Edwina Williams set to the task of adjusting as best she could, despite the children's evident misery during the first months. Their first address was a crowded boardinghouse on Lindell Boulevard, a busy thoroughfare that could not have provided a sharper contrast to the quiet streets of Clarksdale. "At the boardinghouse, Mother had to do no cooking — which was fortunate, since she still couldn't make anything except her old standard, angel food cake. In Mississippi, the cooking and chores and

child-care were largely taken care of by Ozzie, or by Grand. Now everything was different," as Tennessee Williams's younger brother recalled.
But the boardinghouse was soon abandoned for slightly larger quarters,
at 3 South Taylor. As her pregnancy advanced, and as the summer heat
lengthened into a torrid autumn, Edwina appreciated the proximity to
Forest Park, and to Barnes Hospital.

In September 1918, Tom was enrolled at the Eugene Field elementary
school, where he soon suffered verbal and physical abuse from the other
children because of a squeamishness and delicacy that had surrounded
him at home. Forbidden by his mother to engage in any sport because of
his diphtheria-weakened heart (a diagnosis never substantiated by a doctor then or later), he relied more and more on himself, his story-spinning
with Rose, his fabrication of short, sometimes grotesque tales, and his
refuge of solitary reading.

"I preferred to play by myself," he said of those early years in St. Louis.
"I had already stopped making connections with other boys." By the
time he was nine, he had put some of that solitude to good use: he had
read at least two novels by Dickens, some of the Waverley novels of
Walter Scott, and generous selections from Shakespeare. At the same
time, Rose absented herself more from classes, often on the pretext of
helping at home. She often sat quietly alone, in the dark, waiting for Edwina knew not what — perhaps just for Tom to return from school.

On February 21, 1919, the third and last child was born to Cornelius
and Edwina, and his mother insisted on the names Walter Dakin; the
first name was ignored almost from the first day. Immediately following
her release from St. Anthony's hospital, Edwina fell ill, and not long after
she contracted the Spanish influenza that ravaged much of America. Cornelius took her farther west for treatment in a warmer climate, and
Grandmother Dakin came from Clarksdale to care for Rose, Tom and
Dakin.

Her arrival was the happiest moment Rose and Tom had known since
the previous July. Grand was a benediction in their lives: "Her coming,"
Tennessee Williams wrote later, "meant nickels for ice cream, quarters
for movies, picnics in Forest Park ... 'Grand' was all that we knew of
God in our lives!" Her sweetness, her generosity and her unselfishness
embraced them for all the years until her death. "Grand cared for us in
every crisis," Dakin remembered, "from Mother's Spanish influenza
through a series of operations she had in the 1920s and 1930s. Even my

father had a great respect for her and was polite and courtly around her. He recognized quality in ladies, after all."

After about two weeks near the West Coast, Edwina and Cornelius returned to St. Louis. She was not entirely recovered, however, and her features were pinched and drawn. But there was something else that struck Rose and Tom about their parents. The cool politeness that characterized Cornelius's visits to his family in the South, the enigmatic distance that seemed to separate him emotionally from his wife and children, and Edwina's resentment of his drinking and gambling and carousing — these now seemed to have frozen the couple in a mutual hostility. Grand returned to Clarksdale, the Williams family moved to a dark apartment at 4633 Westminster Place, and life at home turned chillingly sour.

The new apartment had only two small windows, in the front and rear rooms, and a fire escape blocked the smoky light from a back alley. Edwina, nevertheless, did what she could to make it habitable.* She told the children that better days were ahead, that this was only a temporary stopping-place. Again, she tried to learn to cook, and again the results were not happy: her neighbor Mrs. Katzenstein could succeed only in helping her to perfect a variation on her standard cake.

As if life had not darkened enough, in 1921 Edwina miscarried her fourth child and had a long and difficult recovery. From this she returned to her children with amazing energy and determination, and it is easy to admire the courage and cheer — most of which was carefully and generously manufactured for the benefit of her children — that this small woman brought to an increasingly unhappy life. The rector's daughter, accustomed to a gentler society, a more elegant atmosphere, a servant and well-bred, courteous neighbors and the thousand details of life among the Southern gentry, was sustaining a terrible demotion.

Over the next several years, the family moved almost a dozen times; there were more moves, in fact, than there had been in Mississippi. By the time Thomas Williams was fifteen, he and his mother and sister had lived in more than sixteen different homes. This certainly contributed to the pattern of geographical instability in his later life, when a kind of gypsylike impermanence and wandering characterized even his most successful years.

---

* The rooms at 4633 Westminster Place are the setting for Tennessee Williams's first professional success, and the building was later named "The Glass Menagerie Apartments." The situation and time of the play, however, and the ages of its characters, are based on the life of the Williams household about a dozen years later, and at a different address.

There was, of course, a severe housing shortage at the end of World War I. In addition, more than once Cornelius gambled away his salary, or spent household money on liquor, resulting in the family's inability to pay back rent. Yet another reason was that Edwina was obsessed with the idea that somehow they would be able to live, even in St. Louis, in the more elegant manner they had once known — the manner befitting what she thought was their aristocratic station.

"The many moves we made," Dakin said years later, "were motivated by mother's desire to find something a little bigger and better than what we'd had. And somehow we always seemed to be following in the footsteps of the Jameson family. Paul Jameson was my father's boss at International Shoe, and he showered my family with attention. Much of the furniture in our apartment came from the Jameson house, or was a gift from Paul. He paid for mother's recuperation trip when she had influenza. I inherited some of his son's clothes and his bicycle, and even, before that, his baby-carriage. Paul Jameson became something of a protector and a provider to my family — especially when my father became less and less responsible — and this was certainly due to his very warm feelings toward mother. The Jamesons went for picnics with us to Forest Park almost every Sunday. This was one way for mother to get away from Cornelius, and there was no way he could prevent it."

Nothing more than warmth of feeling should be assumed about this friendship, however, regardless of what other desires may have been present. Edwina Dakin Williams was too much the Victorian belle to have permitted the emergence or release of anything but the most innocent affection, and Paul Jameson, according to Dakin, "was a very moral man, too, with a family he cared deeply about." Years later, Edwina often spoke openly about the friendship, about the attentive generosity that meant so much to her when her own marriage ceased to have any meaning and when she found it difficult to provide necessities — much less luxuries — for her children. She spoke to her own mother about it, and she spoke to her daughter-in-law, Joyce Croft Williams (Dakin's wife), about it. She hid nothing because there was nothing to hide. But there is no doubt that Paul Jameson was, in the strictest sense of the term, Edwina's gentleman caller.

This relationship was the only light in the dark years of the early 1920s, when life became increasingly dismal. Over the period of the next dozen years, after her miscarriage, Edwina suffered at least eight illnesses requiring surgery, one of them life-threatening and resulting in a total hysterectomy. Each time her mother went to the hospital — and eventually each time a doctor's visit was announced — Rose was almost paralyzed with terror. If her mother died, she would be at the mercy of a father whose airy unconcern and drunken moods kept her in a constant state of anxiety. For a long while, Rose identified with her mother to the point that she would develop simultaneous aches and pains, and suffer identical symptoms. She claimed, with increasing agitation and unreason, that the food was poisoned, that she was dying, that strangers were going to kill them all, and her unhappy state often effected an upset stomach, a sick headache or a fainting spell. And Tom, from age ten, could do nothing but watch, confused and fearful, as the family that had known such genteel peace in Mississippi was thrown into a bitter destiny from which rescue seemed impossible.

Cornelius was a shrewd businessman, popular with his peers and respected by his superiors, and the records of the International Shoe Company reveal that by January 1922 he had been promoted to a managerial position at the warehouse on Washington Avenue. But he was also increasingly alcoholic, a passionate poker player and something of a wildcat. Had he not squandered so much of his money, his family would not have had to live so frugally.

Cornelius was not only volatile and unpredictable and frightening to Rose and Tom, he was also positively intimidating. "He took no joy in the children," Edwina wrote, "seeming to consider them just a nuisance, as though he wished they had never been born. All but Dakin; he and Dakin would listen for hours to the ball game on the radio. Because Rose and Tom did not care for baseball, they were a total loss. . . . Because Tom preferred to read, or write, or go to the movies rather than play baseball, his father contemptuously called him 'Miss Nancy.' Cornelius proved little better than the boys at school who taunted him with cries of 'sissy.' " Of this time in his life, Thomas Lanier Williams said later about his father, "I hated him."

"Life at home was terrible," according to Dakin, "just terrible. By the late 1920s, mother and father were in open warfare, and both were good combattants. He came home drunk and picked up a bill — perhaps for Tom's clothing or schoolbooks — and he'd fly into a rage. 'How dare you spend money on Tom — books! a coat!' and he'd scream something terrific and there'd be a vicious row and finally mother would do her famous fainting act — always managing to fall on the couch, of course, so that she wouldn't hurt herself. Once, however, it was so terrible that she ran into the bedroom and locked herself in. He broke down the door, and in doing so the door hit her and broke her nose. That time she really fainted."

One brief time of calm intervened. "There had been a sex party of some kind among some employees of International Shoe," Dakin continued, "and my father and another employee had contracted gonorrhea from a prostitute. That was a big deal, and it was only because Dad told the truth that he was allowed to keep his job once the word got out at the office. The other fellow lied and was fired." For weeks, Cornelius crept in and out of the apartment in silence — and nearly on his knees, for sheer embarrassment and contrition.

This unhappy scenario took a greater toll on Rose than on either of the two boys. "In her transition to St. Louis, removed from security and thrown into a world of alarm and despair, Rose had hideous inner turmoil in trying to cope with life. She was fragile and sensitive, and she couldn't cope." So Tom remembered his sister's gradual entrance into an inner world of darkness and unreality and, eventually, complete psychotic breakdown.

"Rose was caught in the middle of all this," Dakin agreed. "Her first ten years of life were more peaceful, in Mississippi. Then here they were in St. Louis, and everything conspired for the poor girl's illness. We had very little money and no status, and people in the neighborhood had nothing but contempt for people like us 'poor whites.' The change was a great shock for Rose."

There were some fruitless attempts to bring some pleasure or peace to the girl during her teens, but everything seemed doomed. For a time Edwina took her parents' advice — and some of the savings her mother offered — and arranged for Rose to have violin lessons. On a December evening in 1922, the Elise Aehle School of Music offered a "Costume Violin Recital" at the North Side YMCA Hall. The second item on the program was Rose Williams's rendition of Papini's "Romance," which turned out to be a musical and emotional disaster. She froze in terror, repeated several passages, and finally stopped abruptly in the middle of playing. Her family took her away shaking and in tears.*

Finally, the only refuge seemed escape.

After a brief time at Hosmer Hall — a private junior high school for which Grandmother Dakin once again contributed tuition money — Rose was sent to All Saints, an Episcopal junior college in Vicksburg.

* The events surrounding this are fictionalized in Tennessee's short story, "The Resemblance Between a Violin Case and a Coffin."

The Reverend had been offered a pastorate there for a year, and Rose, at about the age of seventeen, was sent for a formal introduction to society.

"She was doing fine there," Dakin remembered, "but father and Aunt Belle insisted that she be sent to Knoxville for her debut, and it was a catastrophe. She was from out of town, and so no one came. Then, as she was returning, she was delayed at a train station because of floods. Apparently she was approached by a drifter, who made a pass at her or said something vulgar, and by the time she got back to St. Louis she was almost hysterical."

Her mother, soon after, enrolled her at the Rubicam Business College, hoping she would learn to be a stenographer, but that did not turn out well either — she could sustain neither the pressure nor the group contact — and after being hired as receptionist for a dentist she was very quickly dismissed. At home, she soon developed a chronic sick stomach, but none of the tests at Barnes Hospital revealed a physical cause. "It was just the trauma of living in that warring household," according to Dakin. "Things were much worse for her and for Tom than for me. I was Dad's favorite, he took me out and ignored them. Also, I had been raised in St. Louis, in that unfortunate environment, from the start. There was no abrupt change for me — I had been toughened for it. But it shattered Rose's mind, and it affected Tom deeply too."

At the same time, however, there was for Tom the beginning of a more creative refuge. Again with contributions from her mother to the household pocketbook (from which Cornelius took generously for his card games and illegal liquor), Edwina bought Tom a used portable typewriter, thinking it would aid in schoolwork. "It immediately became my place of retreat, my cave, my refuge," he wrote later. At the typewriter he transformed the confusion, the bitterness, the longings into poems, and for a time he clacked out a diary in which he recorded little anecdotes about St. Louis street life. The poems became reflections of his acute observances of everything from a stranger's funny hat to the folds of a flower.

Soon the first writings by Thomas Lanier Williams were published — in the newspaper *Junior Life,* at Ben Blewett Junior High School, which he attended from 1923 to 1926. In October 1924, his short ghost story "A Great Tale Told at Katrina's Party" was considered suitable for the Halloween issue. Not long after, two poems appeared, the first probably inspired by a brief summer visit to his grandfather (then almost seventy), the second an example of the nature ode that every aspiring adolescent poet in every generation seems compelled to try.

"Old Things"
In the silence of the garret,
'Midst rusted things of long ago,
Aloft from the clamor of life below,
Old things — sallowed and hallowed,
Grayed in the gloom;
Things from the old life
In the dusk of their tomb.
This is the place for him and his dreams,
His old gray head bowed over the remnants
Of days that are dead.
The silver candelabrum blazes anew,
And the tapestry blooms to a brighter hue.
The melodeon chimes
A faint caprice,
And the whole world dims to a softened peace.
Eyes gently shine through
The dusk of years
Old faces he sees
Old voices he hears
Amidst the rusted things of long ago.

"Nature's Thanksgiving"
The Bob-White is whirring
And beating, and throbbing;
The wood-brook is singing
And happily sobbing;
The carnival leaves
In resplendent descent,
Fall in a glory o'er merry content.
The wood has all colored,
And flaunting in pride,
Is swaying and laughing
Before they subside
To the sleep —
And the dark —
Of the winter.

When the fledgling, thirteen-year-old poet brought the school newspaper home, his mother thought his contributions were charming, and his grandparents' reply to a copy he sent was a hearty encouragement, and a dollar. In June 1925, the Ben Blewett yearbook printed Thomas Williams's essay "Demon Smoke," which addressed the problem of factory fumes in downtown St. Louis (not the dangers of cigarettes).*

That summer, Edwina — again with help from her mother's purse — took her three children to Elkmont, Tennessee, a mountaintop resort, and they detoured on their return to visit the Dakins. During those weeks, Rose seemed more calm than at any time since they had moved to St. Louis. This respite would not last long.

From 1926 to 1928, while life at home alternated between merely tense and openly awful, Tom wore out generous supplies of typewriter ribbons. When he transferred to Soldan High School (after still another family move), he at once began contributing to both the newspaper and yearbook, and his review of the film *Stella Dallas,* which he saw with a girlfriend, became the English class topic for several days.† Bored with school, he preferred his poetry, his movie reviews and his brief essays on St. Louis life. The only other activity that engaged his enthusiasm was swimming, which Aunt Belle taught him in Memphis during the summer of 1926.

Edwina, meanwhile, was convinced that Rose's "trouble" would yield to prayer and hymn-singing, and she marched her children to church every Sunday while Cornelius slept off the effects of the previous night. "Mother," Dakin recalled, "became something of a fanatic about Protestant religious things, even though the only church nearby was Presbyterian and she had been raised 'high church' Episcopalian. Her voice floated loudly above the others, and of course Tom and I had to join the choir, which we weren't very keen on." The church-going had no apparent effects on Rose's turmoil, however. She was a delicately pretty young woman with a sweet, slightly vacant expression, but the men who came to the Williams apartment to visit or date her rarely returned or called a second time, for they were greeted either with a scowl and a sarcastic remark from Cornelius, or by a teary-eyed Rose, who had just been through some mysterious, unpleasant ordeal.

By the last years of high school, Tom and his family were living at

---

* Three years later, he won a five-dollar prize in the essay contest sponsored by a group called the Citizens' Smoke Abatement League. St. Louis was apparently having serious industrial pollution problems, and concerned residents were publicizing the dangers.
† His review treated the 1925 silent version of *Stella Dallas,* which was directed by Henry King and starred Belle Bennett and Ronald Colman.

6254 Enright, in five small rooms of a three-story, depressing red brick apartment. At University City High School, to which he had transferred, a great deal soon became clear about him.

First, it was apparent that he was not interested in formal education or the ordinary St. Louis adolescent social life. "Tommy Williams was not socially inclined toward the group," one of his teachers remembered. "He had too many thoughts of his own. His grades were average. There was no evidence of brilliance in his work. I fear he was not well-adjusted. In the period I knew him [1927–1929] he was never clear about tomorrow's lesson."

But he was clear about his writing, and where he wanted it to take him. He had won a five-dollar third prize for a letter that answered the intriguing question, "Can a Good Wife Be a Good Sport?" His reply, published in the national magazine *Smart Set* in May 1927, was a resounding negative; he wrote in the style of a young man who finds that his wife, bored with home life, is dating other men. If being a good sport means "drinking, smoking, and petting . . . I don't think that a wife can be that kind of a 'good sport.' " The editors could not have known that the letter was an ingenious fabrication.

A more innocent, real-life "good sport" was the girlfriend he had taken to see *Stella Dallas*. Hazel Kramer, the daughter of a man who reported to Cornelius at International Shoe, was a tall, slightly plump but pretty classmate who became Tom's constant companion. She was, he insisted for the rest of his life, his one great female love — but the love was strictly Platonic. "Tom and Hazel were extremely close all through the last years of high school," Dakin said. "They were always in each other's company — running around together, dating, laughing, going to the Tivoli and Variety movie theatres near by, or to the museum or the library. With her he was open, he had fun. But Father felt that if they went away to college together, as they planned, they'd get married. This, he said, would ruin Tom's chances for financial independence. So he determined to put a stop to that friendship."

Tom wrote later that Edwina was opposed to Hazel, too, but on other grounds:

"My mother did not approve of my attachment to Hazel . . . nor for that matter had Miss Edwina ever seemed to want me to have any friends. The boys were too rough for her delicate son, Tom, and the girls were, of course, too 'common.' . . . [And she] disapproved more of Hazel's mother."

He claimed that their friendship ripened into romantic but sexually unconsummated love, and that it lasted eleven years. In fact — in this as in so many memories that were freighted with feeling — he exaggerated, turning the pleasantly unexceptional into the melodramatic. He and Hazel knew each other well for about three and a half years. Then, not only because his parents disapproved but also because they were both changing rapidly and developing other interests, they drifted apart. Something of her remained in his heart forever, nonetheless — something perhaps more fraternal than romantic. He could enjoy with Hazel the pastimes and diversions that had become impossible with Rose.

"She married another man," Williams reported later, "but killed herself when she was still very young." His memory of her is represented, however, in the reference to a woman named Rose Kramer — in his one-act play *Hello from Bertha,* written shortly after Hazel's death — whose name and fate combine the physical and mental conditions of both his sister and his friend.

In 1928, however, two happy events brightened Tom's life.

He had submitted to the editor of a "pulp" magazine called *Weird Tales* a short story, "The Vengeance of Nitocris." It was a surprisingly lurid account of an Egyptian queen who avenges the execution of her brother, who had been guilty of sacrilege, by inviting those responsible for his death to a dinner. She floods the banquet hall, drowning all the hapless guests and thoroughly enjoying herself in the deed. The idea had come to him from class readings (there is a similar story in Herodotus's *History*), and the style mimics the worst kind of schoolboy translation. ("Hushed were the streets of many-peopled Thebes," he began. "Weird, high-noted incantations of a wailing sound were audible through the barred doors.") But the story has a sure sense of horror, and the final scene is worthy of the magazine's name, as the wickedly loyal Nitocris watches the death agonies of her victims ("Much pleasure might she derive by recalling that picture . . ."). He later thought that the story "set the keynote for most of [my] work that has followed," a reference no doubt to its shocking finale rather than to its patent lack of poetic diction.

By the time the readers of *Weird Tales* received the issue with his story, in August, Tom had joyfully departed St. Louis for a long summer holiday. Up to that time, his only excursions had been with his mother, or to visit the Dakins, or to summer camp with his brother. But for the summer of 1928, Reverend Dakin had coordinated a European tour for members of his parish, and Tom was invited to come along without cost. It would be one of the great experiences of his life, for at seventeen he had seen only small parts of three states.

"His great affection for his grandfather was sealed with this trip," according to a later friend. "The Reverend opened the world to him, and somehow all his later returns to Europe were associated with this earlier, brief journey. And windows were opened — perhaps the only windows during those early, formative years."

Tom traveled to Clarksdale to meet the tour group, and a lavish party was given for their farewell by the Dakins' neighbor Mrs. Wingfield — a name Tom would later borrow for one of his most famous characters. The *Clarksdale Daily Register* reported that "the hospitalities [were] marked with charm and distinction, and sustained Mrs. Wingfield's well-known reputation as a most gracious hostess."

From there the group went by train to New York for four days. Grandfather took him to see *Show Boat* on Broadway, and Tom was bedazzled by the staging and deeply moved by Helen Morgan's plaintive singing of "Bill." On July 6, they all departed the Biltmore Hotel and boarded the *Homeric*. For the first two days at sea, Tom was violently ill. Then he recovered, in time for the glamour of shipboard life to which Grandfather gaily introduced him.

Chapter Two

GHOSTS
(1928–1937)

There's freedom, Joe, and freedom's the big
thing in life. It's funny that some of us don't
even get it until we're dead.

— Mother, in *The Long Good-bye*

ON FRIDAY, July 13, 1928, the *Homeric* docked at Southampton. Tom wrote home that in spite of Grandfather's permission to have a Manhattan cocktail, he preferred ginger ale. But two days later they were in Paris, and at once he was captivated by the City of Lights: he drank a whole glass of champagne, he said in another letter to his mother, and he found it very refreshing indeed after a day trip from the Hotel Rochambeau to the Louvre and Versailles. Next day, Grandfather took him and a few selected members of their group to the Folies Bergère and to Moulin Rouge. Tom assured Edwina that the spectacles noted for scantily clad dancing girls were more artistic than immodest and that, after all, conventions learned at home had best be forgotten when in Paris. Then he described a lavish production of Gounod's *Roméo et Juliette* at the Paris Opera, which had a powerful effect on him. Shakespeare's lovers came alive, the composer's melodies echoed in him for days, and — though he thought the acting wooden — the romantic atmosphere corresponded to something deep but untapped within him.

Marseilles was their next stopping-place, and soon they were in Monte Carlo for a day's swimming in the transparent blue waters of the Mediterranean. By August 4 they had not only toured the doge's palace in Venice but had also shopped for souvenirs with money saved by skipping an occasional meal. Then they reversed their journey, visiting Milan and then proceeding to Montreux and to the castle of Chillon, where the signatures of Byron, Shelley, Dickens and Harriet Beecher Stowe were scratched on the walls. Almost two weeks were spent making excursions from Interlaken, and at last they traveled by steamer along the Rhine to Cologne, where Tom was stunned by the beauty of northern Europe's largest Gothic cathedral.

By late August he was back in St. Louis, and Edwina greeted him with an envelope containing a check for thirty-five dollars from the Popular Fiction Publishing Company, representing payment for "The Vengeance of Nitocris." But Tom did not need remuneration to go on with his writing. As he began his last year of high school — and when he should have been devoting time to mathematics and history — he set to the task of transforming his "Trip Diary" into a series of travel articles. From October through April, the University City High School newspaper regularly featured the colorful, detailed accounts of his European holiday.

The records for the school commencement that year indicate Thomas Williams's rank was fifty-third in a class of eighty-three — hardly a foretoken of collegiate success. At his father's insistence, he enrolled even before graduation in two additional correspondence courses in typing and shorthand; neither the money nor the talent for more education was in sight. His mother preserved an exercise page on which he had typed five times: "There is a difference between talent and genius. Talent does what it can. Genius what it must. But it is the little more that makes the difference." This she thought an extraordinary insight. It is doubtful, however, that she recognized it as an excerpt from Bulwer-Lytton's "Last Words of a Sensitive Second-Rate Poet."

For it was in fact poetry and poets that claimed his attention that first half-year of 1929, and that certainly accounted for his disappointing record in French and civics (his fourth year of Latin yielded surprisingly good results).

During the summer, there were happy and painful moments. Grandmother sent money for the incidental expenses of a year at college, Cornelius agreed to his attendance, and Tom saw a move to the University of Missouri at Columbia, one hundred fifty miles west, as a great leap toward his goal of becoming a poet. The excitement enabled him to endure a gruesome accident. He slipped on a diving board at the Bellerive Country Club (where his father had a guest membership), hit the cement, and opened his eyes to see a puddle of blood and all his front teeth on the grass before him.* A bridge was hastily fitted before his departure for Columbia, but several readjustments were necessary over the years before permanent dentures were inserted.

Less than a three-hour automobile ride from St. Louis in later years, Columbia was in 1929 difficult to reach from the eastern part of Missouri.

---

* The country club, with a slight orthographic change, gave its name to the DuBois estate (Belle Reve) in *A Streetcar Named Desire,* years later.

"One had to go by a sort of Toonerville Trolley, through Centralia, or by hitchhiking, or by another branch line through McBaine," recalled David Loth, who had graduated a few years earlier. "The townspeople there were mostly very poor black people who worked in its enormous shoe factory, and of course the university was restricted to whites — it was as quietly prejudiced as mainstream St. Louis society."

The academic reputation, however, was something for alumni and students to celebrate. The University of Missouri at Columbia has America's oldest school of journalism, founded in 1908 by the country printer Walter Williams, a man of astonishing vision. Soon it began issuing the daily campus newspaper, the *Columbia Missourian,* and thereafter the major urban newspapers of America always numbered a percent of their staffs as Columbia alumni.

For the first two years, students enrolled in general liberal arts courses prior to the concentration in journalism, and every young man was obliged to enroll in the Reserve Officers Training Corps (ROTC) military training program. Tom may have wanted to be a poet, but Cornelius rightly predicted that would be a short route to poverty, and insisted on journalism. And even before Tom had arrived on campus, his father had also decided that his son should apply for admission to Alpha Tau Omega house, a new fraternity whose enthusiasm for sports and healthy male competitiveness in school and social life Cornelius believed would correct his son's shyness and sensitivity.

"There were no Jews in any fraternities, of course," Loth remembered, "since all the Greek fraternities were restricted. Men there, who paid seventy-five dollars a month for room, board and dues, lived somewhat better than those in the dormitories, where life was very Spartan for the rest of us. There were gradations in the fraternities, too — Beta Theta Pi was considered the most prestigious, and was comprised mostly of society men from St. Louis, those with old money." He remembered that school life was strict and serious, and students were expected to formulate clear professional plans quite early. Loth, for one, was already on his way by 1929 to writing a long and distinguished series of historical biographies — *The Brownings, Lorenzo the Magnificent* and *Royal Charles* among the most noted.

There was at Columbia a nominal academic fee of forty dollars a term (to cover library, health clinic and incidental fees), and over the next three years Rosina Dakin provided this sum. When Tom was a month into his first year, the great stock market crash was announced, and school life for some of the 3300 students and 250 journalism majors terminated abruptly. But the Dakins' generosity enabled Tom to remain and, to his father's satisfaction, to accept the pledge to Alpha Tau Omega, whose new residence was just completed and ready for the forty men who prepared to move in. In a happy letter to his parents in October, Tom wrote that fraternity life looked exciting. The only unhappy note is his expression of concern for Rose's "long trouble," which had by this time necessitated confinement in a private sanatorium.

In addition to his courses that first term — English composition, citizenship, intermediate French, geology and ROTC — there was a great emphasis on social life. Nearby were two two-year women's colleges, Christian College for Girls (staffed by members of the Church of Christ) and Stevens College (founded by Baptists).

"Campus life was free and easy," according to David Loth, "but there was very little sexual license. Women's dormitory rules were very strict, at the two women's colleges and at Columbia, and there was no such thing as parietal hours or visiting women's rooms. Social life consisted mostly of going to one of the two movie theatres in town, or to campus dances, or to a concert or sports event — usually in foursomes or sixsomes. Relations between the sexes were very formal, virtually no one had a car, no one had liquor, and drugs were of course unknown. There were occasional rumors of sexual activity among a few notorious students, but it would have been extremely clandestine, and certainly not generally acceptable conduct."

By the end of the year, Tom's small circle of friends included two fraternity brothers who took the same classes, and a girl who lived at the Alpha Chi Omega sorority. Her name was Esmeralda Mayes, and their friendship — based on a shared poetic sensitivity — continued for the next two years. They read aloud together, took picnic lunches off campus, discussed art and literature and love and the future. Tom's few brief surviving entries about her in notebooks are simple records of meetings, readings, talks about school.

Cornelius was unimpressed with the report for the 1929–1930 academic year, however. Although there were B's in composition and citizenship both terms, a B and a C in French, and C's in geology and literature, the performance in the area his father considered most important was poor — the record showed a D in ROTC the first term, and F the second. Tom was warned about this, and about the eighteen absences that had earned him an additional negative credit that year. Cornelius acted as if the modest sums for Tom's education were coming exclusively from his own pocket — but worse, his son, the son of a Spanish-American War veteran, was not on his way to a military commission.

Tom was, on the other hand, on his way to being a serious writer, and his poems occupied the greater part of his time. In the spring of 1930 he had also submitted to the Dramatic Arts Club a one-act play, *Beauty Is the Word,* which was soon staged in competition.

"We went through the plays and found that Thomas Lanier Williams's was not submitted in the correct format," remembered Professor Donovan Rhynsburger, who was one of the contest judges. "But I thought it showed promise and was worthy of honorable mention." And so it was reported, in the *Missourian* dated April 12, 1930, that *Beauty Is the Word* was the first freshman play to be selected for citation. The paper added that it was "a play with an original and constructive idea, but the handling is too didactic and the dialog often too moralistic." Preserved in the library of the university, the original twelve-page typescript of the first play by Williams contains a simple hand-drawn stage diagram, character descriptions, and the short text.

The story concerns a South Pacific missionary and his wife (improbably and perhaps satirically named Abelard and Mabel); their servant and the wife's niece and her husband. The play both endorses the minister's life and corrects his tendency to Victorian prudery: after the missionary refers to the "shameless nakedness of the natives," the young niece insists that "fear and God are the most utterly incompatible things under the sun. Fear is ugliness. God — at least *my* God — is Beauty."

In May, his name was again in print — this time for a less controversial product, the short story "The Lady's Beaded Bag," which appeared in the campus literary magazine. At the same time, another one-act play was ready for production — an eight-page family melodrama he called *Hot Milk at Three in the Morning,* in which a young married couple argue about their poverty, their infant and their feeling of entrapment. "I thought, when I read it," said Donovan Rhynsburger years later, "that it was quite consciously modeled on [Eugene] O'Neill's [one-act play] *Before Breakfast*" — in which a hero is driven to suicide by his nagging wife.* Whatever the source, the text is strident and expresses the motif of emotional confinement that would emerge in all his great full-length

---

* It is equally possible that Williams's play was inspired by Strindberg's *The Stronger* (a two-character play in which only one speaks), which was almost certainly the model for O'Neill's *Before Breakfast. Cf.* Louis Sheaffer, *O'Neill: Son and Playwright* (Boston: Little, Brown, 1968, pp. 351–352 *et alibi*).

plays. Production of *Hot Milk* was, however, postponed until the spring of 1932.

Back in St. Louis for the summer of 1930, Tom renewed his friendship with Hazel Kramer, in spite of his parents' clear disapproval. Cornelius still resented the attachment on purely professional grounds — love and school, he insisted, were incompatible. Edwina, on the other hand, resented the relationship for a more subtle reason. "The fact is that she was jealous of any woman to whom Tom was friendly," according to a writer who knew her well.

He was glad, therefore, to return to Columbia in September, although the gap separating his academic performance from his personal preference continued to widen. That year, one of his fraternity brothers and house-mates came to know him probably better than anyone at the university. Elmer Lower had just joined the Alpha Tau Omega house, and for two years he saw Williams daily on campus. (After receiving his degree in 1933, Lower began a remarkable career in journalism and broadcasting; from 1963 to 1974 he was president of ABC News, and continued, even afterward, to teach and write as a visiting professor at his alma mater.)

"There were forty of us in the house that year," Lower recalled, "and we considered ourselves very lucky indeed. We ate well, thanks to Ola Crews, our affable and skilled cook, and our house-mother, Blanche Eckard, was a kindly widow who was very good to us all. In addition to the house-mother and house cook, there were two waiters who worked for the free meals that came with their job, and two houseboys who did all the chores — even to making our beds."

Tom Williams, according to Lower, was certainly not an exceptional student or fraternity brother, and could not be called gregarious. "Our friendship was based on a mutual enthusiasm for journalism, which we also shared with a third student, Harold Mitchell, a happy, smiling country boy from the small town of Lancaster, Missouri." This boy gave his name, some years later, to a major character in *A Streetcar Named Desire*.

In classes, however, the enthusiasm of Tom Williams was not so evident. That year, he accumulated thirty-six absences, which certainly contributed to a dismal record at end of term — two F's in military science, C's in zoology, history, composition, journalism and logic, D's in Greek history and French, and one B, in literature. Prudently, he avoided a visit home.

"His father visited him once, however," according to Lower, "either deliberately, because of the terrible record Tom was compiling, or because he had to go to the shoe factory nearby. ROTC was required of everyone only during the first two years on campus, but Tom's father announced that *his* son would have two additional years of it. That meant two days a week of class in military science, and a Wednesday afternoon parade on the quadrangle. For this, all ROTC men had to dress in the prescribed uniform of white trousers and a blue coat. But Tom, who was known for being absentminded, constantly forgot his white trousers, and bystanders would look over the parade to see one pair of blue trousers among eight hundred white. He looked a little ludicrous, which is how he often looked when something derived from his absent-mindedness."

That absentmindedness, in fact, typified his schooldays, and fraternity brothers took advantage of him when he forgot his books in the common living room, or left a sweater in the dining hall. "Everybody thought he had two left feet, and he was gently picked on — but he took it all in good humor and without anger, and he never fought back. He kept very much to himself apart from some socializing with me and Harold Mitchell."

Socially, Lower remembers Williams as being almost unbearably shy. "He was too shy to ask a girl for a date, so Mitch and I had to find someone for him so we could have a triple-date for a dance or sports event. Tom wasn't a typical frat man or buddy, and he seemed awkward in groups, even during the simple and brief socializing that was permitted when we brought girls back to the frat house living room for a while. They had a ten o'clock curfew and were only allowed into the house if Mrs. Eckard were there in the parlor as chaperone."

But anyone who spent even an afternoon with Tom Williams discovered that his shyness did not mean a lack of humor. Everything and everyone seemed to amuse him, and he entertained his fraternity brothers with brief, spontaneous scenes of Southern life, his voice rising and falling as he enacted two or three roles in an impromptu skit. "He had a quietly ironic wit," as Lower recalled. "His small monthly allowance came in a letter from his father,* and at mail call Tom held up the check and announced, 'Ah, the Red Goose [the name of his father's branch at International Shoe]! The Red Goose flies again!' "

---

* Lower is correct: although the Dakins were paying for college fees, Cornelius supplied small sums for monthly expense, ROTC uniforms, etc.

The demands of school and his quiet preoccupation with his writing did not, however, diminish his concern for his sister's health. Tom wrote thanking Rose for a gift package of soap, oranges and a tie she sent in January 1931 and asking if she would visit him before May. But travel was beyond her endurance, and both brother and sister were disappointed.

So was Cornelius, who reacted to his son's poor grades by putting him to work at International Shoe in St. Louis for the summer of 1931; the employment files at 1509 Washington show that he was a temporary office clerk in the Continental Shoe Division from June 23 to September 15. Tom hated it — he had hoped to spend the summer with Hazel Kramer and with his poetry notebooks, but he felt he could put up with the warehouse those few months. What he found even more tiresome than the clerical work, however, was the time he had to spend with his father:

"It's true that Dad never seemed greatly concerned about Rose and me," he reflected later, "but in my case, I can't help feeling it wasn't all his fault. If Mother hadn't held me so fiercely close to her, the situation might not have got so bad between us that I *froze* when he entered the house. I might even have got to know him as a man — and I sometimes feel he *wanted* to know me, but the trouble lay in the fact that, knowing I *was* afraid of him, he resented that knowledge so much he turned against me."

Living with his parents that summer was made even more awkward, in addition, by the rides with Cornelius to Washington Street each day. "We used to drive into work every day.... I used to try to think of something to say to him. I would compose three sentences in my mind ... something like, 'The smog is heavy today,' or 'The traffic is bad,' and to each one he would grunt in some disparaging way [as if to say], 'What's this son-of-a-bitch trying to talk to me for?' ... We were just so tongue-tied with each other." The admixture of fear, resentment and muted longing that prevailed between father and son was soon satirized in Tom's writing, for within a few years he had written the first draft of a one-act play about a shoe salesman with his own father's first two initials: Charlie Colton, in *The Last of My Solid Gold Watches,* is a pathetic man, out of step with time and himself.

Back at Columbia in September, he was admitted into the school of journalism, and there occurred what Elmer Lower called "one of the most amazing and amusing things of the year." Never a participant in sports, Tom was urged to help maintain the honor of Alpha Tau Omega by competing in a wrestling match; the prize would be a silver cup for the house. "At 115 pounds, and with his natural timidity, this augured disaster. The event pitted him against two wiry farm-boys, and Tom — after lots were drawn — was chosen for the finals. A few days before the match, a new aspect of his character and humor emerged, however. He attached a sign on the house bulletin board — 'WILLIAMS ULTIMATUM: LIQUOR! LIQUOR! MUST HAVE LIQUOR TO FORTIFY MYSELF AGAINST THE AGGRESSIVE AGRARIANS!' So we got hold of some bathtub gin or some moonshine from the gin-runners up-state. Tom lost, in two falls, but he tried hard, and his efforts helped the total house score." ("I attacked my adversary with great fury," Williams said years later. "I used activity to conceal my lack of skill. I lost the match, but afterward I was known in the house as Tiger Williams.")

That autumn things happened quickly. Although his grades for the term never rose higher than C's, he was writing feverishly and was one of eleven to receive honorable mention out of fifty-five entrants in the Mahan Story Contest. And the writing was accompanied — and perhaps even precipitated at this point — by what must have been a strange and terrifying possibility for him, as it would have been for any Missouri student in 1931. "I was deeply in love with my roommate," he said long afterward, "but neither of us knew what to do about it." According to his very different account in *Memoirs,* the roommate knew very well what to do about it — and offered more than indirect hints — but Tom shivered with anxiety and aborted any sexual contact.

"None of us ever had any inkling of homosexual tendencies in him or his roommate during those years," according to Elmer Lower, "and it would have been certainly difficult to cover it up. Any such activity would have had to be very discreet, and very private, and there simply wasn't very much privacy. Heterosexual sex was rare enough, and mysterious enough, and alternatives weren't even a topic for conversation." The account in *Memoirs,* while perhaps not a deliberate distortion of the truth, probably represents Williams's confusion, at the time of writing, between 1931 and a crucial period in his sexual development that occurred later in the decade.

Oddly coincidental with this time of his life was an artistic experience that he found overwhelming. Just when his literature professor was lecturing on the plays of Henrik Ibsen, a touring production of *Ghosts,* starring the legendary Alla Nazimova, came to campus. "It was so moving that I had to go and walk in the lobby during the last act," he remembered. "I'd stand in the [doorway] and look in, then I'd rush back to the lobby again. I suppose that play was one of the things that made me want to write for the theatre."

Up to this time, Ibsen had been a fascinating and vaguely frightening playwright to Tom, but with *Ghosts* his interest became more personal and emotional than academic. From this time forward, the professional and artistic and personal links between himself and several major writers seemed very clear to him, and he quite consciously identified with those writers — not only in patterns of work, but also in the histories and destinies of their respective lives.

Ibsen was the first of these writers with whom he felt a special, deep bond. He learned that the Norwegian poet and dramatist, who lived from 1828 to 1906, had a youth very like his own: an early dislocation from the comfortable and the familiar to inhospitable new residences; the familiarity with a church and an asylum; undistinguished academic performance and an attempt at journalism. Shy in personality, withdrawn and embarrassed with peers, the outline of Ibsen's life up through his twenties resembled the contours of Tom's, and what appealed to him about Ibsen's *Emperor and Galilean* and *Ghosts* was the attempt to bridge the gap between flesh and spirit, and the obsession, through the stylistic convention of the "guilty secret," to disclose moral truth.*

For a paper that term, he wrote that the central theme of *Ghosts* concerned much more than a simple social problem. Through the use of inherited venereal disease as a symbol, Ibsen established a drama of ideas in which he could reflect on the tragedy of those who cannot liberate themselves from a dead past. Thus Tom came to an understanding that the title referred not only to the spirit of the once profligate, now dead Captain Alving, but to a psychologically bankrupt world in which there is no truth or freedom, a world in which moral diseases inherited from the past affect the living. He did not have to reflect long on his father (almost a duplicate of Captain Alving, with the drinking and the venereal disease), and on the condition of his sister Rose, to find the repetition of Ibsen's characters, his life and his spirit in himself and his own family.

* The disclosure of moral truth by unmasking a "guilty secret" is the major motif of a number of plays by Tennessee Williams: *A Streetcar Named Desire, Cat on a Hot Tin Roof, Suddenly Last Summer, Sweet Bird of Youth, The Night of the Iguana.* It also appears in a number of his short plays and stories.

At the same time, he was discovering the work of the Swedish playwright August Strindberg (1849–1912); Williams's examination books and class notes reveal more than just poetic empathies with Strindberg — they demonstrate an almost mystical feeling of spiritual brotherhood. In Strindberg he found, too, a tortured life, particularly with regard to his relations with women. From Strindberg he learned the dramatic potential of a harsh family background, and one passage in *The Link* struck him as astonishingly relevant to his own situation with his parents: "There is room in me," says the baron to the baroness, "for both love and hatred, and while I love you one minute, I hate you the next." Very soon, it would be from Strindberg that he would take (as did Eugene O'Neill) the dramatic sense of those whom Louis Sheaffer has called "bound by the closest of ties as both victims and torturers of one another."

In Strindberg's life, however, Williams found additional dramatic material that suggested to him links between art and daily reality: the emotional insecurity of a poor childhood, and a connection with organized religion in his family; the attempt at journalism — and then a public rejection for blasphemy. Strindberg's mental crisis almost led to madness, and his revolt against social conventions was accompanied by a deeply personal, mystic vision, periods of alcoholism, and mental instability. That season Williams read Strindberg's *Miss Julie,* whose tone of sexual antagonism and class conflict, brutal action and terse dialogue certainly influenced everything he wrote thereafter, especially *A Streetcar Named Desire.* As his life progressed, Williams noted, in conversations with friends and frequently in letters, that he and Strindberg had an unusual kinship.

But his absorption in the lives and writings of the two great Scandinavian dramatists that year, while it had a profound effect on his inner life and the development of his art, had a more concrete and less constructive effect. In the spring semester of 1932, his pleasure at seeing *Hot Milk at Three in the Morning* was dampened by his D's in journalism courses and political science, C's in English and another journalism course and — the last straw for Cornelius — his fourth F in ROTC. In the last weeks of the term, perhaps knowing full well that the grades to be sent home would be dreadful, he cheerfully wrote to his father about Journalism Week and his place on the Greet and Guide Committee. The letter, dated May 9, 1932, is signed, "Lovingly, Tom." But within weeks he was out of school for good.

"Father used the excuse of poor grades to pull Tom out of Columbia," according to Dakin, "but the real reason was money. In 1932 our family was in a very bad way. Of course Tom's low grades in military education were especially repellent to Cornelius, since he had been in the Spanish-American War."

And so Tom had to leave the sanctuary of Columbia, his camaraderie with fraternity brothers and the intellectual routine of campus life. It was not, to be sure, the classes that ever held his interest; it was the freedom that he began to explore here, the reading and writing, and the first tentative steps toward an understanding of his own complex personality.

"There was absolutely no indication that Tom would become America's greatest playwright," according to Elmer Lower. "He was unremarkable in every way, and when he left he was simply doing what many had to do in the Depression. At the same time, Harold Mitchell left — and, like Tom, he later turned up to finish his degree at the University of Iowa. We remembered Tom Williams as a not especially colorful chap with his head always somewhere up in the clouds. He failed more than one examination because he forgot to appear at the right time and place, and his constant state of disorientation was finally fatal to his career at Columbia."

He had also to see Esmeralda Mayes for the last time. "He had been writing poems to her all along," Donovan Rhynsburger recalled. "In some way they were very devoted to each other. They read one another their poems and it was clear there was some kind of deep sharing, and then he was gone." But like Hazel Kramer she, too, is celebrated in his work — the simple, sensual character Esmeralda in *Camino Real* is given one of his loveliest speeches, and Esmeralda Mayes is also transformed into the odd, marginal Flora, the student poet's girlfriend in his short story "The Important Thing."

What followed was an arid, bleak time in the life of young Tom Williams — and so rudderless that in the telling over the years he exaggerated its most frustrating aspect. To the end of his life he insisted that immediately after the spring 1932 term at Columbia, his father put him to work in an odious, menial capacity at International Shoe, and that this job lasted for two years or three or four years (his dating of the period, and of events in general, was always at best an approximation). And virtually everyone who ever read about him or knew him had the idea of a three-year period in servitude to the warehouse, a time of such anxiety, such creative repression, that he was worn to total physical and mental collapse.

Although there is no doubt about the final toll the period of work took on him, the fact is that he did not work as a manual laborer, carrying huge, heavy boxes of shoes, nor was he employed for three years. The employment records show that he did not actually begin work there until June 24, 1934 and left on April 30, 1935 ("Ill Health" is marked on his card in the personnel office). Apart from the summer of 1931, then, his total period of employment at the warehouse was actually ten months. The remainder of the time, he read, wrote poetry, and endured the insufferably confining atmosphere of family life.*

There was good reason why steady, full-time employment could not begin in 1932. International Shoe was not hiring in that year, which was the lowest ebb of the Great Depression and the year in which one in four American workers was unemployed. Cornelius's position as a sales manager could not, as he had hoped, win his son a job, even if (as was not the case) Tom had had marketable skills to offer the company. Instead, he sent his son for almost a year to night classes in typing and shorthand, against the day when a clerical post might again become available. As late as October 1933, Tom was writing to the Dakins — who had retired to Memphis — that his father assured that a stenographic position would open if he passed the secretarial courses.

His writing, however, continued uninterrupted. Several months after he had resumed life in St. Louis, the alumni magazine of Columbia awarded him honorable mention in the second Mahan Story Contest. And by this time the English department there realized the talent they had lost. On December 10, 1932, Robert L. Ramsey, chairman of English, wrote: "Your absence from the University this year has been a matter of real regret to all of us who knew the excellent work you did here the last few years, especially in the field of creative writing. I hope very much you will be able to return and finish your course." He concluded by offering to submit Tom's story "Big Black: A Mississippi Idyll" to a St. Louis or Kansas City newspaper. It is hard to know who that perceptive group might have been "who knew the excellent work"

---

* The employment files suggest, however, that he may have been engaged on a *per diem* basis, paid perhaps by his father from petty cash or department budgets, but not as a full-time contracted employee for a three-year period. In addition, he seems to have performed what the factory called "piece-work," for which the company paid even anonymous workers in those days on a daily cash basis.

he had done, but universities and their spokesmen often have an astonishing hindsight in appreciating an outstanding former student.

An extraordinary fertile time then occurred, right in the middle of the national and familial Depression, in spite of — and perhaps, again, to some extent because of — Tom's unhappiness at home, boredom at business classes, anxiety for the declining health of Rose, and chafing under his mother's formality and his father's tyranny. "Mother was an extremely difficult and demanding person during those years," according to Dakin, who was working hard in high school. "She was so overly attentive to us, and was clearly the model for Amanda in *The Glass Menagerie.*"

Tom wrote poems, by the score, often on the streetcar by day and at the kitchen table or on the front steps or in his room at night. For the two-year period from early 1933 to early 1935, he received word that his poems were accepted by publications around the country: *Neophyte* published "October Song" in its Christmas/New Year 1932–33 issue; *Inspiration* gave him first prize in the spring of 1933 for two poems, "Under the April Rains" and "Her Heart Was a Delicate Silver Lyre"; his lyric "Modus Vivendi" appeared in *Counterpoint* for July 1933; *L'Alouette* accepted his poem "Ave atque Vale" for its October 1933 number; *Voices,* in New York, bought rights to "Cacti" and "After a Visit" and ran them in the summer of 1934; and several other magazines and journals, suddenly aware of the new St. Louis poet who was being compared to Sara Teasdale, wrote actively soliciting the right to publish his work. This leavened the long months at Enright Avenue, and also enabled him to turn over some money to Cornelius and Edwina. The poems themselves are of doubtful merit and give little indication of the gifts that would flourish later in his plays. Most of them seem written under the influence of Teasdale, the St. Louis poet whose short, personal lyrics were extremely popular. Her suicide in January 1933, at the age of forty-eight, shocked her student-admirers especially deeply.

During the summer of 1934 he worked at fever pitch on a short story he called "Stella for Star"; it was the twenty-third submission he made to the editors of *Story* magazine, and since he had at last been given a position as temporary office clerk at International Shoe, he had to polish the story at night. His mother remembered finding him in the morning as she had left him hours before, slumped at a table in a haze of cigarette smoke, a large, empty coffee pot at his side. There were many weeks when he somehow survived on only an hour or two of sleep nightly.

While the editors at *Story* were considering the latest submission, however, he was told that the St. Louis Writers Guild — to which he had also (and imprudently) sent "Stella for Star" — had awarded it first prize among seventy-six submitted in the Winifred Irwin short story contest, and the ten-dollar check was given to him in a brief ceremony in early 1935. Edwina was delighted, Cornelius made no comment, and Rose for once did not share her brother's joy — for she knew that Winifred Irwin had committed suicide after receiving what she thought was one too many rejection slips in her efforts to become a published writer.

At the same time that Tom was drifting into a black mood over his job at the warehouse, Rose was inhabiting almost exclusively a darker and more frightening inner world, for her two confinements in a private sanatorium had effected only slight, temporary respite from sudden attacks of hysteria and unreason. Tom tried to alleviate her misery, but his efforts were futile. He took her to a dance on Halloween of 1933, but the costumes and gaiety upset rather than lifted her spirits. That same season, a series of gentlemen callers Edwina had lined up for Rose caused emotional trauma, too. Elmer Lower recalled that "the very handsome Jim O'Connor, who was with us at Columbia, had met the Williams family, and apparently Tom's mother tried to set him up with Rose." Of this proposed match nothing is known except that there was only one, brief social call — and it may well have been just as it was later described in *The Glass Menagerie,* when the gentleman caller named Jim O'Connor is brought home to meet the lame, shy sister of the poet Tom.

Rose's phobias and obsessions multiplied throughout late 1934 and early 1935. For a time, she would eat only Campbell's tomato soup, saving the labels as if they were coupons for future discounts. (This example of her inexorable descent into unreason is exactly recalled in the case of Miss Collins in *Portrait of a Madonna.*) Edwina still hoped Rose's erratic behavior would pass if she met the right man. Cornelius seemed to have neither the time nor the interest to consider what was happening to his daughter, but it must also be remembered that Edwina denied him virtually every opportunity to share the family's problems.

"Rose became increasingly unhappy and threatened and depressed," according to Dakin, "and even Paul Jameson [Cornelius's superior and the generous provider for the Williams household] no longer interfered. We were at a real time of crisis. The fighting still continued at home, Dad's scandalous behavior wasn't stopped, and he had reached a halt in his upward mobility, professionally and socially. Tom and Rose became terribly fragile at the same time."

But in the unpredictable nature of such things, it was not Rose but Tom who first alarmed the family so severely that they knew a dramatic change was at once necessary.

He had, first of all, become increasingly absentminded, both at home and at the warehouse. It was only several months after a customer repeatedly complained about nondelivery of a $50,000 shipment that the staff traced the error to Tom; he had been given the data, put it in his pocket before lunch, and there it remained. In addition, there was a dramatic weight loss noticed by his mother. Insufficient sleep, high intake of caffeine, excessive smoking and a terrible inner turmoil — not only about his work, but about homosexual feelings and inclinations he only dimly understood (or refused to acknowledge) — conspired to put him on the verge of complete collapse.

A friendly co-worker and an evening at the movies figure as elements in the final weeks before Tom was sent away.

At International Shoe, there was a dark, burly, amiable worker assigned to a job near Tom. He was everything the young poet was not — at ease in crowds and with strangers, sure of his strength and confident of his ability to charm the ladies. He became Tom's closest companion at the warehouse, and with him Tom apparently felt accepted, even protected from some of the harshness that otherwise surrounded his life. Soon, however, the man married, and about ten years later he died. His name was Stanley Kowalski, and his family survived in St. Louis for many years after. It is perhaps hard to know how much of his character and personality are represented by the character with that name in *A Streetcar Named Desire,* but the attraction to him by Blanche DuBois is certainly something that the playwright himself first knew. There is no evidence of a realized homosexual affair between Williams and Kowalski, but according to Dakin it was clear that Tom had a powerful erotic and romantic attachment to Kowalski: Kowalski's name was often mentioned by Tom, and to see them together was to see a love-struck hero-worshipper and the idol of his dreams.

Very soon after Stanley's departure, which depressed him even further, he took Rose to see the film *The Scarlet Pimpernel* — on March 24, 1935, two days before his twenty-fourth birthday. Because they both became nervous in crowded streetcars, they returned by service-car (a kind of taxi-van). But during the ride, as if someone had thrown a switch inside him, Tom's heartbeat increased dramatically, he broke into a sweat, and he thought he was going to die of a stroke or a heart attack. "It was a terrible crisis of nerves," Dakin remembered, "a fierce anxiety attack which he thought forever after was a real heart seizure. That was the onset of his breakdown."

He was taken at once to a hospital, where tests determined that there was no cardiac incident, no sign of dangerous hypertension — in fact, nothing remarkable beyond evident exhaustion and underweight. During the next month he stayed home from the warehouse several days, and Dr. O. P. J. Falk made house calls to Enright Avenue at Edwina's urgent summons. But if Tom's physical condition was not so alarming, it was clear to doctor and family that he was in an acute state of emotional distress, and two unstable adults in one small apartment was certainly too much for them. Tom's resignation from International Shoe was accepted at the end of April, and in May he began a four-month recuperation in the warmth of the Dakin home at 1917 Snowden Avenue in Memphis.

His grandparents welcomed him with their usual generosity, without asking questions. Tom passed the first weeks lazily, enjoying Grandmother's rich meals, taking long walks through the streets of Memphis in the full bloom of springtime, and indulging himself in afternoon naps. But as he had scribbled in a notebook the previous season, "Words are a net to catch beauty," and he could not for long avoid working at his nets.* His rapid recovery is a testimony to his extraordinary resilience — a trait that characterized his entire life — and at this time it was given great forward momentum by a renowned writer and by a forgotten one.

Before the end of May 1935, Tom had visited the local branch library, and then the central and school libraries of Memphis, where he was enthralled by the life and writings of Anton Chekhov. From then on Chekhov, like Ibsen and Strindberg, was a spiritual mentor — and Chekhov's life he later saw as yet another model for his own. (Asked which playwrights he thought most influenced his work, he usually replied Strindberg and Chekhov.)

After reading at last *The Cherry Orchard* and *The Sea Gull* (which had been on a Columbia reading list he took with him to Memphis), he was soon engrossed in the three volumes of letters that had been translated by Constance Garnett and Louis Friedland. Although no full biography was yet available, these letters and Oliver Elton's *Chekhov* gave him a sense of kinship with the great Russian fabulist and playwright. Perhaps it is not

* The aphorism is put on the lips of Myra in "The Field of Blue Children," a short story he soon began and which was published in 1939.

too strong to say that in time Chekhov's life and destiny were in a deep, interior way assumed by Tom Williams.

After a mediocre school record, Chekhov had discovered the delight of private reading, theatregoing and the pleasures and rewards of writing comic sketches. He took a medical degree, but his writing always dominated, and as he developed the short story form he devoted himself more to serious tales of human struggle and physical illness. "A Dreary Story" and "The Steppe" and *Ivanov,* all written in 1888–1889, were certainly inspired by his experiences as a doctor. The failure of his play *The Sea Gull* in 1894 wounded him deeply, and he claimed at that time he would abandon the stage altogether — a promise which, fortunately, was broken two years later. Tom responded at once to the painful tone of the letters about Chekhov's childhood, seeing perhaps in the Russian writer's hated town of Taganog everything he resented about St. Louis. But it was Chekhov's gentle, elegiac explorations of the secret motives of characters that impressed him, and the tragic vision even within the comic sense that satirized the lack of human sharing. University professors were beginning to speak about Chekhov and a new psychological realism; in May 1935 Tom not only discovered the terms of that for himself, he found a dramatic mood that gripped his imagination and challenged his powers.

He admired most deeply *The Sea Gull,* for this was just the right time in his own life to appreciate its feeling for the sad extinction of youth and talent in an oppressive environment. Its sensitive characters moved him, and at the same time, without the pressure of college papers and examinations, he absorbed the technique of using real objects symbolically in a play: the sea gull, after all, represents not only the triumph of the spirit over adversity, but even the commoner fact of life then known to him — the killing of beauty by those ignorant of it. (In 1981 he wrote a free adaptation of *The Sea Gull,* called "The Notebooks of Trigorin," which was staged in Vancouver and later in Los Angeles. *The Sea Gull,* he thought, showed Chekhov as "the most moving writer." The young New Orleans writer in Williams's short play *The Lady of Larkspur Lotion,* when asked his name, cries out "Chekhov! Anton Pavlovitch Chekhov!")

The theme of beauty threatened or destroyed — already introduced in his college plays and in sheafs of unevenly written poems — he also found in *The Cherry Orchard,* whose title had the same symbolic resonances. And in that play's character of Peter Trofimov, Williams met himself: the university outcast; the threadbare, comic idealist; the eternal student and eternal adolescent; the marginal dreamer who works toward the realization of his dreams.

By June his outlook and energy had greatly improved, and in an affectionate letter to Dakin dated June 25 he congratulates his brother on good high-school grades and then explains an additional reason for his own cheerfulness: a neighbor's daughter, Bernice Dorothy Shapiro, had asked Tom to collaborate on a one-act play for her amateur theatre group. As it turned out, Bernice wrote only the prologue and epilogue, and Tom contributed the rest, a four-scene comedy about the troubled love affairs of two sailors. The play — called *Cairo, Shanghai, Bombay* — took the characters on an imaginary trip around the world in an effort to untangle their romantic anguish. With Miss Shapiro's name preceding Tom's, the play was performed by the Memphis Garden Players in the yard of its organizer, Alice Rosebrough. It was the first nonschool production, however modest, of any play by Thomas Lanier Williams, and its somewhat naïve romanticism does not eclipse its simple and credible descriptions, or the touching sweetness of the two young women characters. The leading lady, Tom added in the letter to Dakin, shouted so loudly that she sounded more like a fishmonger than an actress, but the production was great fun, it was turning his life around, and he was even making a brief, silent cameo in it.

It was perhaps, then, Chekhov and this play and the gentle encouragement of his grandparents in Memphis that summer that sealed his decision to write words for actors, and to create funny and dramatic scenes that could move an audience. From these months he could date himself as a working playwright, and it is actually at this time — long before he took steps to use a new name — that he thought of himself no longer as Thomas Lanier Williams, the quite ordinary son of a mismatched Southern couple, but as a new branch on the Williams tree, one that first flourished in Tennessee.

In September he was ready to return to St. Louis, and to enroll at Washington University — but at first only as an auditor, in a noncredit, less demanding situation. "By this time," according to Dakin, "Dad was making $7500 a year, which was a good salary, and we could afford to rent larger houses in better neighborhoods. And so we moved — first to 6634 Pershing Avenue, then to 42 Aberdeen Place, a comfortable, spacious red-brick colonial house not far from Washington University."

The fall of 1935 was on several counts a time of continuing growth, of intellectual stimulation, and of high-speed creative energy. He read the required books for courses in general literature and philosophy — William James's *Will to Believe* and *Varieties of Religious Experience,* Chesterton's *Heretics* and *Orthodoxy,* Santayana's *Last Puritan,* Russell's *Sceptical Essays,* Walter Lippmann's *Preface to Morals,* John Dewey's *Common Faith;* then he went through the works on literary theory and criticism by Clive Bell, I. A. Richards, Max Eastman and T. S. Eliot. In a notebook at that time he reflected at length on the situation of the poetic, intuitive, subjective side of the artist, of intuition drawing largely from the unconscious. Even after constant rewriting of his poems, he thought, a work continued to expand in his unconscious mind and new ideas and feelings forced revaluations and revisions. This self-imposed demand of aesthetic refinement would become a habit as the years passed; until his death, Williams continually revised his produced and unproduced plays, and in some cases (*Sweet Bird of Youth,* for example) there are as many important variations in the text as there are printed editions.

But his school notebooks and theses and examination books never indicate anything other than passing interest in textbook literary theory — Williams was interested in what he could *experience,* what he could *feel* within himself and then enable his readers or audiences to experience and feel. From the start — and most forcefully this season, when he knew more clearly the acuteness of his own sensitivity — he was excited by the enterprise of transforming that inner experience into controlled poetic emotion. His sympathies were with the Romantics, not with modern realists like Sinclair Lewis. And in a paper on Goethe that he submitted in the spring term of 1936, he embarked on a passionate (if tangential) plea for the preservation of human dignity in a mechanical age. Goethe's study of practical anatomy, he wrote, was but a prelude to the German poet's plea for the moral improvement of the human race. (The original draft of his play *Summer and Smoke,* just a decade later, bore the title *Chart of Anatomy,* and its conflicts are very close to a revision of this early student enthusiasm for Goethe. The possibility of salvation and damnation was, for Williams, as for the German poet, largely a question of a terrestrial battle with the demands of both flesh and spirit, of inner light and inner darkness.)

That year his energies as a working poet were encouraged by friendship with another student who was already an established poet and translator — Clark Mills McBurney, who omitted, professionally, his family name. Soon they were joined by a younger undergraduate, William Jay

Smith, and the trio formed an informal circle they called a "literary factory."

"Tom had fanatical and inexhaustible energy in his writing," Clark Mills recalled. "His persistence was almost grotesque. It was Dionysian, demoniac. He wasn't aiming basically at material success. He wrote because it was a fatal need."

Mills's impression of Williams was on the mark. Although he often referred to himself as a rebellious Puritan, Williams actually was a living example of the creative personality who shared the Dionysian or Bacchic impulse. This term, which derives from the ancient orgiastic rituals connected with the worship of Dionysus or Bacchus (the god of wine, revelry and fertility), refers to the unfettered, passionate abandonment of the senses. The cult of Dionysus was a manic explosion celebrating life, sex, the abundance of food and intoxicating drink; it aimed for an ecstatic loss of control. As the classical scholar H. D. F. Kitto tersely wrote, "the worship of Dionysus stimulated . . . the lively dramatic sense of the Greeks," and it is generally believed that these ancient seasonal festivals in honor of the inebriate god were in fact the beginning of theatre. Dionysus — and his cult-followers — were committed to sensual intoxication, sexual frenzy, and the sudden manifestation of passionate art deriving from unbounded irrationality.

During the 1930s, his fierce attachment to writing — this "fatal need," as Mills called it — had as yet no counterpart in his physical or sexual life. Soon, however, there would be the same intensity, the same apparent helplessness in other areas of his life: Tennessee Williams's passion for writing was soon matched by wildly promiscuous sex. In both activities there was always something obsessive, indiscriminate. Writing was never a Puritanic duty — any more than sex was. In a sense he was a possessed man, overwhelmed by instincts and impulses he never sorted out. The most dangerous result of this part of his nature would finally involve him in the twilight world of drug addiction.

Again that season, as his appreciation of artists widened, so did his interior association with their lives. The stories, poems and essays of Rainer Maria Rilke, the German writer who died only a decade earlier at fifty, were being circulated in translation, and that year the *Sonnets to Orpheus* were snatched up by campus poets and professors everywhere. Rilke's *Notebook of Malte Laurids Brigge* startled him with its account of the personal anguish of a Danish expatriate. Tom now felt another association — with Rilke, whose frustrated, unhappy father was ill-suited to his pretentious, aristocratic mother. Both poets suffered the demands of fathers who wanted them to be military officers; both had frail health in childhood; both had emotional collapses in young adulthood. The similarities in their lives struck him as astonishing — forced to enroll in business courses, each was helped by the quiet kindness of relatives. Tom then read Rilke's *Auguste Rodin,* which reinforced his own sense of incompletion about his art: the creative individual must be committed to the ideal of unremitting work — *toujours travailler,* as Rodin called it and Rilke and Williams learned it. The connections between Rilke and Williams would become even clearer in the years ahead; Rilke's guiding spirit, he thought, followed him right up to the end.

But if his creative life was thriving and the material circumstances at home were comfortable, life with Rose was increasingly sad. For a brief time Edwina put her to teaching Sunday school at St. Michael's and St. George's. Rose, who learned that Reverend Carl Morgan Block, the pastor, was half Jewish, mentioned this innocently to friends and parishioners, and the unwelcome news made the rounds of parish gossip in no time. Dr. Block, perhaps because in a strange way he shared the anti-Semitism of the shocked parishioners, dismissed Rose at once. This exacerbated her already fragile condition.

"She then became increasingly sick with imaginary ills," according to Dakin, "and shortly after we had moved into Pershing Avenue a terrible thing happened. Across the street was Roger Moore, whose sister Virginia was a noted local poet. Roger was a brilliant young man who wanted to get into politics, and he was, as it turned out, the last possibility of someone like a beau or boyfriend for Rose. But Roger had some kind of psychological illness, too, and he was put by his family into a private sanatorium in Kirkwood. One night he broke out, ran into the street and was killed by a truck. This was crushing for Rose. Then, about the same time, Tom uttered a thoughtless remark to her. There'd been a party at the house, while our parents were away for a weekend business trip, and Tom had a few beers. Rose, who was obsessive about alcohol because of Dad, said she was going to tell mother about the beer, and Tom lashed out at her, 'I never want to see your ugly old face again!' Of course he regretted that at once, but Rose was shattered, and from this point on she virtually separated herself from the rest of us."

William Jay Smith recalled Rose's eerie isolation, too. "[She] was rarely mentioned when we came to the house, but we knew that she was up in her room, perhaps listening at the top of the stairs. She was very withdrawn, on the edge of complete breakdown."

On Tom's twenty-fifth birthday, the St. Louis newspapers ran the story of another laurel: he had won first prize (twenty-five dollars) in a verse contest sponsored by the Wednesday Club. His three "Sonnets for the Spring" were selected over more than four hundred other submissions.

This, of course, was marvelously encouraging for Tom and William Jay Smith and their little circle.

"The amount of work that Tom turned out at the time was truly amazing," according to Smith. Many of these poems appeared in *The Eliot,* the Washington University literary magazine, and in *College Verse,* the journal of the College Poetry Society. "Even at parties we always talked about writing," Smith added. "That's what we had decided we definitely wanted to do in life, and that is what we were doing." And they continued to do it by forming the St. Louis Poets Workshop, from which they sent their writings to magazines all across the country. In 1936 and 1937, seven poems by Thomas L. Williams were published in *College Verse,* four in *Poetry* and nine in *The Eliot.* "We have been looking for poetry like this for some time," wrote *The Eliot*'s editor. Another member of the staff remembered Williams as "the model contributor: reliable, neat, careful and literate, [but] I regretted his shyness — he usually slipped his poems under *The Eliot* office door."

Thriving on his success as a university poet and apprentice playwright, Tom was still, according to Smith, "the shyest, quietest person I had ever met. His stony-faced silence often put people off: he appeared disdainful of what was going on around him, never joining in the quick give-and-take of a conversation, but rather listening carefully and taking it all in. He would sit quietly in a gathering for long periods of time until suddenly like a volcano erupting he would burst out with a high cackle and then with resounding and uncontrollable laughter. Those who knew him well found this trait delightful, but to others it seemed rude and disconcerting."

His shyness was at least briefly overcome, however, when the university's French department staged Molière's *Scapin* in April 1936; Tom was persuaded to take the part of Argante, and his performance demonstrated another side to his complex personality. "He read his French lines," Smith said, "with a kind of hound-dog ferocity and deliberation, as if he were chewing on a large section of the Mississippi delta. When he moved woodenly across the stage with absolute seriousness, pounding the floor with his cane, small and square in his satin suit, an enormous blond wig flopping about on his shoulders, he gave a performance that a more sophisticated audience would have taken as deliberate high camp. As it was, our local audience had not the remotest idea of when to laugh since [they] had not a clue as to what was going on."

At the end of that month, the Webster Groves Theatre Guild announced that a one-act play called *The Magic Tower,* submitted by Williams, had won first prize (a sterling silver cake plate Edwina cherished forever after) and would be produced by them later that year. At once he summoned his colleagues in the poets' workshop, and insisted that playwriting be included in their efforts and submissions. When they met at the Williams home, however, both work and socializing were made difficult by Edwina's presence.

"She never stopped talking," Smith recalled, "although there was little inflection or warmth in the steady flow of her speech. One topic, no matter how trivial, received the same emphasis as the next, which might be utterly tragic. I had the impression listening to her that the words she produced were like the red balls in a game of Chinese checkers, all suddenly released and clicking quickly and aimlessly about the board."

The summer of 1936 was a busy time for the entire family. Edwina had been accepted into the local chapter of the Daughters of the American Revolution, and she was occupied with social events and, as secretary, with national correspondence. Dakin and Cornelius were frequently off to ball games. Rose made a few final, frail attempts at attending luncheons for neighborhood ladies. And Tom, in his cramped "studio" in the basement, wrote as if this were his last chance. In August, *Manuscript* magazine published his short story "27 Wagons Full of Cotton," which over the next twenty years would be several times revised as a story, two separate plays and a film — each version progressively more shocking for his audiences. In this early telling, it was the story of a woman lounging indolently on the verandah of her Southern plantation, talking to the foreman who flicks a riding whip and suggests they go into the house where it is dark, cool and private. "I don't know what you'll do to me inside," she says coyly, but adds, "Well, all right, but you must promise not to hurt me."

Even for 1936, the sexy tone and the hint of sadomasochism were a bold step by that magazine; "but Mother and Rose are not used to modern writing," Tom wrote to his grandparents, "and they were very displeased with the subject ... and so Mother forbids me to send the magazine to anybody. She thinks it is too shocking. It is supposed to be humorous but she and Rose don't take it that way."

During the academic year 1936–1937, which Tom began that autumn at Washington University, he studied — for credit now — Greek, French, drama, government, philosophy and literature. But his notebooks reveal where his interests were: there are lines of poetry scrawled round the edges of pages, reflections on nature and dreams and young love. Nature and dreams he had come to know, but young love was entirely a matter of theory to him at this point. His sexual preference was perhaps becoming clearer in his mind, but as Smith noted, "There was not the kind of sexual freedom that there is today. Sex was not the subject of intense campus conversation. And there was little tolerance of sexual deviation. One of the editors of the campus magazine had returned from New York and had openly declared himself a homosexual. We all found this quite shocking."

Tom very likely did not share their shock, but at the same time he discovered an American poet whose life and work and destiny would haunt him for the rest of his life, and with whom — as with Rilke and Chekhov and Strindberg and Ibsen — he saw himself as spiritually linked. Hart Crane's *White Buildings* (1926) and *The Bridge* (1930) were controversial manifestos in the form of radically personal poems. Tom stole these two volumes from the university library, protesting later that they had hardly been borrowed at all. Henceforth, Crane became his most powerful American literary mentor, and a photo of Crane (with one of Chekhov) went wherever Tom Williams lived and traveled.

Crane's poetry and poetic theory — virtually a foreign language for most students of poetry in the 1930s and still enormously difficult for readers — depended on nonrational, hallucinatory associations and connotations to join words. His rich imagery found an intense, sustained explosion in *The Bridge,* which he intended as a reply to T. S. Eliot's "The Waste Land." (Eliot was much studied that year in St. Louis, where he had been born in 1888. His grandfather was a founder and chancellor of Washington University and had given his name to the campus literary magazine.) Williams was at once taken by Crane's idea of art as itself an alternate way of life; his poetic and sexual sensibility, like Whitman's earlier, marked a cry of difference from his fellows and a plea for a fresh vision in a new age. Most fascinating was Crane's affirmation of the Romantic era — and of his own personal history — as a "usable past." It is this aesthetic, this insistence on transmuting the raw material of one's own life into the stuff of poetry and drama, that stung Tom Williams as perhaps the single great challenge he was facing, then or thereafter.

By 1936, Crane had been dead for four years. A mad alcoholic, he had committed suicide at the age of thirty-two by throwing himself from a ship en route from Mexico, and Tom Williams, then twenty-five, was awed by his fiery, profligate life and tragic end. The more he read, the more parallels he found to himself: both endured a miserable home life, both rebelled against fathers for whom they were forced to work. While young, Crane made a break, and began a life of wandering in Cuba, Paris, New York, Ohio and Mexico, until his uncontrollable dependence on drink, and his obsessively promiscuous homosexuality, led him to madness. Everything about Crane's life struck Tom, perhaps precisely because it was a life that consistently defied family, social, sexual and artistic taboos, and that, with its own crazy integrity, rearranged all the accepted icons of American poetry.

In October 1936, the Webster Groves Theatre Guild was ready to stage his one-act play, called *The Magic Tower*. The *News-Times* gave him his first enthusiastic review as a playwright, calling the work "a poignant little tragedy with a touch of warm fantasy. It treats the love of a very young, not too talented, artist and his ex-actress wife, a love which their youthful idealism has translated into a thing of exquisite white beauty. They call the garret in which they live their 'magic tower' and are happy there until the artist's belief in his star fails. Then the magic tower becomes a drab garret once more, and tragedy like a gray woman glides in to remain. [The play] was exquisitely written by its poet author."

A month later, The Mummers of St. Louis, an earnest and polished group of amateur performers, presented Irwin Shaw's graphic antiwar play, *Bury the Dead,* which was preceded by Williams's news dramatization called "Headlines" (for which he was not credited). "I needed a curtain-raiser for the Shaw play," director Willard Holland said years later. "I called Tom and said, 'Could you take some of the headlines and statements by people against war and give us about twelve minutes of stuff to get the audience into the mood for *Bury the Dead?*' "

In a matter of days, Tom turned out four very brief and funny episodes using the short blackout-scene technique: there were an Armistice Day address by a local senator (apt for the day of the play's premiere); two satires on local school and social life; and a sendup of a mythic St. Louis politician. Standing at the rear of the Wednesday Club auditorium, he heard the appreciative laughter of the audience at the three performances. This was a new reaction his words could arouse, and he liked it.

His successes continued. In the middle of March 1937, the Mummers produced his first full-length play. The months in Memphis had given him the idea for *Candles to the Sun,* with its socially alert theme of group and individual welfare against the background of the plight of mine workers in a depressed economy. In the play, the sun represents a group consciousness, the candles that of individuals. The action ends tragically, for individuals come to realize that they cannot succeed and find happiness without the group, which demands some sacrifice of their own small lights. Full of 1930s work-and-union consciousness, but badly structured and overwritten, the play was a local success. (It suggests that Williams may have read John Galsworthy's play *Strife.*)

"They were the disorderly theater group of St. Louis," Williams reflected nine years later, "standing socially, if not also artistically, opposite to the usual Little Theater group.... Dynamism was what The Mummers had.... [Willard] Holland [their organizer] was a great director. Everything that he touched he charged with electricity."

Pleased with these premieres of his work, he set aside the school notebooks and Greek homework and plunged into writing another play, to be submitted in a senior playwriting contest at the university. *Me, Vashya* was about a World War I munitions worker and his eccentric wife (Vashya) — the first of the author's wild ladies. Although years later the judging professor, William G. B. Carson, said that Tom "showed much more ability than the usual student," he did not, that spring of 1937, select the play for presentation. And Tom, who had expected to win at school the way he had been winning with the Mummers and at Webster Groves, was furious.

"It was a terrible shock and humiliation to me. It was a cruel blow. I had always thought I was shy, but I discarded all humility. I stormed into Carson's office. He was a good professor. I screamed at him. I surprised myself." (Dakin added that Carson was "very jealous of Tom's talents, and very unhelpful that year. Tom deserved to win the contest — his play was clearly the best of those submitted — but Carson sabotaged his chances.")*

Tom must have surprised everyone else, too, for the perception about him was identical to that elsewhere. "He wore conservative clothes, tweeds and ties and looked like a young bank teller," Holland recalled.

---

* If the play was indeed "the best of those submitted," the competition cannot have been impressive: *Me, Vashya* has some crackling dialogue between husband and wife, but dramatically it is not much of an improvement on *Candles to the Sun.*

"Writing always came easier to Tom than it does to most people — it just poured out of him. His original manuscripts were the length of three full plays. . . . He was enthusiastic and easy to work with and an easy person to talk to. He had no temperament about his plays. Right from the beginning, I thought of him as a professional. . . . There was an immersion in his work that was staggering . . . [and] he had the most inane laugh I ever heard, a high squeaky cackle, a shriek."

Later, Williams always insisted that it was the rejection of *Me, Vashya* that caused his withdrawal from Washington University and his transfer to the State University of Iowa in the fall of 1937. But there was another reason: he had failed Greek that year, and so he was denied the right to graduate. The disappointment was perhaps greater for his mother, who had hoped the commencement exercises might unite them all for at least one happy family occasion, for it would have coincided with Dakin's graduation from high school.

All during this time, Rose's precarious mental health worsened. In November 1936, Edwina had written to her mother that Rose was "very pitiful. I try to excuse all in her, but she *is* a trial. . . . If I could just get Rose into her right senses we would be 'sitting pretty.' " Moody and withdrawn, then suddenly hysterically angry or weeping at an imagined slight, Rose visited several psychologists at Barnes Hospital, but the counseling seemed not to help her rapid decline. "She still says crazy things," Edwina wrote to Mrs. Dakin in December. "The only thing I can see that the doctor has done for her is to start her to smoking."*

In early 1937, the doctors at Barnes urged Mr. and Mrs. Williams to take Rose to the state asylum at Farmington, for consultation and for out-patient treatments. But after two visits, Edwina saw no improvement: "I can't take her back to those doctors," she wrote her mother on January 26. "The last time she went, the doctor told her that what was the matter with her was 'that she needed to get married.' She has been raving on the subject of 'sex' ever since and I was ashamed for Dakin and Tom to hear her the other night."

During the spring, there was a period of calm, after Rose stayed briefly at St. Vincent's, a mental hospital nearer St. Louis. This was, however, followed by even more outbursts — wild hallucinations, uncontrollable

---

* Some of the poor girl's nervousness at home is easy to understand. In December 1936, Cornelius was engaged in a drunken brawl at a drinking party, and his opponent bit off a generous portion of one ear. When the bandages and stitches were removed, according to Dakin and Tom, something resembling a small cauliflower seemed to have replaced the ear.

rages and outbursts of sexual fantasies — and by threats of physical violence against her father.

The final trauma seems to have been yet another alcoholic rage by Cornelius, in which Edwina was cruelly beaten. Rose, horror-stricken and panicky, raved hysterically, and her father, in his attempt to calm her, made some gesture that was (or that she saw as) too intimate, almost sexual. Her hysteria persisted undiminished for several days, and doctors said that she was now a patient beyond their ability to control with medicines or hot baths or temporary confinements in rest homes. Thoughout the summer of 1937, she was admitted and (inexplicably) discharged at least twice from the state hospital at Farmington.

Concurrent with this tragic development, however, was Tom's decision to leave St. Louis for Iowa City — the expenses for which would again be borne by his adored grandmother. "It wasn't only Washington University that finally disappointed him," according to his brother. "St. Louis represented everything he hated — everything was materialistic, everything was valued in terms of money and social status." As Tom told an interviewer twenty years later, "For all the family, life in St. Louis was dismal," and as late as 1975 he was still calling St. Louis "that dreaded city."

The State University of Iowa promised escape, and perhaps even the success away from home that he so much desired. "It was a great drama school," he told an audience years later, "and had a great reputation for training writers. I went there to study with professors like the great E. C. Mabie and E. P. Conkle."*

At Iowa City, there were at once many important developments in his life. After a brief residence at the local chapter house of the Alpha Tau Omega fraternity, he moved to a two-room apartment with his own kitchen, at 325 South Dubuque, and from there he kept the Dakins informed of his progress and enthusiasm and newly cherished independence. Here he had the privacy he needed to tackle the serious business of his heavy first-term schedule, which included courses in Shakespeare, experimental dramatic production, modern drama, speech (which he failed) and English literature. But he continued his own

---

* Mabie later taught playwriting at the New School for Social Research, New York City, where Erwin Piscator ran the famous Drama Workshop from 1939 to 1951. Conkle's play *200 Were Chosen* had been staged on Broadway in November 1936, and his play *Prologue to Glory* was a successful offering sponsored by the WPA Federal Theatre Project.

writing as well, for the Mummers were eager for a new play for their tenth season.

His first decision was to send them one of the plays he was writing for the dramatic production course — *Spring Storm,* a Southern love story that drew from Professor Mabie the cool criticism, "Well, I guess we all have to paint our nudes!" The play was awash in obvious melodramatic sentiment, lacking in narrative subtlety and devoid of an original touch. Instead, Tom sent Willard Holland another effort, *Not About Nightingales,* a violent play based on an incident in which many men died hideously in a Pennsylvania county prison; the event had been a national scandal and provoked a federal investigation. *Not About Nightingales* was postponed and remained unproduced — not because of its unpleasant subject matter, but because later the Mummers disbanded.

But while he was writing papers, attending classes (with unaccustomed regularity and punctuality), directing and appearing in a campus production of *Hedda Gabler* and writing poems, he completed his revisions for a full-length play called *Fugitive Kind,* which the Mummers at once accepted, believing that it justified their conviction that "Mr. Williams has an important contribution to make to the American stage."

Fugitive Kind* — which was performed at the Wednesday Club on November 30 and December 4, 1937 — is the drama of drifters trying to shake off the repressions and restraints of a bourgeois society. Terry Grady, a criminal on the run, finds in Glory, the adopted daughter of a flophouse keeper, the embodiment of his youthful idealism. Set (obviously, though it is unstated) in St. Louis, its action takes place from Christmas Eve to New Year's Eve, and the *St. Louis Star-Times* published a major review, calling it "a vital and absorbing play . . . several cuts above ordinary amateur efforts. . . . Thomas Lanier Williams is a playwright to watch, [a writer] with first-rate theatrical craftsmanship . . . [who,] like [Sidney] Howard and Ben Hecht and Maxwell Anderson, wants to say something forceful and true about the chaos of modern life."

But Williams was not only advancing his own playwriting career and moving closer to his college degree. He also had his first (and last) affair with a woman — a classmate at Iowa named Bette Reitz, to whose passionately aggressive advances he briefly yielded. "I was a terrible puritan . . . and I remained a puritan until my late 20s," he said later. "I was a

---

* The play has no relation to the film *The Fugitive Kind,* made in 1959; that is based on Williams's play *Battle of Angels* and its later revision, *Orpheus Descending.*

virgin with either sex until the age of 26." After the coed ended their brief encounters, a period of chastity was followed by his admission, to himself, at least, that his erotic desires were really homosexual. At ease in the most creative, open and experimental academic setting he had known, and alert to the shifts in a personality he was coming to know and accept as different from most of his peers, he was ready to assert himself, and to do so sexually.

But this awareness remained secret and dormant, and not because of social or psychological pressure. Grief entered his life in a catastrophic way that season, and it overwhelmed every personal or private consideration.

By autumn 1937, the Williamses had been told that Rose's illness was so advanced that she was capable not only of doing herself physical harm, but also of instigating tragedy — perhaps murder, one doctor said. Her fits had become even more violently schizophrenic, and the doctors insisted that a new neurosurgical procedure — called a leucotomy, or prefrontal lobotomy — was the only cure. It was, they said, safe and sure, and since Rose would be one of the first patients to undergo it, the operation could be performed without charge.

Edwina cringed when the procedure was described: her daughter's skull would be opened, and the nerve fibers connecting the thalamus to the frontal lobes of the brain would be severed. This would result in an immediate and total calming of the patient, and a cessation of the fits and hysterics and dreadful fantasies to which she was subject — some of which, Tom said for years, were simple exclamations of sexual desire deriving from the repressions of a sick woman who was almost thirty years old.

But one of Rose's claims was more upsetting, first because there was no way to assess its truthfulness, but also because it was a terrible possibility. One evening, just before Rose's last hospitalization, Edwina had returned home to be met by Rose, who shouted hysterically that her father had come to her room drunk and had spoken and acted in a lewd, provocative way: she insisted, wildly, that Cornelius wanted her, his own daughter, to go to bed with him. This was something unthinkable, unutterable for Edwina. When Rose could not be calmed after two more nights, she was returned to Farmington.

"I was a freshman at Washington University that autumn, when the operation was performed," Dakin remembered. "My father was too involved with his drinking and golf-playing and poker parties to be interested in Rose, so on weekends I drove mother to the state hospital at Farmington to see her. It was of course dreadful, going to that public institution to see your own sister so sad and forlorn, with wild patients screaming all around. It was a real snake pit."

Tom was not told of the operation until he came home for the Mummers' production of *Fugitive Kind* in November. For years he openly blamed his mother: "She gave permission to have it done while I was away. I think she was frightened most of all by Rose's sexual fantasies. But that's all they were — fantasies. . . . She is the one who approved the lobotomy. . . . My sister was such a vital person. She could have become quite well by now if they hadn't performed that goddam operation on her; she would have come back up to the surface. My mother panicked because she said my sister had begun using four-letter words. 'Do anything! Don't let her talk like that!' "

In *Remember Me to Tom,* Edwina wrote that the final decision was made by her husband. She also said that the operation, she later realized, was a grave mistake that might have been substituted for by therapy and medication. The lobotomy soon became virtually an unknown operation.

From then on, the spirit of his sister haunted his life, her personality trapped in a childish permanence like a pinned butterfly. From his earliest one-act plays in 1938 to the end of his life, the name and image of Rose and her beloved roses pursued him.*

In a calm, reflective mood, he could speak with an almost stoic resignation about this irreversible tragedy: "I don't think I would have been the poet I am without that anguished familial situation. . . . I've yet to meet a writer of consequence who did not have a difficult familial background if you explored it."

But his deepest feelings were more anguished, less academic. "She was the best of us all, do you understand?" he wept to a friend years later. "More beautiful, more intelligent, sweeter and warmer than anyone. Not one of us was fit to stoop and tie her shoes."

* A few select examples: the proliferation of rose imagery in *The Rose Tattoo;* Aunt Rose of *The Unsatisfactory Supper,* and her roses; the roses "of yesterday, of death and of time" in *The Milk Train Doesn't Stop Here Anymore, Camino Real, The Last of My Solid Gold Watches* and *Something Unspoken;* the wild roses of *The Case of the Crushed Petunias;* the roses of Picardy in *Moony's Kid Don't Cry;* the mystic rose of *Now the Cats with Jewelled Claws;* the smell of roses in *The Mutilated,* the wild roses of *Will Mr. Merriwether Return from Memphis?* and the roses in *Small Craft Warnings, The Two-Character Play,* etc. He also painted images of roses in astonishing profusion — both quick sketches and carefully rendered representations.

* * *

And so Rose Isabel Williams survived from 1937 to the end of her long life, which outdistanced her brother's. She inhabited a timeless twilight, in which — when she was asked her age or the date or the events of the time — she would always reply that she was twenty-eight, that her brother Tom was twenty-six, and that her world revolved around visits from "that man, Cornelius Williams." She was free of physical pain and fear and emotional distress at last, but no human communion was possible. For years she was treated with exceptional gentleness and generosity by her only friend, her brother Tom, who had collapsed once and lived in terror of collapsing again. For the rest of his life, he saw in her the tragic figure that he, too, could have become, and might yet. And twenty years later, he wrote one of his great plays, *Suddenly Last Summer,* which includes so many of the real-life details of 1936 and 1937.

The deepest poignancy of her life was never known to her, for ever after she was never quite sure just who she, or her brother, was; worse still, she seemed, in her detachment, never to care very much. Little of Thomas Lanier Williams's life after 1937 is comprehensible without appreciating the awfulness of that Christmas season, when the open warfare in family life was stilled forever, along with the last possibility of life as a complete family.

Chapter Three

IN TRANSIT
(1938–1944)

People enter this world without instructions
of where to go, what to do, so they wander a
little. . . .

— Silva Vaccaro, in *Baby Doll*

H
E HAD a charming personality, a consistently gentlemanly demeanor, and he was full of traditional Southern charm." So was Tom Williams, in the spring of 1938, described years later by a classmate at Iowa, Anthony Dexter.

"Tom was in a small clique of people studying under E. C. Mabie, one of the great directors of all time, in my estimation. He was known to everyone as The Boss, and one day Tom said to me, after a playwriting class, 'The Boss says my work needs a touch more humor. What do you think?' And I said, 'Well, that might not hurt it.' "

The other mentor under whose guidance Williams flourished was the playwright and theorist Elsworth P. Conkle. "I have only one really good student this year," he recalled telling his wife. "He's poor and shy and very talented." Mrs. Conkle's interest in young Williams was at once very keen, for her husband did not often bring home praise for aspiring writers. "Go and see if you can get him to talk to you," he urged her. Virginia Conkle attended a rehearsal of one of Tom's short plays, then in studio production for class.

"Tom Williams was in the front row and I sat down near him. When the curtain came down and the lights went up he took one look at me, recognized me as the professor's wife, and quickly ran away. My husband wasn't there to introduce me, and he was simply too shy to greet me himself. That was my only chance to meet Tom Williams."

"The course also required the students to work only with dialogue, to write radio scripts for reading over the Iowa station," E. P. Conkle added. "I always selected Williams's for broadcast, and for a simple reason: they were the best. At the end of the school year, I recommended to Mabie that Tom be kept on as a graduate student on scholarship, but Mabie's enthusiasm for his work had cooled. 'I've read his new stuff and I don't like it,' he said." This, it turned out, was a minority report, for Conkle and other teachers — especially Edwin Ford Piper, who directed the creative writing seminar — realized they had a unique talent with them that year. Conkle and Piper worked with him, briefly, on a manuscript about the most troubled period in the life of Vincent van Gogh, which Williams wanted to call *The Holy Family;* the project, about artistic aspirations and the danger of madness, was abandoned after several weeks.

During the spring term of 1938, it was clear to Williams that playwriting, and not poetry, would dominate. *L'Alouette* published two final poems that season, as did *The Eliot.* On February 22, the *Daily Iowan,* listing Thomas Williams as a charter member of Pi Tau, the honorary writers' fraternity, mentioned only his plays, for that is what he and his department were emphasizing. Word had got around the campus that he had sent *Candles to the Sun* for consideration in a contest sponsored by the Dramatists Guild in New York, and while the Guild's evaluation was not wildly enthusiastic, a summary report praised the author's pronounced individual style.

In April, he also made another stage appearance — as a footman in the first part of *Henry IV,* a performance that did not help him either in the Shakespeare or the stagecraft course.* His report at Iowa — although he had B's in literature, experimental drama and creative writing — was lowered by D's in classical and modern drama and in zoology, and he had to enroll in the summer session to graduate at last, at the age of twenty-seven, on August 5, 1938. The degree conferred was a bachelor of arts with a major in English. The expenses connected with the extra term were diminished by a work plan: the university had a cooperative program with the state hospital whereby needy students could receive compensation for services. That summer, Tom worked as a dishwasher in the doctors' cafeteria. In a letter to his mother, dated June 4, he thanked her for a wristwatch needed for the job, reported that he got three free meals daily at the cafeteria, and said the new attic apartment he had taken (at 126 North Clinton) at least included clean sheets every week.

A time of poverty, nevertheless, was beginning. The Dakins could no longer afford to help support Tom, and Cornelius had no interest in subsidizing what he considered laziness. Tom departed Iowa shortly after the summer graduation, with very little pocket money and a change of name to mark what he felt was a dramatic new time of his new dramatic life.

For the next forty-five years, Tennessee Williams told interviewers that

---

* In *Memoirs,* Williams claimed he played a page-boy in *Richard of Bordeaux;* university records, however, are more accurate.

Thomas Lanier Williams "sounds like it might belong to the sort of writer who turns out sonnet sequences to spring" (which of course is just what he had done). The transformation to "Tennessee," he sometimes said, was suggested because the Williams clan had fought the Indians for Tennessee, and the idea of the defense of a stockade against a band of savages was consistent with a writer's hard life.

On other occasions, he said he got the name from classmates, that it was not his own choice at all: "the fellows in my class could only remember that I was from a Southern state with a long name. And when they couldn't think of Mississippi, they settled on Tennessee. That was all right with me, so when it stuck I changed it permanently."

The truth of the matter lies, as so often with Williams, on a level of feeling — not on a logical, academic-ancestral decision, nor on the accident of others' confusion. From the summer of 1935, when his health, his outlook and his confidence were given healing encouragement in Memphis, he had associated everything that followed with that time and place. And so it was not basically from his *father's* family that he took the name, but from the cherished summer he linked with a turning from emotional collapse to an emergence as a creator of character and dialogue. In the state of Tennessee, with his beloved grandparents, he had become well enough to write his first play produced outside school, and that memory, to which he would often return as to an epiphany, was most deeply responsible for the name some, at time time of its adoption, considered whimsical, ludicrous or hopelessly fey.

Conkle urged Williams to travel first that autumn to Chicago, where the Works Progress Administration's Federal Writers' Project still survived. Aimed at providing employment for writers, editors and researchers, the project at its peak helped over 6,500 young writers, most of whom had assisted in the preparation of the famous *American Guide* series for every state and major cities, as well as ethnic and folklore studies, nature guides and more than a thousand books and pamphlets celebrating history, art and culture in America. At various times, Conrad Aiken, Richard Wright, Ralph Ellison, Nelson Algren, Frank Yerby and Loren Eiseley were among those who benefited from this employment. (Federal sponsorship ended, by an act of Congress, in 1939, but states were free to extend individual programs through 1943.)

When he arrived in Chicago in September, however, Williams was told that there were fewer positions available than he or Conkle had hoped — and in addition, his family was not on the welfare rolls. He argued that he was as close to destitution as anyone could get, but the administrators saw his family's address — a private home in a St. Louis suburb — and he was sent away.

They recommended, however, that he travel to New Orleans, where the Writers' Project apparently needed a larger staff and was not so demanding about family status. He took the long bus ride south, stopping briefly at home when he was told the Dakins were visiting. The autumn chill had settled in Chicago and St. Louis early that year, and he was soon eager to move on. The WPA had bad news for him in New Orleans, however, and even after six weeks there was no chance of anything like a writer's job for him.

But with his usual optimism and endurance — and because he at once had fallen in love with New Orleans — he stayed on, waiting tables in the French Quarter, distributing handbills for jazz clubs, accepting day jobs. The city itself, he felt, was providing incomparably rich ingredients for his writing, and also a heavy counterweight to whatever Victorian shyness about sex may still have lingered in him.

"It was a period of accumulation," he reflected years later. "I found the kind of freedom I had always needed, and the shock of it, against the Puritanism of my nature, has given me a subject, a theme, which I have never ceased exploiting."

From a room at 431 Royal Street for which he paid three dollars a week late that autumn (and for which "modest" would be too gentle a word to describe its cell-like squalor), he went forth each day and evening to absorb the spirit of what is for many people America's most colorful city — especially in its old Vieux Carré, the French sector that has become synonymous with the birth of the blues, the consumption of catfish and bourbon, and the death of virtually every social and sexual taboo.

At first sight, he loved the heterogeneous, unplanned coexistence of architectural styles, the wrought-iron balconies, the interior and exterior spiral staircases, shuttered doors and windows, the verandahs and quiet courtyards with fountains and exotic plants, and the ethnic diversity of the Gallic streets (Dauphine, Burgundy, Bourbon, Dumaine, Chartres, Toulouse) and those named for saints (Ann, Philip, Peter, Claude) and for the order of nuns who founded the first schools in French Canada and French New Orleans (Ursulines).

The French quarter was, for the man who registered in boardinghouses as "Tennessee Williams, Writer," everything that St. Louis was not. It had something of the South he knew as a child, where the climate was hospitable and there was an air of faded gentility, and where his accent aroused no startled reaction. But there was also a vague tincture of decadence, and this was a marked contrast to the Victorian prudery that was taken for granted in his youth — and which, as if she were overreacting to years with Cornelius's rudeness and indignities, Edwina had in the last several years been exaggerating in her own manners.

In the haphazard mixture of cultures in the French Quarter, there were the mobility and eclecticism of a port town, and the cultivation of a kind of creative indolence. Whitman had been fascinated by the city, and in their turn Mark Twain and Sherwood Anderson, William Faulkner and John Dos Passos. And the marginal society there was, in 1938, not quite so self-conscious as later, when it would wear a carefully tended garland of eccentricity for the benefit of tourists. For the first time in his life, Williams lived among those whom his family and neighbors in Columbus and Clarksdale and Clayton would have rejected: pimps and their prostitutes, gamblers, alcoholics, drug addicts — as well as good-natured, indigent musicians, the wandering minstrels who had survived the Depression, sailors just passing through and ready for a day of relaxation and a night of whatever pleasures were offered, working girls of uneven virtue, and — as easily as if the rest of America did not care — a significant population of homosexuals.

For all the excitement, the novelty and the sensuality of New Orleans, he continued to write daily — mostly short stories and one-act plays based on those he met, the lost and abused, the forgotten and the emotionally maimed; they would all, sooner or later, find their counterparts in the characters of his plays.

In addition, the easy juxtaposition of charm and sensuality soon affected him, and as 1939 was rung in — at an impromptu party at the Royal Street boardinghouse — his sexual inhibitions were abandoned and there was a rush of erotic energy.

His first homosexual experience, he claimed, was unforeseen, and with a stranger for whom he at once developed a tender affection. When the stranger vanished before dawn, Williams was confused and a little sad — but only for a few hours. It was a new year, after all, and he was at an important new stage of self-awareness.

Before the week ended, he had moved to an attic apartment at 722 Toulouse Street that he considered wonderfully bohemian. At a rent of ten dollars a month he could afford to take an occasional brandy

Alexander at Victor's Bar nearby. And he could, he wrote to his mother, find a satisfying ten-cent breakfast, and dinner at a good cafeteria near Canal Street for fifty cents. Oysters, at twenty cents a dozen, were often a filling meal. But every morning — sometimes as early as four o'clock, if he had not dallied late the previous evening — he wrote, and from those private times came the scenes of New Orleans life that would later be polished as one-act plays (*The Lady of Larkspur Lotion, Auto-Da-Fé, Lord Byron's Love Letter, Suddenly Last Summer, The Mutilated*), as short stories ("One Arm" and "Desire and the Black Masseur" and "The Angel in the Alcove") and full-length plays (the great *A Streetcar Named Desire* and, near the end, his memory-play *Vieux Carré*). If he had had a particularly tiring day working at the small table in his room, he would treat himself to a hot supper at Alpine's La Bohème Restaurant, which Sherwood Anderson and William Faulkner had frequented.

For a very short time, he worked at a typical eatery, where he conceived the idea of advertising "Meals in the Quarter for a Quarter," which pleased the cook, Mrs. Nesbit, until she decided that the restaurant business was not worth its headaches. She went to Florida at the end of January, and Tennessee was, only by default, a full-time writer again.

During those warm winter weeks he continued to hope that the WPA would be sufficiently impressed with his revisions on *Fugitive Kind* to see that his social conscience was a delicate one and that they could well use his talents either in New Orleans or in Florida; and now, in addition, he could demonstrate authentic indigence and not a penny of family support. While he waited for a reply, he continued to enjoy the heady sexual freedom the Quarter permitted. Sometimes, too, there were parties in the ground-floor apartment of the artist-photographer at 722 Toulouse; one of these revels went on so loudly and so late that the impatient landlady, Mrs. Anderson, poured a bucket of scalding water through the floor-cracks, thereby scattering the guests. (The incident is recalled in his play *Vieux Carré*.)

In February, however, it became clear that the WPA would be of no help to him, and as soon as he heard that the Group Theatre in New York was sponsoring a play contest, he sent them four one-act dramas, as well as *Not About Nightingales* and *Fugitive Kind*.

The Group Theatre had been throughout the 1930s a vital force in American culture, and from its early guidance under Harold Clurman, Cheryl Crawford and Lee Strasberg it had produced vivid and timely plays — among them John Howard Lawson's *Success Story*, Sidney Kingsley's *Men in White,* several plays by Clifford Odets, including *Waiting for Lefty, Awake and Sing!* and *Golden Boy,* plays by William Saroyan and Kurt Weill, and Irwin Shaw's *Bury the Dead.* Everyone who followed serious theatre knew the importance of the Group, which encouraged the talents of these writers, developed the skills of actors and directors like Strasberg, Clurman, Stella Adler, Elia Kazan, Ruth Nelson, Luther Adler, Morris Carnovsky, John Garfield, Sylvia Sidney, Karl Malden and Lee J. Cobb, and evolved a unique style of production and performance that continued to influence Broadway and Hollywood long after the Group's dissolution in 1941.

There was one impossible stipulation for Williams in the contest rules, however: the entrants must be under twenty-five. And so on his application he wrote "Tennessee Williams — Born March 26, 1914." This made him twenty-four instead of twenty-seven and started a little fiction that persisted twenty years, until a scrupulous press unearthed the truth.

While he awaited a reply, even the minimal rent and daily meals became problems. When another boarder offered him a free ride to California, he thought he might be able to find a scriptwriting job in the movies. And so he and Jim Parrott (a young clarinetist who wanted to work with a jazz band in Los Angeles) set out in a battered jalopy. "I was desperately poor," he told an interviewer in better times, "and I had to hock everything but my typewriter to get by."

On February 18 they began their long trek, and three days later Tennessee wrote (always as "Tom") to his mother that after the New Orleans Mardi Gras they found San Antonio, Texas, as quiet as a tomb. They were sleeping under the stars at night, in an army tent, and were cooking on open fires at roadside. Fifty cents a day was keeping him alive. Edwina was horrified at the thought that her son was becoming a drifter, and she fired off a note to *her* mother, which of course resulted in a ten-dollar bill to be forwarded to the travelers. From El Paso they made two short trips across the Mexican border, to Villa Acuna and Juárez, and by March 1 a blinding dust storm had pushed them on to Phoenix.

Williams was now fully aware of, and enjoying the sight of, the "able-bodied and attractive young men" (as he commented to Jim Parrott) he noticed in Mexico and the Southwest, and to whom they sometimes gave rides through desert country. But he was touched by their predicament — they were almost invariably poor wanderers, family men with exhausted wives and hungry children, begging for work. His sympathies and his admiration for their courage, reflected in letters home, were as deep as his appreciation for their physical appeal. Jim Parrott, unregenerately heterosexual, felt that his sidekick had an unusually empathetic and delicate conscience, and he was impressed when Williams shared their rations with the pathetic children they so often met.*

Cornelius, of course, approved of none of this traveling — least of all with no job prospect. He contacted Sam Webb, a colleague at the West Coast branch of International Shoe, and asked for help in finding employment for his son.

For Parrott, things were easier as soon as they arrived in Los Angeles on March 7. Although the jazz band mysteriously disappeared, he found temporary work in an airplane factory. In southern California, Tom wrote to his grandparents, the talk was only of war, and planes were being built in great quantity. He, however, could not pass the physical examination for such a job — a cataract was forming in his left eye, the result of a childhood injury and the gradual scarring after diphtheria. Instead, he took a job as a ranch-hand just outside the city, where he plucked and killed pigeons and squabs and shoveled manure — a task, he told Parrott, that would prove a good preparation for writing movies.

This unglamorous outdoor work occupied him almost eighteen hours a day for a month; he usually spent the nights in a nearby cabin. A temporary suspension in his writing thus occurred, and perhaps because his artistic sensibility had to have some release, he accepted an offer of free painting lessons from Parrott's mother, who gave them a room and a hot meal once a week when they bicycled down to visit her in the part of Los Angeles known as Hawthorne. He might, he wrote home, return wearing a beret.

Back in New York, the decision of the Group Theatre had been announced. A reader and member of their administrative staff, Molly Day Thacher, recognized at once that the gifts of this oddly named Tennessee Williams were rare and deep. "There's a wonderful young playwright riding around southern California on a bicycle," she told her husband, the actor and director Elia Kazan, who recalled years later that this was the first time he ever heard of Tennessee Williams. "Molly was charged with the task of finding plays for the Group Theatre, and she asked [Harold] Clurman if she could offer a special prize of one hundred dollars to Williams. She had an extraordinary gift for discovering new talent; she had

---

* Williams's memories and attitudes about the poor "drifters" are reflected in a story outline he eventually gave playwright Lanford Wilson in 1973. In February 1974, "The Migrants" was presented as a television drama, "teleplay by Lanford Wilson, suggested by a story by Tennessee Williams."

done the same for Irwin Shaw, she was doing it then for Williams, and there would be others later, like Robert Anderson."

On March 20, 1939, Molly Day Thacher wrote to Williams that although the five-hundred-dollar first prize was awarded to another writer (Ramon Naya, for *Mexican Mural*), the one-act plays he had sent under the collective title *American Blues* were "so outstanding that [they] deserved special recognition," and she enclosed a check for one hundred dollars.

By this time, Cornelius and his friends had made the appropriate shoestore contact, and before the end of the month the playwright of whom everyone spoke at the Group Theatre was busy working at Clark's Bootery in Culver City, where he was paid $12.50 weekly for a sixty-hour stint as a clerk-salesman. However, his bicycle died of exhaustion after long hours on the Los Angeles roads, and, after replacing it with a younger and stronger substitute, he tendered his resignation from Clark's (after only two weeks), and he and Jim headed south for Tijuana.

The money from New York and Culver City was quickly spent for beer, chili and tire patches, and by mid-May they had taken a vacation cabin back in Laguna Beach, south of Los Angeles, where for $7.50 a month they each had a room, and shared a shower, cooking gas and a small garden from which Williams tried to coax tomatoes. He set himself as rigorous a schedule as he would ever have, writing each morning (among other stories "The Mysteries of the Joy Rio" and "The Vine" were first drafted here); afternoons, he swam in the Pacific; and in the evenings he worked at a bowling alley, where he replaced pins. It was, he said afterward, one of the most carefree times of his life, and least complicated by any excesses — there simply was no time for pursuing anything remotely resembling the life of the sensualist.

But the vigilant Molly Day Thacher was pursuing a more serious career development for him. She sent the one-act plays to an agent she liked and respected. "And that," as Kazan remembered, "is how Tennessee Williams came to the legendary Audrey Wood."

Thus began one of the most lengthy, remarkable, loving and finally tragic creative relationships in American theatre history. Audrey Wood, six years older than Williams, was one of the few artists' representatives who did more than negotiate contracts and process fees; she assumed many practical responsibilities for some of her clients. In 1939, she and her husband, William Liebling, managed the Liebling-Wood Agency, at Rockefeller Center.

Almost at once, Audrey sent agency contracts, formally defining the relationship between Williams and herself. Weeks passed, and finally Williams wrote that several New York agents had leaped to the mails after the Group Theatre's special award. He was considering her offer. This amused Audrey: "After all, we were an established agency — even in California people knew who Liebling-Wood, Inc., was — and here was a struggling author with no credits whatsoever!"

But Williams did not want to appear too eager, and he was just hesitant enough to play for time to read the contract — an enterprise which, with one eye now unusable, took weeks. On June 20, Audrey wrote again, asking for the countersigned agreement and adding the good news that *Story* magazine had accepted a piece of short fiction Molly had sent along, called "The Field of Blue Children." It would, she wrote, appear in the September–October issue that year — and, as he insisted, under the name "Tennessee Williams." The story was a delicately written account of a college girl who, after once sexually consummating her friendship with an awkward young poet of average gifts but guileless personality, marries a solid provider. It was also one of the clearest examples of the author reflecting on his own college experience, for he is at once the passionate and pragmatic Myra and the shy poet Homer. Audrey loved the story, ignoring Williams's curious reply (on July 30) that he was pleased with the news of publication but that it did not banish his terror of madness. He enclosed the countersigned agency contract.

Toward summer's end, Williams had grown weary of Los Angeles, and he was eager to be part of the New York theatre world. But cross-country travel was out of the question, since he had but a few dollars left to his name. Audrey came to his rescue (for the first of many times) and advanced him, against *Story*'s autumn payment, the price of a bus ticket.

On August 25, he stopped in Taos, New Mexico, to visit D. H. Lawrence's widow, Frieda, to introduce himself as an admirer of her husband, and to pay homage to the place Lawrence had visited in 1922. "Tom's great god," according to William Jay Smith, "was D. H. Lawrence." This is perhaps an inflated assessment of Williams's hierarchy of favorites, but there can be no doubt of Lawrence's influence on Williams's early prose and poetry — particularly regarding the mystic confluence of sex, nature and power. Audrey, aware of the controversy over Lawrence at that time, at once discouraged Williams from writing (as he had promised) a play about him; she suggested instead a play about Vachel Lindsay (as he had originally planned).

But the visit to the widow Lawrence had a different effect. A few days later, stopping to see his family in St. Louis, he was writing first drafts of two one-act plays reflecting Lawrence's life and thematic iconoclasm. *I Rise in Flame, Cried the Phoenix* dramatized the English writer's death, and *The Purification,* a verse play suggesting also the influence of García Lorca, reveals Williams not only adopting a Lawrentian boldness, but also turning it into autobiography.

The central concern of *The Purification* is a confession of incest as direct cause of a woman's death: while a sister and brother slept together, her husband killed her (the play occurs as a trial after the fact). Written hastily and in tense confusion during another visit to St. Louis since Rose's operation, it concerns a man's guilt over his sister's fate: he drove his sister "beyond all fences"; the girl was subject to parental misunderstanding, and "Not even . . . knocking down walls with two blue brutal bare fists . . . could ever . . . enclose such longing as was my sister's!" The mother cries, "I, his mother, must share in this public censure."

The play is a shout of outrage about the Williams family madness, a cry of hatred against his parents for what they had done to Rose; a plaintive wondering about the terrible final battle between Cornelius and his daughter that may, as she claimed, have ended in a gesture too intimate; and it is suffused with guilt for what might have been his own feelings toward his sister. Greek in its conventions but completely personal in its story, *The Purification* is full of anguished longing. (According to Dakin, his brother did not visit Rose in Farmington on this visit — and not, in fact, until several years later.) "Weave back my sister's image," the son cries. "She's lost, snared as she rose. . . . Irretrievably lost . . . too far to pursue. . . . For nothing contains you now, no, nothing contains you, lost little girl, my sister."

Before the end of September, Williams arrived in New York, where he first took a room in an apartment hotel on West 108th Street; at $4.50 weekly, it was one of a block of studios rented to aspiring artists and theatre people who have always flocked into Manhattan. The first week, he wrote to his grandparents on October 2, he was almost paralyzed with loneliness, and when he heard that a Kentucky woman he had met at Iowa was near by on Morningside Drive, he moved in with her. (This was Marion Galloway, for whose book *Constructing a Play* he would, ten years later, write a brief foreword.)

Finally, on October 11, he presented himself at the Liebling-Wood offices. Asking to see his agent, Audrey, he was told to wait with the small crowd who gathered daily, hoping for acting jobs from Liebling, who was a casting agent. Shyly, he took a seat, and when Liebling told him that there was no part for a young man that day, he finally spoke up and announced himself. At that moment Audrey was passing from the outer to the inner office, and heard his name.

The problem they discussed that day was not the acceptance of a story or the production of a play. "His primary need was survival," according to her. "It was unending struggle to stay alive and fed until we could find a producer who would give his work a production. Tennessee needed every penny of the sustenance we could find him." That sustenance included not only trying to sell poems and stories, but also convincing backers or actors to pay option money on his one-act plays. Hume Cronyn recognized the talent behind the short plays, and he advanced money and tried to interest others.*

"I was just beginning to become interested in production and direction," Cronyn recalled. "I peddled these plays around without any success, [but it was] difficult to persuade people to invest in a bill of one-act plays. . . . And there was no such thing as off-Broadway. There was really nowhere else except the commercial theatre to do those plays. . . . I was going to give them up, but Audrey asked me if I could manage to hold them under option for an added six months," because of Williams's financial hardship.

"That was truly an act of faith on Hume's part," Audrey wrote later; "the money came out of his own pocket, not from backers." (Almost eight years later, after a few brief, intermittent meetings, Cronyn and Williams would visit under more auspicious circumstances, after Cronyn had married Jessica Tandy.)

The doling of option money, the small fees from poems and stories and an occasional addition of a few dollars from her own purse — these were managed by Audrey, as well as constant attempts to get him work even outside the theatre. She arranged for him to attend Broadway rehearsals meantime, and she persuaded friends like the wife of theatrical lawyer John Wharton to pass along used warm clothing from her family as autumn turned colder.

---

* Cronyn paid an option fee of fifty dollars a month, which gave him production rights for nine one-act plays. "These plays were extremely poetic and they were very different from the theatre of the time," he said years later, "— the realism, the naturalism. They were plays that haunted me."

"Audrey came to act as a surrogate mother, or perhaps an older sister, to Tennessee," according to playwright Robert Anderson, who a few years later became another of her most successful clients. "I was shocked, for example, to learn that by the mid-1940s she had already, for a long time, been taking care of his personal finances, paying his bills, answering his mail — sometimes even getting him out of trouble. He frequently called her at strange hours and she rushed to his aid when he was in some difficulty. Now this was not entirely exceptional in those days, when an agent's function was more personal — but Audrey was certainly an extreme example of personal care in the case of Tennessee Williams. I think she liked it, actually — after all, she and her husband had no children, and there may have been something in his dependency that she liked."

In spite of her tireless efforts as guardian angel that fall of 1939, however, the money to survive in New York was not forthcoming, and after a brief stay at the Men's Residence Club on West 56th Street — where the five-dollar-a-week room fee included use of a pool — he had no choice but to return to St. Louis. It was a visit he made with considerable reluctance, for it seemed to justify his father's disapproval. His only contact with the writer's life, from November to January, was his correspondence with Audrey, and his completion of a new long play that had been taking shape for several months within him. By year's end, he complained to Audrey in several letters, he was exhausted from alternate moods of rapture and despair from work on the play; he added that it might be his last, for his nerves could not sustain the creative agony.

But just as he was sending these poignant cries, she was sending happier news: the Dramatists Guild, through a grant from the Rockefeller Foundation, had awarded him a writing fellowship of one thousand dollars — which, she added, she would parcel out to him in monthly payments of one hundred dollars.

Once again, his fortunes and his journey were reversed, and early in January 1940 he was back in New York, where Molly Day Thacher joined Audrey in taking the cause of his new play to the Theatre Guild. The noted critic and theatre historian John Gassner was then an administrator at the Guild, and at once he offered Williams the opportunity to attend, without charge, his playwriting seminar at the New School for Social Research. By this time, E. C. Mabie had emigrated there from Iowa — with the recent arrival of Erwin Piscator's Drama Workshop — and the New School's writing and performing classes were regarded as among the most prestigious in America. (The New School's bulletins from the late 1930s through the late 1940s list among the faculty Robert Frost and W. H. Auden, teaching poetry; Hannah Arendt, philosophy; Paul Tillich, theology; Erich Leinsdorf, directing an opera workshop — a long, impressive list of artists and scholars in all fields.)

The New York theatre season was then also at its peak, and through the help of Gassner and Theresa Helburn at the Guild, Williams was able to see Guild productions of *The Philadelphia Story,* with Katharine Hepburn, Saroyan's *Time of Your Life,* Odets's *Night Music,* and rehearsals for Hemingway's *Fifth Column.* In class with Gassner, he polished revisions on a one-act play, *The Long Good-bye,* and on his new full-length play begun in St. Louis — whose title he had changed from *Something Wild in the Country* to *Battle of Angels.* Gassner, who liked the passion and poetry in the latter play, at once took it to the Guild again for consideration as a production later that year.

In his tenth-floor room at the West 63rd Street YMCA, Williams continued to write; from it he went forth to swim, to attend Guild plays and rehearsals, and to wander through Central Park and midtown. From these excursions there very quickly came a substantial number of acquaintances and of casual sexual contacts (often with men he met at the YMCA pool or steam room); he also found a small number of friends. First among them, and one whose camaraderie he would enjoy for some time to come, was an aspiring Southern writer ten years younger named Donald Windham. Their friendship became a creative collaboration within a few years and was sustained by a remarkably fecund and frank correspondence.

"He put writing before knowing where he was going to sleep or where his next meal was coming from," Windham said of Williams in the early 1940s. In spite of late nights in the cheaper bars of Times Square, Williams managed to produce a constant outpouring of manuscript pages. At the same time, Gassner, Piscator and a cast of nine were ready to present *The Long Good-bye,* and the first New York production of a play by Tennessee Williams was staged at the New School on Friday and Saturday, February 9 and 10; it was so well received that an additional performance was set for the following Wednesday.

The Long Good-bye, almost certainly modeled on Thornton Wilder's *Long Christmas Dinner,* was an experiment for Williams. It is his first memory-play, stretching time and space as a struggling young writer relives crucial moments in his past with his irresponsible father, dead mother and wandering sister. No one — not Gassner, not Audrey nor

Theresa Helburn nor Donald Windham — knew very much about his family at this time, and so no one could have known how personal the play was, how lightly veiled a psychological and emotional family and self-portrait. The brother's alter ego is his sister (named Myra, as in "The Field of Blue Children" and in the play to come next), who makes sexual contacts at a swimming pool, and who both attracts and repels him. The mother constantly moves from house to house and urges her son to stop writing and care for the sister. A friend tells him that his state of mind is abnormal, "starin' off into space like something's come loose in your head." The young poet, however, is more realistic — almost fatalistic: "You're saying good-bye all the time, every minute you live. Because that's what life is, just a long, long good-bye — to one thing after another!"

But the New School's endorsement and the Theatre Guild's evident interest in *Battle of Angels* did not send him back to his portable typewriter with increased confidence in his future; in fact, as he wrote to his mother, he fell into a frighteningly arid period. Through the spring, he took refuge in an increasingly depressing series of distractions that were mostly sexual (about which of course he did not write to his mother).

While he awaited news from the Guild on *Battle of Angels,* he left — for Mexico, he hoped, but he got only as far as Memphis and his grandparents: in early May the Guild sent Audrey a one-hundred-dollar option on the play, and the prospect of immediate casting and an early production drew him back to Manhattan. But at once there was difficulty finding actors for this strange and curious play full of ideas, myths and social-sexual decadence, ostensibly a story of the psychological interplay between a drifter in a Southern town, a dying storekeeper, his frustrated wife, a local seer and a religious fanatic. While Gassner, Audrey and Guild executive Lawrence Langner tried to smooth the way to a production, Williams, in disgust, left for a week of swimming at Lake George.

On his return, he deepened another important friendship which, like that with Donald Windham, never had to finesse the complications of romance. Paul Bigelow, one of the most trusted men in the theatre and a creative adviser on the Guild staff, supported Williams with his compassion and prudence and amity for forty years.

"I had an apartment on East 73rd Street at that time," Bigelow remembered. "We had met through the Guild, and since according to the drift of his fortunes he often had no place to live, I offered him a sofa, or he would curl up in the corner of the living room when he needed lodging. Often enough, he had a knack for finding stranger places to stay, but he stayed with me, irregularly, for considerable periods in the early 1940s. I recognized his talent — his needs no one could ignore — and as we became friends I was pleased to welcome him when I could."

For one weekend in June, Williams was the houseguest of Langner and his wife, actress-producer-director Armina Marshall, at their farm in Weston, Connecticut. "He was a charming guest," Langner wrote in his memoirs, "[who] rapidly completed his work [revising *Battle of Angels*], using a little summer house to write in." His return to New York was almost as brief, for he was restless about the Guild's inability to find a cast and fix a date.

"And so," according to Bigelow, "I put him on a train to Provincetown almost at once. It seemed the best thing for him — to get away to a place he could write and swim, and that welcomed serious writers. He was very rootless in New York, and never happy there. He had to come back, of course, because of Broadway, but it was never his city. At this time in his life, he had what I can only call an unformed emotional persona, and he did not deal very well with the pressures of city life." None of the pressures — urban or professional or personal — were alleviated by the worsening of the cataract that month. Bigelow thought the beauty and the creative life at Provincetown would help Williams's nervous spirit, his often alarming restlessness.

Not yet the overcrowded summer tourist haven of later years, Provincetown was a lively community at the extreme end of Cape Cod, a port of great natural charm and a place — like New Orleans — where Williams could find artists, writers, musicians and those whose sexual preference usually made them unwelcome elsewhere. And of course from 1916 it had been the locale for the famous and important Playhouse, from which Eugene O'Neill was presenting a series of dramatic works that altered the contours and possibilities of the American stage.

Williams took a room, for twenty dollars a week, at Captain Jack's Wharf, Commercial Street, an unpretentious array of small cottages on a pier overlooking Provincetown Harbor, facing east and the Long Point lighthouse. There he wrote, swam and went to the Provincetown Players' summer offerings — Molnar's *Liliom,* Shaw's *Heartbreak House,* Wilder's *Our Town,* O'Neill's *Diff'rent,* and Paul Vincent Carroll's *Shadow and Substance.*

*   *   *

One of the first in Provincetown to befriend Williams was the artist Fritz Bultman, a painter and sculptor from New Orleans who was studying with the legendary Hans Hofmann. Bultman, who described himself as "one of the irascibles among the founding fathers of abstract expressionism and of its manifesto," remembered Williams that summer of 1940 as "very hopeful and eager, but at the same time knowing and sophisticated about the theatre world and about people. At the same time, he was not a professional person of the stage, and he was a bohemian in his way of living. Up to that time, and often later, he lived from hand to mouth, by doing odd jobs. He was very amusing and witty, and he could be absolutely charming. But there was an undercurrent of self-absorption."

Ruth Hiebert, whose family managed Captain Jack's Wharf and who was there at the time, remembered Williams as earnest about his craft, "just like the other writers and artists who came to Provincetown to work in peace." But she also had "some unpleasant memories," and those no doubt concerned the key element of summer 1940 in his life. It was, in short, a time of considerable sexual activity.

"My left eye was cloudy then because it was developing a cataract," he said later. "But my right eye was clear. It was like the two sides of my nature. The side that was obsessively homosexual, compulsively interested in sexuality. And the side that in those days was gentle and understanding and contemplative."

The "compulsive" interest in sexuality was not only manifested in a quick succession of partners in the first several days. In addition, there was a steady companion during those weeks — a young Canadian dancer who had assumed the name Kip Kiernan. He had been born in Toronto to a family of devout Russian Jews, and he derived his new first name from his uncle, the Ukrainian opera singer Alexander Kipnis. Williams could never remember Kip's family name; in fact, Kip was slow to reveal it to anyone, for he was an illegal alien who earned money that summer modeling at the Hans Hofmann art school in Provincetown. By his own admission, Williams's sexual demands on Kip were relentless.*

"Kip was a very solid, straightforward young man," according to Fritz Bultman, "and he became quite devoted to Tennessee." But although

---

* At the end of July, Williams wrote to Donald Windham a detailed account of a typical night with Kip, who (he told Windham) sometimes had to sleep on the beach to get an hour away from the sexually insatiable Williams. "It was an intense, strange kind of relationship," according to Paul Bigelow, in whom Williams confided later in New York, "but then all Tenn's sexual relationships were intense and strange."

the relationship was intensely physical, Williams was not interested in permanence or exclusivity. Later, he claimed that the end of the affair was "shattering" for him, and that it was precipitated by Kip's fear that his dance career would be jeopardized and his status as an alien draft-dodger would mean deportation if it became known that he was a practicing homosexual. But the truth of the matter is that Williams was as avid in his search for other partners as he was in his need to write intensively, daily. Work and sex were feverish, necessary.

By mid-September he had taken the remaining Rockefeller Foundation money and traveled to Mexico City — and then on to Acapulco, where he met Jane and Paul Bowles, both writers (and he also a composer) whose collegiality and friendship he would enjoy for many years. From there he went on to the Costa Verde, a hillside hotel over the stillwater beach called Caleta.

Until late September he enjoyed the steamy languor of the place and its motley crew of guests, who ranged from a party of German guests (exultant over early Nazi victories) to a few wandering writers and artists, like himself. That summer he later called "a desperate period. . . . I expected to be dead before [it] was over" — not because he had fallen ill, but because he was convinced that the Guild had dropped its option on *Battle of Angels* and because the wound left by the dancer was still fresh in his heart.

"But it's during such times that we are most alive," he added, and indeed, he felt enough vitality to write the first draft of a full-length comedy, *Stairs to the Roof,* and of a short story, "The Night of the Iguana." The story (incomplete until 1946 and bearing the merest hint of a resemblance to his great play of 1961) incarnates, in the character of the spinster Miss Jelkes and her unlikely experiences with a homosexual couple, the summer's tensions, from whose grip the writing was refuge.

By early October he had retraced his journey as far as St. Louis, and he visited for the first time the new family home at 53 Arundel Place, a comfortable, eight-room brick colonial with garden. Here he learned that screen actress Miriam Hopkins had agreed to return to the stage in *Battle of Angels* (a part he had actually written with Tallulah Bankhead in mind); the Guild was ready to proceed. For ten days, this kept him in a panic of inactivity, and he remained with his family — a dubious sanctuary at the best of times. He had regarded the manuscript as only a first draft, on which he would have time to work on substantial revisions with a director and cast; according to the director, in fact, "he had been secretly appalled when ... he had read in *The New York Times* that the Guild was about to put it into rehearsal. He knew he lacked the technical expertise to make alterations on demand, as the Guild so often required, and he was dazed by all the haste."

On October 24, he was back in a room at the 63rd Street YMCA, New York, going to meetings at Audrey's office and at the Guild offices with Langner and his assistant Theresa Helburn, and with director Margaret Webster.

"Why they should have thought of engaging a young, English woman director who had never been farther south than Washington to direct this work, I cannot imagine," Webster admitted. "[Rather,] the local color and the poetic prose in which it was written called for a director who was at ease in the medium of poetry.* ... I read the play, and thought that it wasn't, and never would be, a very good one, but that there was power in it and some splendid, multicolored words, and I believed the author would one day live up to his obvious potential talent and write a real dazzler. I also thought the Theatre Guild was very brave to do it. So did they."

There was not, after his trip to Mexico, money left for his living expenses from the option on the play, and Williams had to await box-office receipts for any profit on the work. He took a job at the Gotham Book Mart, a favorite stop for bibliophiles on West 47th Street, but he proved himself so inept at wrapping packages that he was dismissed after one day.

But rehearsals were beginning in New York in November, prior to a scheduled opening on Monday, December 30, at the Wilbur Theatre in Boston; after two weeks there they hoped to proceed to New York. Williams was summoned to the first rehearsal, and Margaret Webster recalled "a short, sturdy young man with crew-cut hair, pebble-thick glasses and an even thicker Southern accent, dressed in a shabby corduroy jacket and muddy riding boots. He greeted us amiably; Miriam [Hopkins] said she hoped he had enjoyed his ride; he replied that he never went riding but that he liked the boots. He then sat down on the spotless yellow satin chaise-longue [in Webster's hotel suite] and put them up on it. We started to talk about the play; he didn't seem much interested; once, when Miriam became a little vehement, he prefaced his reply with 'As far

* It was precisely because she was "at ease in the medium of poetry" that the Guild selected Margaret Webster, a noted director of Shakespeare and, in 1939, supervisor of Shakespeare productions at the New York World's Fair.

as I can gather from all this hysteria . . .' This is what is known in the language of *Variety* as 'stoperoo.' . . . [Williams] was, in fact, stupefied by the maelstrom of the Broadway theatre into which he had been flung quite suddenly and unexpectedly," and he responded by withdrawing into himself, by lying down and closing his eyes. This was often mistaken for haughtiness and incivility — in fact it was sheer terror.

Williams himself described *Battle of Angels* as "a mixture of super religiosity and hysterical sexuality co-existing in a central character," and that is true enough.

The action describes several complex relationships. Myra, in her midthirties, is trapped in a loveless marriage to Jabe Torrance, an older man who is dying of cancer. Into her life comes the young, virile, itinerant poet Val Xavier, who is hired to work in the Torrances' shop and who stirs up the town. Besides Myra's attraction to him, Val has to cope with the blandishments of the sexually obsessed Cassandra Whiteside, and the repressed sexual hysteria of Vee Talbot, a painter and a religious eccentric who is also wife of the local sheriff. Val becomes Myra's lover, she learns that she is pregnant, Jabe discovers this and announces that it was he who had killed Myra's father years earlier, and the play ends in multiple acts of violence: Jabe shoots Myra, and Val is hung and burnt by the sheriff's posse. Passionate and symbol-congested, it is clearly the work of a novice (if serious) craftsman, intrigued with Christian symbolism, Dionysian myth, Freudian motifs and D. H. Lawrence (to whose memory it is dedicated). In spite of a dense structural tangle, *Battle* nevertheless introduced all the major concerns of Williams — the urge for life, expressed in the desire for freedom and constant flight ("You and me," says the prophetic Cassandra to the hapless drifter Val Xavier,* "belong to the fugitive kind. We live on motion. . . . Nothing but motion, motion, mile after mile, keeping up with the wind."); the inevitability of sexual tension and jealousy, and the desire to be both immersed in sex and free of its demands; the interweaving of Lawrentian body-mysticism and the Christian yearning for transcendence; the necessity of sacrifice and atonement; the eternal struggle between truth and mendacity. At the same time, the play contains the basic theatrical methods through which these concerns will be more maturely treated in the later plays: material

---

* Val Xavier's name was derived from that of a distant ancestor in Williams's paternal grandmother's family, whose name was changed to Sevier in England. If, as some have claimed, there is a connection to the Spanish-French Xavier lineage, then it is possible (as Williams sometimes liked to think) that an earlier branch of the family tree was grafted onto the same family from which came the famous Spanish Jesuit missionary, St. Francis Xavier. See p. 164.

experimentation and technical innovation; the counterpoise of supporting characters; naturalistic dialogue that is somehow penetrated with poetic diction.

But of immediate concern to the producers, director and cast were the
mammoth technical demands Williams's script made: sound effects,
lightning and thunder, guitar music and songs, and a great fire at the
end, which is to burn up the entire setting. Smoke pots were called for,
but the effect at rehearsal was weak. By December 30, everyone was in a
barely suppressed panic.

They had, it turned out, good reason to fear. Many at the opening
night, unaccustomed to plays that dealt so bluntly with connections between religious hysteria and unacknowledged lust, and with the unsubtle
innuendoes in the dialogue, abandoned the theatre long before the final
moments. And those who remained were very nearly subjected to as-
phyxiation, for the smoke pots worked all too well, and both cast and
audience were enveloped in a thick, choking smoke.

For years after, the impression was given by Williams and others that
Boston critics and the staid Boston censors at once closed the play as
morally objectionable. But the critics were, in fact, genuinely (if cautiously) in favor of it. Alexander Williams, writing in *The Boston Herald*
the day after the opening, called the play "astonishing.... [It was] our
privilege to see it.... The scene where the religious fanatic discovers that
she has painted Valentine Xavier as Christ is uncomfortable, but that is
due to our own scruples and the playwright's uncompromising realism at
this point." And Elliot Norton, in *The Boston Post,* called the author's talent "most interesting," the characters "credible," and the playwright
"compassionate, [with] a gift for vividness." (The New York-based
critic from *Variety,* on the other hand, called the play "sordid and amateurish," and farther south, the *Clarksdale Register,* whose critic did not
see the last act, attacked it as a dirty drama about the author's home.)

Battle of Angels did, however, run for its scheduled two weeks, by
which time a member of the Boston City Council, responding to a few
complaints from irate theatregoers, decided to become involved. "Then it
was," Williams wrote soon after, "that censors sat out front and demanded excision from the script of practically all that made it intelligi-
ble, let alone moving."

Williams was overreacting as sharply as the few severe critics, however,
and it was, at last, much ado about not very much: one council member
did indeed denounce it as "putrid.... This show is a crime to be

permitted to run in the city of Boston," but his exact objections will never be known. He did not see the play, and later he refused quite rightly to elaborate. Then a minor politician took up the cause, and his tirade forced the police commissioner to call in the city censor himself, but he was out of town at the Sugar Bowl football game. Finally, an assistant from his office attended the January 7 performance and reported to the police commissioner that yes, there were a few offensive lines. The Guild ordered them dropped from the next evening's performance. And so it could be in the more stringent conditions of 1941.

But the real damage, done mostly by society's word-of-mouth, was fatal. Miriam Hopkins, exhausted but not dispirited, called a press conference, defended her appearance in a serious drama, and suggested that the City Council be flung into the harbor with the historic tea.

There was no question of bringing the play to New York, and the Guild drafted a letter to its subscribers, explaining its original enthusiasm for the play, praising its experimental style and its psychological honesty, as well as the author's real poetic gifts. But they admitted that it was not, in the final analysis, dramatically successful.

William Jay Smith was in Boston for that opening, and he thought the play, although terribly uneven, had tremendous power. And Audrey Wood never for a moment lost faith in her client's future success, even after the next morning, when a meeting was held at the Ritz-Carlton and the decision not to move to New York was announced. "Tom asked me to stay on with him for a while," Smith remembered long after the depressing meeting, "and indeed he appeared so depressed that I hesitated to leave him. He said nothing about *Battle of Angels* but went to his suitcase and took out an anthology of poetry and asked me to read aloud to him the poems of John Donne, which I did for the next few hours."

The months that followed were as rootless and displaced a time as he would ever feel. "Wherever he went, even then, as he has done all his life, he worked long and hard, totally dedicated to his craft," Audrey Wood said of those early years. "To say that he struggled is an understatement." And Donald Windham, with whom Williams spent long evenings in 1940 and 1941 touring Manhattan bars, affirmed that "although *Battle of Angels* had failed and he could not get his stories or poems published, his devotion to his writing remained. He was penniless, borrowing when he could, no longer living in the comparative affluence of option money and grants."

The business of survival — not to say the maintenance of creative energy — was further complicated by an extraordinary unworldliness. Companions from the early 1940s remember retrieving from laundry sacks the small checks from Audrey. Appointments would be forgotten, conversations unattended and meetings blithely dispatched to oblivion. Paul Bigelow described him as "just not being with you during most of his visits with you"; he counted on the alertness, the alacrity and the care of those he knew to see him through the practical and the emotional hurdles of life — both when his fortunes were grim and when they were glorious.

Continuing his efforts to help a career in which he very much believed, John Gassner reported to the Guild that producer Cheryl Crawford had taken a lively interest in a trio of one-act plays Williams had left with him in January: *At Liberty* dramatized the situation of a once successful actress who has returned to her Mississippi home as a consumptive profligate, deluding herself that she can return to the stage. *This Property Is Condemned,* a variant of the first, was the portrait of a lonely girl whose promiscuous sister died of tuberculosis and who deludes herself into thinking she has acquired the sister's boyfriends. And *Port Mad,* or *The Leafless Block,* told of a deranged spinster living in poverty and with her memories of a former lover. "All three possess sensitive writing," Gassner wrote to the Guild, "and the last is deeply affecting. . . . From all this productivity an evening of one-acters could be made." (Eventually, *At Liberty* and *This Property Is Condemned* were combined into a double bill, called *Landscape With Figures — Two Mississippi Plays,* published later in 1941 in William Kozlenko's collection *American Scenes. Port Mad* was revised three years later as *Portrait of a Madonna.*)

At the same time, Williams planned to work in another warm, beachfront, tolerant refuge — this time Key West, which had been a refuge at a time of dejection for his beloved Hart Crane. (Crane's *Key West: An Island Sheaf* had been published posthumously in *College Verse,* at the same time as Williams's own poems were appearing in it.)

Stopping in New York en route from Boston to Key West, Williams received his selective service classification card; even had he been younger he would not have been a fit candidate, for his wretched vision at once demanded a medical exemption. ("His eyesight," as Margaret Webster wrote, "was such that he could not distinguish an enemy soldier from a friendly tank.") The cataract in his left eye was so advanced that an operation was performed in New York that month. It was only partly successful, and even after several later submissions to surgery he would never have good vision in the damaged left eye.

"I had a small apartment on Morton Street, in Greenwich Village," Fritz Bultman recalled, "and since Tennessee had nowhere to stay when he was recovering from his eye surgery, I put him up for a while. He made a quick recovery, and began working on the revisions of *Battle of Angels*, which Erwin Piscator and Herbert Berghof wanted to produce at the New School. As it happened, Piscator wanted the play reworked as a social drama about life in the South, and Tennessee saw at once that they could never see eye-to-eye and that his play would never be done by Piscator.

"That winter," Bultman continued, "I saw that there was another side to Williams. He had this great sweetness and charm and humor, and then he could be cold and abusive as ice. Very soon it was a nuisance to have him in the apartment. He would drag home a stranger during the night and then expect me to get rid of the fellow later. This went on when he visited again the following winter, but then I had to ask Tennessee to leave." Beside any other consideration, of course, the nightly wandering through the streets near New York's West Side piers was more than unhealthy in midwinter; it was just plain dangerous. But the daily work on his play and the nightly search for sexual excitement continued throughout January and into early the following month.

By February 12, with help from a five-hundred-dollar grant from the Rockefeller Foundation, he had checked into the Trade Winds, a century-old Key West house with separate, small guest cottages. The compound was owned by the widow of an Episcopal minister, Mrs. Cora Black, who had trotted from rectory to rectory as long as her husband was alive and had now settled into a more relaxed life. With her were her son George and her daughter Marion, who at once became Williams's friend and confidante. Five years older than he, she had been in the 1920s a governess to the daughter of Florenz Ziegfeld and Billie Burke; now, she was a delicate, soft-spoken, gentle, alcoholic nymphomaniac. During his intervals from working on the revisions of his play, he shared with Marion glasses of bourbon and stories of sexual escapades. (She became the model for the character named Cora, in the short story "Two on a Party," in which the homosexual Billy is a clear surrogate for Williams; and in 1957, when a new draft of *Battle of Angels* was finally staged as *Orpheus Descending,* it was dedicated to Marion.)

The life of the Black family was financially improved by Marion's wedding, not long after, to Regis Vaccaro; after his death in the late 1950s, he left her a fortune from his investments with a fruit-trading company. Eventually, she built a lavish mansion in Coconut Grove, on Biscayne Bay, and to the end of Marion's comfortably pathetic life she was known to Williams and his friends as "The Banana Queen of Coconut Grove," a double entendre she much relished.

But the genial Cora and Marion and George could not provide Williams with escape that season from a terrible storm of failure that raged inside him. Nor was his unhappy mood alleviated by Key West and Miami parties, where he met Max Eastman, John Dewey, James Farrell, Elizabeth Bishop and the former Mrs. Ernest Hemingway. His shyness and poor vision mostly kept him confined to the corner of a room. Again, his alternations of mood were as severe as his alternations of hope and finances. Physical and creative vision were failing him, and he wrote to Audrey Wood that he was continually harassed by "blue devils" that made him almost suicidal. Alarmed, his agent prevailed on him to take some of the Rockefeller money for a vacation, or to return to New York with the revisions of the play. He chose New York, but the Guild admitted they had by now lost interest, and *Battle of Angels* was quietly shelved.

The return to New York was not by a direct route. He stopped in Miami again, in St. Augustine and in Georgia, where he visited wandering theatre people like himself, those he had known in New York. He then paid another visit to St. Louis, where his father thought at first that he was now ready to settle down at last with a serious job, and to haul firewood to the backyard. After a few days he fled to Manhattan and to its (comparative) acceptance of him.*

Partly because Paul Bigelow and other New York friends found him almost unbearably depressed throughout the early summer of 1941, Williams was encouraged to revisit New England. In July he wandered along the coast of Massachusetts, at last settling into a Harvard dormitory with a brilliant twenty-year-old law student named Bill Cannastra. Extraordinarily handsome and manically bisexual, Cannastra was an addition to Williams's growing list of unusual contacts: alcoholic from an early age,

---

* Early in the spring of 1941 his first published play appeared, in Margaret Mayorga's *Best One Act Plays of 1940* (this was also his first appearance in a book rather than a magazine). The play was *Moony's Kid Don't Cry*, a revision of *Hot Milk at Three in the Morning*, to which he had added some dialogue about a man's psychotic breakdown and confinement to an asylum. The Kozlenko book, containing *Landscape with Figures*, appeared later that year. Total payment for the two was under fifty dollars.

his looks and talent and sexual availability provided access to circles that included W. H. Auden and Chester Kallman and Jack Kerouac. His preferred form of erotic activity was, it seems, a strange mixture of voyeurism and exhibitionism, which Williams found amusing.

Half the summer of 1941 Williams spent in a haze of sexual and alcholic confusion that he finally realized was decreative and dangerous. He returned to Bigelow's East 73rd Street apartment at the end of July, avoided liquor long enough to converse sensibly with Audrey and a few magazine editors, and again left for the South. One of the poems he left with his agent was written the night before the meeting, at Bigelow's kitchen table, and it included a description of his obsessive nightly wanderings through New York's streets:

> Then I must that night go in search of one
> unknown before but recognized on sight
> whose touch, expedient or miracle,
> stays panic in me and arrests my flight.

New Orleans could, he hoped, provide freshness once again. From late September through late October he stayed at no less than four boardinghouses, either alone or with those he had met casually at bars or at the New Orleans Athletic Club. The renovation of the French Quarter was continuing in the early 1940s, under the inspired supervision of Lyle Saxon and Elizabeth Werlein, with whom Williams often took breakfast at the famous Morning Call Coffee Shop; they were sometimes joined by writer Roark Bradford, to whom Williams first told the story of his meeting with two bizarre people at the Athletic Club — a sadistic black masseur who had found a willing partner in a frail white masochist. He was already beginning a transformation, into short fiction, of this curious pair. Later he completed his gruesome tale "Desire and the Black Masseur," which concludes with the literal devouring of the masochist by the sadistic masseur.

Letters to Audrey Wood from New Orleans paralleled his production of poems and stories that autumn. He asked for cash, and for some hope: Did she think Hume Cronyn would renew the option on his one-act plays? Would Cronyn be interested in a long drama about D. H. Lawrence, or one based on Lawrence's fiction? What about the Guild, or another fellowship?

He interrupted the New Orleans sojourn once, in early November, when word reached him about his grandmother's illness. She had gone to

her daughter in St. Louis to consult specialists about terrifying symptoms
that would begin two years of suffering before her death.

Literally penniless and needing a second eye operation, he returned to
New York at the beginning of March 1942, and after a harrowing day on
a surgeon's table he recovered enough to take a job: he recited his poems
and served patrons at the Beggar's Bar in Greenwich Village. There he
sported a patch with an eye brightly painted on it, and Valesca Gert, the
Polish-German refugee proprietor, welcomed this new addition to her
crew of eccentrics. "The Beggar's Bar was a mess of a place," according to
Fritz Bultman, "but there Tennessee stayed. Valesca was just wild and
eccentric enough for him, and she even provided him with a young playwright he had an affair with. The writer went back home to Germany
after the war." As for Valesca Gert, she turned up in Federico Fellini's
1965 film *Juliet of the Spirits,* as the hermaphrodite prophetess of sex-as-
wisdom.

Tennessee's acquaintance with the demimonde of wartime Greenwich
Village was also highlighted by meetings with artist Olive Leonard ("a
pathetic lady who therefore was psychologically attractive to Tenn," according to Bigelow); she later became the model for the mad female artist in his 1975 novel, *Moise and the World of Reason.*

Partly because of his growing obsession with the life and spirit of
D. H. Lawrence, and also because he was at this time often in the company of (more or less) serious artists, Williams began to sketch (as
Lawrence had done). Almost all his artwork, then and later, celebrates
the primitive and the sensual, and reflects the daily and nightly experiences of that winter.

The insistence that dedication to the private life of the senses is itself
an art antedated Lawrence, he knew (and in this regard Williams did not
read Lawrence quite accurately). But in early 1942, he seems to have considered the life of the senses as if it were a new religion. That year, as he
told Donald Windham, was a period of selfish, blind hedonism he could
interrupt only by the hours he was traveling from city to city. And in a
poem written in February he confirmed the association between sensuality and religion:

> . . . our blood is sacred; to the mouth
> the tongue of the beloved is holy bread . . .
> as earth divides, our bodies meet and burn
> and in our mouths we take the holy bread.

It was at this time that Fritz Bultman had to ask Williams to find other lodgings.

Williams's connection with Lawrence was concrete as well as psychological by the spring of 1942. Windham had completed an outline and several scenes of a projected play based on Lawrence's short story "You Touched Me," and after reading it Williams suggested they collaborate on a full-length comedy.

By the end of May, however, Williams had not even the price of a room at the YMCA, and there was no option money in sight for the first draft of *You Touched Me*. Bigelow was about to leave New York for a visit with friends in Macon, Georgia, "and just a few days after I left him alone at 73rd Street," Bigelow recalled, "he wrote, saying he could not bear to be alone and that if we would have him he would join us in Georgia. Of course I replied at once, and by mid-June he arrived, tired and nervous." He had not been encouraged even by a first-rate production, on June 2 at the New School, of *This Property Is Condemned*, which shared a bill with one-act plays by Synge, Strindberg and Molière.

Board was free that summer in Macon, and Williams used the small attic room to write. He was beginning the short story "Kingdom of Earth"; he completed revisions for the autobiographical comedy he had begun in Mexico (*Stairs to the Roof*, about a young writer in a shoe factory); he dramatized his short story "The Malediction" into a one-act play, *The Strangest Kind of Romance* (which concerns a man and his cat); and he completed more poems. With this impressive productivity, as Bigelow was pleased to see, his nerves calmed, his humor again grew keen.

"He was a real wit — not just that summer, but for most of the years I knew him. He had a constant, quick humor, not just an occasional joke or remark. He was always amused by life, and at the same time he was saddened by it."

The combination of warmth and humor with a kind of wry acceptance of the vagaries of life was maturing in his personality that summer; it would often be reflected in his great plays, and in any case he was always, as Bigelow said, "enormously good fun to be with, no matter what he was working on."

By the end of August, he had earned a small amount of cash by cleaning tables at a Macon restaurant, and so he decided to return to Key West and to the Black family. But he reached only Jacksonville, where he found work operating a teletype machine for the United States Department of Engineers, a division of the War Department. This he held until the middle of November, working mostly nights and writing and swimming by day. (Audrey Wood and John Gassner had suggested major revisions on *You Touched Me,* and he worked on those while writing almost daily to Windham.)

But just as his moods had swung during the previous months, so it was that season. He wrote to Audrey Wood and to friends in New York and Georgia and Massachusetts that since 1938 he had really not known a day of complete serenity, that he lived in continual fear of the world and almost everyone in it, and that the great psychological trauma of his life was the tragedy of his sister. How he would transform these fears and this personal history into his art he did not know. But as he made clear in a ten-page, pencil-written letter to Audrey dated September 15, 1942, the single great threat to his integrity as a writer was the temptation to take the easy way out by not dealing with the things he knew best — family pain, mental instability, emotional obsessions, the conflict between the love of solitude and the desire for human comfort. Better than any woman in his life during the 1940s, Audrey Wood heard his written and spoken laments; better than anyone, she showed him how it was precisely by perseverance in the struggle that the purification he so desired might be effected.

By year's end he was back in New York, pouring out his feelings in person to her, to Bigelow and to Windham, and working (again, for only a few weeks at each job) as an elevator operator at the San Jacinto Hotel, and as an usher in a midtown movie theatre — not the happiest situations for a man of bad eyesight who was also constantly discomposed by his own reveries. One evening Audrey took him to a Chekhov play, thinking this would cheer him; it was the production of *Three Sisters* with Katharine Cornell, Judith Anderson and Ruth Gordon, and with them was his classmate from Iowa, Anthony Dexter.

"It was a depressing night," Dexter recalled. "Tom had his cataract problem, he had not yet had the success he had expected, and he was a most unhappy sight to see. But he showed no sign of self-pity. He was his usual half-laughing self. I believe none of us realized his great potential."

By Easter 1943, boredom and poverty again forced him out of New York — but not before he met the man who would for the rest of his life be his primary publisher. His poems had been passed along from Donald

Windham to Lincoln Kirstein (for whom Windham worked as a temporary secretary at *Dance Index* magazine), and Kirstein gave them to James Laughlin, the publisher of New Directions books. When Laughlin included a selection of Williams's poems in an anthology the following year, it would be the start of an author-publisher relationship that ripened into cordial permanence.

Returning to St. Louis, he found only emotional turmoil and heartache. His beloved grandmother was slowly dying of cancer, but so uncomplainingly and courageously that she brought tears to his eyes as he sat by her bedside or helped her with the small household tasks she insisted on doing. The combination of her valor with the horror of her illness reminded him of Hart Crane, and as he endured the unpleasantness of his father's temper he thought all the more of that poet, driven to suicide. These reflections he put into letters to Audrey, and to Donald Windham.

"He hated being in St. Louis in the 1940s," Paul Bigelow said. "He resented everything about it, and now he worried about his grandmother's dying, and about the future of his eighty-six-year-old grandfather, who found life in St. Louis very painful. He had in some mysterious way lost every cent several years before, and he depended on Cornelius and Edwina, who resented him precisely because of this loss. All this made Tenn's visits home quite painful."

The final and most poignant sadness of those weeks at Arundel Place was a series of letters from Rose, still confined at the state hospital in Farmington. Calm she was, but utterly without clarity or reason. She wrote to her brother that he was lucky to be in prison, like herself, because screaming crowds of hungry people were clamoring at the city gates.

It was precisely the short series of letters from his sister that made him plunge into the first draft of a new play whose title was *The Gentleman Caller*. He was fully aware of its autobiographical nature from the start, for he wrote to Windham that it was taking shape as a personal history of his family. The play would be a tribute to Rose, and a cry from his heart about the serenity they had all gradually lost over the years and were never able to regain.

Then, at the end of April, a telephone call from Audrey Wood altered things dramatically. She had negotiated with executives at Metro-Goldwyn-Mayer, in Hollywood, and had got him a six-month contract as a screenwriter, at the incredible sum of $250 a week. This was so shocking for him that at first he thought that figure represented a monthly salary. But never mind, Audrey exclaimed happily, he should simply come to New York to sign the contracts and to gather whatever manuscripts he wanted to take with him, and then proceed at once by train — by train! — to Los Angeles. He had taken, she assured him, his last bus ride. At the same time, she prudently sent to M-G-M a detailed list of "properties owned by Tennessee Williams" prior to this contract, so that he would always retain rights to what he had written before May 1943. The list included ten long plays, twelve "long short" plays, seventeen one-act plays, nineteen short stories and over two hundred fifty poems.

Film studios were engaging novelists and playwrights in great numbers in those busier days of multiple productions. At various times William Faulkner was part of the group of American writers Hollywood contracted, as were F. Scott Fitzgerald, John Steinbeck, Clifford Odets, Thornton Wilder, Maxwell Anderson, Robert E. Sherwood, Sidney Howard, John O'Hara and Katherine Anne Porter, as well as Lillian Hellman, Nathanael West and Samson Raphaelson. When he went to the Liebling-Wood offices on May 4 to sign the contract with M-G-M, he felt in good company and in high spirits. Three days later he was on his way to Los Angeles, under very different circumstances from the 1939 trek that ended at a pigeon ranch.

The contract specified that his first assignment was the screenplay of *Marriage Is a Private Affair,* which was to star Lana Turner. By May 17, he realized that there was no route by which he could appreciate the story or the requirements for what he bitterly called a "celluloid brassiere" for Miss Turner, but he had no choice except to give his superiors the impression he was hard at work on it.*

Nothing could have been farther from the truth. During the days before he reported to the M-G-M offices in Culver City, he had contacted David Greggory, a friend from the earlier days in New York. Greggory had gone to Hollywood to work in films and now gave him a hearty welcome, helping him get a driving license and a used car. Together they rented rooms in a boardinghouse at 1647 Ocean Avenue, Santa Monica, with a spectacular view of the Pacific and less than a minute's walk for swimming.

But Williams had no typewriter, and since Greggory was about to em-

---

* Years later, in his play *Small Craft Warnings,* Williams has the elderly writer Quentin say that Hollywood found him "too literate for my first assignment, converting an epic into a vehicle for the producer's doxy, a grammar school dropout."

bark on a cross-country motor trip, he asked him to return by way of St. Louis and bring the old one he had left behind.

"I went to Clayton and met Miss Edwina," Greggory recalled, "and it was a very formal and Victorian interview. I remember that she questioned me about his behavior and his health — in that order. She gave me a letter to deliver to him, and when I got back to Santa Monica he showed it to me. 'It is my opinion,' she had written, 'that anyone who wishes to make a living as a writer should be able to provide his own materials.' And she had enclosed with it a clipping about Edgar Allan Poe, and how he had died a gutter alcoholic. She wasn't thrilled about his occupation as a writer."

The resumption of the camaraderie with Greggory was important to Williams. "We found the apartment quite by accident," Greggory added, "an old frame building with several apartments for boarders. Ours was a large L-shaped studio. The landlady was a remarkable, well-preserved woman, and very freewheeling. She always had a couple of young male admirers courting her." Within days of meeting this formidable landlady — who was partly, Williams told Greggory later, the basis for the character of Maxine Faulk in *The Night of the Iguana* — he had begun a short story she inspired. This became "The Mattress by the Tomato Patch." Simultaneously (as he was always able to do) he began or polished a number of other stories — "The Coming of Something to the Widow Holly," "Chronicle of a Demise," "The Angel in the Alcove," a verse play based on Robert Browning's "My Last Duchess" (which he called "The Balcony in Ferrara") and poems that reflected his nostalgia for New Orleans and his anguish over his grandmother's imminent death.

Life at Ocean Avenue was relaxed and this Williams needed, for he was soon chafing under the M-G-M servitude. "I visited his office there," Greggory said, "and he simply couldn't lick the problems of the Lana Turner film. There in his office was a picture of Chekhov, so it wasn't hard to see how different his intentions were from writing a 'celluloid brassiere' for her." Instead, Williams began to draft film treatments, proposals, outlines and sample scenes for films he wanted to submit to Pandro Berman, a producer of major films at M-G-M; most of them were, of course, based on Williams's own short stories or plays.

On May 31, Audrey Wood received by mail a nine-sequence outline for a film to be based on his short story "Portrait of a Girl in Glass," and the play he had begun which was based on it, *The Gentleman Caller*. With its indication of dissolves and image-overlays, its insertion of musical motifs and its plastic, dreamlike construction, it was conceived as a film of memory. "This is what he most wanted to see realized on the screen," according to Greggory, "and he hoped M-G-M would take it in lieu of *Marriage Is a Private Affair*." Throughout May and June he continued to work on it (while the studio expected him to be occupying himself with the Turner film), and by late July he had prepared a detailed scenario. He also had selected the right actress to play Laura, the surrogate for his sister Rose: it was written expressly, he told Audrey, for Teresa Wright, the Oscar-winning star (for *Mrs. Miniver,* in 1942) and one of the busiest and most popular players in Hollywood.

The reaction to *The Gentleman Caller* was instantly negative, however; M-G-M was not interested in a story about Southern women — *Gone With the Wind* had served up enough of them for a decade, he was told. And so it was that the studio lost the opportunity to buy all rights for what would soon be called *The Glass Menagerie*.

"This really hurt him at the time," Greggory said. "He asked me if I thought he'd be paid each week even if he didn't show up at the office, and I said it was worth a try — things at studios were generally rather loose, and writers simply had to say they were working at home. Sure enough, for a few weeks he got paid even though he didn't go in at all." The paychecks of course were forwarded to Audrey, who, at Williams's request, doled him an allowance and sent most of the rest to St. Louis — for his grandmother's medical care, and for Rose, who was permitted the summer at a North Carolina rest home. He kept little cash on hand for his own amusements.

But for diversions only very little cash was needed. He was making new friends; he swam and wrote daily — these were always his two scheduled activities — and he also pursued the easy life he said had been denied when he had lived in Los Angeles in 1939.

The first of the friendships was with the writer Christopher Isherwood. "He just showed up one day at my house in Santa Monica," Isherwood said, "and we very quickly became good friends. He was very outgoing with me. There was no veneer of a false manner. It was only after we met socially that he mentioned that he wrote poetry, and when he showed me a selection I must admit that I wasn't exactly knocked senseless by them. But after all, a lot of inferior work is produced by great artists, and his poems are nothing like his great plays. Then he told me he was writing a play and a screenplay about his sister, and he confided some of the family history to me. About that history he was incredibly creative."

Isherwood, then deeply committed to exploring the history and practice of Eastern religions, was one of the first to learn something of Williams's private life in Santa Monica. He visited Ocean Avenue and found him "sitting typing a film story in a yachting cap, amidst a litter of dirty coffee cups, crumpled bed linen, and old newspapers. . . . Tennessee is the most relaxed creature imaginable: he works till he's tired, eats when he feels like it, sleeps when he can't stay awake. . . . Since the coastal area had been put under a wartime blackout, the park at the top of the cliffs had become a sex jungle at night, full of servicemen and their hunters. Tennessee was in his element there. I walked with him a little way into the thrilling darkness but didn't join him in the hunt."

David Greggory elaborated life along the Pacific Palisades in those days. "It was wartime, and all bets were off. Everybody who had any money at all was spending it. There was an attitude that was partly desperation and partly the feeling that life had better be enjoyed right now. You couldn't walk a block in Santa Monica without meeting people who wanted to be 'friends,' and quite often many of them were sailors in port. People made friends and short-time lovers all over; the spirit was 'Eat, drink and be merry, for tomorrow —' and this was especially the attitude of the sailors and those who were attracted to them." And according to Isherwood, "In his private life he was very bold, very spontaneous, whereas I was very British and complicated. He made contacts with people very easily."

"He always had strong and governing sex urges and impulses," Paul Bigelow said. "It was a burden, his sexual drive. He once said to me, rather pathetically, that he hoped with the passing of time it would lessen in intensity. He saw his libido as a painful burden, and he discovered later that in his case it did not in fact lessen with time. With Tenn it was a persistent, driving urge that accompanied him through life."

What Isherwood, Greggory and Bigelow (among others) witnessed over the years was in fact a deep, poignant disconnection in the life of Tennessee Williams — a vast space between his artistic vision and his personal reality. From his late twenties to the end of his life, whether he had a stable relationship or not, he sought sexual partners incessantly.

In this regard, the Dionysian side of him — manic, wild and ecstatic — revealed a Byronic romanticism. Rejecting order, clarity and serenity, such a romantic typically abandons logic and revels in chaos. He takes flight in excess — and sometimes in flight itself, constant travel. And often, especially in the case of the romantic who is sexually uninhibited, he seeks his satisfaction in the body of another. But such satisfaction is doomed precisely because no other human can perpetually appease an infinite need and an endless yearning, as any reflective romantic can attest. The search, then, becomes endless, the disappointment inevitable. And because he insists on the possibility of satisfaction in sensuality, there occurs a cycle of futility. He moves on, forever restless, betrayed by himself.

To observe this pattern in one's own life or the life of another is not to pass judgment. It is to assess a derailment that neither precludes great artistic achievement nor forecloses the possibility of great spiritual achievement. Such an assessment does, however, help to identify a real threat to emotional stability and to happiness — a threat that had dire consequences in the life of Tennessee Williams.

By the end of July, it was clear to M-G-M that Williams was not going to produce a screenplay for Lana Turner. Accordingly, he was first given a story about Billy the Kid, and when nothing came of this he was asked if he would write something for child star Margaret O'Brien. He replied that the "something" he had in mind for Margaret O'Brien was unprintable, which did not endear him to the studio after several months of uncooperation. On August 9, M-G-M suspended him without pay for six weeks because of his consistent refusal to work on assigned material.

But another reason for his lack of interest in studio work was the arrival in Los Angeles of the producer to whom Audrey Wood had sent *You Touched Me,* on the final emendations of which Williams and Windham had at last agreed. Margo Jones was an energetic woman from Dallas who had already directed Chekhov's *Uncle Vanya* in Texas, and who was therefore already virtually acceptable to Williams as producer. Strong-willed, magnetic and fiery with enthusiasm for the play, and for the reams of Williams manuscripts Audrey had also sent, she blew in "like a tornado," Williams reported to friends. Henceforth, she was called "the Texas tornado" by his entire circle.

It was Jones's plan to stage *You Touched Me* first at the Cleveland Playhouse in October, then to move west to the famous Pasadena Playhouse (or even to its more intimate performing space, the Playbox). By this time, she felt sure, they would have raised sufficient interest and money to bring it to Broadway.

During the layoff period from M-G-M, Williams and Jones (without the benefit of Windham's collaboration) revised, polished and restructured the play. This was almost certainly the first breach in the friendship with Windham, who felt left out of the final deliberations over a work on which they were to share not only equal credit but also equal compensation. (He was shocked to learn later that he was expected to sign an agreement forfeiting a percentage of his royalties in favor of Williams, who claimed that *You Touched Me* was more his than Windham's.)

While Windham awaited word from Santa Monica, Williams felt a new rush of optimism for the future. "From the day Margo arrived, he had a strong feeling that his success would lie in New York, with the theatre there," according to Greggory. "Much to the credit of Audrey Wood, whose communications to him were not only monetary but also full of affectionate encouragement, he saw hope for his future. Audrey and Margo made it absolutely clear to him that Broadway was in the cards."

By the end of September, Jones had been to New York for casting and had proceeded to Cleveland for rehearsals. Williams had hoped to accompany her, but by this time M-G-M was ready to give him another chance, and he needed the salary after six payless weeks. Windham instead went on to the first performances.

You Touched Me, although originally suggested by Windham, gave Williams an opportunity to formalize his affinity for Lawrence, and to endorse Lawrence's celebration of the flesh's triumph over Puritanism. The story follows Lawrence's with some embellishment: the arrival of a young man wins a repressed young woman away from her prudish aunt. To a rather straightforward romantic comedy Williams added the clear references to Lawrence's *Fox,* with its hen-house attacker. The play — even after its 1943 and 1945 alterations — has a dated quaintness about it, but it is perhaps too innocent for its own good. The overthrow of everything the aunt represents, and the sudden (and not entirely consistent) liberation of the girl, comprise thesis material more than compelling seriocomic action. Williams was prudent to write it in collaboration, so it would not bear his name alone. He seems, despite his somewhat disingenuous protest of devotion to it, to have known that it was a minor exercise — essentially a valentine to D. H. Lawrence.

As his M-G-M contract was about to expire, he added to his list of friends two whose fidelity and affection would remain precious in all the years to come, despite the occasional absences forced by professional obligations. The architectural designer and artist Tony Smith, whom he had met in Greenwich Village and who, working in Los Angeles, had also taken a room at Ocean Avenue, asked Williams to be best man at his wedding to the actress and singer Jane Lawrence, and on September 25, with a taxi-driver as the only other witness, the ceremony was held. Jane Smith remembered Williams's humor and candor and compassion, and his marvelous capacity for life.

It was only a few friends like the Smiths who buoyed him through the last days in Hollywood and the nervous anticipation of the opening of *You Touched Me*. On October 21 he was off the M-G-M payroll, and the same week the *New York Times* reported that the Cleveland press had liked the play, but had suggested a "tidying up" of loose ends before a Pasadena opening. From early November until the opening night, that suggestion was taken up, and Williams worked as if his life depended on it.

By the time of the play's opening at the Pasadena Playbox, however, there was a new wrinkle in his relationship with Margo Jones; quite simply, he suspected that she intended to become his wife.

"Tenn was in absolute terror that Margo would somehow bring about a marriage against his will," said Paul Bigelow, with whom Williams was in constant contact. "Just how this might occur he never specified, but it was clear that she certainly had her eye on him, even at this early stage. She had a remarkable vitality and a toughness of character, and her desire to become Mrs. Williams persisted through later years of their professional association." She was not the last woman to hope that Tennessee Williams's sexual preference could be altered on her account, and in this she shared a belief more widely endorsed years ago as a theory of homosexuality — namely, that by a simple act of will one might change one's orientation. In any case, Margo Jones's intention was particularly problematic, since she not only knew of Williams's preference but was herself quite openly lesbian.

The opening night, November 29, was a gala event, with Ruth Ford in the leading role, and her husband Peter van Eyck and the Smiths among Williams's friends there. This group contrasted sharply with the only guest Williams escorted to closing night, December 5: his father, who happened to be in Los Angeles on business. Afterward Cornelius joined playwright and producer for dinner. "Son," he said when they were alone, "there are two things we've never had in our family — a sober man and a drunken woman." He was afraid that his son (whose sexual preference he may have surmised but never acknowledged) was going to yield to Miss Jones's iron-willed, boozy blandishments.

Next day, the two Williamses and Margo Jones drove to Santa Monica, with a friend of the producer's who came along for the ride: Burl Ives, the singer and archivist of American folk music, was appearing in the touring company of Irving Berlin's *This Is the Army*. "Tennessee was very quiet during the ride from Pasadena to Santa Monica," Ives remembered, "but his father went on and on about Jews and finally said, 'That Irving Berlin must be a *good* Jew — he didn't take a cent for that show!' And Tennessee was mortified — he just shrank back in the seat and said nothing the whole ride."

Before Christmas, Williams went on to St. Louis, but alone, since he wanted to stop near Taos for a visit with Frieda Lawrence at her ranch in the Lobo Mountains. There he stayed two days, alternating vivid conversation with almost religious periods of veneration at the little chapel nearby where Frieda kept her husband's ashes. A few hundred yards from the house, on a small knoll, a white temple had been built, surmounted by a golden phoenix, which was Lawrence's own symbol.

He arrived at his parents' home for the holiday, and in time to see Dakin, who had been called to war duty in the Orient. The holidays were full of boredom, tension and finally grief, for his grandmother was clearly in a protracted death agony; the atmosphere in the house was Chekhovian, he wrote to Windham.

Finally, on January 6, 1944, death came to the woman he loved more than anyone in the world after his sister; the courageous, tireless woman who had sacrificed so he could have money for school and holidays and treats was at last too weary to fight. She was, he wrote, "a living poem . . . all that we knew of God in our lives," and her final hours were a bitter and bloody struggle for breath.

He could not endure the services that were planned, and he quickly arranged to have another eye operation in St. Louis on the day of the funeral. It was the most successful of the procedures to correct his cataract, and with thick lenses he could soon work well and long. The period of recovery and an improved ability to read and write would perhaps distract him from the weight of death. Like most escape routes through which we attempt to flee an inner landscape of sorrow, however, his writing under these circumstances led him nowhere. He could not concentrate. Family once again meant loss and pain and a deep, incurable wound.

At last one night in late January, alone in his room, he allowed a beginning of the healing process. For all of them — for Grand; for his forlorn grandfather and confused mother; for his father, drunk and isolated; for his brother, who was now somewhere in the war; for Rose, who knew nothing of any of them; and for himself and his last six years of wandering — he wept.

Chapter Four

FAMILY AFFAIRS

(1944–1947)

In these trying times we live in, all that we
have to cling to is each other.

— Amanda Wingfield, in *The Glass Menagerie*

H E REMAINED in St. Louis almost until spring 1944, but his work there reflected the continuing antipathies about home, family and that city. "Oriflamme," a short story he completed (which was a revision of an earlier one called "The Red Part of a Flag") accurately described his own feelings that winter, in terms of a disoriented woman who selects a rose-patterned dress to mark and move forward her liberation from a confining tradition. ("The city had never pleased her. . . . Her hope had died in a basement of this city. Her faith had died in one of its smug churches.") Not a fully drawn portrait, the story is a sketch for a later short work ("The Yellow Bird") and for a major play (*Summer and Smoke*). After reading Chekhov's short novel "My Life," he completed another story, "The Vine," whose psychological texture combines the Russian writer's mood and his own that winter. In it, Williams stated as clearly as he ever would his abhorrence of being alone:

"When you really thought about it, when you got down to it, what was there to live for outside the all-encompassing and protecting intimacy of marriage? And yet a great many women like Jane Austin [*sic*] got on without it. There were also men who got on without it. But he, he could not think of it! Going to bed alone, the wall on one side of you, empty space on the other, no warmth but your own, no flesh in contact with yours! Such loneliness was indecent! No wonder people who lived those obscenely solitary lives did things while sober that *you* only did when drunk. . . ."

But enough was, apparently, too much, and by mid-March he was back in New York, staying in single rooms and men's residences and forgetting to keep Audrey Wood quite aware of just how he could be contacted from day to day. New Directions presented him with an advance copy of *Five Young American Poets,* marking his first book appearance as a poet, and this was heartening enough to send him back to his verse note-books — but not before death again claimed a loved one.

A message came for him at Audrey Wood's office, the same day in late March that he kept an appointment with her. Kip Kiernan, the ballet dancer from Canada and Provincetown, who had regularized his status by marrying an American, had no sooner begun a career in New York than there was a diagnosis of inoperable brain cancer. Then about twenty-five, he was blind and near death in a Manhattan hospital, sending out calls for "Tenny Williams." And so Williams, who had undergone eye sur-gery rather than attend his grandmother's funeral, now sat by Kip's bed-side, scarcely recognizing him. Kip's hands reached out for his, clasping and gripping as if to keep from slipping out of this world. But within days of Tennessee's arrival, Kip was gone. The event of a former lover's death would be repeated, with startling and chilling congruence, twenty years later.

The visit to Kip found a place in his poetry that spring, however:

> ... Beneath me your breathing face
> cried out, Return, return ...
> Return, you called while you slept.
> And desperately back I crept
> against the ascending fall ...
> ... and only your voice calling, Stay!
> But my longing was great
> to be comforted and warmed
> once more by your sleeping form,
> to be, for a while, no higher
> than where you are,
> little room, warm love, humble star!

It was a season of violent shifts in New York, and not only in surpris-ing alternations of temperature, of warm sunny days with sudden midspring blizzards. For Williams, the pleasure over publication of his poems was muted by the awfulness of Kip's final hours, followed by yet another radically different motion of his life. On April 27, he was told that a grant of one thousand dollars was awarded to him by the Ameri-can Academy of Arts and Letters, "in recognition of his dramatic works, which reveal a poetic imagination and a gift for characterization that are rare in the contemporary theatre."

Rejecting an offer to come to Pasadena, where Margo Jones was staging *The Purification,* he then withdrew for the summer to Provincetown to complete *The Gentleman Caller.* *

After weeks of concentrated effort — and, he wrote to Margo, a strange combination of fear and pain — the play was ready for Audrey Wood and, he hoped, a Broadway producer. On October 17, it was announced that actor-producer-director Eddie Dowling's new project would be a play by Tennessee Williams; he was the first to read the manuscript, and, after an afternoon conference with the quietly persuasive Audrey, he convinced businessman Louis Singer to join him in financing a production.

That month, the details moved together swiftly. Dowling, who had directed actress Julie Haydon in *The Time of Your Life,* convinced her that (although she was thirty-four) she would be credible as the lame, fragile Laura, a character at least a decade younger. She, in turn, took the play to her friend and mentor (later her husband), the formidable critic George Jean Nathan, whose approval she felt obligatory. At the same time, the forty-nine-year-old Dowling announced — without a smile — that he would play young (twentyish) Tom, the shoe-warehouse clerk and aspiring poet; for the role of the gentleman caller, Anthony Ross was hired. The remaining role to be cast was Amanda Wingfield — the "little woman of great but confused vitality," as Williams described her in the play, "clinging frantically to another time and place." The role demanded not mere competence, but the nuances of dramatic greatness. Nathan suggested Laurette Taylor. Dowling and Wood and Williams saw his wisdom; they also panicked.

Laurette Taylor, then sixty, had been up to the 1930s one of the great ladies of the American stage. Those who had seen her in *Peg O' My Heart* (in 1912) or *The Furies* (in 1928) or *Outward Bound* (in 1938) knew her gifts. But for almost ten years she had herself become a woman of great but confused vitality, and a confirmed alcoholic.

At that time, Taylor was living in sad withdrawal from the theatre, at a hotel on East 60th Street, where she was daily attended by a drama student named Eloise Sheldon. In return for acting lessons, the young woman cared for the practical details of Taylor's life and offered devoted companionship. The play reached Taylor by the circuitous route of

---

* In his original draft of *Memoirs,* Williams wrote that it was during the summer of 1944 that he met and caroused with Bill Cannastra, the alcoholic and voyeurist Harvard law student. But by this time Cannastra had apparently moved to New York, and the evidence suggests that in fact their meeting took place, as described above, in 1941.

Wood to Dowling to Haydon to Nathan to Sheldon to Taylor. It also bore a new title — *The Glass Menagerie.*

"Of course her first reaction was to turn it down," Eloise Sheldon Armen recalled years later; "she thought her career was over. But we prevailed on her to see that no one could bring this character to life the way she could." At last, with the loving encouragement of Eloise — "a small flame," as Laurette Taylor's daughter appreciatively wrote of the young student, "guiding [Taylor] back to the paths of everyday life" — she accepted the part. She did not, however, stop drinking, nor did she seem to give much attention to memorizing lines before or during rehearsals.

In November, Dowling (with, Williams insisted, Margo Jones as co-director) began rehearsals in New York prior to a scheduled Chicago try-out at the end of December. Terrified that something like the history of *Battle of Angels* would be repeated — not because of the new play's content (which could not have been more different) but because he no longer believed the play was anything but "rather dull, too nice" — Williams fled New York for St. Louis. There he was interviewed on his life and work and hopes by the drama critic of the *Star-Times,* a man named William Inge. The resulting article was full of inaccuracies, half-truths and Williams's typical alterations of personal history; the resulting friendship was much more intense and dramatic.

But Audrey and Dowling would not allow Williams to be an absentee author, and in December he was summoned to Chicago. The situation, he quickly realized, was as bleak as the fierce winter that had already descended.

First of all, Laurette Taylor — with only a week remaining before the December 26 premiere — attended the final rehearsals in what can only be called an alcoholic stupor, barely summarizing the dialogue and so broadly defining the woman's Southern accent and character that, as Williams wrote to Windham, she made the play sound like the Aunt Jemima Pancake Hour. In addition, Jo Mielziner's stage designs were being followed with great difficulty, and the music Williams had commissioned from his old acquaintance Paul Bowles sounded harsh through the theatre's crude sound system. Luggage had not arrived; a winter storm raged; the Civic Theatre was inconvenient to Chicago's main theatre district; there was no budget for advertising or publicity; and everyone in the company (except Eddie Dowling and Julie Haydon) — cast, crew, author — submerged the fear of failure in strong drink. Margo Jones, Williams wrote to Windham, was like a scoutmaster leading a wayward and desperate troop to their doom.

Edwina Estelle Dakin,
about the time of her marriage

Cornelius Coffin Williams

St. Paul's Rectory, Columbus, Mississippi

Thomas Lanier Williams

Rose Isabel Williams,
at Westminster Place

In Europe, summer 1928

Edwina Dakin Williams, 1936

Cornelius Williams, 1937

Rose and Dakin Williams,
in Forest Park, St. Louis, 1935

Rose, with a friend and Tom

Rose, just before surgery

In Santa Monica, 1943

The Reverend Walter Edwin Dakin

About the time of *The Glass Menagerie*

Audrey Wood and clients: Williams, William Inge,
Maurice Valency and Carson McCullers

With Frank Merlo, Elia Kazan and Charles Feldman,
during filming of *A Streetcar Named Desire,* 1950

1431 Duncan Street, Key West, about 1952

With Donald Windham, Tanaquil LeClercq (dotted dress), Gore Vidal
and Buffie Johnson, in the garden of Café Nicholson, about 1951

As late as Christmas Eve, the lines of the play had been neither "frozen" (fixed by the producer and playwright to be performed as written) nor completely memorized. Laurette Taylor managed only a martini mumble, Dowling was demanding rewrites, and the cast was stumbling into props and one another. "Mr. Dowling," Williams said quietly that night, "art is experience remembered in tranquillity. And I find no tranquillity in Chicago."

The night after Christmas, *The Glass Menagerie* was somehow performed for a small, diffident audience. By the afternoon of the twenty-seventh, the box office had taken in only four hundred dollars, and the producers prepared a closing notice. But then Audrey telephoned them to read two brief reviews: critic Claudia Cassidy, writing in the *Chicago Daily Tribune,* said the play had "the stamina of success . . . [it] knows people and how they tick. . . . If it is your play, as it is mine, it reaches out . . . and you are caught in its spell." And Ashton Stevens, in the *Herald American,* said *The Glass Menagerie* "has the courage of true poetry couched in colloquial prose."

Before the end of that day, the mayor of Chicago, at the urging of the Civic Theatre's management, authorized a fifty-percent ticket subsidy for municipal employees. On the third night, Laurette Taylor was not simply discharging a half-formed role, she was creating a legend; she had begun to draw a more wonderful portrait than anyone could have imagined — not Eddie Dowling (who resented the critics' subsequent raves about her), not Tennessee Williams nor Audrey Wood, not anyone connected with the play.

"Actually," according to the playwright, "she directed many of the scenes, particularly the ones between mother and daughter, and she did a top-notch job. She was continually working on her part, putting in little things and taking them out — almost every night in Chicago there was something new, but she never disturbed the central characterization. Everything she did was absolutely in character."

The closing notice was removed — not, however, because box-office business dramatically improved, but because Claudia Cassidy and Ashton Stevens had been championing the play, returning almost nightly and telling and writing about it almost daily. "It gripped players and audiences alike," Cassidy wrote on January 7, 1945, "and created one of those rare evenings in the theatre that make 'stage struck' an honorable word." By the middle of the month, no tickets were available. In an unusual example of journalistic salvation, a play was for once not lost but kept alive because of critical support.

The author's spirits were raised also by the admiration and attention of William Inge, who came to Chicago to spread the good news back to St. Louis. What he did not share with the folks back home, however, was the fact that during his short visit to Williams the two men had an impromptu and intense sexual affair, never resumed in their later friendship.

The search for a New York theatre continued even as Williams and Dowling and the cast refined the play, perfected the lighting and music and mood, and tried to keep Taylor away from liquor. They succeeded in everything but the last. But when the curtain rose, something other than alcohol dominated the woman. A grace and gravity changed her, and through her the other actors.

No one was more happily surprised by the sudden turn of fortune than the author, who had tried to prepare himself for another failure. On March 2, he wrote to his mother from the Hotel Sherman that his income from the play was a thousand dollars a week; soon afterward, he wrote again, he had arranged for half the royalties to be assigned to her. For the rest of her life, Edwina Dakin Williams would never lack material support. The play she had unwittingly inspired would give her considerable financial rewards and finally enable her to have the one thing she had so long desired — her independence from Cornelius.

But sudden affluence and increasing fame did not alter the basic texture of Williams's life — yet. In Chicago he began scenes for a new play about a younger, faded Southern belle he named Blanche, who (like Amanda Wingfield) was lost in memories of the old South, and who survived brutality by her own illusions. *The Glass Menagerie* was a gentle lament for missed opportunities; the new play would be more violent, beginning in a character's loss of home and respect and family fidelity, and moving through sexual decadence to lunacy. Writing disjointed scenes for a projected play he then called *The Moth,* with Tallulah Bankhead again in his mind as the doomed heroine, he found the subject sufficiently frightening that he stopped work on the manuscript after a week.

Instead, he tried to relax into Chicago life — mostly campus life, as it turned out, since there were one-night stands with attractive, admiring undergraduates at the University of Chicago, young men to whom he read Hart Crane and who offered the passion typical of students — eager, sexually dynamic, emotionally petulant and less dependable than Chicago weather. The fickleness of young men, he wrote in his poetry notebooks, was like fox's teeth in the heart — a phrase he employed with increasing frequency in poems of the following years.

* * *

By his thirty-fourth birthday (not, as everyone thought, his thirty-first), on March 26, the company had moved to New York. Five nights later, on Easter eve, the curtain rose at the Playhouse Theatre; when it finally descended, after the twenty-fifth appearance of the cast for bows, "the reluctant Mr. Williams," as Laurette Taylor's daughter noted, "was persuaded to show himself at the side of the proscenium arch and bowed low to Dowling and Laurette, presenting a modest behind to the cheering audience." But during the performance, which moved many to tears, Eloise Sheldon (who was appearing that season in *Harvey* and had arranged to have her role taken by an understudy that night) stood just in the wings, holding a bucket for the terrified Laurette Taylor, who took advantage of every moment offstage to vomit. No one in the theatre suspected anything other than what turned out to be the actress's great triumph. But she was not simply suffering the effects of drink; she had contracted cancer. Nevertheless, every performance, for those who saw her, was an experience of great art, of theatre history.

One of the few autobiographical plays in American theatre to reach a common depth of understanding and compassion for the human condition, *The Glass Menagerie* transforms the Williams family of St. Louis into the Wingfield family of St. Louis. The narrator, who bears the author's own name Tom, informs the audience at the outset that "the play is memory," and he leads a series of scenes in family life. He lives with his mother, Amanda, and his sister, Laura. Amanda, a doting, manipulative woman full of good, strong will, is also caught in a net of memories: she reminds her son and her daughter that in her youth she was the quintessential Southern belle, always attended by scores of gentlemen callers. Laura, whose slight limp is both a cause of her shyness and an excuse to capitalize on her fragile emotional state, is unable to sustain the pressures of the outside world and (like her prototype, Rose Williams) has taken refuge in old gramophone records and in tending her collection of glass animals — her glass menagerie, which is a symbol of her difference and her delicacy. The father is absent from the family: he is described by Tom as "a telephone man who fell in love with long distances."

Forced to help support his family by working in a shoe factory, Tom longs to break the ties and become a wandering poet. Before he can try, however, his mother prevails on him to bring one of his co-workers from the factory home to dinner; she is desperate to re-create her own past — and to help her daughter graduate to adulthood — by finding a gentleman caller, a suitor for Laura. When they entertain a young man named

Jim O'Connor, however, it turns out that Laura had been attracted to him in high school earlier, and that now, in fact, he is engaged to be married. With his departure, any lingering hope for Laura's future seems broken, just as her beloved glass unicorn was broken after an impromptu parlor-dance with Jim. At the conclusion, it is clear that Tom will make his own way through life, but that he will always be haunted by the memory of his sister, who will very likely be excluded from any emotional fulfillment.

"The events of *The Glass Menagerie*," according to Dakin Williams, "are a virtually literal rendering of our family life at 6254 Enright Avenue, St. Louis, even though the physical setting is that of an earlier apartment, at Westminster Place. There was a real Jim O'Connor, who was brought home for my sister. The Tom of the play is my brother Tom, and Amanda Wingfield is certainly Mother." Indeed, the portrait of the woman in whom, as Williams wrote, there was "much to admire . . . and as much to love and pity as there is to laugh at" is inspired by Edwina from the first moment. ("Honey, don't *push* with your fingers. If you have to push with something, the thing to push with is a crust of bread. And chew — chew! . . . Eat food leisurely, son, and really enjoy it. . . ."*)

"We all knew that this play had some correspondence with his own life," according to Randy Echols, one of the key members of the play's technical staff. "Tennessee — and only Tennessee — laughed aloud at lines every time he came to a performance, lines that didn't seem to amuse anybody else." And although Edwina admitted in her memoirs that she had an obsession with proper eating habits, Williams thought she "never understood how much of her was in Amanda."

The correspondence goes deeper than mere details, however. The prevailing tragicomic tone of the play — with a poignancy reminiscent of Chekhov's *Cherry Orchard* — projects the unreconciled ironies of family life far beyond the contours of the Wingfield/Williams group.

"All work is autobiographical if it's serious," he reflected some years later. "Everything a writer produces is his inner history, transposed into another time. I am more personal in my writing than other people, and it may have gone against me." *The Glass Menagerie* so permanently established his fame and fortune that it could not be said to have "gone against" him. But he knew that it never represented the real network of

* There is an identical moment between mother and son in *Auto-Da-Fé*.

feelings, the deepest pain, about Rose, and it was this that he had hoped to exorcise in the play. "It's human valor that moves me," he told an interviewer after opening night. "The one dominant theme in most of my writings, the most magnificent thing in all human nature, is valor — and endurance." A requiem for unhappy lives, this first great success for Tennessee Williams was in a sense an ending as well as a beginning. "I may not have any more nice things to say. I must have known unconsciously that I would never write that kind of tender play again."

Because of its simple structure, *The Glass Menagerie* is often produced by professionals and amateurs on the stage; it has also been filmed and adapted several times for television. Precisely because of its directness and emotional accessibility, it can be misconceived and misrepresented. Compassionate for the misguided devotion of an unrealistic mother and for the unworldliness of a sister who is somehow forever marred, the play is as appealing to read as to see enacted, and its final moments are a summary of the honesty and dignity with which the author met his own memories:

"Tom's closing speech," he wrote in the stage directions, "is timed with what is happening inside the house. We see . . . that Amanda appears to be making a comforting speech to Laura, who is huddled upon the sofa. Now that we cannot hear the mother's speech, her silliness is gone and she has dignity and tragic beauty. Laura's hair hides her face until, at the end of the speech, she lifts her head to smile at her mother. Amanda's gestures are slow and graceful, almost dancelike, as she comforts her daughter. At the end of her speech she glances a moment at the father's picture. . . ."

And Tom's final words are the clearest memoir Tennessee Williams left to the American theatre:

> Not long after that [evening of the disappointing dinner with the gentleman caller Jim O'Connor] I was fired for writing a poem on the lid of a shoe-box. I left St. Louis. I descended the steps of this fire escape for a last time and followed, from then on, in my father's footsteps, attempting to find in motion what was lost in space. I traveled around a great deal. The cities swept around me like dead leaves. . . . I would have stopped, but I was pursued by something. It always came upon me unawares, taking me altogether by surprise. Perhaps it was a familiar bit of music. Perhaps it was only a piece of transparent glass. Perhaps I am walking along a

street at night, in some strange city, before I have found companions. I pass the lighted window of a shop where perfume is sold. The window is filled with pieces of colored glass, tiny transparent bottles in delicate colors, like bits of a shattered rainbow. Then all at once my sister touches my shoulder. I turn around and look into her eyes. Oh Laura, Laura, I tried to leave you behind me, but I am more faithful than I intended to be! I reach for a cigarette, I cross the street, I run into the movies or a bar, I buy a drink, I speak to the nearest stranger — anything that can blow your candles out!

[*Laura bends over the candles.*]

For nowadays the world is lit by lightning! Blow out your candles, Laura — and so goodbye.

[*She blows the candles out.*]

The play is, then, what its author knew at the time of its first production — his tenderest delineation of his feelings about the Williams family and their collective past. Transmuted through his memories of Rose's own glass collection is the purest poetic light — an arc of forgiveness (of fate and of his mother), a ray of apologetic celebration of his sister's tragedy, a beam of understanding for himself and his own painful needs. Stronger plays would follow, works considered by many to be more successful in dramatic content and structure and richness of character. But nothing Tennessee Williams ever wrote after *The Glass Menagerie* has its wholeness of sentiment, its breadth of spirit and its unangry, quiet voice about the great reach of small lives.

The New York critics followed their Midwest colleagues. Even George Jean Nathan, who considered it "less a play than a palette of sub-Chekhovian pastels brushed up into a charming resemblance of one," admitted that *The Glass Menagerie* "provides by long odds the most imaginative evening that the stage has offered in this season." Some reviewers (John Mason Brown, George Freedley, the writers for *Time* and *Life* and *Newsweek*) attributed the success of this fragile play to the genius of Laurette Taylor, but there was unanimity on the value of the whole — the writing, according to Brooks Atkinson, had "pity for people, coolness of perspective, poetic grace." And playwright Arthur Miller, years later said, "It is usually forgotten what a revolution his first great success meant to the New York theatre. *The Glass Menagerie* in one stroke lifted lyricism to its highest level in our theatre's history, but it broke new ground in another way. What was new in Tennessee Williams was his rhapsodic insistence that form serve his utterance rather than dominating and cramping it. In him the American theatre found, perhaps for the first time, an eloquence and an amplitude of feeling. And driving on this newly discovered lyrical line was a kind of emotional heroism; he wanted not to approve or disapprove but to touch the germ of life and to celebrate it with verbal beauty."

With the block-long lines at the theatre on Monday morning, life began to change in a way that it had not in Chicago; "and new problems developed with success," as Williams was the first to admit. The following week, the New York Drama Critics Circle voted *The Glass Menagerie* the best play of the year on its first ballot. Late in April, Edwina and Dakin came to New York, were brought in great style to suites at the Royalton Hotel, and were honored at a reception. (Cornelius had seen the play while in Chicago on business, the resemblance to his family entirely eluding him.) Interview followed interview, and party followed reception that spring; the last of several awards was announced in June by the Playwrights Company (the creative consortium of Maxwell Anderson, S. N. Behrman, Elmer Rice, Robert E. Sherwood and John Wharton), who awarded Williams the Sidney Howard Memorial Prize of fifteen hundred dollars. By this time — after another operation on his left eye — the socially beleaguered playwright had departed for Mexico. With a weekly income almost equal to the prize money, he could afford a private berth on the train, and to book at a first-class hotel. From his impecunious past, only the old portable typewriter on which he had worked on the final draft of *The Glass Menagerie* remained among his new, well-stocked luggage.

At a guest-house about thirty miles southeast of Guadalajara, he settled into the pleasant rhythms of life at the popular fishing resort of Lake Chapala. Strolling the borders of Mexico's largest inland body of water (over four hundred square miles), swimming, drinking rum-cocos with native boys, he decided to extend his visit through early August. Never a man to rest idly, however, he wrote compulsively each day for at least three hours.

The visit, he found, released a flood of more memories. Even as his fame was now established, and other American guests stopped to introduce themselves to the celebrated young playwright, he was still gazing backward to the two Roses in his life, his sister and his grandmother. In

"Recuerdo," a poem written one cool morning at Lake Chapala, the two women joined hands with him over an arch of painful years:

> And he remembered the death of his grandmother . . .
> In childhood's spectrum of violence, she remained pale . . .
> My sister . . . vanished completely —
> for love's explosion, defined as early madness,
> consumingly shone in her transparent heart for a season
> and burned it out, a tissue-paper lantern!

In "The Jockeys at Hialeah," however (which he had begun in Chicago), memory collides with the bluntness of sensory pleasure — and this poem, he knew, failed precisely because of coyness and imprecision.

But the sojourn at Lake Chapala was extended for a more serious project. He returned to work on *The Moth*, which he now called *Blanche's Chair in the Moon*. The image-basis, he said later, was simply that of a woman, sitting with folded hands near a window, while moonlight streamed in and she awaited in vain the arrival of her boyfriend. During the warm, dry Mexican summer so high above sea level, he relived many personal and family memories, and they clashed with the satisfaction of purely physical desires (which were being readily satisfied by cheerful native boys). The new play, in such circumstances, took on a fusion of sensuality and nostalgia and violence new to his writing. The first indication of this violence was in scenes involving men at a poker table.

"During the New York run of *The Glass Menagerie*," according to Randy Echols, "Tennessee wanted to learn how to play poker. He invited some of the crew from the play to his hotel room, provided cards and chips and liquor and foods, and then he went from player to player taking notes. We found out only later what he was doing and why he needed to learn." Following the method of Chekhov, Williams wanted to learn more background detail than he would use. During the summer, the play — its title soon changed to *The Poker Night* — took shape as a contest between the crude sensibilities of working-class poker players and the delicacies of two Southern women. After several weeks, however, he had only card scenes; there was considerable atmosphere and dramatic tension, but the narrative was undeveloped.

By mid-August he had traveled north to Dallas, for a visit with Margo Jones. Her single-minded loyalty and outspoken confidence not only encouraged him; she virtually demanded that he complete a short story that had remained unattended for three years. And so in one intense afternoon he wrote the final sections of "One Arm," the grotesque but oddly touching story of a young, cynical male hustler in New Orleans, homeless and mutilated, who just before his execution for murder realizes that he needs to respond — once, with wholeness of feeling — to the emotions so long buried in an avalanche of ill fortune. The story affirms a communion between those whom accident and desire have made marginal people. And for perhaps the first time, Williams wrote compellingly of the fight between the aphorisms of sectarian religion and simple, ordinary human needs — and his empathy is at last not with the poor, confused minister, afraid of his own sexual storm, but with the doomed and drained Oliver Winemiller, the boy whose youth was lost long before an arm.

Late in August he arrived in Boston for the rehearsals and pre-Broadway tour of *You Touched Me!* — to which the producer, in Williams's absence, had insisted on adding the provocative exclamation point — and which was having some problems in the playing. The success of *The Glass Menagerie* had encouraged director Guthrie McClintic and his cast — Edmund Gwenn, Catherine Willard and Montgomery Clift — and the late arrival of the tanned and cheerful author, with several final additions to his text, gave them even more enthusiasm. (Among Williams's last-minute personal addenda were a character's dedication of a poem to Hart Crane; the fact that the wife of the Reverend Melton — named for Windham's former roommate Fred Melton — was born and died on the same dates as Williams's grandmother; and the physical ailments of the Reverend, which represent several of Williams's own.)

In the role of the dark and handsome young wartime flier was the dark and handsome young actor Montgomery Clift, who at twenty-five was at the start of a promising career. There was a mutual assessment by actor and author, which Williams later reflected on: "I never knew him well because I wasn't sexually attracted to him" — a statement of a strange logic indeed, or an ambiguity (which he never clarified) as to which of the two men associated depth of acquaintance with sexual activity.

At the end of September, *You Touched Me!* opened at the Booth Theatre in New York; the critics found it genial, pleasant and clearly inferior to its neighbor, *The Glass Menagerie*, three blocks to the north. The comedy seemed too calm and pale in a Broadway season that thrived on *Carousel, Oklahoma!, Bloomer Girl, On the Town, Song of Norway, A Bell for Adano, The Late George Apley, Dear Ruth, Harvey, I Remember Mama, Life with Father* and *The Voice of the Turtle.* From his room at the Hotel Shelton, Williams read the reviews of his and Windham's efforts, and began work on a more serious treatment of sexual liberation, which *You Touched Me!* had introduced perhaps too gently for his increasingly confident voice.

The first pages of a new play had, for a time, the title *Chart of Anatomy,* and were a loose development of his story "Oriflamme" and another story in progress, "The Yellow Bird." After a week, he abandoned the play as hopeless: all he had was the thesis of a woman's erotic awakening to the raucous charm of a doctor she had known from their childhood; the characters, however, were ciphers. And so, as he had done with the inchoate life of *The Poker Night,* he put it aside in favor of short fiction and poems.

In November, *Story* magazine published "The Important Thing," his fictionalized account of the college friendship with Esmeralda Mayes. In the first draft, the marginal, rejected, poet Flora of the story had been named Laura, revealing perhaps a connection between Williams's feelings about his girlfriend and about his sister (who would become Laura in *The Glass Menagerie*); in any case, the tender story is an elegy to the marginal world that author, friend and sister inhabited.

Audrey Wood, meantime, was having her usual difficulty keeping track of her wandering client; on a few hours' decision, he left the Shelton, sending a cable next day that he was back in Boston, or in Washington, or Chicago, or Atlantic City, or simply "in transit." He was reading his poems to a gathering at Harvard; he was meeting a group of students at Northwestern University; he could be contacted at the 92nd Street YMHA in New York, en route to St. Louis; he was off to New Orleans.

Paul Bowles, who saw Williams frequently during these active years, thought that "he was more eager to get away from where he was than he was to get to another place. . . . I think very much it [was] an eagerness to leave the people . . . he [was] suddenly fed up with a place and the people in it and [felt] that somehow any other place, or nearly any other place, [was] more acceptable at that moment than the place he [was] in. So he [left and went] — it doesn't matter so much where, because he always [changed] his mind at the last minute anyway . . . he [was] inherently extremely restless." And William Inge, who had at first followed him from St. Louis to Chicago, agreed that Williams was "a restless person, physically restless. . . . I think he [did] need the diversion that travel [gave] him."

For a time he settled down to serious work — and to the always equally pursued serious life of the senses. And once again he found that the right place to pursue both needs was New Orleans. By December 18 he had taken a suite at the Hotel Pontchartrain, where he wrote to Donald Windham that New York and Broadway were dangerous for the ego — the way the Hotel Shelton was coming dangerously close to being his bordello, he admitted — and that New Orleans felt less intense, and he more relaxed in pursuing both his writing and his private life. "If I can be said to have a home," he wrote for a Liebling-Wood press release, "it is in New Orleans, which has provided me with more material than any other part of the country."

On New Year's 1946, he took a short-term lease on an apartment at 710 Orleans Street — three small rooms on the second floor, where he wrote a long one-act play called *Ten Blocks on the Camino Real* (a fantasy in the style of Strindberg's haunting *Dream Play*) with Kilroy as the archetypal American, a vagrant whose voice is that of the peripatetic Williams. In a comic rearrangement of characters historical and fictional, Kilroy meets Camille and Casanova, Don Quixote and Sancho Panza, a weird assortment of street people, and Esmeralda, the daughter of a Gypsy. Formless and experimental, it was clearly a vehicle for the extreme feelings about the visit to Mexico — the relish of freedom one moment, the retreat to a more rigorous life the next. Audrey Wood counseled him to wait with this one.

Before the end of January, upsetting letters were reaching him from St. Louis. Cornelius had officially retired from International Shoe, and, with nothing to occupy him other than drink and cards, he was making life miserable for his wife and father-in-law. Reverend Dakin, then almost ninety, was virtually blind and found little comfort with a daughter who continued to harbor a strange resentment against him. Edwina, Williams wrote to Audrey on January 15, was a monument to all the psychological hazards of her time, a woman whose endurance and once fine qualities continued to flourish alongside a narrowness of perception and only the dimmest awareness of human feeling. But her self-styled martyrdom to her husband's callousness was about to end with the economic freedom provided by *The Glass Menagerie;* now, Williams hoped, he had only to deal with the misery of his grandfather.

This consideration could not be managed at once, however, for his own living situation had at the same time become more complicated, if happier, simultaneously more satisfying and more raucous. During his last visit to New Mexico, he had met a desk clerk at La Fonda de Taos Hotel, a dazzlingly handsome young man named Pancho Rodriguez y Gonzalez. By the middle of February, Pancho had visited Williams in New Orleans twice and had then moved into the new Williams apartment on Orleans Street. From Williams's more or less protracted affairs and from his array of sexual partners, one had elicited an emotional response deep enough to warrant risking the complexities of a shared life. Thus began a relationship full of warm passion and emotional fire. Pancho was strong and helpful, adoring and enthusiastic — and these qualities Williams needed in a partner. But Pancho was also emotionally insecure, capable of sudden bursts of temper, and afraid of losing Williams to the charms of fame — and Williams could be both impatient and manipulative of those fears. Pancho wanted a sexually exclusive, one-to-one relationship; Williams, as he admitted in letters to friends like Donald Windham, insisted on keeping his own counsel with a variety of bedtime partners.

"Pancho was a terribly nice man," according to Fritz Bultman, who saw a good deal of the couple in New Orleans that season, "but he was a primitive and I'm afraid Tennessee wasn't very good to him. He was too promiscuous for Pancho, who really wanted a stable life. But Tenn insisted on going out cruising almost every night. His life had not changed very much, in that way, from what it had been in [Greenwich] Village several years before. Pancho was a very simple young man who really loved Tennessee and he couldn't get used to the idea that his love wasn't reciprocated, or that their relationship might come to an end. He was a remarkably sweet man, and a religious man. And I think he had a terrible time explaining Tennessee to his family."

At the outset, there was reason for celebration with their New Orleans friends, a circle that now included the poet and teacher Oliver Evans as well as some city administrators who found congenial the often wild and anonymous parties at the Williams apartment. In February, champagne was poured to mark the publication of Williams's collection *27 Wagons Full of Cotton;** the distance from New York perhaps enabled him to read with detachment the generally unenthusiastic reviews by Joseph Wood

---

* In 1946 this anthology contained the one-act plays *27 Wagons Full of Cotton, The Purification, The Lady of Larkspur Lotion, The Last of My Solid Gold Watches, Portrait of a Madonna, Auto-Da-Fé, Lord Byron's Love Letter, The Strangest Kind of Romance, The Long Good-bye, Hello from Bertha* and *This Property is Condemned.* Others would be added in later reissues of the volume.

Krutch (who decried the "romantic pessimism") and of the *New York Times Book Review* (whose reviewer found the plays full of "sentimental ... disembodied emotionalism").

That same month, he and Pancho and Fritz Bultman were invited to visit Bultman's sister at her home on Louisiana Avenue, a great residence built in 1852. To this house in the legendary Garden District of New Orleans was now added a three-story enclosed greenhouse. With its giant ferns and ficus trees and exotic vines, the "Green Room" at once impressed Williams with its potential as a dramatic setting. Within the decade, it became the model for Violet Venable's terrifying garden in *Suddenly Last Summer* (the second play of *Garden District*), his brilliantly harrowing play that united family history and personal confession. "Tennessee was such a restless soul in those days," Muriel Bultman Francis recalled. "He was always on the move. But he was a gentle man and not one of those writers who felt that he always had to spice a conversation with witticisms or profundities."

The wit and depth were poured, that season, into his work. By April, *Ten Blocks on the Camino Real* was complete, along with the short story "Desire and the Black Masseur." This remains one of his bitterest allegories about what people do to each other, and was in fact a thematic sketch for *Suddenly Last Summer*. There is a fierce guilt about sadistic homosexuality in it. As a celebration of pain and the mute inevitability of self-sacrifice, it has a calmness about universal horror unparalleled until the later *Suddenly Last Summer,* in fact. (The fact that Williams began this story at the height of World War II and completed it just after may explain the theme of universal horror.)

He then began the short story "The Night of the Iguana," which derived from his visits to Mexico, and which introduced the character of Miss Jelkes. Unsatisfying in its early stages as at its completion, it has none of the narrative consistency, character logic or breadth of vision that he would give to a play with the same name in 1960.

Meantime, life with Pancho was becoming more problematic. Pancho could not understand the writer's need for solitude; Williams could not always understand (much less respond to) the young lover's need for reinforcement and attention. The one was passionate and devoted, with the eager conceit of youth; the other was more than a decade older, serious, established, but unwilling to offer emotional stability. He needed Pancho's need; he resented Pancho's neediness.

"Tennessee behaved very badly toward Pancho," Fritz Bultman remembered, "and he did so by using Pancho for real-life scenes which he created — and then transformed them into moments in *A Streetcar Named Desire.*"

By the end of April, it was clear that some brief separation was necessary, and so Williams bought a car and drove from New Orleans to St. Louis. Pancho was sent ahead to Taos, where they were to meet for a holiday in early May. The situation at Arundel Place was more painful than ever: Cornelius spent the daytime in bars, the nights in rages or stupors at home; Edwina was gloomy, if not taciturn; her father was a virtual recluse in his room. This unhappy arrangement Tennessee endured as long as he could, and then, although he felt ill, he resumed his auto trip to New Mexico.

But the sickness he had in St. Louis was not, it turned out, simply psychosomatic. Abdominal pain increased, a fever would not subside, and he had to go to a hospital in Wichita, Kansas, where after a cystoscopic examination doctors found neither a kidney stone nor any acute infection. Diverticulitis was diagnosed, and the likelihood of appendicitis. Williams, however, refused to accept treatment in a strange setting, with only strangers around him; he insisted on proceeding to Pancho in Taos. On May 16 he finally arrived and was brought in acute distress to Holy Cross Hospital where two surgeons, Ashley Pond, Sr., and Albert M. Rosen, correctly interpreted the problem.

Williams was in fact suffering from an intestinal anomaly found congenitally in less than two percent of the general population. Called Meckel's diverticulum (after the eighteenth-century German anatomist), it is a residual sac like the vermiform appendix, whose inflamed and infected state it mimics; impacted, it causes obstruction and requires surgical removal. The procedure is neither complicated nor life-threatening once properly diagnosed. "It wasn't a particularly long operation, and the patient was not near death," Dr. Pond recalled years later. Within a week, Williams's abdominal stitches were removed and he was discharged from the hospital, into Pancho's attentive and tireless care.

But the episode provided Williams with a marvelous bit of melodrama after the initial fear had been dispelled. He wrote at once to Audrey, he wired his family, he telephoned friends near and far, that he was at death's door, and that he had made a will naming Pancho as sole heir. None of this was true, but it did insure the attention and manifest alarm from everyone he contacted. And it coincided perfectly with his tendency to hypochondria and exaggeration; he knew how dramatic emotions are necessary for the artist, and no one but he could manufacture — physically, if necessary — the small scenarios that elicited from those around him the reactions he could transmute into drama.

There was perhaps an additional reason for Williams's little construction of melodrama at this time of his life. He had just finished rereading selections from Chekhov, and letters which recounted how, at the age of thirty-five, he accepted the fact that he was dying; and how, for what would be his last five years, the acceptance of terminal disease colored his work. Tennessee Williams, also thirty-five, saw another link between himself and the Russian writer, and although the doctors in Taos pronounced him entirely healed, he refused to believe that he was anything other than a dying man. It took almost two years for him to see that the parallel was not to be realized; even after that, however, he protested that he was harboring a fatal disease no surgeon was alert enough to diagnose. He was, according to the poet Gilbert Maxwell, who knew him then, a "hypochondriacal being who lived in dread of physical and mental illness," and who was always "morbidly, pathologically frightened" of death. At the same time, however, he realized fully that it was the possibility of death, and the omnipresent danger of accident, that gave life and art — in both content and style — an urgency of feeling.

From New Mexico, he and Pancho passed through New York to visit friends before proceeding for a summer on the island of Nantucket. He met briefly with Audrey Wood, stopped in at the Playhouse Theatre to see the first act of *The Glass Menagerie,* and bought some books for summer reading. One of them he read while in New York: *The Member of the Wedding,* by the Georgia-born Carson McCullers, touched him with its gentle compassion and offbeat family ironies. Eager to meet the twenty-nine-year-old author, he wrote a letter praising her book. And the next day he expressed this admiration to Paul Bigelow and Bigelow's friend and companion, Jordan Massee. As it happened, Massee was McCullers's cousin, and they offered to arrange a meeting between the two writers after Pancho and Williams had reached Nantucket. They had rented for the summer a wind-battered, gray two-story house with an extra bedroom, they told Bigelow and Massee. There would be room for a weekend guest.

"The meeting between Tenn and McCullers happened this way," according to Bigelow. "Alfred Kazin [the literary critic, whom McCullers had met when she was a student at Columbia University] and his daughter had planned to take Carson on a motor trip with them through New England. Tennessee genuinely admired her work, so it was arranged that the Kazins would leave Carson at the ferry on Cape Cod, whence she would proceed on to Tennessee in Nantucket. I had the impression that she always planned to stay on with him, and that she didn't have quite the spontaneity that the more innocent have supposed."

And so began one of the most affecting and strange friendships in American literary history. Williams and Pancho, one Saturday afternoon in mid-June, went to the Nantucket harbor to meet their guest, "a tall, slim figure wearing faded blue dungarees, white moccasins, a man's shirt, and a wide-brimmed straw hat," as her biographer described her appearance that day. At once the two men recognized a member of the group of people with whom they felt at ease. McCullers — married but sexually ambivalent, shy but demanding — was eager to ingratiate herself with the playwright who had achieved the kind of fame she coveted.

From mid-June, she was welcomed, with Williams's easy generosity. He was fascinated with her crooked grin, her ability to spin weird anecdotes for projected novels and stories, her swift infatuation for women visitors, her taste for liquor and for the poems of Hart Crane. They swam together, toured the island on bicycles, had long candlelit dinners preceded by long cocktail hours, and sang at the battered upright piano in the parlor.

"Pancho was of course crazed with jealousy," Paul Bigelow recalled. "Tenn told us later how difficult things got that summer." Without reason, Pancho feared that Carson was out to capture Tennessee as a husband, or at least as a temporary lover. He need not have feared her effusiveness; it was part of her "Southern guff," as Bigelow called it — and in any case, Carson moved from emotional turmoil over one woman visitor to near hysteria over another: "Carson went wild and raved about [a woman visitor's] beauty, poise and elegance," Pancho remembered years later; at the time, however, he feared most of all that she would alienate Williams's affection.

As for Williams, he wrote each day — and in so doing set an example for McCullers, who at once set herself the task of transforming *The Member of the Wedding* into a play. In this, he encouraged her, and daily they sat at opposite ends of the dining room table working, she taking as a model *The Glass Menagerie* (which she had not seen but had read) and he busy on the first full draft of *Chart of Anatomy*. Still convinced that he

was under a death sentence, he complained of chest pains and heart palpitations, of rapid pulse and erratic breathing. All this, however, was actually being experienced not by him, but by the heroine of his
play — Alma Winemiller, the repressed daughter of a Mississippi minister, the "singing nightingale of the Delta" whose unrequited love is for
the wild young doctor to whom she complains of her "palpitations." But
she is finally rejected by him, and this leads her to cast off the fetters of
her strict background and to go off — for one evening, at least — with a
young traveling salesman.

Chart of Anatomy took final shape quickly, with an increased appetite
for life on Williams's part that summer that was no doubt due in part to
the even zanier attitudes of Carson McCullers, and precisely because of
her veneration of him. There are, after all, few stimulants like worshipful
praise.

At the end of June, she left for her home in Nyack, New York, returning several days later with her husband, Reeves McCullers, an equally
anguished soul given to bouts of alcoholic schizophrenia and a bisexual
experimentation that his wife stoutly encouraged. (The people in Tennessee Williams's circle could never be accused of following bourgeois
convention.) But poor Reeves was uncomfortable in this group, and despite the interesting visitors at a Fourth of July party (designer Oliver
Smith, actress Rita Gam and choreographer Jerome Robbins) he soon
fled back to Nyack, to the comparative calm of his mother-in-law.

Late in July, Carson left with the first draft of the dramatized version
of her novel. Acquaintances of both writers then and later were aware
not only of their mutual affection and respect, but also of a strange and
unfounded rivalry that sprang up between them. For her part, she quietly
resented his increasing success. But Williams, always lavish in his praise,
could afford to be generous: even after her play won the New York
Drama Critics Circle Award in 1950, her frail health, her infrequent publications and her gradually debilitating strokes and decline into a private
world of unreason prevented her from reaching anything like a full flow-
ering of her always fragile talent. That did not always, however, prevent
him from wondering if *his* fiction were as good. . . .

"From that summer," according to Paul Bigelow, "despite his kindness and warmth and coming forward to help her in her career, Tenn was
very realistic about her. He recognized an iron determination underneath
all that Southern guff."

The friendship with McCullers has, however, another aspect, which

should perhaps be considered in light of a gift he made to her that summer: a small jade ring that had belonged to his sister Rose. In his collegial support of her — especially as her physical and mental health
declined in a series of strokes and alcohol dependence while she was still
in her early thirties — he saw an opportunity to do for McCullers what
he could not have done for Rose, to help keep her demons at bay, to sustain her unpredictable moods and her almost pathological selfishness.
Even he was horrified at her callous indifference to her husband's neurotic dependence on her (Reeves eventually committed suicide while
alone in Paris), and he endured her moods and pretenses and emotional
demands that he would never have endured from any man. The play he
worked on that summer (with an epigraph he took from Rilke) was
dedicated to Carson McCullers in memory of the weeks they shared. But
half the royalties from it were assigned for the care and benefit of his sister Rose, to insure her more frequent holidays from the state hospital in
Farmington, to buy her clothes and treats. Forever in his mind and memory, the ornery and ill and finally pathetic Carson McCullers — until her
death at fifty in 1967 — was associated for him with Rose, from whom
he was still separated by time and distance.

Before the summer's end, Williams gave a reading from his one-act
plays to the summer residents of Nantucket. Thornton Wilder and actress Patricia Collinge were among those in the audience who especially
liked *The Unsatisfactory Supper* (one of the bases for what would later be
the controversial film *Baby Doll*), and on September first and third there
were staged performances of *Moony's Kid Don't Cry* and *The Long Good-bye*
at the Nantucket Straight Wharf Theatre. Two weeks later, with Williams suddenly and gruesomely ill, he and Pancho departed the island for
New York, and for almost a month they were detained in the city; after
an array of gastrointestinal tests, it was discovered that he had somehow
become the unwilling host to a monstrous tapeworm, which took several
weeks to be coaxed from his system. Quite irrationally, he insisted it was
another indication of terminal cancer.

By the time he was discharged, Williams had arranged — through
Pancho, who again preceded him and who was working hard to satisfy
Williams's caprices — to rent a new apartment in New Orleans. From
the end of October through the winter, they remained in quarters beautifully furnished with antiques collected by the owner, Richard Orme, at
632½ St. Peter Street. There he completed the first revision of *Chart of*

Anatomy and sent it along to Audrey with the suggestion that someone like the English star Celia Johnson would be right for the role, or the American actress Josephine Hutchinson. There was no immediate reply from Audrey, but there was from friends to whom he read it one evening, and their negative comments were enough for him to put it away and to return to the still only half-understood figure of Blanche DuBois, the lady of *The Poker Night.*

"I live," he wrote in an essay that autumn, "near the main street of the Quarter. Down this street, running on the same tracks, are two streetcars, one named 'Desire' and the other named 'Cemeteries.' Their indiscourageable progress up and down Royal Street struck me as having some symbolic bearing of a broad nature on the life in the Vieux Carré — and everywhere else, for that matter." *The Poker Night,* indeed, was taking shape as a treatment of the clash between desire and death; its two major characters — a faded belle (Blanche DuBois) caught in the web of her own illusions and hypocrisies, and her crude brother-in-law (Stanley Kowalski) determined to shatter those illusions at any price — were on an ineluctably tragic course. He completed revisions within days of learning of another death — this time, Laurette Taylor's. She died in New York of cancer at the age of sixty-two, four months after the final performance of *The Glass Menagerie;* her courage and her art had had a large part in validating his own, and her death moved him deeply.

"She was neither a well nor a strong person at any time during the run of the play," he wrote in a tribute that December. "Even when throat trouble made it painful for her to speak she continued in her demanding part and I have never seen her physical suffering affect the unfailing wonder of her performance." Comparing her favorably with Eleanora Duse and Sarah Bernhardt, he saw in Taylor "hints of something that lie outside the flesh and its mortality. I suppose these intuitions come to many people in their religious vocations, but I have sensed them more clearly in the work of artists and most clearly of all in the art of Laurette Taylor." Her death also confirmed his intuition about his own imminent death from what he insisted was pancreatic cancer. But *The Poker Night* must be produced first, and to that end he devoted what he thought were his last energies.

The arrival in New Orleans of Reverend Dakin, who had begged to visit his grandson as a refuge from the unpleasantness of Arundel Place, was a happy interval. On January 9, 1947, Williams wrote to Audrey Wood that Grandfather was no longer able to read, but was quite content to sit quietly with the radio. At this time, a noticeable change occurs in the tone of the correspondence between Williams and Wood; his letters are more open, more self-revealing, less guarded. They are signed "with love" or "devotedly," and betoken an exchange between son and mother more than between client and agent. And she often wrote only about family matters. To be sure, Audrey's services on his behalf now included her complete management of his financial life and the preparation of his income taxes. But her personal discretion about his private life was equally important to him; she understood without archness of condescension the complexity of the relationship with Pancho Rodriguez, she was willing to run interference with members of his family, and she spoke out clearly when his self-confidence failed.

On his side, there was no detail of his life that was not submitted for Audrey's approval. He was, he wrote in January, paying $150 each month for the St. Peter Street apartment; he was spending the same amount weekly for food and medicine; he had bought another new car for $1400, and that cost $20 a month to keep in a local garage; he was paying Pancho $200 each month (which he insisted was a bargain) — everything was sent to New York for Audrey's scrutiny, and nothing escaped her judicious comment.

The visit of Reverend Dakin improved not only the old gentleman's mood; Williams and Pancho had a new peace between themselves, too, after a month of acrimony and sometimes open fistfights because of Williams's extracurricular romances. The obligations connected with the care and comfort of a ninety-year-old forced them to temper the eruption of domestic melodramas to the more tender concern for another.

"Whenever I'm disturbed or discouraged with my work," Williams said at the time, "I just go and sit near [Grandfather]. Sometimes we don't speak at all, but even as we sit in silence I seem to get a great spiritual solace from him." Part of the comfort was undoubtedly due to the fact that the Reverend was, in his grandson's words, "an extremely liberal man. . . . He didn't disapprove of indulgences of the flesh. He played bridge and enjoyed his cocktail," and he never raised a disapproving eyebrow about his grandson's private life; in fact, the bonding of homosexual men always seemed to him rather an elite and stylish manner of living. No one enjoyed the gay bohemianism of New Orleans more than the Reverend; no one was more welcome to its colorful conceits than this quiet Southern cleric.

Which at least partly explains why Williams felt free, in mid-January, to take his grandfather from the drizzly chill of New Orleans on a motor trip southeast, to the warmth of Key West. They took several rooms at La Concha Hotel, with a wide view over the Gulf of Mexico. Miriam Hopkins, newly remarried, celebrated their arrival with a lavish party, but for most of the time Williams remained in his room, working on a final draft of *The Poker Night* while Pancho escorted the Reverend for walks in the sunshine.

The major problem Williams was battling seemed to be the ending for his play: would the distraught and crushed Blanche, robbed of her illusions and of any chance for happiness and social acceptance, simply leave her sister Stella and brother-in-law Stanley for more wandering, with no destination? Would she, like Anna Karenina, throw herself in front of a train? Or would she be removed to a lunatic asylum? During a short visit to New York in late February he was still unsure, and Audrey prudently withheld her opinion; she knew how deeply the tragic nature of the play was working itself within him, and she would not intrude on the natural term of his creativity. She heartily approved, however, his decision not to attend the revival of *Stairs to the Roof* in Pasadena, which Gilmor Brown presented at the end of February for a disappointed press and public.

At the end of March, when Grandfather and Pancho and Williams had been back in New Orleans for several weeks, *The Poker Night* was sent to Audrey for forwarding to prospective producers. Simultaneously, Margo Jones was ready to proceed with a summer production of *Chart of Anatomy* at her theatre-in-the-round in Dallas — but not until Williams insisted (and not until he had Audrey's favorable reaction) on a change of title — to the poetically more apt *Summer and Smoke*.

In April, when it became clear that the details and preparations for theatre productions would take Williams north for much of the year, Reverend Dakin decided to move on to Memphis, where he could be tended by friends and cousins without the necessity to move constantly. This freed Williams to accept Audrey's suggestion that he come halfway north to meet the producer she had interested in *The Poker Night* — Irene Mayer Selznick, the daughter of one legendary movie producer and the wife of another. She had come to New York to pursue an independent career as a theatrical producer, and Audrey felt, quite rightly, that her sensibility and her good taste (not to say her first-rate creative and financial connections) would make her the proper one to lead the play to success. To keep the meetings and negotiations quiet, Audrey suggested they meet away from New York, and she chose Charleston, South Carolina, a town of happy memories connected to her late friend and client DuBose Heyward (whose first novel, *Porgy,* became the basis for a play, an opera and a motion picture).

Williams and Selznick (whom he would often refer to, with ironic deference, as "Dame Selznick"), after a cautious and unsure meeting, were convinced of one another's seriousness. There was no doubt she loved the play and was moved by its tragic grandeur and its sharply etched portraits of men and women in conflict; and she agreed with Williams that the ideal man to direct was Elia Kazan, who with his wife Molly Day Thacher had been following Williams's career with great interest. Williams, Selznick and Wood had been equally perceptive in following Kazan's, for he was by then regarded as one of the most important talents in American theatre and film, and so he would remain. He had acted in the 1930s, made his directing debut in 1935, and within recent years had been highly praised for his direction of *The Skin of Our Teeth, Harriet, Jacobowsky and the Colonel* and *Deep Are the Roots,* among other plays. In addition, he had just directed Arthur Miller's first successful play, *All My Sons,* which had opened in January to great acclaim (and he would soon be awarded the first "Tony" for best direction).

But from Hollywood, where Kazan had had equal success directing the film of *A Tree Grows in Brooklyn,* and where he was completing direction of *Gentleman's Agreement,* word came that Kazan's first reaction was lukewarm — not indeed to the play, but to his directing it. Williams told Selznick that his second choice was John Huston. But by early May, Williams had changed his title to *A Streetcar Named Desire* — which his associates loved — and after being guaranteed major credit and twenty percent of the play's profits, Kazan agreed to direct.

Until Kazan arrived in New York, however, and while Selznick set to the producer's array of duties, Williams decided to break away from the dither of New York. He and Pancho drove to Provincetown, where he made still more changes on *Summer and Smoke.* On June 16, he wrote to Audrey that he had a summons from Margo, who wanted him in Dallas at once for pre-production. She was planning a July 8 opening at the Gulf Oil Playhouse, a theatre without proscenium. This invitation he flatly rejected, reminding Audrey (who, after witnessing several unpleasant scenes with Pancho in New York restaurants, hotel lobbies and suites, was hardly uninformed about such matters) that what he euphemistically called his unconventional private life would be unappreciated in Dallas.

With both plays ready for production, he was content, for the month of June, to enjoy Provincetown; decisions about casting would depend on Kazan's schedule in any case, and the leading ladies whose names were mentioned for the role of Blanche did not appeal to him — Margaret Sullavan, Bette Davis, Pauline Lord, Fay Bainter and — he laughed when he told Pancho — Mary Martin. As for Stanley Kowalski, the quintessential semi-Simian representative of undiluted virility, there was talk of John Garfield or Burt Lancaster.

But there was different talk in Provincetown that month; in the ongoing script of his own domestic disharmony a new name was now introduced. Frank Merlo was a twenty-five-year-old, New Jersey–born navy veteran, a self-educated, second-generation Sicilian. Short, muscular and strikingly handsome, Merlo was that summer at the end of an affair with lyricist John LaTouche; Williams felt that he, too, was near the end of an affair. He and Merlo spent a night together on the Provincetown dunes, but since Merlo was disinclined to a ménage or to the uncertainty of Williams's months ahead, they parted with intense mutual regrets and longing. The parting, however, would be only for a time.

By early July, two things were clear. First, the situation with Pancho was becoming intolerable. Jealous rages followed long nights of drinking by one or the other of them, or by both; outbursts of frightful, tearful hysterics followed the jealous rages; a day's disappearance followed the hysterics. In a letter to Donald Windham, Williams said he understood the reasons for Pancho's emotional immaturity: the young man had known no security as a youth, and now he was afraid of losing his only link with respectability, permanence and glamour. But there was also the report, carried through mutual friends from that summer, that Frank Merlo had returned to New York complaining how he missed Tennessee Williams. Pancho Rodriguez's days in Tennessee Williams's life were thenceforth numbered.

But because he still considered himself a dying man, Williams was cool to the idea of traveling alone on an imminent trip to California, which was necessary to consider an actress for the role of Blanche; accordingly, he postponed plans to send Pancho away with a cash settlement and a letter of employment recommendation.

The previous January, Hume Cronyn had produced a quartet of one-act plays for the Actors' Lab, a small professional company in Los Angeles. Three of the four plays were by Williams and one of them, *Portrait of a Madonna,* was directed by Cronyn. In it, his wife, Jessica Tandy, had starred as the tortured, deranged Miss Collins, living in a world of romantic illusions and finally carted off to an institution. Cronyn had hoped to have Williams travel out to see the play that previous winter; it took until July, with the urgency of a scheduled opening for *Streetcar* in New York before year's end, for Williams to agree to the trip. But he would not travel without Pancho's companionship, he required guarantee of a hotel pool or nearby beach, and he demanded that the stay be short.

The generous Irene Selznick had arranged for him to have his choice of residences — at her house on Summit Drive, at a beach-house, or at a small bungalow in Malibu. Over the period of a month, Williams — sometimes with and sometimes without Pancho — stayed in all three. And his companion, thrilled to near delirium with the movie capital, maintained socially exemplary behavior, so that Williams felt easy about prolonging the stay, while Cronyn restaged *Portrait of a Madonna* for his especial benefit. A single performance, at which Williams was joined by Selznick and Kazan (who had just finished editorial supervision on the film *Gentleman's Agreement*), was enough to settle the matter of who would play Blanche DuBois. There was no argument that it must be Jessica Tandy, who had acted in her native England and in America for almost twenty years, and whose career now had seemed tediously mired in unexceptional films. Cronyn's early faith in Williams and his appreciation of his wife's great gift were at once vindicated and rewarded.

The first of August, tanned and overfed, Williams and Pancho left for Dallas and Margo Jones, who swept round them with *passionate* announcements about the reactions to *Summer and Smoke,* and how *clearly* she understood Williams's vision, and how *glad* she was that Kazan had been engaged for the new play, but that she thought, *really,* she would be *thrilled* to come back to New York to direct *Summer and Smoke* there, and other Williams plays thereafter.*

"Margo Jones wanted desperately to be Tennessee's producer and director after her work as codirector of *The Glass Menagerie*," according to Randy Echols. "All she had to do was say to him, 'Your new play is magic, Tenn, it's sheer magic,' and she had him eating out of her hand. But of course when she finally directed *Summer and Smoke* it was an absolute disaster."

---

* On May 3, 1947, Margo Jones had presented the first offering of her new repertory company "Theatre 47": it had been, at Williams's urging, William Inge's *Farther Off from Heaven,* which Williams had referred to Audrey. *Summer and Smoke* followed.

And so it was, with her curiously imprecise direction. Brooks Atkinson, however — who made the trip from New York, where he was drama critic for the *Times* — recognized it, in spite of production flaws, as a deeply affecting play. He suggested that there be major changes before they come to New York.

Margo piled suitcases, and her friend and assistant Joanna Albus, into the car with Williams and Pancho and drove with them back to Cape Cod, chattering about the casting for *Streetcar* and making her usual bold suggestions — now mostly about the role of Stanley Kowalski. When he arrived in Provincetown, Williams found a letter informing him that excessive demands were being made by their first choice, John Garfield, who wanted a guarantee for a subsequent film of the play as well as the right to withdraw from the play if a good movie offer arose. These and other stipulations seemed even to the novice Mrs. Selznick as unconscionable, and Garfield was left out of subsequent negotiations.* This infuriated Williams. "A play is my life's blood!" he shouted over the telephone to Audrey. "What is Dame Selznick up to? I have more reverence for Miss Margo, who is here with me now. . . . I am more interested in getting Garfield back than in talking about another actor. . . ." And so on it went, for several nights at the end of August.

At this point Bill Liebling made a suggestion to Audrey; she thought it was inspired, and she wired Kazan and telephoned Irene and Williams at once. A twenty-three-year-old former New School student in Erwin Piscator's Drama Workshop had impressed Liebling with just four Broadway appearances — as the son in *I Remember Mama,* in 1944; in Maxwell Anderson's *Truckline Café,* directed by Harold Clurman (and co-produced by Clurman and Elia Kazan) in 1946; in Ben Hecht's salute to Israel, *A Flag Is Born,* with Paul Muni, also in 1946; and in a revival of Shaw's *Candida* with Katharine Cornell. His name was Marlon Brando. The last week of August, Brando was persuaded to travel to Provincetown to read for Williams.

"I never saw such raw talent in an individual," Williams recalled. "Brando was a gentle, lovely guy, a man of extraordinary beauty when I first met him. He was very natural and helpful. He repaired the plumbing that had gone on the whack, and he repaired the lights that had gone off. And then he just sat calmly down and began to read [the role of Stanley in *A Streetcar Named Desire*]."

* Audrey and Irene had sent Williams a list of names for consideration, some of them more amusing possibilities than others: Van Heflin, Edmund O'Brien, John Lund, Gregory Peck, etc.

The effect on everyone in the room — Williams, Margo, Joanna, Pancho — was instantaneous enthusiasm. "Get Kazan on the phone!" Margo shouted, leaping around the room. "This is the greatest reading I have ever heard — even in *Texas!*" As it happened, Kazan had already known and worked with Brando — but he had reservations about the actor's detached style, his frequently uncooperative moods, his unique but unpredictable acting method. Williams insisted that Kazan hear Brando read, in New York. "He is a God-sent Stanley," Williams told Audrey; he felt Brando's reading caught the humanity of the character, and the character of *A Streetcar Named Desire* as a play of misperceptions, of the callousness and insensitivity of youth. Brando's sensuality, Williams added, and his immediate physical appeal, would enable audiences to react with more appropriate complexity to the tragic ironies and shifting identifications he wanted them to feel.

By September, Jessica Tandy and Marlon Brando had, with some mutual wariness, met at a first reading under Kazan's confident, quiet guidance; Kim Hunter and Karl Malden were signed for the roles of Stella and Stanley's buddy Harold Mitchell (whose name and character were based on Williams's Missouri classmate). Irene Selznick fixed a December 3 opening at the Ethel Barrymore Theatre in New York, after previews in New Haven, Boston and Philadelphia.

"Tennessee was quite shy during our early rehearsals," Elia Kazan remembered, "but he became less so as time went on. He never interfered, but he was always there for us, always available if there were a question about the text." As the first performances drew near, rehearsal time increased — and by mid-October there were eight hours of work at night, at the New Amsterdam Theatre roof rehearsal hall, in addition to two hours of work each morning. At Williams's insistence (and with Kazan's quick approval), the script was frozen — as much because there was no need of alteration as because the author said this was his last play, that he was dying, and that he had no energy for any more work. But he looked quite well, and he ate heartily and kept late hours. The cast knew not what to think.

Two decisions by Tennessee Williams during the pre-Broadway tour suggested that he would not be so quickly departing this world. First, the dissension with Pancho had reached a critical stage when he tossed Tennessee's typewriter from a hotel window and then tore up the curtains. That was impossible to forgive. Williams gave Pancho a train ticket to New Orleans. To this he added two months' pay to assist him in a new life; there could be no question, however, of a resumption of their relationship. Williams was on the verge of an important moment of his career, he said. This was the first indication in months that he did not, after all, expect to be buried just before (or after) opening night in New York. The second was that he booked passage on a ship to depart America on December 30 for a long holiday with friends in Europe.

"At the end of his affair with Pancho," Fritz Bultman said, "I saw something I didn't like — something opportunistic and abusive in Tennessee. I must say that I thought he mismanaged things with Pancho, and I didn't trust him after that. Later, my wife and I met him in Paris, but he was more callous than I'd imagined anyone could be. After Kip and Pancho, something seemed to go sour in him, to harden. And I felt he was beginning to lose his friends. There were plenty of hangers-on, but Oliver Evans [the poet and teacher] was probably the only deep friend from the old days he saw regularly in the years after."

In New Haven Williams offered a spirited defense of the play and its characters to his colleague, the venerable Thornton Wilder, who came to a rehearsal and objected to Williams that the situation of Stella DuBois Kowalski was incredible: a genteel Southern girl like her, he objected, would never link herself with the scornful, proud, violent physicality of Stanley.

"This man," Williams said to the bystanders when Wilder had stepped away, "has never had a good lay!" Quite apart from presumptions about Wilder's private life, Williams's intention was, of course, to indicate the nature of Stella's perseverance with her husband. No one appreciated the comment more than its speaker, whose piercing cackle could be heard in every corner of the Shubert Theatre. He expected Wilder not to join them in New York for the Broadway premiere, and he was right.

But an enormous crowd did — the audience at the Barrymore on December 3 applauded for a full half-hour, Williams was called to the stage, and the critics rushed off to their typewriters to hail a brilliant new American drama. From his subleased apartment on East 36th Street, Williams hosted an after-theatre party, and the guests awaited anxiously the first newspaper reviews. They need not have worried, then or for the next several weeks, for the theatre had not only a solid commercial success but a play almost universally proclaimed great. Brooks Atkinson in the *Times* called *A Streetcar Named Desire* "a quietly woven study of intangibles. . . . [Williams's] knowledge of people is honest and thorough and [his] sympathy is profoundly human. . . . Out of poetic imagination and ordinary compassion he has spun a poignant and luminous story." Howard Barnes, in the *New York Herald-Tribune,* described it as a play of "heroic dimensions. . . . Williams is certainly the Eugene O'Neill of the present period. . . . [*Streetcar*] is a savagely arresting tragedy . . . a work of rare discernment and craftsmanship." John Chapman, critic for the *New York Daily News,* wrote that it was "compassionate, heart-wrenchingly human. It has the tragic overtones of grand opera." For George Freedley of the *Morning Telegraph,* the play was "a drama of great and compelling honesty, [and the author] a dramatist of stature." And *The New Yorker*'s critic, Wolcott Gibbs, called it "deeply disturbing . . . a brilliant, implacable play about the disintegration of a woman, or, if you like, of a society."

The story of *A Streetcar Named Desire* is simple; its themes are complex. Blanche DuBois, a sad, thirty-year-old Southern belle who has suffered the loss of her ancestral home, arrives in New Orleans to visit her sister Stella, who has married a crudely forceful man, an archetype of machismo named Stanley Kowalski. Blanche's airs, her affectations and illusions about herself and others, her lies about a tragic and sordid past, are ruthlessly exposed by Stanley. It is revealed that — far from being a respectable schoolteacher who would only consider a chaste courtship prior to an old-fashioned wedding — Blanche has a reputation for seducing teenage boys, and has been the scandal of her home territory. Prior to her wanderings (and perhaps precipitated by guilt), she had been briefly married to a young man whose homosexuality she accidentally discovered and then deliberately and cruelly exposed publicly; as a result of this, he at once took his own life.

In a desperate attempt to salvage her sanity and the last vestiges of self-respect, Blanche hopes that Harold Mitchell, a crony of Stanley but bound to his own mother, will rescue her and provide some kind of emotional refuge. Stanley discloses her sordid past and then rapes Blanche, and this is the last act of retributive cruelty that seals her doom. At the end, the complexities of life and death are italicized: Stella has given birth to Stanley's baby and (contrary to what her sister had hoped) remains with him. Blanche suffers a complete breakdown and is led away to an asylum, now dependent in a new way — as before in a promiscuous way — on what she calls "the kindness of strangers."

The connection several critics pointed out — between the forlorn, tainted Blanche DuBois and the dying culture of the old American

South — Williams himself admitted: "I write out of love for the South.... [It] once had a way of life that I am just old enough to re-member — a culture that had grace, elegance, an inbred culture, not a society based on money. I write out of regret for that.... I write about the South because I think the war between romanticism and the hostility to it is very sharp there." He had treated the passing traditions of that culture before, to be sure — in Charlie Colton's diatribes of *The Last of My Solid Gold Watches,* for example.

But the social-cultural framework of *A Streetcar Named Desire* is just that — a framework, not a schematically proposed thesis. The loss of Blanche's homestead is more than a cultural consideration. For Williams, it is the play's first narrative marker of its major concern — that the hal-lowed things of the sensitive are cheapened and destroyed by contact with the brave new world whose brutish instinct can neither understand nor sustain what is fragile. (In this regard, *A Streetcar Named Desire* has a certain nostalgia that testifies to its author's veneration of Chekhov and his tragic seagull.)

But after all the critical and scholarly appreciations have been set down, we are left with the fact that Tennessee Williams brought from himself a play he was convinced was to be his last — that he would never have the energy for another long play — a work whose conflict (of desire and sensitivity against brutality) he associated with death. In his creative struggles with himself and in his domestic struggles with Pancho, in his desire for security and in his inclination for multiple and casual sexual partners, he met both the protective and the destructive Stanley, and the gentle, needy, spiritual but manipulative sensualist Blanche. And he was convinced that death was the term of his struggle.

"I draw all my characters from myself," he said later. "I can't draw a character unless I know it within myself." And as Elia Kazan well under-stood, "Blanche DuBois, the woman, *is* Williams. Blanche comes into a house where someone is going to murder her. The interesting part of it is that Blanche DuBois-Williams is *attracted* to the person who's going to murder her.... I saw Blanche as Williams, an ambivalent figure who is attracted to the harshness and vulgarity around him at the same time that he fears it, because it threatens his life."

In fact it was Kazan's unspoken understanding of the deeply personal complex of feelings in Williams's life at this time that made the staging of the play possible. "Kazan," Williams said, "has always given me con-fidence and always brought out the best of me." Instead of confounding his inner anxiety with explosions of guilt and with a paralytic remorse, Williams dealt with his conflicts the only way he knew — creatively.

The acuteness of perception and the truth of those shifting associations between Stanley and Blanche could be set down for audiences because Tennessee Williams first knew the battle and the shifting identifications within himself. He looked to Pancho Rodriguez for strength and protection against passersby and against the harsher tradesmen of the theatre; he needed him for traveling companion and he came to him for comfort and for tenderness when he was exhausted from work. Like Stanley toward Stella, he also needed someone to comfort and to protect, and in Pancho's insecurity he found the perfect recipient — perhaps too perfect, which is why he could finally no longer sustain the blunt demands that the younger man made, and that made him paradoxically so dependent that it was suffocating to Williams.

"Tennessee liked Pancho," Kazan reflected years later, "for the same qualities he saw in Kowalski — that he'd break up the joint if he didn't like what was going on." An admirer of brute strength and its often impolite, ungenteel manifestations, Williams nevertheless took more often the part of Blanche: he learned to yield to the temporary soothing of alcohol and to the comfort of strangers' arms.

But just as Williams was donor and receiver of the protectiveness, the encircling strength of Stanley, so was he prey to the crazy, ungentle animal instincts of both Stanley and Blanche. As he wrote to Donald Windham in March 1947, and to others throughout the year, he felt the need to supplement intimacy with Pancho with other sexual contacts — as he had during the time with Kip; he felt like the Blanche who went from bed to bed, and whose encounter with a newspaper-boy is the mirror image of Williams in those critical years, eager, like Blanche, to be affirmed by strangers.

But at last, he believed, this conflict between Stanley and Blanche leads to death — thus his conviction, even while he was depending on Pancho and driving Pancho away, while he was giving to and receiving from Pancho — that desire, unreined, leads to death: "They told me to take a streetcar named Desire, then transfer to one called Cemeteries," is Blanche's first line in the play.* He was himself convinced that the clash of desires in him was leading him to a literal death; and although time proved him wrong, there was a deeper awareness that with unchecked

* He has, with poetic license, modified the direct streetcar route of the French Quarter to suit his own purposes.

desires something always dies. He was, he felt in 1946 and 1947, Blanche herself — at the end of the line; and death, and maybe Elysian Fields, lay ahead. This inevitability, he felt, was due to the free play that desire had had, up to this time, in his life.

The part of him that was Stanley rebelled, and protected Stella, the sister who saw the necessity of compromise; the part that was Stanley wanted to tear away the mask of illusion and the drab phoniness that Blanche brought into his life. And there lay the heart of the battle, for although the part that was Blanche lied, wore a deceiving garb, clung irrationally to a dead past that could not be revived, yearned for a style that had already gone to rot, she still wore the mantle of a tragic dignity; she was still aware that "there has been some progress . . . art, poetry, music . . . such kinds of new light have come into the world . . . some tenderer feelings have had some little beginning."* She was still aware, finally, that although she had not pursued those tenderer feelings as she might, and had squandered and falsified her emotions, there were still rations available to her — and if too late for her, available to Stella, and to others.

Viewers and readers of the play (and the audiences of the brilliant film of it directed by Kazan in 1951) sense that *A Streetcar Named Desire* dramatizes the eternal clash within everyone. Williams knew it most deeply in himself: his sister had been broken by conflict, he was always being *almost* broken by it. In the play that many still consider his masterpiece, he revealed not what all life is like, but what some of life is like, and what all life is in constant danger of becoming — a willing ritual sacrifice of humanity at its gentlest to the fierce demands of carnality. An empty immolation, it leads only to death, or to madness.

Accepting and mistrusting the praise for his play, he left for Europe by steamship at the end of 1947. He was exhausted and nervous but alone, and for once he was pleased with the solitude of a single room.

---

* In *The Glass Menagerie*, Amanda Wingfield praises "Superior things! Things of the mind and the spirit! Only animals have to satisfy instincts! Surely your aims are somewhat higher than theirs!"

Chapter Five

FIDELITIES

(1948–1952)

I always say that life is such a mysteriously complicated thing that no one should really presume to judge and condemn the behavior of anyone else.

— Alma Winemiller, in *Summer and Smoke*

HE HAD EXPECTED Paris in 1948 to be glamorous, happy, open, daring and full of international artists, as it had been in 1928. But from a damp and chilly room at the Hotel Lutetia, on the Boulevard Raspail, Williams wrote to Audrey Wood, Donald Windham and others that the city had on the contrary depressed him, and he had a bad cold and a sick stomach. Could Audrey send cans of condensed milk? She did. Would she write to Dr. Emmet Hoctor at the state hospital in Farmington, to arrange for a paid companion for Rose, so his sister could have more frequent outings? Audrey at once took the matter to the Missouri authorities. Could she send instant coffee, which would be less strong on his excitable heart? Audrey wrapped several jars and forwarded them by air mail.

By the end of January, Williams's Paris excursions had taken him to a few required tourist attractions and to the gathering places of the homosexual population there. At least once, he was robbed by a companion he had brought back for the night. Windham and Wood urged caution, and she added that walks in Montmartre at night were unlikely to be safer than those in Central Park (which, she knew, had already been disastrous for him). Audrey was also concerned at his report that his cold had turned to hepatitis and mononucleosis, and that he was confined to the American hospital in Neuilly, a suburb of Paris. But by the time she had sent a cable asking if she should go to him, he had been discharged with a prescription for cough syrup and was back at his hotel; as usual, he interpreted his symptoms as signs of grave illness.

In February, he began to retrace the journey he had taken twenty years earlier with his grandfather, traveling by train along the Riviera; then, without stopping, he proceeded through Italy to Naples and Reggio di Calabria, and went over for a brief visit to Sicily. Alone and unable to speak Italian, he at once returned to Rome, where he spent two weeks in a small apartment, completing revisions on *Summer and Smoke* for a Broadway production later that year.* It was the last attempt at serious work for many months, and it began the first protracted hiatus in his writing since adolescence. The outcome of such uncreative indolence was unfortunate.

In his new apartment at 45 via Aurora, his life was all play and no work. "His trip," according to Paul Bigelow, "recalled the earlier vacation with his grandfather. But now he could find more sexual freedom than he had found anywhere else — and a social and creative freedom when he wanted that, too."

The social and creative freedom of postwar Rome came as a surprise, both to the American colony and to the somewhat bewildered, struggling Romans. "In 1946 and 1947 Europe was still out-of-bounds for foreigners," as Gore Vidal remarked. "Rome was strange to all of us. For one thing, Italy had been sealed off not only by war but by Fascism. Since the early thirties few English or American artists knew Italy well." Very quickly, however, things changed, as an influx of artists — and the welcome American dollar — altered the pattern of Roman day and night life.

The invasion was chronicled by, among others, Harold Acton, who came from his house in Florence in March 1948 to observe what he called "a bohemian annexe to the American Academy [in Rome]," and where he met Williams ("a pudgy, taciturn, moustached little man without any obvious distinction"), composer Samuel Barber, Vidal (whose *The City and the Pillar,* the first serious novel of homosexuality by an American, was soon to be published), the poet-novelist Frederic Prokosch, and even the occasional heterosexual, like Orson Welles. Acton was not the only historian-observer to be struck by the Americans' creative zest and by their boldness in pursuing unconventional sexual mores. And pursuing is what they did with a vengeance; Williams, for one, wrote letter after letter to Donald Windham boasting of what he admitted was an excess of sensuality. Part of this was because a little money went a long way, and Roman boys and young men would, for the price of a meal or a coat, be available.

Typically, however, it was not long before Williams felt less calloused, warmer feelings. By the end of March, when he hosted a reception at his

---

* At the same time, he quickly drafted the short story "Rubio y Morena," a heterosexualized (and much sentimentalized) account of his travels with Pancho. The story concerns the lonely writer Kamrowski and his doomed affair with the Mexican girl Amada.

apartment, he had taken a young Italian lover named Salvatore (who was called Raffaello in Williams's *Memoirs* and letters). Williams at once found himself full of tender affection — a sentiment, he told Windham, he had very much hoped to avoid after the Pancho era.

Vidal — alert, serious but gifted with a keen, patrician humor — later recalled that in 1948 Williams had an "indifference to place, art, history. [He] seldom reads a book and the only history he knows is his own; he depends, finally, on a romantic genius to get him through life. Above all, he is a survivor. . . ." And surviving was what Williams intended during his remarkably sensual life that year; he discovered that he was not in imminent danger of death, and that the busy, affable crowd of Americans in Rome would not tolerate such ridiculous protestations to the contrary. With the Roman spring he caught the spirit of *dolce far niente,* of sweet indolence; a short story or two was occasionally attempted, but most waking hours were otherwise given over to wandering. He planned to stay as long as he could, at least until it was necessary to return to New York for *Summer and Smoke.*

In the midst of what he still often insisted was only a temporary escape from his death sentence, the good news came from Audrey: *A Streetcar Named Desire,* on March 31, received the award for best play of the year from the Drama Critics Circle, and on May 3 the Pulitzer Prize was added to its honors. Audrey wrote that his income was spiraling, and she recommended serious investments. In 1948, as international companies produced his plays and *Streetcar* continued to sell out in New York, his revenue was so great that he had to pay more than $100,000 in taxes.

From the end of April to early June, Donald Windham and his friend and companion Sandy Campbell came to Rome and joined Williams and Salvatore all day every day. They could see his restlessness, however, for a fierce promiscuity — in spite of Salvatore — was manifested that season: he was getting an appetite (Williams's word) for blonds, and said he might go north. (Sebastian Venable, in the later *Suddenly Last Summer,* becomes "fed up with the dark ones and was famished for blonds . . . that's how he talked about people, as if they were items on a menu. . . .") In a letter to Audrey Wood on April 19, he quoted at length from the Episcopalian act of contrition and added his own awareness of the sins of his life. Perhaps because he had almost completely stopped working that spring, the pull of the flesh was more strongly felt than ever.

Audrey replied to his letter, but changed the subject: in May, Jerry Wald, at Warner Brothers Studios, was hastening negotiations by reporting that Samuel Goldwyn was simultaneously trying to buy the rights to *The Glass Menagerie,* in which he hoped to star Teresa Wright and Dana Andrews, who had been so popular in his production of *The Best Years of Our Lives.* Warners, at Wald's behest, acted quickly and Goldwyn lost the rights.

Glad of the visit of his American friends and for the most part content with the longest vacation he had known, Williams was, precisely because of the gnawing sexual tension within him, glad of the news of Margo Jones's imminent arrival. A visitor he might otherwise have tried to avoid, she was due in Naples in early June to discuss the final revisions and production plans for *Summer and Smoke.* The consistency of feeling, the congruence between his own struggle and that of Alma Winemiller, the play's heroine, could not have been more exact if he had written literally about himself instead of about his surrogate, the minister's daughter. The complexities of his life with Pancho had been transformed into *A Streetcar Named Desire;* the conflict continued, unexpectedly, with the Italian boy Salvatore. And the last draft of *Summer and Smoke* — prepared for Margo's arrival that spring — reveals the shift in feeling, the deepening of the conflict far beyond what the play had dramatized in its earlier version, for now Miss Alma's conflict had a knife-edge poignancy, her Puritan guilt a breathless urgency.

By June 8 he and Salvatore had met Margo and traveled briefly to Capri and Ischia; the islands in the Bay of Naples would, Williams said, be relaxing for them all while necessary work was done on production plans. But Margo was uncharmed by Mediterranean beauties geographic or human, and so, after depositing Salvatore in Rome, he went with her to London. Margo returned to New York shortly thereafter, and in his suite at the Savoy Hotel Williams — energized by the contagious enthusiasm of "the Texas tornado" — resumed daily writing and met with the producer (Hugh Beaumont) and the director (John Gielgud) who were preparing the London version of *The Glass Menagerie,* in which Helen Hayes had agreed to star as Amanda. Also at this time he met the young Russo-English aspiring actress Maria Britneva, whom he often visited in London and whom he often entertained in America. A woman of strong loyalty and vitality, she was appointed by Williams as a cotrustee of a trust created by the terms of his will.

But the essential loneliness of London, which he detailed in letters to Audrey, was sharpened by the sudden awareness of how deep was his feeling for young Salvatore, whom he had at first tried to keep distant and who broke the unwelcome news that he might soon realize his dream of emigrating to America — in the company of an American woman he intended to marry. It seemed to Williams like the repetition of his relationship with Kip Kiernan, the Canadian dancer. But from the calm — almost stoic — observance of this, he shaped the final scenes of *Summer and Smoke:*

"Yes, it had begun that early, this affliction of love," Alma says to John Buchanan, the doctor she has loved, spurned and then after changing her mind and heart must at last lose, "and never let go of me since, but kept on growing. I've lived next door to you all the days of my life, a weak and divided person who stood in adoring awe of your singleness, of your strength. And that is my story! Now I wish you would tell me — why didn't it happen between us? Why did I fail? Why did you come almost close enough — and no closer?" As he knew, it was with the doctor as it was with himself — the distance, and the loss, were really due to the nature of Alma, and the nature of Tennessee Williams.

It was at this time that he met someone who suggested that he supplement the chemical effect of liquor with mood-altering pills. By the end of June, he admitted to Audrey, this dangerous combination had become a frequent indulgence. It was perhaps the next step in a life of increasing abandonment to sensual experience, even at the risk of health.

This experience was sufficiently frightening to him that he departed London and returned to Paris, where he took two rooms at the Hotel de l'Université, renewed his friendship with Gore Vidal and Frederick Prokosch, and his acquaintance with Truman Capote. Then a twenty-four-year-old whose first novel, *Other Voices, Other Rooms,* had caused some literary excitement, Capote regaled Williams with anecdotes about his birthplace, New Orleans. Williams found that Capote's boyish looks and fey humor took some time to appreciate. There was more substantial distraction at a luncheon given for Williams, Vidal and Prokosch by Jean Cocteau, who wanted the French rights to *A Streetcar Named Desire* for Jean Marais to act in.

"I came along as translator," Vidal recalled. "Marais looked beautiful but sleepy. Cocteau was characteristically brilliant. . . . Tennessee knew no French. He also had no clear idea just who Cocteau was, while Cocteau knew nothing about Tennessee except that he had written a popular American play with a splendid part in it for his lover Marais. Between Tennessee's solemn analyses of the play and Cocteau's rhetoric about theater . . . no one made any sense at all except Marais who broke his long silence to ask, apropos the character Stanley Kowalski, 'Will I have to use a Polish accent?' "

Meanwhile, the London premiere of *The Glass Menagerie* was set for July 28. Edwina and Dakin arrived, and Audrey Wood hosted them at the Savoy. Then they — with Gielgud and the cast — awaited the scheduled arrival of the playwright. The afternoon of the premiere came, but no Williams; the first performance and a lavish reception followed, but still no Williams. Then Edwina was handed a telegram from her son, dated from Paris: "Take a bow for me." She was furious, Audrey was embarrassed, and Helen Hayes was perplexed. In a letter the actress received three days later, Williams begged pardon for his childish behavior, and explained his rudeness by detailing a condition of exhaustion, overwork, frayed nerves, emotional paralysis and — Alma Winemiller's complaint — constant heart palpitations. His failure to arrive, he wrote, was due to an accidental overdose of the sedative barbital he had taken to quiet a nerve crisis; he then fell unconscious for five hours and missed his train. He deeply regretted his gaucherie and felt that the patient and understanding Miss Hayes would forgive what his own mother would not. She tried, as did Audrey, to ignore the event, and with their good humor they kept Edwina off his track.

On August 4, Williams departed from Genoa for New York, having delayed as long as he could his return for the rehearsals of *Summer and Smoke*. It is not known whether there was a final meeting with Salvatore.

Back in New York, his friends Tony and Jane Smith had been on the alert for an apartment he might sublease, and they had arranged for him to move to 235 East 58th Street, which Tony had recently redesigned for its tenant, the artist Buffie Johnson. The Smiths welcomed him warmly, as did Paul Bigelow. But at once Williams began to complain that he was dying of heart disease — shades of Miss Alma yet again.

"I got tired of all this talk from Tenn about his imminent death from one malady or another," Bigelow remembered. "This time he insisted it was a heart condition, so I took him to a friend of mine who was a distinguished cardiac man. After several consultations, the doctor said to me, 'I think it would be better if you didn't disabuse Mr. Williams of this illusion about a serious illness — it would make him very unhappy to think he was in perfect health, and it might even bring about a heart attack!' We both smiled over that, and of course I never told Tenn what the doctor said. After a few days with his friends, however — all of whom took little notice of his hypochondria — he was for the most part his old self, full of fun and deviltry."

On October 6, *Summer and Smoke* opened at the Music Box Theatre, and most of the critics gave it a chilly reception: "a pretentious and amateurish bore" and "a juvenile and sadly delinquent effort" and "almost unendurably lengthy" were the kinder remarks, and even his mentor John Gassner thought the play represented "the weaknesses I have suspected in its author for a long time — an insufficient exertion of intellect." Among the few who praised it was Brooks Atkinson, in the *Times:* "It's tremulous with beauty . . . a work of art . . . the gift of a poetic and creative writer." Only Atkinson felt that the failure of *Summer and Smoke* was due to Margo Jones's unfortunate direction, and not indeed to any deficiencies in what he felt was an important play.

In fact, *Summer and Smoke* is one of Tennessee Williams's masterworks for the stage, a play of the eternal conflict between flesh and spirit — although these are often schematically represented by the heroine, Alma Winemiller and the man she has known from childhood, John Buchanan. She is the soul, or smoke, of the title — the exponent of something "immaterial — as thin as smoke," as John says of her — while he is represented by everything that refers to the body, to summer's heat, and to the plain, flat acceptance of physicality which he recommends to her and which he literalizes in his profession as a doctor. The story is straightforward: from his youth as a hell-raiser and womanizer, John is transformed into a serious and devoted physician, a change which occurs partly as a result of Alma's example and partly because his irresponsibility causes the death of his own father. By the time of his transfer of energies, however, Alma, too, has changed: she has come to know that an exaggerated, hermetically sealed angelism is inhuman. But when she is ready for a healthy life of the body, it is too late: John — who alone, over the years, has been her real heart's desire — is ready to marry a sturdy, uncomplicated girl from the town. "The tables have turned with a vengeance," Alma observes, in Tennessee Williams's most poignant assertion that balanced unions between the right mates are very rare indeed.

The objection that Alma and John are created as characters so extreme as to be incredible is perhaps not a fair one. It is in fact precisely because they are extreme people (like the two aspects, wild and sensitive, of their creator) that they are doomed to estrangement. Everything about Alma

Winemiller is too removed from the things of earth and body; everything about John is too involved with the things of earth and body.
They should complement one another, but complementarity is rare —
which is why not even the passionate Rosa Gonzales can win John,
either: she is as sensual as he, and cannot balance him. And it is Alma's
years of extreme living that lead her to a single dramatic gesture at the
final curtain: she meets a young man in the park, by the statue of the
stone angel, and agrees to go off with him for a night at the Moon Lake
Casino. There is nothing to suggest entrance into a life of promiscuity
(as some have presumptuously believed); it is simply a single gesture of
reversal and defiance, a single attempt to correct a habit of an unbalanced
nature.

At the opening (which, according to those present, brought tears of
emotion from many in the audience) were two people who were becoming increasingly important to Tennessee Williams, and each for a different reason. He had invited, for a center seat and a place of honor at the
party following, the woman to whom the play was dedicated — Carson
McCullers. Earlier that year, from Italy, Williams had written to Paul
Bigelow that he hoped he could do something concrete to help the frail,
unstable Carson — something, he said, that would atone for the selfishness that marked his life in Rome. But he added that he knew he could
not give up the "irregularities" of his life and nature, and that he feared
this would add to Carson's unhappiness. Now, back in America, he was
about to make a bolder suggestion: that he and she take Rose from the
hospital to live with them in a kind of family situation.

This was, of course, an impossible (if poignant) fantasy. For a time,
however, Carson and Williams spoke as if it were no more unlikely than
a winter picnic. Privately, however, she told friends that she was nervous
about Williams's nerves; and privately he told friends that he was nervous about her nerves. They were both, on the other hand, romantically
attracted to the other's fragility.

But if Williams was disappointed with Margo's handling of *Summer
and Smoke,* and unsure how to establish the little family of Williams,
Williams and McCullers, he was buoyant and rock-sure about the other
friend at opening night. Walking along East 58th Street, he had met
Frank Merlo. Before the end of October, Merlo had moved to Williams's
apartment, and so began the longest and the deepest intimacy of his life.

On the fineness of Frank Merlo's character there is simply no dispute, nor on the devotion and dutifulness with which he gave over his life to Tennessee Williams's. "Frank was the best person Tom ever lived with," according to Dakin. "My brother left every practical detail of his life to Frank, and he discharged everything wonderfully well. He cared for Grandfather equally well. Frank was a unique man."

"We were all very pleased when Frank moved in with Tenn," Bigelow remembered. "Frank was a warm, decent man with a strong native intelligence and a sense of honor. Those of us who cared about Tenn realized that Frank wanted to care for him and to provide some order in his chaotic life. Tenn had what I call 'artist's order,' which is something else — but he needed someone to look after the ordinary logical structure of everyday life. And with great love, this is what Frank did."

Christopher Isherwood agreed: "Everyone who ever met Frank Merlo found him a marvelous man. He was a support to Tennessee; he made everything work for him. He ran the house, he looked after him in a way that was uncanny. He was no goody-goody. He was just plain good. And he wasn't just some kind of faithful servitor. He was a lovable man with a strong will. We have a saying in Britain — 'He kept his wig on' — that is, he was a man who kept cool, even when he and Tennessee were exposed to the most appalling pressures of social and professional life."

Williams and Merlo had no sooner settled his belongings into the apartment than the playwright set out for a brief visit to St. Louis. Dakin — who was now acting on his brother's behalf in legal matters relative to the family — drew up the terms of a trust that his brother wanted for Rose. In addition to half the royalties from *Summer and Smoke,* he arranged for regular deliveries of gifts and clothing to her. And then, for the first time in over ten years, Tennessee went to see her at Farmington — on her birthday in November. The remainder of his short visit to St. Louis passed quietly. Only Edwina and her father were now at Arundel Place, Cornelius having moved first to live with his sister in Knoxville, and then to an apartment hotel nearby. Several afternoons in St. Louis, Williams worked on a tentative first draft — not more than very rough scenes, in fact — for a play called *The Big Time Operators;* it would form, after much time and development, the thematic and narrative basis for *Sweet Bird of Youth.*

Back in New York with Frank, Williams realized how fortunate he was to have so attentive, efficient and loving a companion. Frank had rearranged the furniture in the apartment so that Williams had uncluttered and private work-space, and he had assumed innumerable small duties designed to free him from daily concerns and smooth his writing and social schedule. This he did with easy grace and unselfconsciousness, and Williams was so touched and appreciative that he suggested they leave almost immediately for a long trip together, a kind of celebration of their new, shared life. The only place to go, of course, would be to Italy and Sicily, since Williams had loved the island on first sight earlier that year, and because Merlo's family had emigrated from Sicily. Before their departure, he wrote to Audrey, telling her he could be reached simply "in care of American Express, Rome," and assuring her that the important part of himself coveted not Broadway and fame, but a deepening of his creative life without concession to the demands of celebrity. Audrey and Dakin were seeing to the professional, legal and financial aspects of his life; now he could add to this pragmatic dependency the devoted attention of Frankie. Neither before nor after this was Tennessee Williams ever surrounded with so much protection and support.

And so in early December they boarded the *Vulcania* from New York, and a week later were met in Tangier by Jane and Paul Bowles. It was the first meeting since 1940 between Williams and the hapless Mrs. Bowles, who resembled no one so much as Carson McCullers — she was exactly the same age, with the same delicate talent, the same complexity and ambiguity and unusual personality, the same scratchy persona.

"In appearance she was a lovely girl," Williams wrote, "small, piquant, darting between humor, anxiety, love and distraction. I had met nervous girls before, but her quicksilver animation, her continual cries, to me and herself: 'Shall we do this or shall we do that? What shall we do?' showed such an extreme kind of excited indecision that I was skeptical of its reality — intrigued, certainly, but still somewhat incredulous.

"Used to it as Paul [Bowles] must have been, he stood there, simply smiling in a bemused sort of way. It seems to me that Frank Merlo took command of the chaotic situation, much to the relief of us all. . . . All the indecision was a true and dreadful concern that she might suggest a wrong move in a world she had correctly surmised to be so inclined to turn wrongly."

In the company of one or both Bowleses, Williams and Merlo spent three weeks touring the charming and the seedy corners of Tangier, Fez and Casablanca. With the new year they crossed to Marseilles, retrieved a car they had shipped ahead, and drove across the Riviera and down to Rome, arriving January 7 at the via Aurora apartment which they made their base until mid-April. Almost immediately, as if the prospect of another long holiday were more nerve-racking than refreshing, he set in motion a series of anxious letters to Audrey and Dakin regarding Rose. Before departing America, he had sent money to Edwina through Audrey, to help arrange the final details for Rose's transfer from Farmington to a private sanatorium — with luck, permanently; but at least, he hoped, for several days weekly.

Fortunately, an assistant in Audrey Wood's office named Elizabeth Schauffler was the daughter of a Missouri physician, and he corresponded with Dr. Hoctor at Farmington; the exchange clarifies the patient's status but not the plans for removal. Rose Williams, Dr. Hoctor replied to Dr. Schauffler, had been diagnosed as suffering from dementia praecox, had insulin and electroshock therapy regularly since her lobotomy, and although her condition had shown some improvement, the prognosis was considered poor. He added that she remained a sweet and gentle patient, grateful for the help she had received. The irony of the final remark did not escape Williams's notice. Not long after, he had Rose moved to a clinic in Connecticut, and soon thereafter to a more expensive, more attractive institution in Ossining, New York.

Instead of setting up a regular writing schedule in Rome, Williams inquired about the possibility of collaborating on a screenplay with Italian director Vittorio De Sica; this would, he hoped, provide an immediate and substantial cash income to support himself and Merlo through the term of their European stay, and to support Rose at home. But an Italian deal did not materialize.*

In addition, Williams hoped to be able to send money to several needy friends in America — Donald Windham among them, whose literary fortunes were uneven and for whom Williams still had an amiable concern. In fact, he had an unselfish attitude about money even when he was worried about his own income, and friends of Tennessee Williams knew that as long as he had anything at all to spare they could turn to him for several hundred dollars in time of emergency. This was such a time for several of them, and he responded quickly.

He might have suspected, of course, that very good times were imminent for himself: very soon, contracts were negotiated providing hand-

* In a letter to Audrey Wood dated March 1, 1949, Williams listed his four favorite films: Visconti's *La Terra Trema*, Eisenstein's *Alexander Nevsky*, and De Sica's *Shoeshine* and *The Bicycle Thief*. In 1952, Williams was asked to improve an English translation of Visconti's script for *Senso*, for the English-speaking players. On this he worked with Paul Bowles; only the original Italian version has ever been released, however.

some compensation to him for the screen rights to both *The Glass Menagerie* and *A Streetcar Named Desire*. From these and from the foreign royalties of his plays came Williams's fortune, the bulk of which was established before 1965. And from this fortune came Rose's permanent care and his assistance to indigent actors, friends in need of surgery and anonymous young writers who applied for his help through the Dramatists Guild. Not ignored were the needs and requests of Frank Merlo and, in later years, more demanding companions.*

But much of this was still to come in early 1949. In February, Frank went ahead to visit relatives in Sicily and to arrange details for Williams's arrival in late spring, and for their motor trip across the island. Williams wrote several poems (which later found a place in his collection *In the Winter of Cities*), but most of them were unsatisfying and he turned instead to the outline of his first novel.

The image-basis for the novel's opening was a poem, "The Interior of the Pocket," which he wrote one drizzly morning in London the previous summer and which he now revised. The novel was at last called *The Roman Spring of Mrs. Stone,* a lightly veiled autobiography in which a middle-aged American actress is at once frightened of and attracted to the faintly cruel machismo of Italian gigolos. She ends an affair with a particularly handsome and particularly exploitive one and turns to another, a stranger who has been following her, and who is invited into her apartment where "the nothingness would be interrupted, the awful vacancy would be entered by something."

At about this time, his old friend from Santa Monica, David Greggory, arrived on holiday in Rome, and Williams told him, "I'm writing a novel — but I don't know why!" On reflection, however, he might have guessed. It was not only to pass time creatively while waiting for Merlo either to return or to send for him; it was also because, as soon as Merlo had left for Sicily, Williams had resumed his affair with Salvatore, and an obsessive pursuit of casual sex — much of it furtive, some of it dangerous. *The Roman Spring of Mrs. Stone* was virtually a journal of this time, although Karen Stone's adventures at fifty were considerably less frantic than Tennessee Williams's that year, when he was thirty-eight.

But his attitude about this interlude was neither cavalier nor callous;

* Williams's continuing concern for the situation of his friend Donald Windham is revealed in a letter dated June 21, in which he asked Audrey to speak to producer Charles Feldman about Windham being engaged as the screenwriter for *The Glass Menagerie*. That this did not happen was not the result of any lack of effort on Williams's part, or Audrey's.

what is notable, however, is that he *thought* his attitude was cavalier and callous. In a letter to Donald Windham dated February 20, he praised Frank Merlo for his remarkable qualities, but admitted that he himself had not altered his own personal habits much, and had continued to pick up sailors even while his most regular companion during Merlo's absence was Salvatore. Mrs. Stone's Roman spring was not much happier than his; he felt that he, too, was just "drifting," the word repeated no less than twenty-three times in the novel's last four pages.

By early March, Frank returned, after recovering from an intestinal illness that kept him housebound in Sicily for several weeks. They accepted an offer to drive south with Truman Capote and his friend Jack Dunphy, and from the Excelsior Hotel in Naples the four planned a visit to the island of Ischia. A spa for the wealthy international set had set up headquarters in the section known as Forio. Ischia again pleased Williams, but he quickly became bored with the company. There were unpleasant scenes with Capote, which, Williams admitted in letters to Audrey Wood and Donald Windham, were largely the result of his own foul mood. At the end of the month he had not only succeeded in alienating his travel-mates, but had also (by writing several hours each night) counteracted the boredom by completing a number of scenes for three plays in progress. But this work was not going well, and his increasing depression was exacerbated by his suspicion, expressed in a letter to Windham dated March 23, that the relationship with Frank would probably end in grief and tears. Already Merlo had mentioned to Williams that he resented Williams's "dependence" on him. There had been more than one loud shouting match.

The emotional scenes with Merlo and with his friends, set in splendid spas and great cities, the confession of soap opera sentiments, the dramatized illnesses and the attacks of palpitations, the periodic fabrication of domestic vendettas more typical of nineteenth-century melodrama — all these characterized Tennessee Williams's life from the late 1940s. Some of this is easy enough to understand: the dramatist who draws directly from his personal history must first keep his responses sharp, his controls clear; and nothing ensures that so well as casting his companions in the roles of characters in a real-life pre-Broadway tryout.

In April a visit to London was necessitated by the imminent production there of *A Streetcar Named Desire;* Irene Selznick had arranged for meetings with Laurence Olivier (who would direct) and his wife Vivien

Leigh (who would star), and there was already discussion about the film version. Williams took to London theatre folk the way he had the previous year — which is to say that, in spite of Merlo's company, he was not at ease with politeness and what he thought was affectation. But he loved the Oliviers' home, a former abbey, and he appreciated the special attention Vivien gave Frank.

Even before a journey to Hollywood later that year, the unpleasant memories of his time at M-G-M were already having a strange reprisal. Returning to Rome, he received the first draft of a screenplay for *The Glass Menagerie* which Warner Brothers had submitted, requesting his comments. He was outraged at the gross transformations, and in a letter to Audrey on May 13 he complained that Amanda Wingfield had been robbed of all dignity, poetry and pathos; that she had become a cheap and brassy caricature. Worse, he found unconscionable the reversal of the play's conclusion, entirely shaped to accommodate Hollywood's insistence on a happy ending. How different had been his recent meeting with Vittorio De Sica, he wrote, who thought that *The Roman Spring of Mrs. Stone* deserved a faithful, bold transformation to the cinema, and that it might be the right vehicle to tempt Greta Garbo from retirement.

Very soon after, Irving Rapper, who was contracted to direct the film, arrived in Rome for meetings with Williams. "I found him terribly shy and withdrawn," Rapper recalled, "partly because I think he felt great pressure about the film and about the Hollywood considerations of casting and treatment — but also because it was his nature to withdraw socially. In our conversations I always had the feeling that he wasn't really listening, that he became lost in another world, a more interesting inner world somewhere. He was not anti-social or unpleasant — far from it, he was a sweet, patient gentleman. And in spite of his concern for what might happen to his *Glass Menagerie,* I think he really preferred to continue relaxing in Italy, swimming, socializing with his Italians. His personal happiness and contentment were, I think, more important to him than any consideration of Hollywood movie success."

By mid-June, a larger concern than the fate of the film had settled into Williams's life. He was nearing forty, and he was feeling the pangs of creative, social and sexual anxiety that he projected onto Karen Stone at fifty. His poems, he thought, were awkward and selfconscious (not a harsh judgment); his stories he considered unimaginative (a shallow assessment in many cases); and the early drafts of his new plays, he was sure, were hopelessly unfeeling (in this, he was dead wrong). While working on screenplay revisions with Rapper (which he alternated with improvements on a new comedy tentatively called *The Eclipse of May 29, 1919*), he resumed an indiscriminate use of pills; he wrote to Audrey asking to have a New York physician send, via air mail express, tranquilizer tablets, which were then unavailable in Rome. Within the week, a month's supply arrived; within two weeks, the pills were consumed, and Frank cabled New York for a refill. No one suspected that this might be the beginning of a dangerous habit.

On the first of September Williams and Merlo returned on the *Saturnia*. In New York, Audrey greeted them with the good news that Feldman and Warners were agreeing to her terms for a second contract; for a half-million dollars, they would have the rights to *A Streetcar Named Desire*. This somewhat sweetened the prospect of an imminent trip to Los Angeles, where, everyone felt, the final script for *The Glass Menagerie* would benefit from Williams's contributions. Williams was especially glad to hear that Elia Kazan would almost certainly direct the film of *Streetcar*.

"By the time he and Frankie got to the studio," according to Irving Rapper, "it seemed to us that he really didn't want to have much to do with the picture. He said he didn't want to come on the soundstage — 'You people have all the experience, you've been doing pictures for years,' he said. 'If you want me or need me for anything, I'll help out.' And then we didn't see much of him."

They did, however, begin to hear from him when the first photographed scenes were screened in October — not because he disapproved of Rapper's direction, but because the script was so much Hollywood and so little Williams, moving along a predictably romantic course to the upbeat finale. The studio executives sensed his displeasure — and they feared it, since they would need his cheerful presence to publicize the film on release. In a memorandum from Warner Brothers executive Jerry Wald to producer Charles Feldman, it was admitted that writer Peter Berneis was, at their demand, adding an ending about which Williams knew nothing (regardless of what he suspected). At the same time, Williams was complaining to Audrey about the movie's Tom being shown on a ship, with the story told in a romanticized flashback; he wondered if Gertrude Lawrence, woefully miscast as mother to Jane Wyman and Arthur Kennedy, would appear on skates.

The situation was not helped when Williams read letters from Joseph I.

Breen, vice-president and director of the production code administration of the Motion Picture Association of America, who tended to see mud where there was hardly dust. He was demanding an irrational sanitizing of the film: "The room in which Laura seeks refuge should not be labeled 'LADIES,' nor should there be any toilet fixtures evident in the set. We think it would be better to establish this as a lounge, rather than as a lavatory."

Bored and disgusted with Hollywood, Williams took Merlo and left for St. Louis, collected Reverend Dakin and his suitcases, and headed for Key West, where they spent the winter. On November 25, they took a six-month rental on a house at 1431 Duncan Street, a modest three-bedroom cottage. Now virtually blind, Reverend Dakin learned his way about the house easily, for there was no clutter of furnishings such as Edwina had accumulated on Arundel Place. Frank set the rooms in neat order, prepared the meals, drove playwright and parson out to dinner, over to acquaintances, down to the beach. "Tom is so good to me," the Reverend wrote to Audrey Wood. "I love him."

According to Paul Bigelow, "They stayed the winter not only because they liked Key West life. The most compelling reason was that his grandfather loved it there. It was his refuge from St. Louis, and Frank saw to it that he was treated with deference by one and all and that no comfort was lacking. There was a homey atmosphere in Key West. Tenn wrote each day at one end of the dining room table, Frank cooked and ran the house, the Reverend was a respectable addition to the household — it was all very much a family."

The following year, when Williams finally bought the Duncan Street property, it was really for the sake of his grandfather. Never inclined to assume the material responsibilities connected with ownership, he felt that with Frank's management it was a worthwhile purchase. In September 1950 he bought the house from Lee and Katherine Huyck Elmore of New York, and over the years there were added a patio and swimming pool surrounded by palm trees and privacy-insuring shrubbery, and a small studio and guest cottage at the opposite end of the property. Also added eventually was a small gazebo to the left front of the house — "The Jane Bowles Summer House," he called it — to which he later attached small brass plates with the names of friends. The memorial plaques bore the first names of Marion (Vaccaro), Maria (Britneva), Bette (Reitz, the passionate coed at Iowa), Hazel (Kramer), Andrew (Gunn, a former sentimental attachment from the Macon summer of

1942), Kip (Kiernan) and Little Horse (his affectionate nickname for Frank Merlo). By the time of his death the once modest cottage was part of a tract valued at nearly $100,000, which was ten times what he paid.

As Christmas approached, so did a period of depression. Frank planned to visit relatives in New Jersey, and this gave Williams the chance (as he wrote to Donald Windham) to dip into his little book of names for casual sex partners. (Once, as he wrote to Paul Bowles, some Key West sailors became frisky with cutlery and had to be turned out. The Reverend's reaction has not been documented.)

He was also, that season, writing to Audrey, asking for fresh supplies of Seconal (a brand of secobarbital) and Syntropan (a brand of phenobarbital) — both central nervous system depressants, which he was by now taking regularly to counteract tension and insomnia. But he also often took them with gin-spiked grape juice. The effect was a predictable lethargy he offset with strong coffee. And the depressants, in 1949 and 1950, were almost as freely available as coffee — and were not thought to be any more harmful.

He continued, nevertheless, to devote the morning hours to his writing, and although he was angry with the quality of his work, he had finished by Christmas a first revised draft of *The Eclipse of May 29, 1919,* which he had for a short time called *Stornella* and then, after considering more possibilities, *The Rose Tattoo.** Audrey knew he would be cheered by the end-of-the-year report on the Broadway version of *A Streetcar Named Desire* (which had closed on December 17, 1949, after two years and 855 performances): it had won both the Pulitzer Prize and Drama Critics Circle award; it was doing brisk business on tour across America; and there were foreign companies presenting the play in London, Paris, Rome, Brussels, Stockholm, Zurich, Mexico City and Buenos Aires. *The Glass Menagerie* was before the cameras in Hollywood, the contract for Kazan to direct the film of *Streetcar* was signed — in short, Tennessee Williams was the richest and most famous playwright in America, and he was not yet forty years old.

But still he was not happy. Before Christmas he wrote to Donald Windham that ordinarily his life was fifty percent work and worry about

---

* Among other temporary titles: *The Vigil Light, Novena to a Rose, A Candle to a Rose, A Rose for Our Lady, The Grace of Our Lady, A Rose from the Hand of Our Lady, Perpetual Novena to a Rose.* There was not so much a religious obsession gripping him that season as there was a cultural interest in Sicily and a growing concern for Rose.

it, thirty-five percent a struggle against madness, and fifteen percent devoted to friends and lovers. But that season he felt eighty-nine percent of his energy went to worry about his work, ten percent to the fight against madness, and a scant one percent to love.

The New Year 1950 arrived without celebration, and after bringing in a companion for his grandfather, Williams went north to see Carson McCullers's play *The Member of the Wedding* and William Inge's *Come Back, Little Sheba,* of which he had been a champion for some time. Everyone was calling Inge a protégé of Williams, who had furthered with Margo Jones the cause of Inge's first play and who had recommended him to Audrey Wood. Williams accepted the designation, for he was indeed personally proud of Inge's rising star — but only for the present.

He and Frank returned to Key West, resuming a more settled household routine without (as Williams complained to Donald Windham) the variety of sexual contacts he had enjoyed in Frank's absence. In this regard, one of the few matters over which Williams and Merlo continued to argue was that of exclusivity: Merlo was willing to offer a companionship that was stable, committed and sexually monandrous — without other partners — and he hoped for the same in return; Williams thought that was a quaint Old World convention, but not realistic, and even dreary as a serious goal.

In February, *Flair* magazine published one of Williams's most autobiographical stories, "The Resemblance Between a Violin Case and a Coffin," which lightly fictionalizes the stages of Rose's illness. She is not named (although the brother-narrator is, as Tom), "Grand" and the Reverend are represented, as are the nursemaid Ozzie and a traveling father. There is an elegiac wistfulness (but not a sententious sweetness) to the story. It interweaves the author's inchoate homosexuality without disturbing the balance between a Chekhovian gentleness and a socially dreadful "secret" worthy of Ibsen. "The Resemblance Between a Violin Case and a Coffin" — with "Portrait of a Girl in Glass" and "Completed" — forms a trilogy-tribute to Rose Isabel Williams.*

A number of other stories are also based on direct personal history: "Grand"; "Two on a Party" (a celebration of wild weeks on the road, sharing liquor and men with Marion Black Vaccaro); "The Important

---

* Two late, unproduced screenplays — *The Loss of a Teardrop Diamond* and *Stopped Rocking* — were inspired, respectively, by Rose's awkward social life in her youth, and her confinement in institutions. But the characters are less closely modeled on Rose herself than those in the above trilogy.

Thing" and "The Field of Blue Children" (memories of school times and delicate friendships); and "The Angel in the Alcove" (an account of New Orleans life in 1939). But others of his stories are more overtly grotesque, more blunt in their narratives about sex, the emotional (or literal) cannibals or the erotically (sometimes pathologically) repressed personality. In this last category must be included "One Arm," "Chronicle of a Demise," "Desire and the Black Masseur," "Hard Candy" and "The Mysteries of the Joy Rio." The last two are variations on the theme of furtive sex in a movie theatre.

Most often, however, Williams used the form of short fiction as a sketchboard for his longer plays: "The Night of the Iguana" prepares for the play of the same title; "The Yellow Bird" for *Summer and Smoke;* "Three Players of a Summer Game" for *Cat on a Hot Tin Roof;* "Man Bring This Up Road" for *The Milk Train Doesn't Stop Here Anymore;* "Kingdom of Earth" for its later namesake. The best of his efforts in the short story reflect not merely an intensity of poetic diction, but also the intuition that human struggle is mysterious but surely not absurd nor without final significance.

This awareness is found especially in the extraordinary story "Three Players of a Summer Game." Unique among Williams's efforts at fiction, it comes very close to being mystical, and it joins the carefully interlocked style of Henry James with an almost religious sensibility. Compassionate but calm in its wonder about the mystery of spiritual anguish and emotional impotence, it suggests that there was a latent capacity for almost philosophical reverie that in Tennessee Williams did not flourish.

"The Resemblance Between a Violin Case and a Coffin," however, elicited a surprised and surprising response: Cornelius Williams wrote to Audrey Wood, objecting to the story's "very detrimental remarks about me."

"It was a very poor story," he continued, "and most of it is untrue. . . . I started to bring suit against these people [the publisher] including Tom. . . . I don't know his address — if he ever refers to me in any of his writing I will make him regret it as long as he lives. During the depression the last two years he was at the University of Missouri in Columbia I borrowed $1000 each year so he could go back. As far as I know I have never done him an unkind act and to me he has proven himself the most detestable of all persons — a liar and an ingrate. I want nothing further to do with him. I would appreciate your conveying this message to him, and he will also find there has been no insane people [sic] in the Williams family, but more than one on the immediate Dakin side."

There is no record of a reply from Audrey or her client. Cornelius's rage may in the final analysis not have been evoked by any particularly unflattering portrait of himself; the worst allusion to him in the story is that "my father . . . was a devilish man, possibly not understood but certainly hard to live with." The deeper anger may, on the other hand, have been because of his son's outspoken admission, in the story, of homosexual preference: Tennessee calls himself a "monster of sensuality" and a "devout little mystic of carnality" as he describes with great detail and appreciation the chest and arms of another schoolboy. This, for the likes of Cornelius Coffin Williams, must have been more dreadful than any detached observations about the Williams side of the family, in whose tradition of rowdiness his father always gloried.

Not two weeks after he had received word of this letter, Williams must have been amused by the ironic contrast of another letter from his family. Dakin wrote with the announcement that they were all descended — also on father's side! — from St. Francis Xavier. For the sake of his brother, Tennessee replied that he was simply delighted with the Xavier-Sevier connection. He may not have known that it was distant and doubtful; but the accumulating ironies of his family and their supposed traditions must have touched him as wonderfully funny.

There was other family correspondence gracing the Williams–Dakin postboxes that season. The Reverend dictated a letter (written by Frank) to his daughter, saying he had never been happier in his life, that the social whirl of Key West — he gave as an example dinner at Martha Hemingway's — he found delightful, and that Tom and Frank were the best companions.

"Apart from Rose," David Greggory said, "the Reverend was the only one Tennessee mentioned regularly. He was totally devoted to his grandfather, who was a man who offered him love and asked nothing in return, was not critical of him and really knew what Tennessee was all about. He wasn't just a nice grandfather being nice to some image of a nice grandson. He really understood Tenn, and his work. He was such a liberal spirit, and it was rather strange to all of us that his daughter should be so different."*

---

* "All his plays have a poetic foundation," Reverend Dakin said of his grandson to an interviewer that year, "and he is more interested in developing his characters than he is in the stories" (cf. the *Nashville Banner,* July 19, 1950).

At the beginning of May, Williams and Merlo deposited Grandfather at the Hotel Gayoso, Memphis, after assuring that he would be cared for by a companion and the amiable staff he had come to know on a regular basis over twenty years in that city. They then proceeded to New York, where they took a suite at the Sherry-Netherland and went to several receptions, private parties and news conferences announcing that Cheryl Crawford would produce *The Rose Tattoo*. They also went to the City Center where, two months after the final tour performance of *Streetcar*, the play reopened for a limited run with Uta Hagen and Anthony Quinn. At the end of the month, they boarded the *Ile de France*. Jane Smith traveled with them, for she was en route to furthering her career as an opera singer in Europe. She recalled hilarious nights aboard ship, with Tennessee and Frank as her two dancing and singing partners.

By early June Williams and Merlo were dining in Paris with Anna Magnani (on whom and for whom Williams based the image and the role of Serafina delle Rose, the leading character of *The Rose Tattoo*) and with Carson McCullers (who had taken a house in the French countryside). The formidable Magnani they at once adored, and she relished the adoration and returned it with a raucous affection that was both sisterly and maternal. As for accepting a Broadway role, she promised to discuss it further with them in Rome later that month: she liked the play, but was frightened at the prospect of English. McCullers — by this time significantly called his "Sister-Woman" by Williams — was not nearly so much fun to be with, for she was becoming more frail and ornery with the years and, although only thirty-three, looked much older after her first debilitating strokes.

By the second week in June, the two men had made the first of two summer excursions to Sicily. From the balcony of their room at the Belvedere Hotel, Taormina, they overlooked the Ionian Sea and the tourists and natives on the streets below the nearby plaza. Williams wanted authentic Sicilian dialect in *The Rose Tattoo*, but in true Chekhovian fashion he learned more than he used. Frank prudently convinced him that excessive foreign language in a play would only annoy the audience.

But the scenery, people and heritage — a colorful mixture of Greek, Norman, north African, French and southern Italian traditions — found a permanence in Williams's affection. He loved not only the elegance of Taormina, but the crowded, poorer streets of Catania and Palermo, too; not only the climate and palm trees and general "Southernness" of towns like Giardini di Naxos (which he found very like the rural villages along the Gulf of Mexico), but also the wildness of the hill country, the grandeur of Mount Etna, with its almost perpetual thread of white volcanic smoke, and the mysterious, ancient atmosphere of Cefalù, with its blend of Greek, Byzantine and Norman influences. Never had he felt so embraced by a land and its people; he would have preferred a Sicilian relative to a Sevier, a Williams or even a somewhat intimidating sixteenth-century Spanish missionary-saint.

On June 26 they moved to an apartment on via Firenze, Rome, after planning for a return to Sicily later that summer. That same day, he wrote to Cheryl Crawford that he felt restless, incomplete, dissatisfied even after the delights of Sicily, and he could not understand those feelings. Nevertheless, he added, he was working well on the revisions of *The Rose Tattoo,* tightening its classical allusions and unities and giving it more compactness. His producer had no doubt, after reading a second draft, that the play would fulfill its promise of being a serious comedy.

"I had been really rather upset about not having *Streetcar* submitted to me several years earlier," Cheryl Crawford said years later. "So I was delighted to have *The Rose Tattoo,* even though I learned that in fact Irene Selznick had a first look at it and turned it down. I never thought badly about Audrey for this, since she was, as always, thinking first of Tennessee, and she felt Irene should have it for first consideration."

The Rose Tattoo would be but the first of a quartet of plays by Tennessee Williams to be produced by Cheryl Crawford. From her earliest experience with the Theatre Guild in the 1920s, she became one of the founders of the Group Theatre, where she directed a number of plays in the next decade. Since 1938 she had also built a reputation as one of the theatre's most respected producers: by the time Audrey negotiated with her on *The Rose Tattoo,* she had produced *One Touch of Venus* (with Mary Martin in the leading role), *The Tempest* (starring Vera Zorina), two revivals of *Porgy and Bess,* and with Eva LeGallienne and Margaret Webster she had founded the American Repertory Theatre. She was also, with Elia Kazan and Robert Lewis, a founding director of the Actors Studio.

By the middle of July, advance copies of *The Roman Spring of Mrs. Stone* were available, and the intolerable heat of Rome was matched by the angry fire of critical and collegial resentment over his first novel. To escape the Italian capital and a platoon of inquiring journalists and photographers, Williams departed for Vienna. Defending himself against his critics, he wrote to Cheryl Crawford that his goal in chronicling the decline of Karen Stone was to arouse compassion for a sensitive nature, and how the awful obsession with power and fame change a once fine person into a caricature. If once you examine any honest nature, he concluded, only the distortions necessary to survive a mad world — or dullness incarnate — will be revealed.

But intentions do not structure a novel, nor do they invest its characters with credibility. *The Roman Spring of Mrs. Stone* is a book full of its author's emotional and spiritual fears, and it represents the battle being waged, in 1948 and 1949, in the corners of Tennessee Williams's soul.

The story could not have been simpler: following the death of her husband, the American actress Karen Stone settles in Rome, where after some hesitation she yields to the blandishments of an adoring but abusive gigolo. When her affair with him ends, she seems on the verge of an endless cycle of similar liaisons.

Williams knew that an irreversible decline into decadence was possible to him; he could identify with the insecurities of a celebrity who questions the reality of her talent and the rapid advance of time. The prevalent motif of the novel (which has a tripartite dramatic form) is artistic and sexual prostitution, and it is an amalgam of prostitutions that spells the final doom of the hard-hearted Mrs. Stone: "She looked at sick people with the hard eyes of a bird and her sympathetic tones [with the sick] were produced from her throat. . . . Everything that she did to court the favor of her professional associates, to create the legend of Mr. Stone [her late husband] as a paragon of loyalty and goodness, was directed by the head as distinguished from the heart. The result was that a great many people said *Mrs. Stone is a wonderful woman* in almost the same perfunctory tone with which she inquired of her secretary, 'Who died today, or Whose birthday is it?' "

Karen Stone's Italy is, for Williams, his own Italy: "I have fallen back on a great deal. . . . This country, these people," she says; and he had known what it was to be, like her, "crazily infatuated with a pretty young boy, in fact with a succession of pretty young boys of the pimp or gigolo class. . . ." At the inevitably sad conclusion, Karen Stone yields to what Williams knew all too well: she throws her keys down from her balcony — like a grotesque Juliet or a decadent Rapunzel — so that a stranger may come to stop the drift of meaninglessness with a diversion of the flesh. For his friend Donald Windham, *The Roman Spring of Mrs. Stone* was Tennessee Williams's "first fictionalized self-portrait after his success — and it displays a hair-raising degree of self-knowledge."

*   *   *

The highlight of the summer, however, was the second meeting with Magnani, among the crowd at Doney's own via Veneto. There she said finally that she was committed to stage plays through 1951; but the real reason was her fear of English. She did agree, however, to appear in a later film verson, since the English dialogue could be rehearsed and recorded in small pieces.

"Magnani first said she would only sign on for a four-month run because of Italian commitments," according to Cheryl Crawford. "This, in addition to her nervousness about English, made it impossible for us to put her in the role of Serafina."

This news led to the advancement of two other major careers, continuing a hallmark of the Williams plays, which seemed to rejuvenate a major talent (Laurette Taylor) or to deepen a talent already established but not yet fully realized (Julie Haydon, Jessica Tandy, Marlon Brando). In the fall of 1950, those favored were the young actors Maureen Stapleton and Eli Wallach.

"Tenn had written it for Magnani," Stapleton recalled, "but when she couldn't do it, I was asked to read. Up to that time, Eli and I hadn't done so much in the theatre, so everyone was a little cautious about us — which is I guess why there were so many readings before casting was settled."

The season had other events for Williams besides agreeing on a cast and on the director, Daniel Mann (who that year had with such distinction directed *Come Back, Little Sheba*). Williams gave a party for the English poet Edith Sitwell, who was on a lecture tour in America, and he came to the Museum of Modern Art on November 16 with Carson McCullers and poet Marianne Moore for a bizarre presentation of *Macbeth,* with Sitwell improbably reading Lady Macbeth and the novelist and poet Glenway Wescott in the title role. Williams and Sitwell had met before in New York, at a famous photography session at Frances Steloff's Gotham Book Mart on West 47th Street. In the fall of 1948, Steloff had arranged for a *Life* magazine photographer to attend a reception at her shop for Edith and her brother Osbert Sitwell. In attendance were Williams, Stephen Spender, William Rose Benét, W. H. Auden, Horace Gregory, Richard Eberhart, Gore Vidal, José Garcia Villa, Elizabeth Bishop, Marianne Moore, Randall Jarrell, Delmore Schwartz and Charles Henri Ford. It was, as Sitwell biographer John Pearson wrote, "something of a classic exercise in elegantly engineered publicity.... The resulting photograph has something of Aquinas's Vision of the Heavenly

Host, with poetry's angels and archangels grouped around their virgin queen [Edith]."

There were other New York parties that autumn, and they helped to distract him from some especially unpleasant news. Bill Cannastra, the brilliant but disturbed Harvard student Williams had been attracted to several years earlier, had come to New York to pursue both his career as lawyer and his strange sexual habits. In a grotesque accident, he leaned through the open window of a moving subway car, apparently to follow the glance of a smiling stranger. A steel pillar neatly decapitated him.

By November, Williams and Frank had gone to Memphis to meet Grandfather, and the trio arrived in Key West for Thanksgiving. It was not a happy day, since Reverend Dakin was atypically withdrawn and depressed — he had submitted to radiation treatment for minor skin cancers, and although there was no doubt of his complete cure, he was a proud man and his blindness did not help him believe that he looked quite fine.

On Christmas Day, the company of *The Rose Tattoo* left New York for a Chicago premiere four days later. Williams did not intend to go to Chicago (his brother cheerfully represented the family at the first night at the Erlanger Theatre). He did, however, send several pages of script revisions. "We were performing every night and working on new business all day, every day," Maureen Stapleton recalled. "Everyone was weary, but the play had so much life, and put so much life into us, that we were revived by it every night."

There were, however, structural problems with *The Rose Tattoo;* the local critics (the faithful Claudia Cassidy among them) were quietly warning the producer and director, while the roving reviewer for *Variety* openly reported trouble in Chicago. Williams was finally summoned, and for several nights the ending of *The Rose Tattoo* was played with variations of the script at each performance.

But this is precisely the purpose of an out-of-town preview, after all: to see how a play plays, to hear how an audience reacts, to see what knots in dialogue or staging need to be untied. By the time they were ready to open in New York, according to Donald Windham, "Tennessee was counting the laughs in each scene and, when there were not enough to make him feel 'box-office secure,' [he suggested] the insertion of gags." Windham and his friend Sandy Campbell recalled sadly that, beginning about this time, "encounters with [Williams], although unlikely to be dull, were unlikely to be pleasant." He was not, it seems, coping well with what he had called "the catastrophe of success," and the single-minded devotion of Frank Merlo did not satisfy him.

"Frankie gave his entire life — without any reservation, without hesitation, and God knows without very much compensation — to the life of Tennessee," according to their friend Johnny Nicholson. When *The Rose Tattoo* opened in New York at the Martin Beck Theatre on February 3, 1950, Nicholson was in the audience; he was the proprietor of a popular café directly across from the East 58th Street apartment and had befriended his new neighbors from the start. In time, he found them another New York residence, and his good-humored support became particularly precious to Frank in later years.

From the time of the Chicago run of this play to his death, Frank Merlo had no closer friend than Maureen Stapleton; and as in the case of Johnny Nicholson, Williams did not always appreciate the kind of loyalty Frank elicited from others when he, sometimes, could not. "Frank Merlo was a man everyone adored," according to Stapleton. "It's really as simple as that — everyone loved him. I became a friend to Tenn by being a friend of Frankie. He was the liaison officer between Tenn and the rest of the world. He was at home with everyone, easy to be with, uncomplicated and understanding. And he loved and protected Tenn and did everything for him."

Although there were serious reservations about *The Rose Tattoo*, it was an instant commercial success. Some critics objected to the heavy-handed, profuse symbolism of the rose and the simplistic psychology of a Sicilian-American widow, irrationally (and unjustifiably) devoted to the idealized image of her late husband, but quickly restored to vitality (after a long period of mourning) by a slightly dim but sexy truck driver.

The Rose Tattoo is strong on charm and humor, but weak in understanding adult fears and emotions. Taking seriously the charge that he could portray only tragic scenes in the lives of repressed Southern belles, Williams gave his critics comedy. But since he was a searching poet at the same time, and not really intimate with the inner life of an immigrant woman, the comedy was instead smothered beneath a blanket of ubiquitous rose imagery, and the seriousness of a bereaved woman's predicament is diminished by the play's insistence that sexual response is the answer to life's problems.

In his correlative symbol of the rose, there are rather academic allusions to the mystic rose of religious literature, to the rose window of the medieval cathedral, to the cycle of death and rebirth: "*The Rose Tattoo* is the Dionysian element in human life," Williams wrote at the time, "the lyric as well as the Bacchantic impulse . . . the transcendence of life over the instruments it uses . . . a celebration of the inebriate god."

As it happened, *The Rose Tattoo* fared well with critics and audiences, and in a season that also featured *South Pacific, Darkness at Noon, Guys and Dolls, The Country Girl, Call Me Madam* and *Bell, Book and Candle,* the relatively uninhibited and joyous paean to the erotic in life was apparently another indication that Williams was the playwright attempting bolder themes. *The Rose Tattoo* was awarded the "Tony" for best play, Maureen Stapleton and Eli Wallach were honored for their performances, and Boris Aronson received the prize for stage design.

To the opening night came Edwina, who was embarrassed by the play's explicit talk of sex and lovemaking. Her father, also present, was blind but not deaf, and he thoroughly enjoyed it. "He was," Cheryl Crawford recalled, "quite an old eccentric — a little on the fey side, in fact." He also charmed everyone who met him, and some — like Maureen Stapleton — appreciated another element in the Reverend's personality:

"He was a crotchety old man, but Tennessee adored him. The old man was really a father to him, but what a demanding one! Tennessee took him wherever he could, and he was with us all the time in New York. He loved a good evening out, this old man in his nineties. And he didn't have one bit of trouble with the relationship between Tenn and Frankie, which is saying something, for he was an old-fashioned minister, or so his daughter described him."

As the critics continued a public debate over the merits of the play, however, they could not have known precisely how personal a work it was — and how the life-context of Tennessee Williams endowed it with both liabilities and assets. For it is really not so much the valentine to the world — nor even to "the inebriate god" of the senses that he insisted — it is rather a valentine to two loves, and that is why the rose imagery cannot overwhelm its aroma of death nor make wholly credible the swift and facile happy ending, in which Serafina is freed from her repressions and illusions by yielding to a new man in her life who has acquired a rose tattoo on his chest in imitation of her dead husband. The two loves for Williams in 1950 and 1951 were the spiritual and physical models for the play, and they were, of course, his sister Rose and his lover Frank. And there was a deep sadness in his life about both of them.

By 1951, Williams had arranged for his sister's permanent transfer to a special hospital-residence, Stony Lodge in Ossining, New York, and he was visiting her there often, usually in the company of friends like Johnny Nicholson or Cheryl Crawford.

"I made several trips with Tennessee to visit his sister," Cheryl Crawford remembered. "I always felt he had an enormous guilt about Rose — that he'd done nothing to stop the lobotomy years earlier, and that he felt responsible for the emptiness of her life. There was no question about his concern for her, and of his devotion to her. It was very touching to see them together." Johnny Nicholson remembered that the meetings were not gloomy or sad; Tennessee's sense of humor did not fail him, and alongside any guilt there coexisted an appreciation of her distance from life, and the good humor that distance gave his sister. "He found her special brand of logic very amusing," Nicholson said, "and he catered to her whims when she wanted to shop for an entire case of soap or a dozen bottles of perfume."

His sister in fact haunted his consciousness more than ever at this time, and the play reflects this — not only in its profusion of roses and rose names and rose allusions, but in its plain references to his sister. "Rosa had a very strict mother and wasn't allowed to go on dates with boys," says the sailor Jack Hunter of Serafina's daughter in *The Rose Tattoo,* summarizing the early adolescence of the playwright's sister; and Rosa makes her first appearance (in the play's first minute) as a girl of twelve with a jar of lightning bugs she has captured — a summer evening pastime of Rose and Tom that he had long ago mentioned in a poem whose title was inspired by Ozzie. That poem, "The Couple," fuses all loves into the love of a brother for his sister, whose captured fireflies taught them both death.

But the play really confuses the allusions to the virginal mother of Jesus with those to his own virginal sister. And finally all the jumbled rose imagery is patently sexual — as a universal symbol of sexual ecstasy, or at least sexual capacity. This connection is nowhere clearer than in another Williams poem, also called "A Liturgy of Roses" (which had been the working title of *The Rose Tattoo* for some months), which concludes with a deliberately blasphemous transformation of the Christian doxology, or hymn of praise, into an idolatrous celebration of male and female genitals. The "inebriate god," Dionysus, was never far from his soul.

The further connection he made between his writing of *The Rose Tattoo* and his sister was revealed by his more frequent visits, at this same time, to Carson McCullers, who from their first meeting in 1946 (and his giving of Rose's ring) became a kind of surrogate sister to whom he could offer a creative compassion.

"I spent several occasions with Carson and Tennessee," Cheryl Crawford recalled. "This was a unique friendship, and I think her special qualities of craziness appealed to him. It isn't going too far to say that he really liked and appreciated and understood and was amused by a crew of eccentrics throughout his life!"

Carson's instability was analogous to his sister's, and to his own; Carson's uncertain, constantly shifting sexuality and her self-absorbed, zany retreat into the refuge of alcohol both amused and frightened him. In the imprecise, variegated folds of *The Rose Tattoo,* he expressed his love for his sister, for Carson and for the unfettered freedom all three of them sought. On at least two occasions that winter, Williams brought Rose across the river from Ossining to Carson's home in Nyack. The meeting between the sister and the "Sister-Woman" could not have been more touching and funny. "Kiss me, Miss Rose!" cried Carson, her arms thrown open. "No, thank you," Rose replied politely, "I have halitosis." And when liquor was served before, during and after lunch, Rose — perhaps glimpsing a deep reservoir of St. Louis life-images — stood in a corner, "praying," as Johnny Nicholson remembered, "for drinking sinners."

But *The Rose Tattoo* was also a celebration of Frank Merlo. Thus far, since 1948, Frank Merlo seemed to be his salvation. And it was Merlo's unselfconscious love, his unfettered generosity, his deep attachment and his Sicilian lust for life that Williams so admired, tried to emulate, and celebrated in this play. (*The Rose Tattoo* bears the dedication "To Frank in Return for Sicily.")*

Tennessee Williams saw himself as the emotionally cloistered Serafina delle Rose, caring for a young girl named Rosa, transformed by the passion of a truck driver. Just before he met Williams, Frank Merlo had also been driving a truck (in New Jersey). From the first months of their first trip to Europe, Williams had called Frank — because of his passionate energy and his handsome, equine features — his "Little Horse." And it was in their beloved Sicily that Frank suggested to Williams the inevita-

---

* Frank, in return for himself and Sicily, received not only the dedication of the play that chronicled the psychological renewal of its author. He also received (in addition to a weekly salary of one hundred dollars) ten percent of all the profits from *The Rose Tattoo* and from the two plays that followed.

ble name for the Sicilian reviver of life in the play: the truck driver must of course be known as Alvaro Mangiacavallo, Alvaro Eat-a-Horse.

At the beginning of March, Williams took Frank, the Reverend, Edwina and Dakin to Key West. All of them promptly fell ill with a winter influenza. Frank nursed them all, but Tennessee decided that his mother and brother must return to St. Louis as soon as possible. The day after, he celebrated their departure by getting very drunk and taking his car on the main street of Key West. He had forgotten his license in New York, however, and was at once arrested for drunk driving.

At the end of the month, as if to impose some social order and responsibility on his life, he brought his sister and a nurse to Duncan Street for several weeks. Once again, Frank responded to the needs of the guests. And it was shortly after this that Williams knew a cook-housekeeper was needed. Almost daily when they were in Key West, and for the next thirty years, meals were prepared by Leoncia McGee, a calm, unshockable and devoted housekeeper. In one way, of course, Frank was pleased; but on the other hand he saw this as a first indication that perhaps in some concrete, practical matters he was a dispensable presence — that money would purchase for Tennessee any of the services Frank loved to provide.

In early May Williams was ready to depart again for an extended trip to Europe. By now, Merlo expected but was not entirely accustomed to the impermanence of their life; he would have been content to remain in the relative quiet of Key West. "He loved the stable home-life that they could have in Key West, with the house and the cook and Grandfather to care for," according to Johnny Nicholson. "And everyone in Key West was crazy about Frank and missed him. He was often referred to as 'The Mayor of Key West,' and this didn't always please Tennessee. He sometimes resented Frank's great popularity because he didn't have it."

They stopped briefly in New York, where Williams talked with Maureen Stapleton about a matter to which he had written her in March: he was then hard at work on revising *Battle of Angels,* a play for which he still had great affection. He was unsure of a new title but he thought (logically, after her triumph in *The Rose Tattoo*) that she might play Myra, the lusty wife of a dying man, or even Vee, the repressed, fanatical artist. That same week, he completed a poem that bore the eventual title of the revised play — "Orpheus Descending," a plangent lyric in which he yearned for a perfect art and a perfect mate, things "marked by their nature to be not completed / but only longed for and sought for a while and abandoned."

Before the end of May, Tennessee and Frank were at the Cavendish Hotel, London — the place from which, Williams wrote to Stapleton, Oscar Wilde was arrested. As usual, he complained about his failing health, perhaps because the news they received from America was for several weeks a series of medical bulletins: Audrey had an emergency appendectomy (soon to be followed by more serious surgery from which she needed a longer recovery period); Oliver Evans had an operation on his ear; and Paul Bigelow required surgery to correct a chronic jaw ailment. Both these latter two old friends were helped by checks from the sympathetic Williams, who responded to their need at once.

In mid-June they were in Rome, at 45 via Aurora. His bohemianism, Williams wrote to Brooks Atkinson, once again took a strong hold on his life; he still felt as if he were trying to escape the shackles of an intensely puritanical background.*

The correspondence between Williams and Atkinson that began in 1951 is a curious one. The two men were never very close friends, nor did they meet in person very often or share confidences. But when he sat at his typewriter and sent letters to this admiring critic, Williams became someone like a character in one of his own plays. His descriptions of his life are colored by all the melodramatic exaggerations he perhaps thought Atkinson would appreciate. As time passed, however, his letters have the unmistakable flavor of publicity. In a sense, Tennessee Williams wanted to be considered as controversial as his work, and perhaps even more enduring.

In early July, Williams visited Saint Tropez — while Frank traveled alone to Venice. When he eventually joined Frank in Venice, he completed the first draft of the short story "Three Players of a Summer Game" — about a once-powerful athlete-as-artist named Brick Pollitt, who has become an alcoholic. He has an affair with the widow of his doctor and at the end is abandoned by her and is dependent on the care of his wife, who drives him around in their car "exactly the way that some ancient conqueror ... might have led in chains through a capital

---

* Often, in interviews, essays, and letters to those with whom he was not on very personal terms, Williams dramatized his "puritanical background" — perhaps as a means of fashionable justification for his promiscuity: "What I do I'm not responsible for, it's all the result of my childhood repressions," etc.

city the prince of a state newly conquered." He did not finish the story for ten months; over the next two years it changed form and he added characters, and it became *Cat on a Hot Tin Roof.*

Williams could write that summer about the debilitating effects of alcohol on a middle-aged artist because so much of his own time was spent under its influence. On July 22, he was speeding north from Rome, drunk, when he lost control of the Jaguar. Had he never believed in miracles before, his mind might have been changed: the car was completely destroyed, but he walked away with a slight cut on his forehead.

Not for the first or last time, Frank came to the rescue. He drove them in a rented car to Göteborg, for the Swedish premiere of *The Rose Tattoo.* By the end of August, disagreeing over friends and travel plans, Tennessee and Frank agreed to separate — the latter went back to Rome and the former went on to London. Soon after, he was invited to luncheon at the Garrick Club by his publisher, James Laughlin, who was visiting T. S. Eliot. The American expatriate poet, playwright and essayist had won the Nobel Prize for literature in 1948 (an honor that somehow always eluded Williams, and whose omission in his life he greatly resented). The meeting between Eliot and Williams was very cordial, and not nearly as difficult as one with Carson McCullers, who was in London at the same time, more ill, more psychoneurotic and more demanding than ever. On August 29, Williams wrote to Frank that she was drinking heavily, apparently out of unrequited love for the sister of her British publisher.

By September 8 he was at the Hotel d'Angleterre, Copenhagen, for another premier of *Tattoo;* the trip, he wrote to Cheryl Crawford, was part of a sustained effort to avoid confronting himself, his responsibilities, his work and his relationship with Frank. He hoped to return to London for a November opening of *Summer and Smoke.**

The rest of the autumn was a fevered series of steamer bookings, short flights, long hours on trains, parties with strangers and virtually no productive work. He was by now smoking more than two packages of cigarettes daily, and, because of constant travel, he was not exercising regularly. After additional brief visits to London, Stockholm, Paris, Barcelona, Amsterdam and Rome — never for very long, and never with much interest in the art or tourist attractions — he and Frank returned to

---

* He had prepared, he said later, a major revision of that play, but he arrived when the original was already in rehearsal. More than twenty years later, the second version was finally produced — as *The Eccentricities of a Nightingale;* the critics and public received it even less warmly than the original Broadway version of *Summer and Smoke. Cf.* note below, on p. 317.

New York aboard the *Queen Elizabeth,* on November 7. They took Reverend Dakin to Key West for Thanksgiving, and at Christmas were in New Orleans.

"When I saw him in New Orleans that year," David Greggory recalled, "he was really depressed. He was drinking much more, and more heavily. I think he felt terrific pressure after his first few successes. His periods of depression didn't last long, but they were formidable when they did occur."

Somehow, work was resumed in New Orleans, and in spite of his increasing use of alcohol and various pills for sedation and alertness, a revised draft of the lengthened *Camino Real* was ready by the end of January. More than ever a wild, hallucinatory fantasy, combining characters from history and fiction as well as incidents from his own experiences in Mexico, Rome and New Orleans, the play had been structured as if it were modeled on Thornton Wilder's *Skin of Our Teeth:* the narrative stretched time and place arbitrarily; the emotional truth of the play was the truth of dream and fantasy, of memory and longing and hope — the truth of poetry, not the truth of verisimilitude.

From the start Williams hoped that Elia Kazan would direct *Camino Real;* this hope, in fact, seems to have influenced the construction of the play, for it was with *The Skin of Our Teeth* that Kazan's directorial career had been firmly established. (*Camino Real* was dedicated to Kazan.) His play, he wrote to Cheryl on February 10, was an extended poem on the romantic attitude to life, and everything that he had drawn from *Camille* and from the memoirs of Casanova had been reshaped according to that poetic ideal. She replied that of course she was interested in it, and before the summer Audrey had negotiated for both Kazan and Crawford to undertake this very delicate play.

At the same time another play was being prepared, and no one could have anticipated the results.

In 1951, a repertory company called the Circle in the Square (so named for its circular playing space in Greenwich Village's Sheridan Square) had staged a production of Lorca's *Yerma.* A young actress named Geraldine Page, who had acted in Chicago and New York and had worked at various odd jobs round the country, had impressed Theodore Mann, the Circle's producing cofounder, and José Quintero, who had directed her in *Yerma* in the role of the pagan crone.

"We were looking for a play that would be just right for her," Mann remembered, "and that would be within our limited range of financial and material resources. We hadn't had a real success in our first year. But then one day José came rushing in, shouting, 'I found it! I found it!' and he showed us *Summer and Smoke*. It had of course been a failure in 1948, and the rights were readily available. So we set to work. We required a fierce ardor from everyone in the company. They worked on props, costumes; they took out the garbage, stoked the furnace, worked at the box office — and for not very much money. But as soon as we were into rehearsals on *Summer and Smoke,* there was excitement among us."

Geraldine Page added that the play was their final choice by a process of elimination. "When we finished *Yerma,* everyone wanted to do a dramatization of Sherwood Anderson's *Winesburg, Ohio,* but we had to get the rights directly from Mrs. Anderson. She was doing a lot of traveling that year, and it was hard to locate her. Then there was talk of a revival of Lillian Hellman's *The Children's Hour,* but she said there was a Broadway version scheduled. And so at last the decision was made to do *Summer and Smoke.*"

Rehearsals proceeded in Sheridan Square. Meantime, Williams was unaware of the extraordinary historic night that was about to occur — not only for the cast and for him, but for what would be known as off-Broadway theatre.

In Key West, he was completing a 120-page screen treatment based on four of his one-act plays (*The Last of My Solid Gold Watches, 27 Wagons Full of Cotton, The Unsatisfactory Supper* and *This Property Is Condemned*). The story — sprawling, funny, bawdy — was something of a tangle, he wrote to Audrey, but he was sure it had promise. In time it became the single most controversial work of Tennessee Williams's career when, more than three years later, it reached the screen as *Baby Doll.*

Audrey, at the same time, was busy in her corner. The imminent revival of *Summer and Smoke* encouraged her to go to Hal Wallis at Paramount with the offer of its film rights, and within the year they were sold, as the rights to *The Rose Tattoo* had been, for $100,000.

March and April were busy in different ways for all those whose lives touched Williams's. Frank supervised construction workers who were building a studio and swimming pool in back of the Duncan Street house. At the same time, Williams flew to Los Angeles for the Academy Awards ceremony. *A Streetcar Named Desire* won Oscars for best actress (Vivien Leigh), best supporting actor (Karl Malden), best supporting actress (Kim Hunter) and best art and set decoration (Richard Day and George James Hopkins). It had also been nominated for best picture, best direction and best screenplay, but Williams himself received no award. He wrote to Cheryl Crawford that he resented his own resentment, that he wanted to be a winner of prizes like this, but he wondered if he would ever develop real humility and a solid sense of values. The letter, dated April 5, 1952, reveals a poignant self-awareness and honesty — until the final paragraph, where (in all seriousness) he expresses his anger over Frank's sexual infidelity. This would perhaps be pathetic if it were not ironic, since in fact it was Williams himself who so actively pursued other partners, and Merlo who kept himself free of such involvements.

"Merlo was a wonderful man for Tennessee," according to José Quintero. "Number one for his devotion to Tennessee, a real devotion. . . . He was enormously sensitive and one of the people that told Tennessee the truth without being afraid of 'Tennessee Williams,' in quotes. In 1952, Tennessee was really being loved and taken care of by Frank, and he needed that a great deal."

Opening night of the revival of *Summer and Smoke* (April 24, 1952) was a glorious event and a resounding success, but it came as something of a surprise to outsiders, and neither Williams nor his friends attended. The next day's reviews changed everything.

"Nothing has happened in the theatre in a long time as admirable as this production," began the review by Brooks Atkinson in the *New York Times.* "You might fairly argue that [*Summer and Smoke*] is a finer piece of literature [than *Streetcar*]. The analysis of character is subtler and more compassionate. The contrasts are less brutal. . . . From every point of view [it is] a beautifully wrought drama."

Atkinson and the other reviewers who came to the performances were right to compare the play to *Streetcar,* for in some senses it anticipated in the character of Alma Winemiller the forces in Blanche DuBois's background. The clash between emotional yearnings and repressions are more delicately explored in *Summer and Smoke;* the overrefined sensibility in conflict with the needs of the body receives a more compassionate treatment. But as with *Streetcar,* the drama derives its force from the depth of feeling that prevailed in the heart of the playwright; the theme of unreasonable idealism, broken open and humanized, was certainly plain in *Streetcar* and *Tattoo.*

"Everything in his life is in his plays, and everything in his plays is in his life," Elia Kazan reflected years later. "He was so naked in his plays, and *Summer and Smoke* is one of the best of them."

Williams admitted that Alma had a close connection to himself: "I think the character I like most is Miss Alma. . . . She is my favorite because I came out so late and so did Alma. . . . Miss Alma grew up in the shadow of the rectory, and so did I."

Summer and Smoke was, first of all, part of a tetralogy about the psychological imbalance in a woman caught between fantasy and reality. In *The Glass Menagerie,* Amanda Wingfield, bound to the traditions of her parish church, has a kind of daffy nobility in spite of her illusions and her envelope of memories. In *Summer and Smoke,* set in the early years of the century, Alma Winemiller — who has the same initials* — is a kind of early version of Amanda Wingfield. As with Amanda, the young Blanche and the older Serafina, so with Alma Winemiller: there is an exaggerated spirituality that must confront her counterpart — Dr. John Buchanan (as Blanche with Stanley Kowalski, and Serafina with Alvaro Mangiacavallo). In the final scene of *Summer and Smoke,* the genteel and the passionate unite as the rejected Alma seeks in the arms of a stranger the love she could not find with John Buchanan. In *The Rose Tattoo,* Serafina learns to accept the new man in her life, and to abandon the idolization of her dead husband. And Blanche DuBois is perhaps one possible term of this — the last route of the habit of sexual confusion and spiritual self-delusion in which the *alma,* or soul, is finally the tragic victim. (In his one-act play *The Dark Room,* first published in 1948, Williams comically explored the theme of repression and its final state in the [unseen] pregnant daughter and the sexually repressed social worker.)

Everywhere the text of *Summer and Smoke* reveals the personality of its author: Alma's "mental afflictions [have] to be brought under control"; and she speaks from Williams's level of personal anguish — "I wonder if they stop to think that I had had certain difficulties and disadvantages to cope with — which may be partly the cause of these peculiarities of mine — which they find so offensive!" And Alma speaks Williams's own final acceptance of life: "I know I'm not dying, that it isn't going to turn out to be that simple."

As soon as Audrey cabled Williams that *Summer and Smoke* was the surprise hit of the New York theatre season, he made a trip north. "I met him in the lobby after the show," José Quintero recalled, "and he rushed at me, put his arms around me, and gave me a terrific hug. I was of course petrified. He was carrying an umbrella with a very sharp point, and because we were standing so close together, when he put it down it

---

* It is perhaps only a curious coincidence that Amanda Wingfield and Alma Winemiller also share the initials of Tennessee's surrogate mother, Audrey Wood.

landed on my foot. Then he leaned on it. Right between my toes. Here
was this great playwright full of admiration for the work we had done.
How could I tell him he was puncturing my foot?"

For his part, Williams made sure the cast knew of his admiration and
gratitude — a trait that became typical, and that of course always delighted the various companies. Later, he went on record in praise of
Geraldine Page as "a talented and beautiful actress. . . . She is the most
disciplined and dedicated."

The next month continued his good fortune. On May 28, he and Carson McCullers, Newton Arvin, Eudora Welty, Louise Bogan and Jacques
Barzun were among a group elected to lifetime membership in the National Institute of Arts and Letters. And with this honor capping the success accorded *Summer and Smoke* (which played to capacity audiences for a
year), he departed on June 11 with Merlo for a summer in Europe.

But Carson was departing at the same time, and she would not accept
his initial refusal to visit the country house she and Reeves had taken at
Bachvillers, a tiny village an hour's drive north of Paris in the Oise val-
ley. To avoid spending time at the house, Williams brought Carson and
Reeves back to Paris for several evenings.

Also in Paris he met Anna Magnani for discussions about the film of
Tattoo. Being with Carson and Reeves was too draining, too depressing
for him; they expected too much, while Magnani gave.

By early July he and Frank had arrived in Rome, and meetings both
social and business-based continued with Magnani. She suggested that
Vittorio De Sica or Luchino Visconti direct the film of *Tattoo.* Williams
thought this inspired, but neither of them had any clear idea of international filmmaking union regulations about such things. (Daniel Mann
eventually directed the film as he had the play.)

Until the end of September, Williams and Merlo remained in Rome,
except for a brief excursion to visit Elia Kazan, who was directing the
film *Man On a Tightrope* in Germany. They discussed the script for *Camino Real,* which was far from finalized and was presenting terrific problems in design and construction.

After a week in London at the end of September, Williams and Merlo
returned to New York on the *Queen Mary*. They attended a Halloween
party at Jane Bowles's rented townhouse on West 10th Street, where she
was the only woman among a wild group of men who finally left her
very much alone with the music and the food while they all crept, in

groups of two or more, to intimate corners of the house. She seemed not to mind at all.

At Christmas, Tennessee Williams and Frank Merlo were in Key West, with only Reverend Dakin and his daughter to join them for a quiet holiday.

Chapter Six

THE NOON-DAY DEVIL

(1953–1957)

You know we live in light and shadow —
that's what we live in, a world of light and
shadow — and it's confusing.

— Vee, in *Orpheus Descending*

CAMINO REAL was scheduled for a mid-March 1953 opening in New York after previews in New Haven and Philadelphia. Williams insisted that the play was "my conception of the time and world that I live in, and its people are mostly archetypes of certain basic attitudes and qualities" he found in that world. In fact, for all its wild and idiosyncratic texture, its experimental and dreamlike progression of scenes, its fierce and funny series of almost kinetic images, *Camino Real* was not only an expression of the time and place Williams believed he inhabited; it was also his first and last frankly political play to open in New York.

The action is introduced as Don Quixote's reverie. In a mythical, vaguely Latin American town are gathered the lonely and disaffected, and those whose lives are synonymous for love, its loss, its pursuit and its varieties — Camille, Casanova, Byron — and the archetypical American, Kilroy. Very little happens in *Camino Real:* the play contrasts repression with freedom, violence with tenderness, despair with hope in alternating scenes of reflective dialogue and boisterous parades. The energy of the characters' struggles builds as the heroes and antiheroes — and finally Kilroy — pass through symbolic cycles of death and rebirth.

There were frantic, late meetings between Williams and Cheryl Crawford, between Crawford and Elia Kazan, and between Kazan and Williams — about sets, costumes and even script revisions — as late as March 1. "He was a more tense man than he had been when I'd worked with him on *Streetcar*," Kazan recalled. "A good bit of that I attributed to the nature of *Camino Real,* however. It was a risky thing. He knew that, and we all knew it."

Happily, the casting was easy. Since so much of the budget was allotted for Lemuel Ayres's sweeping set and for the colorful period costumes for over fifty actors, the producers avoided engaging major "name" stars;

in any case, Eli Wallach was ideal for the tough, naïve hero Kilroy, and Barbara Baxley, who had taken over major roles in long Broadway runs and touring companies, was Williams's first and only choice for the wacky, ingenuous, confused Gypsy daughter Esmeralda. He and Kazan heard her read at an audition, and when she protested that she loved the role — and especially its haunting, lyrical prayer near the finale — but that she was not quite certain she understood it completely, Williams replied, "Honey, you don't need to understand it — you just go do it!"

In New Haven and Philadelphia, the playwright's agitated state and his terror of a critical and popular failure after a series of successes were justified. The production was chaotic, and the audiences found the lack of a traditional narrative disconcerting: many of those who came slammed out of the theatre angry, confused and disgusted. For the sake of his cast and crew, however, Williams affected a detached composure, and he frequently explained his calm by quoting the narrator of his short story "The Angel in the Alcove," who reflects, "I had already learned to make a religion of endurance and a secret of my desperation."

"I was also in Philadelphia, with another show," José Quintero recalled. "I stood in the back of the theatre with Tennessee and watched the people walking out. The play had gotten very bad notices, and that's when I began to sense the enormous strength in this man who was so tender and so sensitive and so gentle. I thought, 'Oh my God. This stampede is going to destroy him.' But I had not counted on his steel." The uncanny, courageous Williams humor was never more evident than at the time of *Camino Real,* whose Broadway failure was almost a foregone conclusion. With a rueful smile, Williams remarked quietly to Quintero as they watched the audience leave in midact, "Well, I don't think they are really taking the play to their hearts, would you say?"

"He was a man who didn't reveal his disappointment," Quintero added. "I knew inside he was bleeding, just like anyone would in his position. But he believed in his creation. He may have found parts that were faulty, but he'd never waver or disown any of his work just because other people didn't like it." And his Southern gentlemanliness never failed him.

For all his public bravery, however, Williams's anguish over the play was clear to his intimates. Merlo coped with his black moods at home, and conveyed his intentions to the cast as the New York opening approached. "Frankie was the communicating line for all of us," according to Barbara Baxley. "He was so perfect about everything — he sensed everything Tenn needed, everything we needed. He was the one who brought everybody back to the reality of life before us every day. He was firm, he gave us all balance. They were both lucky men — Tenn was lucky to have Frank, and Frank was fortunate to be with this great poet."

In spite of later revivals of this experimental, poetic but not obscure play, American audiences would never in fact "take the play to their hearts," as its author suspected. From the typical heroes and heroines desiring freedom ("All of us have a desperate bird in our heart") to the sense of captivity ("Caged birds accept each other but flight is what they long for"), the play leaps to open expressions of Williams's own fears as a middle-aged poet, whose "vocation . . . is to influence the heart. . . . He ought to purify it and lift it above its ordinary level." But at the same time there is the fear that his vocation has been lost in the frenzy of celebrity, lost, like Byron, "among gondolas and palazzos, masked balls, glittering salons, huge shadowy courts and torch-lit entrances, baroque facades, canopies and carpets, candelabra and gold plate among snowy damask." The social subterfuges, the escape routes Tennessee Williams himself attempted in 1951 and 1952, haunted the part of him that was serious craftsman and sensitive chronicler of the human heart. In *Camino Real,* the royal road of glamour yields to the real road of life's demands — thus his insistence that the title be accented on the first syllable of each word, to stress the reality, not the royalty, of the road of life; the hardness of decisions, not the affect of sublimity.

It may be, however, that audiences in 1953 rejected the play not in fact because it was vague, but because it was all too clear in its denunciation of the fascist demagoguery then spreading over the country in the voice, especially loud, of Senator Joseph McCarthy.

"Walter Winchell and Ed Sullivan attacked the play as anti-American," according to Barbara Baxley. "They accused it of being a leftist manifesto. The earlier version of the play — what we performed in Philadelphia, not what was finally printed as the New York version — was an unwaveringly anti-imperialist play. It certainly wasn't anti-American, however — it was anti-fascist. But all references in the play to fascism in America, and to brotherhood and love were cut, since they were thought to be ringing cries of Communist sympathy."

Remnants of this concern appear in the printed version, nevertheless, as Casanova decries the situation in which "the individual becomes an undistinguished member of a collectivist state [under the control of] the maintenance of the military police. . . . Nothing wild or honest is tolerated here! It has to be extinguished."

In spite of lusty humor and a poise between politics and poetics, the play did not succeed even with the most sensitive and admiring among Williams's supporters. Walter Kerr, who was second to none in his respect for Williams as America's premiere playwright, wrote in the *New York Herald-Tribune* that *Camino Real* was "the worst play yet written by the best playwright of his generation." More than a disappointed critic, Kerr was a loyal admirer, and in a long letter the following month he offered Williams extended constructive criticism: the failure of the play, he wrote, was not because people were appalled at what was said, "but that people are simply not able to get through it to your intention at all. Actually, I think they are really outraged by a blank wall, by the play's defiant lack of esthetic clarity. . . . Surely you must acknowledge that your intention is not getting over; and that therefore the play *isn't* clear. . . . What terrifies me about *Camino Real* is not what you want to say but the direction in which you, as an artist, are moving. You're heading toward the cerebral; don't do it. What makes you an artist of the first rank is your intuitive gift for penetrating reality, without junking reality in the process; an intuitive artist starts with the recognizable surface of things and burrows *in*. Don't swap this for the conscious, rational processes of the analyst, the symbolist, the abstract thinker."

To this extended comment the director, Elia Kazan, later added a simple diagnosis of what he thought was the play's problem: "It doesn't have a third act — it doesn't seem to go anywhere at the end. We worked on it, over and over, but we never got it, we were never satisfied. The poetry of it is wonderful, though, the imagery is beautiful and the humor is terrific, as with all Tennessee's plays."

Opening night was a particularly difficult experience for Williams. In a letter to Brooks Atkinson two weeks later — perhaps because Atkinson, almost alone among critics, wrote favorably about the play — Williams admitted that he survived the first night on Nembutal and Seconal, that he was experiencing life like the motley, confused crew of pilgrims in his play, and that he was living among desperate outcasts in Key West, men of passion and endurance and tenderness — and as an artist, he concluded, he was honor-bound to speak for that world since it was what he knew best. The letters of Hart Crane, he told Atkinson, were always by his side; Crane's life was his support and his encouragement.

*   *   *

Within days of the opening, Williams and Merlo in fact returned to Key West, to the "desperate outcasts" with whom they felt more at ease. For several weeks Williams withdrew to his workroom and grappled with depression by working feverishly on revisons of *Camino Real* — not because he hoped that they could be incorporated into the Broadway production and reverse its anticipated demise, but because James Laughlin at New Directions was eager to publish it before year's end, and Williams wanted an improved text to represent him in print. On March 31 he wrote to Cheryl that some of the material he was adding restored the cuts demanded by Walter Winchell's political objections. Posterity could be the judge of his politics — which, he felt, were humanitarian impulses and not partisan prejudices.

There was another reason for his seclusion in the Key West studio in March and April, however. He had agreed to direct Margaret Phillips in Donald Windham's play *The Starless Air* for Joanna Albus's Playhouse Theatre in Houston, and before the premiere on May 13 he was working on staging and corresponding with Windham on structural changes.

"He wanted to try to direct at this point in his life," according to Paul Bigelow, who was then at the Theatre Guild, which intended to sponsor *The Starless Air* in New York after the Houston run. "But he wanted to direct a play far enough away from New York so the critics couldn't have a go at him if he failed. He knew he couldn't stage one of his own, because the press would swoop down on him from everywhere. So he went to Houston to direct a play by Donald Windham. Lawrence [Langner, at the Theatre Guild] said we would wait to see what happened with it there; if it became successful, the Guild would consider producing it in New York. But after a few days in Texas, Tenn called me and begged me to come down. 'Donald is being miserable to me,' he complained. 'He's not allowing me any directorial control.' When I arrived in Houston I saw they were at loggerheads, and the cooperation between them virtually ended then and there." Windham admitted that there were "morbidly sensitive" feelings, from the beginning, although he later wrote that Williams was "an inspired director." Windham, however, felt that he was not being given the consideration due a playwright: "The first thing [Williams] did was to bar me from rehearsals." Soon after, Windham found that Williams was "writing and inserting speeches" into the play.*

* *The Starless Air* never did come to New York — a fact due more to Williams's protracted European journey and his lack of strong support for Windham in negotiations with the Theatre Guild concerning script revisions than to the earnest efforts of Audrey Wood and of

Immediately before the opening, in fact, Williams left Houston and drove north, stopping in Memphis to visit his grandfather, who was planning to spend the year at the Hotel Gayoso. By the end of the month he was in New York, and Frank arrived by train two days before their departure for Europe on June 5; he now knew to expect the sudden announcement that they would pass each summer abroad.

The crossing did not ease Williams's tension, and by the time they docked in Le Havre Merlo was spending more time with their bulldog, Mr. Moon, then he could with Williams, whose nervous condition, constant physical complaints and moodiness were all but intolerable. "I wouldn't be a good person for anyone to latch on to," he had told an interviewer a few years earlier. Of the first month of the 1953 voyage in Europe, only Merlo knew the tension, and only he invented distractions to dispel it.

As soon as they arrived in Rome on June 22, Williams wrote to Paul Bowles in Tangier. They had come to their fourth-floor walkup, he said, right at the start of a suffocating Roman summer. No breezes stirred on either of the two terraces.

They left almost at once for Spain, but on arrival Williams was confined to bed with food poisoning for over a week and he became so restless that when he could eat he insisted on returning to Rome — which they did, only to depart for the southern coast. Then they went on to Vienna, Venice, Zurich, back to Spain, then down to the southern towns of Italy. Over two months — from August to October — Williams and Merlo (and sometimes Paul Bowles) moved from hotel to guest-house to inn, from scenic resorts (at Positano, for example) to cramped fishing villages. At one point, fearful that he had contracted a deadly fever, he drafted a short story that was a kind of last will and last confession in fiction form: "Man Bring This Up Road" is the account of a rich widow in Amalfi who takes in a talented but freeloading young poet. She teases him — with food and with an absurd offer of sex — but her exploitation leads to his weeping, and she dismisses him from her house.

A curiously cold story, related in its confessional motif to the later *Suddenly Last Summer* and anticipating also *The Milk Train Doesn't Stop Here Anymore* in its interweaving of life-force and death wish, "Man Bring This Up Road" reflects the malaise of summer 1953. It was a time

---

Phyllis Anderson (Windham's agent). On the entire sad issue, *cf.* Donald Windham, ed., *Tennessee Williams' Letters to Donald Windham 1940-1965* (New York: Holt, Rinehart and Winston, 1977), pp. 273-289.

he summarized in words he had recently put on the lips of D. H. Lawrence, in a revised version of *I Rise in Flame, Cried the Phoenix:* "All that I ever do is go packing around the world with women and manuscripts and a vile disposition. I pretend to be waging a war with bourgeois conceptions of morality.... What I'm fighting with really's the little old maid in myself." *Camino Real* had certainly been the pretense of a war with bourgeois morality: Kilroy, the archetypal American with a "heart as big as a baby," the wanderer with no sure harbor, was nothing so much as a stand-in for Williams himself. Now, in the summer following, he sought out the usual places in Italy where he might deal with the "little old maid" in himself. By the trick of a certain profligacy of the flesh, the old maid might be put to rest — or at least stung to a savage new vitality.

The result of the wandering — and this he admitted for the first time in his life — was a creative stasis, a writer's block such as he had never before experienced. By early autumn he had gone to Tangier with Bowles, and from the Hotel Rembrandt he wrote on October 14 to Audrey Wood complaining of a mysterious weakness, a fatigue that gripped him a half-hour into his morning work. He was prodding himself with morning liquor, he wrote, but he found that the writing was so forced and artificial he ended even more depressed than the previous unproductive day. He insisted in the same letter that there must have been something physical, something with the body that kept him from working successfully. With the patient and cheerful Bowles, Williams could work or not, wander at will or stay at the hotel, keep his private assignations with familiar or anonymous north Africans, or write letters at the bar. After meeting a small crew of international eccentrics of a particularly gruesome sort, he sailed back to New York on October 27, aboard the *Andrea Doria.**

Meantime, Johnny Nicholson had been alert for a furnished apartment to replace Buffie Johnson's subleased quarters, and he found one for them — at 323 East 58th Street, on the second floor of a house Nicholson simultaneously bought, and to which was annexed his relocated café. He had it beautifully furnished in oriental antiques for his new tenants, and it was ready for their return.

Typically, however, they did not remain long. Williams was eager for a

---

* The odd crew he met that summer inspired the weird assortment in his story "It Happened the Day the Sun Rose," which was published privately in 1981. The story features variations on those he had known in north Africa — exhibitionists, voyeurs, sadomasochistic prostitutes, etc.

warm climate, and they went South, collected Grandfather, and proceeded to New Orleans.

The trip to this city was motivated by neither nostalgia nor because they preferred it to Key West. This time, there was indeed a medical reason; it turned out, however, to be neither dangerous nor incapacitating. In Europe that summer, he had begun suffering with hemorrhoids, and his friend Oliver Evans recommended a New Orleans proctologist who could treat him. He was to be admitted for surgery at the Ochsner Clinic, and within a week he could be discharged.

But he did not undergo the operation at Ochsner. Thomas K. Griffin, for many years a leading New Orleans journalist, cultural historian and archivist, received a call from Williams asking that Griffin arrange for him to be removed to the Touro Infirmary for "emergency surgery."

"But the real reason," according to Griffin, "was that at Ochsner they were very strict about alcoholic drinks, and he wouldn't do without. I didn't know that until I had taken extraordinary measures to have him transferred to Touro. So they did this relatively minor operation there, and he had his liquor."

By mid-January 1954, Williams, Merlo and the Reverend left New Orleans for Key West. To Brooks Atkinson, Williams wrote that the bad time of last summer still prevailed, and that his discomfort was deeper than the lingering surgical discomfort; he had no vitality, no interest. At the same time he wrote to Donald Windham that he was a wreck, fit only for the movies or the beach. Prior to his operation, he had worked with some enthusiasm on the screenplay now based only on two one-act plays;* it was then called *Hide and Seek* — and, briefly, *The Whip Master* and *Mississippi Woman* — and it would soon be called *Baby Doll*. But now it lay untouched on the studio desk in Key West.

His letters to Cheryl Crawford were somewhat more explicit. He and Frank, he wrote, were trying to avoid the transient sailors at the Key West bars. For her part, the loyal Cheryl found Williams in the mid-1950s "courageous and fearful, suspicious and trusting, generous and acquisitive, sanguine and despairing, impulsive and cautious"; she always listened uncritically, patiently, like a prudent sister.

At this time, Key West's bohemianism began to peak. Margaret Foresman, then and for many years later the managing editor of the *Key West*

---

* *The Last of My Solid Gold Watches* and *This Property Is Condemned* did not figure in the last stages of working on the screenplay.

Citizen, recalled that in the 1950s, "although illegal, there was gambling in Key West, and even a brothel on Stock Island nearby, which was eventually closed. There was no open advertising of preferences, but it was certainly a relaxed place to be a nonconformist. Tennessee was honored there by virtue of his successes, and he often showed up at the Casa Marina or the Officers Club. In the 1950s there was no indication of anything like drugs — liquor and sex seemed to be the usual recreations. Tennessee might not have been invited to the blue-haired ladies' parties, but people were certainly respectful of him — if a little distant. For the gay population, young men were always available in Key West. And when the authorities got around to closing the brothel on Stock Island, well, there was always the house on Duncan Street for any sailors passing through. But in spite of his often wild living, and the groups of people tumbling in and out of his house, he was up early in the morning, and he worked until noon."

By early spring, Williams had resumed daily work on the play that would transform, expand and alter the mysterious short story "Three Players of a Summer Game." In the 1954 drafts of this new long play, Brick, the alcoholic ex-athlete married to a woman who keeps him in benevolent subordination, was becoming an enigmatically distant man, still alcoholic but now also impotent, refusing to take any interest in his sex-starved wife or in the machinations of his brother, who is maneuvering to take over the great estate and the wealth of their terminally ill father. The play was becoming *Cat on a Hot Tin Roof:* the wife Maggie was the anxious cat, and Williams saw with greater clarity the characters of Big Daddy and Big Mama, the humorous-pathetic scions to a family steeped in greed, mendacity and self-delusion.

A strange shift was occurring in Williams's writing in early 1954. Whereas *Camino Real* was loud with action, delirious with crowds and vague regarding time, place and purpose, the new play in its earliest development was observing classical unities of place, time and theme, and it entirely subordinated action to a series of very nearly philosophical dialogues. Perhaps because *Cat on a Hot Tin Roof* was dense with a network of personal references and personal fears, he was calling it a comedy of manners. In this play, everything that *happened* had happened before the curtain rose — or it *might* happen afterward. During the summer evening of the play's time, only the characters' reactions filled the stage, only these representative critical moments were held up for the audience.

By April, Williams had had enough of Key West; the doctors at

Ochsner, after he returned for a postoperative evaluation, pronounced him ready for travel. That meant Europe, and so Frank repacked their luggage and arranged for Reverend Dakin to go to St. Louis, either to live with Edwina again or to enter a nursing home. Then ninety-seven, the old gentleman was at last weary and suffering an array of geriatric ailments.

As they prepared to depart, Williams heard that playwright Arthur Miller had recently been refused a passport to attend the premiere of one of his plays in Brussels. On his colleague's behalf, Williams prepared a letter to the Department of State (dated April 1, 1954), in which he stated that he himself had spent the last several summers in Europe and could attest that Miller was highly respected there. Refusing him permission to travel outside America, he continued, could only strengthen Communist propaganda about the lack of artistic freedom in the West; if our country was not persecuting its finest artists, as Russia claimed, then Miller should be granted freedom to travel.

A noble and courageous defense, to be sure — but one of which Williams quickly repented. He admitted later (from Sicily, to Brooks Atkinson, in a letter dated September 4) that he never mailed the statement to the government. Just as he was about to do so, he realized that his own passport — then due for renewal — might be delayed or denied if he were an outspoken supporter of Miller. He decided that prudence was the better part of valor, and, so as not to irritate the Department of State and jeopardize his own freedom, the letter remained in his file.

In early May, Williams was in New York, and Carson McCullers invited him to share a stage with her for an evening. She had been invited to speak on "Twenty Years of Writing" at the Poetry Center of the 92nd Street YMHA, and she thought that Williams — much the stronger and the better reader — should accompany her. He agreed, on condition that a pitcher of martinis be set at his elbow. His intolerance for any substantial quantity of alcohol, and her generous refilling of her own glass, resulted in a strange event. Two of America's most famous writers sat for the evening, interrupting one another, stumbling and slurring over their words, perversely relishing one another's boozy humor as much as they were oblivious to the uncomfortable audience.

At the beginning of June, Williams and Merlo arrived in Rome and at once contacted Anna Magnani, who had promised to return to America with them later that year to film *The Rose Tattoo* for Hal Wallis at Paramount Pictures. She realized that Williams was depressed to a dangerous point, but neither she nor Merlo could convince him to seek help or to return earlier to New York for treatment. Instead, he wrote to Cheryl Crawford that he was passing through the worst nervous crisis of his life, trying to avoid total mental collapse with an almost round-the-clock reliance on liquor, an increased dependence on sedatives and barbiturates, and an incessant round of social distractions that gave him no pleasure.

He was, he told Cheryl, being helped by nothing — not even the affectionate attention he got from the new bulldog, Boffo, that had replaced Mr. Moon, who had recently died. He admitted that he was taking pills and drinking before noon and not stopping before dinner; he could not walk a Roman street unless there was a bar or wineshop. Cheryl would understand him, and how deep was the mental crisis of which, he was sure, this was but a physical expression. For the first time, Williams was admitting that the source of his unhappiness and of his addictions was not disease, but rather a wasting of the spirit. He agreed with Alma Winemiller: "I don't see how I'm going to get through the summer."

This letter was explicit: he was too shy with Audrey Wood, he admitted to Cheryl, to share these secrets. But he was at such an impasse that he must have treatment when he returned to the United States; he had avoided acknowledging this under pretext of the press of work, but now even the work was failing him, and the obsessive travel was no relief. He quoted D. H. Lawrence: "Face the facts and live beyond them"; he would, he promised, return to New York in August to face the facts.

Could Cheryl recommend a psychiatrist for him? he asked. Could Dr. Alfred Kinsey recommend someone, since he and Williams had once met, five years earlier, to discuss the relationship between art and neurosis? He said he did not want the same doctor as William Inge, since Inge — especially since his recent success with *Picnic* — seemed to him complacent and pompous. There was some ray of hope, Williams concluded: he had revised *Battle of Angels,* now called *Orpheus Descending.* It reflected the deeper spiritual crisis of the 1950s, rather than the simple sexual repressions of the 1930s. If he had not been so tormented, he told Cheryl, the play would not have had the ring of authenticity. He looked forward to being with her in New York that autumn.

But for several months he delayed his return, and apparently for no other reason than the distraction of travel across Europe with Frank. At last, on September 22, Williams, Merlo and Magnani left Rome, arriving a week later in New York. The following month, filming of *The Rose*

Tattoo began in Key West (which was to pass for a Mississippi Gulf town), next door to Williams's house. Locals appeared as extras, adoring Magnani, who was at first hesitant about her English and then relaxed among the townspeople. Her screen performance as Serafina would soon be considered the highlight of her career. Hal Wallis, the producer, appeared briefly in a bar scene with Williams, the two watching the furious Magnani stride into the shot. And the short, handsome man who tried to stop the ensuing fight is none other than Frank Merlo. Busy with filming, busy with writing, busy with his social life, Williams seemed to have abandoned the idea of psychotherapy.

By New Year's Day 1955, Audrey Wood had negotiated with the Playwrights Company to produce Williams's next Broadway play, *Cat on a Hot Tin Roof.* (Cheryl Crawford read and admired it, but she thought that there was "no one to root for.") The Playwrights — Elmer Rice, Robert E. Sherwood, Maxwell Anderson, John Wharton and Roger Stevens — had added to their number Robert Anderson, whose *Tea and Sympathy* had opened in September 1953 (directed by Kazan) and had played for over seven hundred performances.

"Audrey may well have been impressed with the Playwrights' handling of *Tea and Sympathy*," Robert Anderson said, "and since I had joined that group she considered it natural to submit *Cat* to them when Cheryl declined to produce it. It had been Elia Kazan and Roger Stevens on my play, and so it was to be Kazan and Stevens again on *Cat.* There was a certain logic to all this, and of course everyone involved was someone with whom Audrey felt confident."

The play is structured as a series of confrontations between members of the Pollitt family: Brick, a former athletic star and current alcoholic; his wife, Maggie, the "cat," who is sexually frustrated because of Brick's mysterious distance from her following the suicide of his friend Skipper; Big Daddy, Brick's father, whose imminent death means the transfer of a vast estate; his confused, loyal, long-suffering wife, Big Mama; and Brick's venal brother and sister-in-law.

Williams came to New York in January to approve the cast and to meet with Kazan, who had a number of important recommendations about the text. Although Williams later felt that the stuctural and character changes Kazan wanted were drastic alterations of his original intentions, he wisely followed the advice: he wanted a success, and an audience for his melodrama about truth and falsehood, about greed and sexual confusion, and he respected Kazan's perceptions.

Specifically, Kazan believed that the character of Big Daddy was too important to vanish after act two; he also thought that as a result of the confrontation between him and Brick some change should be evident in the son; and finally he felt that Maggie should be a more sympathetic person at the end. Williams in some way acceded to all these counsels. "I do think my ending is better," Kazan said years later. "And Tennessee agreed. I gave him every opportunity to override my objections — the Dramatists Guild has rules about such things, after all — but he agreed." For a 1974 revival, Williams kept Kazan's structural changes (in spite of his insistence to the contrary for years before and after). He restored only a risqué joke told by Big Daddy and the ambiguous sarcasm of the last line of the play.

To work on the revisions of the third act, Williams left New York — and he had another reason to do so, for Tulane University in New Orleans had prepared productions of his one-act play 27 *Wagons Full of Cotton* and an opera by Raffaello de Banfield for which *Lord Byron's Love Letter* had provided the libretto. For the premiere of 27 *Wagons,* Williams chose Maureen Stapleton to play Flora, the slightly dim farmwife whose husband, Jake, destroys a neighbor's cotton gin. The neighbor, Silva Vicarro,* subsequently brutalizes Flora in a grim fable of revenge, greed and sadomasochism that Williams called "a Mississippi Delta comedy."

"Tennessee was very brave about this production at Tulane," Maureen Stapleton remembered. "The set they had built was so massive and heavy and awkward that it was impossible to act on or in or around it. And when Tenn and Frank arrived on January 15, Tenn just sat down with the man in charge of the set. He flattered, he cajoled, he offered to pay out of his own pocket for construction changes. Nothing would convince the man. So we finally put a swing downstage, and Tenn directed rehearsals in which I could act on and around the swing, in front of that impossible set, which we just pretended wasn't there." And that is how the swing, and the dialogue that occurs in the famous "swing scene," found its way into the film *Baby Doll* the following year; Williams made a virtue of necessity — a prop became a brilliant symbolic device, the perfect correlative for the reversed fortunes of the two men, and for the gradual erotic awakening of the "baby doll" wife. Quite coincidentally, Tennessee Williams was soon awarded the "Show Business" award for artistry and merit in dramatic construction. (27 *Wagons* came to New

* In 27 *Wagons Full of Cotton,* the name of the character is Vicarro; in the film script *Baby Doll,* which combined this play and *The Unsatisfactory Supper,* he has become Vacarro.

York for a six-week run in April, as part of an evening of various enter-
tainments.)

After a brief visit to Los Angeles to see the first cut of *The Rose Tattoo,*
Williams and Merlo flew back to New York, for on February 7 rehearsals
began for *Cat* — with the revisions Kazan had suggested. Ben Gazzara
and Barbara Bel Geddes were to play Brick and Maggie, the couple
whose marriage is threatened by untruth, denial, jealousy and Brick's
guilt for failing a needy friend who took his life.

"My father had a great gift for phrases," Williams said later. "The title
'Cat on a Hot Tin Roof' comes from him. 'Edwina,' he used to say,
'you're making me as nervous as a cat on a hot tin roof!' "

Burl Ives (who had played the tough-gentle sheriff in Kazan's film of
John Steinbeck's *East of Eden*) at once impressed Williams during casting. Previously best known as a folksinger and archivist of the American
ballad, Ives played Big Daddy Pollitt, the dying master of the Delta
plantation whose combination of raw vulgarity and curious appeal was
partly the figure of Cornelius Coffin Williams. "Tennessee told me," Ives
recalled years later, "that he had written this part after his own father,
and that on opening night he sat in the fourteenth row and saw Cornelius Williams."

The role of Big Mama required an actress who could suggest a combination of fidelity, silliness and a special kind of simple nobility. The
choice was Mildred Dunnock, whom Kazan had directed in Arthur
Miller's *Death of a Salesman.* She later said that "Williams was a dreamer
and Kazan a realist, and they complemented one another perfectly. Williams was really a very shy man and he had to avoid anything that inhib-
ited his creative writing. Kazan helped him to do this, for he had an
extraordinary capacity of leadership and the ability to draw from the players what we didn't know was there inside us. He led us in a way that an
orchestra conductor leads." (Ives used the same metaphor in recalling rehearsals: "Ben Gazzara and I were directed by Kazan as if the play were
an orchestra piece, a fugue — building, building, building in the confrontation between father and son.")

The Pollitt parents indeed are modeled on the Williams parents — but
with great freedom, since of all his plays of the 1950s *Cat on a Hot Tin
Roof* most subjects characters to a system of ideas. There is great subtlety
in the playwright's construction of Brick, the guilt-ridden son with his
foot in a plaster cast and his hand on a liquor bottle; and in Maggie, the
sex-starved, determined wife who stands outside the lies and sees patterns
of weakness and a need for truth.

"I think Maggie is more himself than anyone else he may have pointed to, or who claimed to be the model for this woman," according to Kazan. And Williams himself expressed his admiration for this passionate sensualist, both in the notes to his play and in comments to the press. "Maggie was the only aristocrat," he said. "She was the only one free of greed. . . . I sympathized with her and liked her myself, and [she] had become steadily more charming to me as I worked on her characterization."

During rehearsals in February and March, Kazan denied Williams access to the cast. "Kazan didn't want us talking about the play with the playwright," Mildred Dunnock remembered. "We were all in awe of Tennessee, of course, because his talent surpassed that of other writers. But we had the sense that these characters were not written realistically, and that to discuss them as if we were dissecting neighbors would have been untrue to them and to the play. Tennessee wrote from the inside to the outside of the characters and he did not muddle them by analyzing them to us."

That the characters in *Cat on a Hot Tin Roof* are indeed "not written realistically" is a key to the play's nature and importance. Never before was Williams so clearly in debt to August Strindberg; never before was the machinery of family strife the symbolic canvas on which he painted something like a mysterious sense of the universe. And never before did he so deliberately refuse to explain the dark, tantalizing corners of characters' souls.

"The bird that I hope to catch in the net of this play is not the solution of one man's psychological problem," he wrote in the text. "I'm trying to catch the true quality of experience in a group of people, that cloudy, flickering, evanescent — fiercely charged! — interplay of live human beings in the thundercloud of a common crisis."

More elusive and richer than *Camino Real, Cat on a Hot Tin Roof* is not merely a stinging play about greed, the inheritance of guilt, and the refusal to acknowledge the possible homosexuality of a college friend. The play has the tragedian's sense of the mysterious nature of personality, for Brick's paralyzing guilt is due to his deeper refusal to be true — precisely by open understanding — to a friendship for which he claimed total devotion. Additionally remarkable is that there is finally no villain in this play about moral darkness: there is understanding, compassion and allowance for every conundrum of every character. They are all recognizably human, funny and unforgettable.

That Williams's concerns in this play go beyond one family (his own or the Pollitts) to a consideration of the nature of common guilt is further indicated by his insistence on a nonrealistic set, sparsely furnished — "far less realistic than I have implied . . . the walls below the ceiling should dissolve mysteriously into air; the set should be roofed by the sky; stars and moon suggested by traces of milky pallor, as if they were observed through a telescope lens out of focus. . . ."

Brick Pollitt as idealist, unable to accept the fall of himself or others — the broken foot being the result of a literal and the sign of a symbolic fall — is in some sense a psychological self-portrait of Williams as idealist. But as impassive voyeur, unable to act, to choose or to enter without being led, Brick depends on the stronger Maggie — "more himself," as Kazan has suggested, the one eager to turn lies into truth, and to take the weak-willed by the hand and conduct him, with love.

As if the agony over this play were not poignant enough for him during that rehearsal period, he was told on February 14 that his beloved grandfather had died at Barnes Hospital, St. Louis, at the age of ninety-seven. Generous and uncritical, proud and grateful for his grandson's companionship in the last decade, Walter Edwin Dakin left an emptiness in Williams's life that would never be filled. "He left two small bequests," Paul Bigelow remembered, "one hundred dollars for Frankie Merlo, and one hundred dollars for me. It was all the old gentleman had in the world." Within the year, Williams donated one thousand dollars to the University of the South at Sewanee in his grandfather's memory.

On March 24, *Cat* opened at the Morosco Theatre, and although not all critics agreed about the value of Williams's deliberate ambiguities, there was no lack of praise for the cast or the seriousness of the play's content. And the salty language, an off-color joke about a tumescent elephant told by Big Daddy in the revised third act (and excised on April 4 at the request of the New York City license commissioner) and the psychosexual turmoil sent shock waves through the 1955 audience.

"The postwar theatre was extraordinary," as Robert Anderson said, "but in the galaxy of playwrights Tennessee Williams and Arthur Miller were in a sense the most exciting — not only because they were new, but because their material was different and was presented in a fresh way." With *Cat on a Hot Tin Roof* Williams showed that if he could not experiment with structure for his "fresh way" (as he had tried with *Camino Real*), then he would portray characters in recognizable but unconventional situations. For an audience he considered emotionally hard of hearing, he wanted to shout; for those blind in their smugness, he drew large and startling figures. His enemy was complaisance, and he fought it with shock tactics.

For three weeks in April, Williams took Carson McCullers to Key West. Mornings, they worked on their manuscripts; afternoons, they drank, sat on the beach, welcomed neighbors. French author Françoise Sagan visited, to Carson's special delight, and later Williams announced that they would go to Havana to meet Ernest Hemingway. But after two days of waiting on the island, they returned to Key West: Hemingway had never received the advance telegram, and was not there.

They returned to Key West to receive the news that *Cat* had won the Pulitzer Prize for drama; Williams at once announced that the five hundred dollars would be turned back to the Columbia University Graduate School of Journalism. By mid-June, Carson had departed, and Williams left for his summer holiday in Europe. As Audrey Wood soon wrote to an executive at Warner Brothers, Williams moved from one European capital to another that year with a rapidity and lack of motivation that she found frightening. She was also concerned (as were his other friends) that he was traveling without Frank Merlo, who explained quite openly when she telephoned to Key West. There had been growing tension between the two men, and they both thought a summer's separation would improve the relationship.

Meantime, Williams's arrivals and departures in the great hotels were so capricious and unannounced that it was several weeks before the telegram finally reached him that Margo Jones had died on July 25. The victim of an accident in her home, Margo was only two years younger than Williams — forty-two that year. She had not served his career well in the 1948 production of *Summer and Smoke,* but of her devotion there was never any question. With this news, he felt inconsolable for days and guilty for his neglect of her in the last several years. The remainder of the summer was, as he wrote to critic Kenneth Tynan, a period nearly blacked out by drugs and drink: he admitted to the habit of washing down Seconal tablets with double gin martinis.

In midsummer, he flew from Rome to Stockholm for the Swedish premiere of *Cat on a Hot Tin Roof,* as the guest of Lilla van Saher. She was a Hungarian immigrant to America, and the sister of the psychiatrist Dr. Franz Alexander. Lilla had been a casual visitor to Key West from her New York home since she and her husband saw *Camino Real.* By 1955, Lilla — whom Williams called "the last of the crêpe-de-Chine gypsies" — was a charter member of the curious entourage that surrounded Williams at home and abroad. She somehow managed to turn up wherever Tennessee Williams turned up. A thickset woman of modest wealth but generous eccentricity, she single-handedly took it on herself that September to ensure that Williams would be awarded the Nobel Prize in literature. She installed him in the Castle Hotel and proceeded to announce a series of lavish parties and press receptions to introduce him to Swedish society and those highly connected with both the court and the Nobel committee.

"She had all the press there," according to Williams, who thought that her publicity overkill had alienated the Swedish critics and Nobel executors. "She was like a field marshal! 'You over that way! You over there! You do not approach Mr. Williams until I give you the signal!' Barking out orders. Oh, it was just terrifying. The next morning the newspapers all came out saying Mr. Williams arrived in Stockholm preceded by a very powerful press agent!" And so ended his chances for the Nobel Prize, in his assessment — but not his friendship with the formidable, loyal and colorfully zany Lilla van Saher.

When he returned to New York in the fall of 1955, Williams took advantage of a quiet time at East 58th Street to complete revisions of his screenplay, now firmly titled *Baby Doll*. (Merlo remained in Key West.) He and Kazan exchanged an eager correspondence about it, but Kazan soon noticed that Williams had done all he intended and turned it over to the director. Kazan had worked with the one-act play *27 Wagons Full of Cotton* at the Actors Studio with the young Carroll Baker, and with Karl Malden. There was no doubt in his mind that they were just right for Baby Doll Meighan (the Flora of *27 Wagons*) and her husband (now called Archie Lee), and that Eli Wallach would be right for Silva Vaccaro, and Mildred Dunnock for Aunt Rose Comfort.*

"Then I began working on the movie, a little bit here and a little bit there," Kazan recalled, "and I kept facing the problem of structure. . . . I threw out [the other one-act plays], but I used *The Unsatisfactory Supper* [along with *27 Wagons*]. . . . Here again I was working as a writer in disguise, behind the scenes; when I showed the thing to Williams, he liked it. I said, 'You must work on it, though, you're really a great writer, and

* The subplot about Aunt Rose in *Baby Doll* derives from *The Unsatisfactory Supper,* a short play in which Aunt Rose fails to please Archie Lee with her cooking. Archie Lee and Baby Doll, in *The Unsatisfactory Supper,* are called the Bowmans.

I'm just a constructionist — or trying to be.' And he said he would but he never did much. He was writing another play at the time [*Sweet Bird of Youth*], and he would suddenly write a few scenes and send them to me with a note, 'Insert somewhere.' Some I used and some I didn't; he didn't seem to care. Finally, I was desperate, because I had no ending to it. I had got Warner Brothers to finance it, everything was set up, and I said: 'Tennessee, we have no ending!' He said: 'Well, I promise you I'll work on it.' So I said: 'Well, I haven't got much time now, you'll have to come South with us [for the filming in Benoit, Mississippi].' "

Kazan and his cast and crew were to arrive in Mississippi in December, and to be in a Brooklyn studio for interior filming in early February. Before that, however, Williams said he had to be in Miami, at the Coconut Grove Playhouse. Tallulah Bankhead — for whom he had originally written Myra in *Battle of Angels* and Blanche in *Streetcar* — was at last going to play the latter for three weeks before moving north for a two-week run in New York at the City Center.

At once, an electric tension crackled among Williams's loyal friends. Maria Britneva was visiting from England, and Bankhead, unaccountably, resented her. Donald Windham's friend Sandy Campbell noted at the time, "Tenn is licking his lips with the prospect of an encounter between Bankhead and her." There might well be seeds of a play here, after all; he did what he could to encourage the animosity — one way being to add still more women to his coterie.

Soon Marion Vaccaro arrived — "a sad, lost lady" by this time, as Bigelow described her — a friendly soul whose surname Williams had borrowed for the vengeful neighbor in *Baby Doll*. Next day, Lilla van Saher swept in. Euripides himself, in *The Trojan Women*, or Shakespeare at the opening of *Macbeth*, or Goethe describing a *Walpurgisnacht*, could not have assembled a team more ready for what Jane Bowles called an exercise in feminine wiles. What was crucial for Williams's purpose, as he relished the social tension from the sidelines, was that all these ladies adored him, but none of them liked each other. Physical combat was just barely avoided; mutually hurt feelings, tears, inebriate rages, were not. Only Williams escaped unscathed as this grotesque gavotte was danced around him. "I don't know what Tennessee gets from the Monster Women," Gore Vidal wrote later, "but if they give him solace nothing else matters. Certainly he has a huge appetite for the grotesque not only in art but in life." Jane Smith agreed: "He would allow and slightly gear things to a little drama offstage and then sit back and watch it, [but] his taste was not always reliable — about a number of things, and surprisingly enough, not always about people."

The finale of this brief winter scenario occurred, appropriately, backstage, late in January in Coconut Grove: "After the show last night," Sandy Campbell wrote in a memoir, "Tenn went in to B[ankhead]'s dressing room, got down on his knees, put his head in her lap and said, 'Tallulah, this is the way I imagined the part when I wrote the play.'" But at a party later that evening he told Jean Dalrymple, producer for the imminent move to New York, that if Bankhead "continued to give such an appalling performance he would not allow the play to open in New York. She was 'playing it for vaudeville and ruining my play.'" A reporter from a national magazine was nearby, his remark was published the following week, and a great classical repentance scene had to be enacted in New York (also for the benefit of the press) to soothe the burnt ego of Bankhead and to restore Williams to her favor. The revival of *A Streetcar Named Desire,* alas, was not well received, for Bankhead's fans disrupted her performance with atrocious displays of ill manners. There is no record of the reaction to this theatrical failure by the other ladies in Williams's social circle, but one may perhaps imagine.

While these intrigues continued, Kazan had more important concerns for Williams: he needed him on location for *Baby Doll.*

"He had a dread of going to [Mississippi]," Kazan recalled. "He said: 'Those people chased me out of there. I left the South because of their attitude towards me. They don't approve of homosexuals, and I don't want to be insulted. I don't want my feelings hurt.'" Finally Williams agreed to come, but after several days he announced that he was leaving: "'I can't find a swimming pool.' So I [Kazan] said: 'God damn it, I need an ending to this film! You can't use the excuse of a swimming pool to leave, Tennessee. You're leaving me in the lurch!' . . . The next thing that happened was typical of him — after he's done something bad like that, he does something brilliant. In a couple of days he sent me an ending, which I thought was wonderful."

But his swift departure was not only to escape an unpleasant memory of social ostracism (real or imagined), or the sudden snap of subfreezing weather in Mississippi. Early in January, George Keathley, founding director of a theatre in Coral Gables called the Studio M Playhouse, had asked Williams if there were a new play available for him to produce and direct. Williams sent a very short one-act play, *The Enemy: Time,* about the young gigolo to a retired movie queen. He returns to his hometown, only to learn from his former girlfriend that she had to be sterilized after she contracted venereal disease from him. He is savagely beaten by her brother at the end. Williams returned to Coral Gables from Benoit to meet with Keathley about an April production for what was becoming the first extended draft of (and was now titled) *Sweet Bird of Youth*.

"I found Tennessee Williams in good form in February," Keathley recalled years later. "He was very shy, and he seemed to be drinking too much, but he was full of brilliant ideas and charm. We cast the play and set an opening date without any trouble. He took a room at a hotel in Miami, and he came with new or revised scenes daily. Then we went to the house in Key West, where he continued to work before rehearsals were scheduled."

In Key West, however, Keathley saw that the relationship between Williams and Merlo was indeed — as Merlo had told Audrey — passing through some kind of crisis. "They were having troubles. Once, Tennessee turned to Frank after reading a new scene aloud and asked, 'Do you like it, Frankie?' — 'No, I don't!' — 'Why not?' — 'I don't know, I just don't!' — 'But why *not*? What's wrong with it?' — 'Don't ask me, I'm not your goddamned yes-man!' And with that Frank ran into another room, packed his bags and took off for a few days. There must have been some prelude to all this that I never saw. But after this they separated more and more."

Several days later, about the first of March 1956, Williams suggested to Keathley that they move back to Miami. From this point, Williams in fact spent less time in Key West, "and Merlo held the fort during his absence, entertaining a wide circle of friends," as one of them wrote. In his room at The Towers Hotel, Williams revised his lyric "A Separate Poem," which expressed the sadness over what he clearly recognized as an unbreachable distance that had finally come between himself and Frank:

> Oh, yes, we've lost our island . . .
> Our travels ranged wide of our island but nowhere nearly so far
> as our silence now enters the bare and mountainous country
> of what cannot be spoken.
> When we speak to each other
> we speak of things that mean nothing of what we meant
> to each other . . . a storm of things unspoken . . .

None of their friends was entirely surprised by the gradual separation between the two men. Williams's life had become increasingly affluent, increasingly restless, increasingly full of demands, while at the same time Merlo longed for permanence, for the quiet life. Now money made possible the quick, worldwide acquisition of anything Williams wanted: servants were available at home and abroad; various diversions could be arranged, and various means of pleasure, both chemical and human. The plain fact was that Merlo's usefulness had become obsolete — an unpleasant truth, but a truth Williams admitted to himself and to a few friends. It was one of the reasons he had traveled more. But an easy separation was not ahead for them; a decade of devotion could not be quickly reduced to insignificance. They were both sad, but they could not discuss that sadness. So when they went south they parted, and pretended it was more convenient, while in New York Merlo ordinarily accompanied Williams and socialized with the same crowd. All who knew Williams loved and respected Merlo, now as before.

"During rehearsals for *Sweet Bird of Youth* in March," according to Keathley, "Williams joined us every afternoon following his work and swim. He often spoke of his sister Rose — 'Once she was violent, but now she's just tranquil.' " There was good reason for Rose to be especially in his mind that season. First, the character of the sterilized, abandoned girl in *The Enemy: Time* was originally named Rose (not Heavenly, as in the final script). Also, he had completed arrangements for her to return to Ossining after she had been living on a small farm, cared for by a Missouri couple, and after an interval at a private sanatorium in St. Louis.

The play opened at Studio M on April 16, with Margrit Wyler and Alan Mixon in the leading roles. Calling it a "work in progress," Williams told a reporter from the *New York Times* that it was "an examination of what is really corrupt in life." He apparently thought it was not too strong even for his mother, for Edwina accepted an invitation to attend. "She was a nonstop, talking Amanda," Keathley recalled, "just as he'd led me to expect." Two weeks later, Kazan and Audrey Wood and Cheryl Crawford made the trip, too, with Paul Bigelow and Maria Britneva.

At the same time, *Baby Doll* was ready for the months of editing prior to a winter premiere across the country.

The first version of *Sweet Bird of Youth* set a number of people on edge, with its story of a middle-aged woman who fills up empty hours with young lovers, vodka and a variety of drugs; the emphasis was squarely on the charm of a young lover. Proudest among Williams's coterie of women friends was the unshy Lilla van Saher, who claimed after opening night, "Curtain rises, and I am there, in bed with my trade! Is very clear a play about me!" Lilla's fantasy life was far more active than her rather conventional morals, in fact, but her vivid imagination endeared her all the more to Williams.

The truth is that the inspiration for the leading character was Tallulah Bankhead. The revisions Williams offered Keathley in February and March reflected what Williams learned from Bankhead herself, from her servants and from the press. In 1951, for example, Bankhead had charged her former secretary Evyleen R. Cronyn (then fifty-eight) with stealing more than four thousand dollars from her by forging checks. Cronyn claimed that on the contrary she was ordered to buy drugs, liquor and male prostitutes for Bankhead, but that the actress was in such a drunken condition that she could not sign her own checks and in all innocence Cronyn did. "Of course I drink," countered Bankhead, "but nobody has to forge my checks to buy liquor. And if I had been getting dope, do you think I'd pay for it by *check?* And Gods knows I never had to *buy* sex!"

To this Williams could add a real empathy, for these habits were quite plain in his own life; it is this congruence that gives the character of the "Princess" (as she calls herself) a special poignance. The gigolo remains an empty beauty.

Throughout the late spring and summer of 1956, Williams's emotional crisis deepened. "The Williamses have suffered from nerves for generations," he told Sandy Campbell. "My father was an alcoholic, and I am a semi-one. I drink more lately." He admitted the same in a letter to Cheryl Crawford in May: he was drinking far too much, as an escape mechanism due to a diffuse anxiety attack. Did she think he should stay in New York to confront the problem once and for all — at last — in medical and psychological treatment? He did not wait for a reply, but passed quickly through New York and left alone for Rome, where he pursued the usual summer wanderings — for some of which he was joined by Marion Vaccaro. Merlo again remained in Key West.

On August 3 he wrote to Cheryl, complaining that he could sleep only an hour or two each night and was on the verge of a complete breakdown. His only ray of light was Anna Magnani's agreement to come to

Broadway at last for the revised *Battle of Angels, Orpheus Descending.* Merlo, he concluded, did not care about him any longer, and he had asked friends to find him a separate apartment — something he would never do on his own. He and Merlo would be separated more often now, he wrote, until they had a clear sense of the pain they were causing each other.

What he did not mention in the letter to Cheryl — but which other friends saw — was that Williams's reliance on alcohol and pills only exacerbated his paranoia, which was centered in the conviction that no one cared for him, that everyone wanted him dead, and that everyone else was addicted to drugs.*

"I had heard about a paranoid personality," Maureen Stapleton reflected sympathetically years later, "but I never really knew what it meant until I saw it in Tennessee in the 1950s. He would accuse Frank of something — in Frank's presence and mine — and Frank would prove Tenn wrong. But even then Tenn, while laughing at himself over it, wouldn't believe him. Once Tenn found a used hypodermic in Florida. Now Frank was not in the remotest way a drug-user. But Tenn got it into his mind that Frank was self-injecting drugs. Frank reminded him that some time earlier a doctor had come to give him an antibiotic, and had arranged for vitamin shots to be given later. One of the needles had fallen under the bed. Tenn was not taking drugs intravenously [yet]. It was a simple mistake. But he got it into his head, and the accusation [against Frank] stuck."

In September, Williams was back in New York. All his business he conducted from a subleased apartment high above East 36th Street, since Frank was staying at East 58th. Soon the playwright met with his agent and learned that Magnani refused to appear in *Orpheus Descending* for more than two months because of her fear of English; the producers, logically, turned again to Maureen Stapleton as a replacement. (Ironically, the play ran exactly two months.)

On November 17, *Cat on a Hot Tin Roof* ended a twenty-month run after its six hundred and ninety-fourth performance. National and international companies opened very soon after, and a filmscript was in progress.

But four days after *Cat* closed, an important revival began at the City

---

* In the original typescript of *Memoirs,* Williams wrote that from the summer of 1955, in fact, he wrote only under the influence of artificial stimulants.

Center, one much more favorably received than the *Streetcar* that brought Bankhead there earlier. Helen Hayes charmed audiences and critics in a limited run of *The Glass Menagerie,* and a curious development occurred with the praise that attended this production. The prevalent critical opinion was that this was the kind of play that Williams should continue to write, and that the grotesqueries of *Camino Real* and *Cat on a Hot Tin Roof* — and the rumors about *Baby Doll, Sweet Bird of Youth* and *Orpheus Descending* — were not nearly so satisfying as the values of *The Glass Menagerie.* This assessment was put forth most plainly by none other than Brooks Atkinson, who wrote in the *New York Times,* "Although Mr. Williams has written some overwhelming dramas since 1945, he has not written anything so delicate and perceptive. . . . To see it again is to see how much he has changed." He was joined by other influential colleagues, among them John Chapman, who called *The Glass Menagerie* "Tennessee Williams's finest play . . . [an] affectionate, compassionate and poetic nocturne."

This praise might have worked only in the play's favor, and in Williams's, had not the newspapers been at the same time beginning to report the imminent release of *Baby Doll* — and the emotion-charged meetings among Warner Brothers, the director, theatre owners, reviewers and self-appointed arbiters of public taste and morality.

For the final print of the film, Kazan had agreed to a number of excisions demanded by the Motion Picture Code, which finally approved the film for national and international release. Clear implications of sadomasochism, of madness, and of the awakening eroticism of a young virginal bride were considerably modulated. Code administrator Joseph Breen's requests were satisfied — including the alteration of a scene in which Karl Malden angrily breaks into the bathroom while Carroll Baker languished in the tub. Also tempered was Malden's general appearance as the husband who waits none too patiently for the day his wife has promised to consummate their marriage, as well as a scene in which Eli Wallach pets Baker's legs as she rides a swing and gazes at him with a look that Breen called "orgiastic."

The premiere of the suggestive but essentially comic film was scheduled for the evening of December 18. Two artists had been commissioned to paint Carroll Baker's picture on a block-long billboard over Times Square — an outsize, characterisically 1956 advertisement with eighty-foot limbs and ten-foot eyebrows. Although both the Code and the New York State Board of Censors approved the film, most family and organized religious groups did not. Typical of the thousands of letters sent to Warner Brothers within a month was one from California — "Clean up your productions or cross a family of five off your list of moviegoers!" Warners' archives remain full of similar letters — and those from more confused patrons, like a New York woman who wrote condemning the new film and simultaneously converting it into an Irish epic: "No decent Catholic boy or girl would want to see *Baby Doyle,* a picture underlying Christian morals!"

It was, unfortunately, the ecclesiastical voice of New York that gave the film a national importance: the Legion of Decency, a New York–based group of moral vigilantes, on November 27 gave the film a "C" rating, condemning it and de facto refusing most Roman Catholics permission to see the film. With that, Francis Cardinal Spellman stepped to the pulpit of St. Patrick's Cathedral and (without, of course, having seen the film for himself) condemned it as "revolting . . . a contemptuous defiance of the natural law . . . immoral and corrupting . . . evil in concept. I exhort Catholic people from patronizing this film under pain of sin. . . . Since these degrading and immoral pictures stimulate immorality and crime they must be condemned. It has been suggested that this action on my part will induce many people to view this picture and thus make it a material success. If this be the case, it will be an indictment of those who defy God's law and contribute to corruption in America."*

"I disagree that *Baby Doll* is immoral," Kazan calmly replied when the press appeared at his door, "and I am outraged by the charge that it is unpatriotic. . . . Tennessee Williams and I have tried to see four small pitiable people with honesty and charity. . . . In this country judgments on matters of thought and taste are not handed down ironclad from an unchallengeable authority. People see for themselves and finally judge for themselves. That's as it should be. It's our tradition and our practice. In the court of public opinion I'll take my chances." And Williams told a reporter: "I can't believe that an ancient and august branch of the Christian faith is not larger in heart and mind than those who set themselves up as censors."

Just as Cardinal Spellman expected, the condemnation helped business. But two things are noteworthy about this holiday frenzy. First, the vast majority of critics in the secular press were equally outraged by what they considered the degrading, overt sexuality of the film, and its array of char-

---

* Cardinal Spellman had, to be sure, his secular brothers: *Time* magazine termed *Baby Doll* "possibly the dirtiest American-made motion picture."

acters so very different indeed from those of *The Glass Menagerie*. From every major newspaper and magazine in America came expressions of disgust and dismay. Williams was compared to himself, and they did not like his new style.

It should also be pointed out that Catholics, as well as many other moviegoers, generally made up their own minds, and most who defied a parochial edict found that *Baby Doll* might have been sensual in its implications, but was certainly nothing like pornography. In fact, it is quite an old-fashioned morality piece, in which violent sex (never presented in the film) and greed and opportunism are solidly denounced. The film is played for humanizing comedy — gentle, bawdy, and sad. "There is a sense in which I've always preferred *Baby Doll* to the film of *A Streetcar Named Desire*," Eliza Kazan said later. "It's more ambiguous. It combines passion with farce and tragedy and comedy, and I think it has a real humanity to it. It's not a large canvas, it's a miniature. To this day, it's hard to understand all that furor."

As the snow and the condemnations accumulated in New York, Williams remained in Key West, where he brought Edwina — apparently, as he implied in letters to friends, so that he would not have to confront alone his deteriorating relationship with Merlo. But if Merlo's presence made him uneasy, Edwina gave him a sick stomach, as he wrote to Cheryl Crawford: everything his mother said and every time she looked at him was a cause of guilt. He insisted that he still loved her, but he pitied her too, and she was driving him quite mad.

The "madness," of course, had quite another basis, and by January 5, 1957, he was able to admit (in a letter to Donald Windham) that he needed professional help, since he was tired of living with himself as he had so long been. "I am increasingly restless as I grow older," he told an interviewer at that time. "That's just the opposite of what it should be, isn't it?" But he summoned the courage to write final revisions for *Orpheus Descending*, drawing on his depressed spirit for the insertion of passages about frustration and a hope of purification. "I am an anxious, troubled person," he said that winter. "I can't write about anything I don't feel. . . . I wrote from my own tensions. For me, this is a form of therapy."

This form of therapy continued as he returned to New York for rehearsals. Harold Clurman had been chosen to direct, a choice difficult to understand since he was no avid partisan of Williams's method or vision.

(He had, for example, called *Camino Real* "a fallible minor work of a young artist of important talent.")

"Tenn and Clurman should've got along better than they did," according to Maureen Stapleton. "They hadn't worked together before, and there was just something in Harold's personality that didn't mix well with Tenn's." This polite tension did not help Williams's mood, and for a time Frank Merlo appeared on the scene, to help in any way that seemed appropriate. But not even he could change the fact that the play was in serious trouble.

"When we were rehearsing," Stapleton said, "everyone — producer, director, cast — knew the prologue was not working. I was delegated to tell this to Tennessee! So I went and told him that the whole thing had to be cut — not just part of it, as he thought. By this time we knew each other well enough that I could get away with this, or I neither could have nor would have tried! Tenn seemed a little set back by this news, but he just went away quietly, and next day he came to rehearsal and said, 'Maw [his invariable nickname for Stapleton, who in turned called him "Paw"] seems to think the prologue isn't working, and so I think we should cut it.' " This sort of authorial humility is — as Rebecca West wrote about male chastity — not ordinarily found in vulgar profusion. But Tennessee Williams ordinarily responded to suggestions from colleagues by rethinking and reworking his material. (It should be noted, however, that he reinstated the prologue for the published version of the play.)

On March 21, *Orpheus Descending* — with a program-epigraph from Hart Crane — opened at the Martin Beck Theatre, where once before Maureen Stapleton had brought so much to the success of a Williams play.* But not even her energy and talent were enough to please critics and audiences. With memories of Helen Hayes and *The Glass Menagerie,* and of the *Baby Doll* scandal, fresh in critics' and audiences' minds, the play's sharpened motifs of sexual frustration and spiritual search were not readily palatable. The reviews were only lukewarm when they were not plainly denunciatory. The play closed, after sixty-eight performances, on May 18.

Precisely at this time, Williams began to speak openly about his fear of failure. "My writing has followed a declining line since [*A Streetcar*

---

* Williams had hoped to have Brando in the role of Val Xavier. Brando did play the role in the film, but Cliff Robertson (replacing Robert Loggia in the Philadelphia previews) took the part to Broadway. Lois Smith, who had been Laura in the Helen Hayes *Glass Menagerie,* played the Cassandra figure, now called Carol in *Orpheus Descending.*

Named Desire]," he told the *New York Herald-Tribune* in a woefully inac-
curate self-description. "With *Orpheus Descending* I felt I was no longer
acceptable to the theatre public. Maybe, I thought, they'd had too much
of a certain dish, and maybe they don't want to eat any more." The
"dish" of course, was violence, derailed sexuality, and the submission of
mythology — in this case Orphic mythology — to his own dramatic
purpose.

Orpheus Descending's title suggests that classical resonance and intention. All the Orphic symbolism that was so diffuse in *Battle of Angels* was
intensified here, and this made the play more structurally satisfying but
not clearer, since Williams could not seem to decide whether he wanted
the play to be a story of concrete humans in a concrete situation, or a set
of modern constructs in a universe of archetypes. The play subjects religious to mythic motifs, too: Val's speech about the bird that never settles
on earth equates that bird with spiritual incorruptibility as well as wandering — and thus gives the wanderer almost a pilgrim sensibility. Lady
(renamed from *Battle*'s Myra) agrees that if there is a bird in perpetual
flight, then "God's made one perfect creature." (The image recalls *The
Roman Spring of Mrs. Stone,* when Karen asks Paolo, "Speaking of birds
. . . is it true that the rondini don't have legs and that is the reason they
stay in the air all the time?")

Also from the Orphic myth Williams drew the compelling image of
the wheel on which souls spin, entering alternately the light and the
darkness, death and life, until purified forever for a final transmigration
of souls: "You know," says Vee, the artist, one of the three women
whose sexual frustration at once focuses and destroys Val Xavier's life,
"we live in light and shadow — that's what we live in, a world of light
and shadow — and it's confusing." In 1957, no one found the world
more confusing than Tennessee Williams.

On Wednesday afternoon, March 27, still smarting from the barrage of
negative reviews, Williams was staying with Frank at 58th Street. A
thoughtless friend had left him a copy of that week's issue of *The New
Yorker,* so he could read the review of his play. "The people in it aren't
really terribly interesting," began Wolcott Gibbs. "I could see nothing
but purposeless ruin. . . . I don't believe that he has turned out a coherent
play, or that he was quite sure of what was on his own mind."

As if on theatrical cue, the telephone rang and Dakin Williams told
his brother that their father had suddenly died in Knoxville, at the age of
seventy-seven.

"He always told me over the years that for him his father had long been dead," according to Paul Bigelow. "There was nothing between them." But as so often in such cases of long-term estrangement, the emotions and reactions were more complicated at the time of death. Father and son had met only once or twice, and then by accident, in the last decade. By 1946, Edwina had been able to change her life with her husband, "and cut him out she did," as her son wrote long afterward:

"He had been in a hospital for recovery from a drunken spree. When he returned to the house, she refused to see him. My brother had returned from the latest war, and he would go back and forth between them, arranging a legal separation. I suspect it was not at all a thing my father wanted. But once more he exhibited a gallantry in his nature that I had not expected. He gave my mother the house and half of his stock in the International Shoe Company, although she was already well set up by my gift to her of half my earnings from *The Glass Menagerie*. He acquiesced without protest to the terms of the separation, and then he went back to Knoxville . . . to live with his spinster sister, our Aunt Ella. [But she] wasn't able to live with him, either, so after a while he moved into a hotel at a resort . . . and somehow or other he became involved with a widow from Toledo, Ohio, who became his late autumn love which lasted till the end of his life."

Frequently in his later years, Cornelius and the widow — who, according to Dakin, was a faithful drinking companion but very much a companion, too — flew down to Gulfport or Biloxi, where Cornelius and Edwina had once been happy. He died soon after one such visit.

In Knoxville, the elder Williams's family gathered for the services, and Dakin and Tom sat together for the first time in years. Edwina, unmoved and unmovable, remained in St. Louis.

Almost at once, Tennessee Williams's attitude and statements about his father shifted. "I have changed my feeling about him," he said soon after. "My father was a totally honest man. . . . He had a strong character and a sense of honor. He lived on his own terms which were hard terms for his family but he should not be judged as long as he remains the mystery that he is to us who lived in his shadow. Maybe I hated him, once, but I certainly don't anymore." Twenty years later he still bore the burden of that missed relationship: "In retrospect, I don't think he was that bad. I think he wanted to talk, too. . . . I feel a great affection for him now. He had a tragic life."

If ever people doubted that Tennessee Williams's expressions of compassion, forgiveness and understanding were authentic, they had only to consider his response to the death of his severe, enigmatic father, a man with whom such unhappy, frustrating memories were always associated, and with whom he never had any real communion.

Not long before his own death, he told of a moment after his father's funeral that may have begun the healing of memories that is forgiveness. "Aunt Ella . . . showed me a newspaper photograph of him outside a movie house where a film of mine, *Baby Doll,* was being shown. Along with the photograph of my father was his comment on the picture. What he said was: 'I think it's a very fine picture and I'm proud of my son.'"

His father's death caused him so much unexpected pain that all the usual ailments — hypochondria and a persecution complex — rushed over him with a new ferocity. "Tenn became a terrific hypochondriac that spring," according to Maureen Stapleton. "He thought he had every disease possible, and that he was always on the verge of death. If he'd ever been one-fifth as sick as he thought, he wouldn't have survived any single year of the 1950s. He tried to act very bravely with us during the short run of *Orpheus* — he was always trying to cheer us up, make us laugh when it was hard to laugh. He took us to dinner and was very generous with his time when it was clear to all who were close to him that he was going through a hell of a bad time. His paranoia could surface at the most unexpected times. More than once, we sat at a restaurant table and he would overhear someone nearby say something uncomplimentary — and invariably Tenn thought it was about him. And he'd be ready for a fistfight to defend an imaginary insult! He wasn't the subject of the remark — and he wasn't drunk or disoriented when he imagined all this, it was just his paranoia!"

By June 1957 he could no longer avoid his need for serious professional help, and on the advice of several colleagues he began intense psychotherapy — an hour daily, five times a week — with Dr. Lawrence S. Kubie, a strict Freudian analyst and author of the book *Neurotic Distortion of the Creative Process.* Kubie did not merely listen to Williams's outpourings, he tried to help with constructive advice on how to reassemble his fragmented life. In July the playwright mentioned that he had begun work on an original screenplay, *The Loss of a Teardrop Diamond,* but (according to Williams's description in *Memoirs* and elsewhere) Kubie urged him to put his writing aside for a time. Williams wrote that he was even more shocked when Kubie told him to consider a break with Merlo and to attempt a heterosexual life.

Whether Williams's memory can be relied on here is an open question. But according to Paul Bigelow, "At this point he could no longer take Kubie very seriously, and later, when he moved to another part of town, he changed analysts quite easily. He thought it was very chic to say, 'I'm going to see my shrink!'"

For the first summer since 1949, Williams sacrificed Europe and contented himself with visits to friends in and around New York. He made several trips to Ossining to visit Rose, and frequently he brought her to Manhattan for lunch and a movie or a day of sightseeing and shopping. His own crisis made him even more sensitive to the tragedy of his sister, and he redoubled his efforts to bring her some pleasure.

One day early that autumn, Lilla van Saher went with him to Ossining and, after their visit with Rose, she went back to the car so that he might have a few moments alone with his sister and with a nurse-companion. Williams returned to the car clutching a crumpled ten-dollar bill. Rose had given him the money as he was leaving.

"Tom," she had whispered, "I know how hard you are working at the shoe warehouse. I know you want to be a poet, and I believe in you. I have been saving some change for you, and I hope this will help things to be a little easier. If you will just be patient, I know good things will be ahead. Always remember I believe in you."

He looked at the bill in his hand, and then at Lilla. She started the engine and drove away from Stony Lodge, allowing her friend the privacy of his tears.

Chapter Seven

THE HEALING
OF MEMORIES
(1958–1962)

I know it's a hideous story but it's a true
story of our time and the world we live in.

—Catharine Holly, in *Suddenly Last Summer*

FOR OVER A YEAR beginning in mid-1957, Tennessee Williams underwent intense psychotherapy. And during the summer and autumn of that same year he visited his sister Rose with a frequency that astonished even the administrators of Stony Lodge. The connection between these two activities would not become evident to others until he had completed the play that, in spite of Dr. Kubie's advice, he drew from himself that season — his painfully autobiographical *Suddenly Last Summer*. "I think if this analysis works," he said as the year drew to a close, "it will open some doors for me. If I am no longer disturbed myself, I will deal less with disturbed people and with violent material. . . . It would be good if I could write with serenity."

The doors were indeed opened, but the resulting material was more violent than ever. Williams could not write "with serenity" — not only because his inner life was in turmoil, and undergoing severe scrutiny, but because had he then imposed a blanket of calmness over his writing, he would have been untrue to himself and to precisely what he had to bring to the American theatre. As Harold Clurman wrote that year, some of the greatest literature in the history of the world, "Sophocles, Euripides, Shakespeare, Strindberg, Dostoevsky, etc. — has been far more violent [than Williams]. . . . If critics cannot tolerate unpleasant subjects in contemporary plays, they should disqualify themselves as critics; and if an author feels obliged constantly to apologize . . . he must despair of maturing."

Williams had hoped, at the beginning of his therapy, to conform to the prevailing theatrical and cultural coziness of 1958; but the play that came from him was neither safe nor easy, nor would it be for his audience.

Suddenly Last Summer, written quickly, in something like a confused trance of guilt and remorse, was the most creative result of his psychoanalysis. With his doctor he felt confined and restricted; in the study at the new apartment on East 65th Street, he produced a confessional drama that dealt with his demons not by avoiding them, not by reducing that guilt to insignificance or by denying it, but by *asserting* that guilt and working through it: confession to begin the healing process. His doctor apparently disapproved; audiences, ever since the premiere that winter, were unable to avoid the seriousness of what Williams insisted was a moral fable for our time, drawn from his own history.

In its final version, all the dialogue of *Suddenly Last Summer* prepares for Catharine Holly's final speech. Violet Venable, the mother of her dead cousin Sebastian, attempts to bribe Catharine's mother and brother into having the girl lobotomized. She wants this operation performed because of Catharine's monstrous claims, about which we are fully told at the conclusion: last summer, Sebastian was devoured by urchins in Spain who had (it is implied) sexually prostituted themselves for him.

When he brought his mother to New York late that autumn, rehearsals for the play were in progress. In *Suddenly Last Summer* the formidable Mrs. Violet Venable (surely the most malignant archetype of the Terrible Mother in the Williams canon) seeks to silence her niece by brain surgery, if need be; seeks to "cut that horrible story out of her brain" — just, Williams felt, as Edwina Williams wanted the awful ravings of her daughter Rose cut from her brain in 1937. But Edwina was forever oblivious: "Why don't you write a lovely, long play again, Tom?" she asked repeatedly during her visit. "Like you did before — a lovely, lovely, long play," referring no doubt to *The Glass Menagerie,* of which she always saw herself as the indomitable heroine. What premiered in January 1958 was a profoundly unlovely short play, with the accidents of his life and of Rose's at its center.

By November the play was complete, and Audrey Wood suggested that it be performed on a double bill with a shorter work. He selected *Something Unspoken* as the other one-act play to be staged with it — a work written several years before, an ambiguous dialogue between two women who may or may not be (or have been) lovers but who are certainly bound to one another by a strange psychological dependence. The two works, under the collective title *Garden District* that described their New Orleans setting, would be presented in an off-Broadway theatre. As rehearsals began, Williams grew more and more uneasy: if the sex and violence in both *Baby Doll* and *Orpheus Descending* were rejected by critics and audiences, how would they respond to a play that contained two monologues about devouring flesh, two about seduction, one about lobotomy and a detailed description of sexual exploitation?

"Tennessee was absolutely terrified of this play," according to the actress Anne Meacham, who had several times played the first dramatic representation of Rose Williams, Laura in *The Glass Menagerie*. She was chosen to play Catharine Holly in the new play by the director Herbert Machiz, who had staged one of those early productions, and who knew her deftness at projecting fragility and strength.

"The play was so close to him that he wouldn't allow Audrey [Wood] to be at the casting or rehearsals, and he took a long time before he could show her the play," Meacham recalled. "Audrey was a mother to him in a way that Edwina never could be," and this may account for a hesitation that would otherwise seem inexplicable. In this play he accused himself of "devouring" others by buying sex and by paying for counterfeit emotion; just as he was the model for Sebastian Venable, so was Edwina the model for Sebastian's mother Violet.* Williams's emotional and psychological association with the maternal Audrey, therefore, caused him to delay submitting the text to her as long as possible. "He was so protective of it and frightened by it," Meacham said, "although I think he knew it was one of his best plays, and that in Catharine Holly he created one of the greatest roles ever written for an actress."

Throughout November and December there were daily meetings with the cast, with composer Ned Rorem and with set designer Robert Soule, who had to realize what Williams described in the published stage directions as "a fantastic garden which is more like a tropical jungle, or forest, in the prehistoric age of giant fern-forests when living creatures had flippers turning to limbs and scales to skin. The colors of this jungle-garden are violent.... There are massive tree-flowers that suggest organs of a body, torn out [the reference is to both Melville's devoured sea-turtles, described by Mrs. Venable, and to Sebastian's death, described by Catharine] ... there are harsh cries and sibilant hissings and thrashing sounds in the garden as if it were inhabited by beasts, serpents and birds, all of savage nature." The effect of the setting, Williams insisted, should mediate the core of the play, which postulates that within the genteel arti-

---

* "Venable" is an old form of the word "venal," and as late as the last century it meant both able to buy and able to corrupt, capable of being bribed, of unprincipled character, and associated with sordid and corrupt influences (*cf. Oxford English Dictionary*). And are Violet and Sebastian grotesque revisions of the twins Viola and Sebastian in *Twelfth Night?* Some have thought so: see Mary Lynn Johnson, "Williams' 'Suddenly Last Summer,' Scene One," *Explicator* 21 (April 1963), item 66.

fice of an apparently advanced civilization lie savagery and destruction: we live in a garden of our tending, a garden far from paradise in which we feed living things to living things, fruit-flies to Venus flytrap and one another to one another. Doctors can be bought, relatives bribed, attorneys compromised. The situations of the play are almost mythic. (The model for this grotesque garden was of course Muriel Bultman Francis's fantastic "Green Room" in the Garden District of New Orleans, which years before had so impressed him, and which he waited for years to recreate in this cathartic play.)

The network of autobiographical references is everywhere evident in *Suddenly Last Summer,* and the few friends and associates who knew of his and his family's private lives saw at once how clear the parallels were — most of all between Catharine's threatened operation and Rose's surgery, a connection suggested to him by his own sorry life in the 1950s: Sebastian Venable's pattern of exploitation was the pattern of his own: "Yes," says Catharine, "we all use each other and that's what we think of as love," and for Sebastian/Williams sexual exploitation had masqueraded as love, and had become a kind of human devouring. The final horror of "Desire and the Black Masseur" was at last narrated in the extreme: "We were going to blonds, blonds were next on the menu," Catharine says. "He was famished for blonds, he was fed up with the dark ones and was famished for blonds . . . that's how he talked about people, as if they were items on a menu. 'That one's delicious-looking, that one is appetizing,' or 'that one is *not* appetizing' — I think because he was really nearly half-starved from living on pills and salads."*

Williams made the connection between himself and Sebastian even clearer: they both had the habit of "popping little white pills" because of a "bad time with his heart . . . he had rheumatic fever and it affected a heart-valve . . . and [he] was frightened about it." And although Violet claims that Sebastian, like the author, "dreaded, abhorred false values that come from being publicly known, from fame, from personal exploitation," she admitted: "Time after time my son would let people go, dismiss them."

There is a brutal paradox that must be faced in coming to terms with the life and work of Tennessee Williams. On the one hand, of all American dramatists he is the one most deeply sensitive to the inequities, illu-

* On April 10, 1948, Williams had written to Donald Windham that after two months in Italy he was getting an appetite for northern blonds, since he was tired of the Romans who were mostly dark. See above, p. 147.

sions and potential exploitations in intimate relationships. In his plays he went deeply to the truth of love and its absence. Yet from his late twenties to the end of his life he pursued sex — for its own sake, as a quick, anonymous diversion — with a vigor recalling Casanova or a Byronic figure. Later, in *Small Craft Warnings,* he put a summary of this on the lips of Quentin, the aging homosexual writer: "The experiences are quick, and hard, and brutal, and the pattern of them is practically unchanging . . . like the jabbing of a hypodermic needle . . . more and more empty of real interest and surprise."

"The remarkable aspect of Tennessee Williams," Robert Anderson said, "is how he transmuted his anguished life into great plays. Wasn't it Faulkner who said that a writer needs experience, observation and imagination? Williams had them in abundance, and these qualities enabled him to turn his private pains into public art."

Nowhere was the art more confessional than in *Suddenly Last Summer,* in which Tennessee Williams gave as clear a perception of derailed creative energies and the abuse of love as any moralist could ever proclaim. Obsessed with what the play calls "the trails of debris" that he believed had characterized so much of his life in the 1940s and 1950s, he wrote a play that wept for the waste — most of all because he felt that he had abused the freedom of the creative life, and of life itself. He had squandered what had been denied to his sister. He always knew that the only thing that kept him from sharing Rose's fate was the hair's breadth of accident; they had, after all, both endured breakdown. According to the artist Vassilis Voglis, who had by this time known Williams socially for several years and would see him frequently to the end of his life, "He was devoted to Rose, but in a way she was an extension of himself. *He* could have had the lobotomy. *He* felt the outsider, marred in some way. He really cared for her, and perhaps he never really cared for anyone else in this life, ever. And I think he knew it."

Sebastian Venable's exploitation of others, his empty, decreative life, and his abuse of his cousin Catharine were for Williams the clearest portrait he could draw of his own remorse. The play is, then, both confession and act of penance. He perhaps misjudged his own best gifts and the healing effects of those gifts when he told the interviewer that he hoped to have done with violence, and to write with serenity. "*Suddenly Last Summer* is a play he would have liked to have back — as if he regretted writing it," said Joseph L. Mankiewicz, who directed a brilliant film of it the following year. "There is something not only of confession in the play, but of wish-fulfillment, too. Tennessee might have liked to have a garden with statues like Sebastian's, a study with paintings like Sebastian's. If he had a distaste for anything, it was for his own aging and his own humble background and circumstances. *Suddenly Last Summer* enabled him to have what he despised, in a way. And Mrs. Venable is certainly a composite of the women who defended and accompanied him all over the world."

Garden District opened in New York on Tuesday, January 7, 1958, at the off-Broadway York Playhouse on First Avenue. In the unpredictable nature of such things, the most influential critics surprised Williams (who later said he expected to be run out of town when *Suddenly Last Summer* was performed). Atkinson wrote that no other American playwright used "ordinary words with so much grace, allusiveness, sorcery and power. . . . *Suddenly Last Summer* is further evidence of Mr. Williams's genius." Walter Kerr agreed, calling it "a serious and accomplished work."

But even as favorable reviews were appearing, Williams prepared to leave New York. Although he had just moved to East 65th Street and was due daily at Dr. Kubie's office near by, he arranged for the rent and the doctor to be paid. Very likely in an effort to disconnect himself from the current of pain and tension which this play caused (right up to opening night, according to Anne Meacham, whom the reviewers all hailed), he went to Key West. Meantime, Audrey was concluding negotiations for a screen sale of *Orpheus Descending,* and she was trying to locate as collaborator for the screenplay a young writer who had impressed her and her client. Williams, for his part, was eager for sun and water in midwinter. By late March he was back in New York, calmer and apparently not so indulgent with alcohol and little white pills, and he told Audrey that a revision of *Sweet Bird of Youth* would be ready for Cheryl Crawford to consider. Before he departed for Europe, he formally ended his visits with Dr. Kubie.

At the same time, Random House published the text of William Inge's recent play, *The Dark at the Top of the Stairs,* which had opened on December 5, 1957. This was a revision of Inge's *Farther Off from Heaven,* which Williams had recommended to Margo Jones and to Audrey Wood; Inge and Wood now suggested that Williams write an introduction to the published version, since it was dedicated to him. He was lukewarm to this idea, however, since he said that he was entirely too occupied with his own plays and screenplay treatments. "Audrey," he told her, "it is one thing to type three words — 'For Tennessee Williams' — on a dedication page. It's quite another thing to write several pages of introduction."

But Audrey prevailed, and the text was submitted. It is one of the strangest pieces Williams ever wrote, best described as praising Inge with faint damns. He implies that Inge's life was a better drama than Inge would ever write.

The sudden emergence of a jealous, hostile streak toward Inge must be seen against the background of their respective fortunes in the 1950s. After *Farther Off from Heaven* in Dallas in 1947, Inge had his first New York success with *Come Back, Little Sheba,* which in 1950 ran for six months. But then in 1953, *Picnic* opened, ran for 477 performances, and won for Inge the Pulitzer Prize and New York Drama Critics Circle Award. The following month, *Camino Real* opened and failed, after only sixty performances.

At that time, Inge had invited his former champion to lunch. "Tennessee," he asked gently, "do you think you're blocked?" That was all Williams had to hear from a writer he still considered an apprentice. He replied that he would break through the block, as always; but later, in a classic transference, he wrote that his friendship with Inge began to cool at this time because "Bill's problem was one of pathological egocentricity: he could not take a spell of failures after his run of smash hits: so eventually he was cared for by two male nurses." But the fact is that in the 1950s Inge had an uninterrupted series of successes. On March 2, 1955 (three weeks before the premiere of *Cat on a Hot Tin Roof*), Inge's *Bus Stop* opened, directed by Harold Clurman. It ran for 478 performances. Although Williams's play won the Pulitzer and Drama Critics Circle Award, the quiet contest continued. Then virtually all friendly exchange between them was severed (until Inge's illness years later) when in 1957 *Orpheus Descending* (directed by Clurman) opened in March and ran eight weeks, while later that year *The Dark at the Top of the Stairs* (directed by Kazan) ran for 468 performances. In January 1958, in Key West, Williams said he hoped Inge would not win any awards for that play; in fact he did not.

"Williams was very jealous of Inge's success," according to Meade Roberts, who worked with Williams later that year on a screenplay. "He was, after all, Audrey's client, and Tennessee himself had introduced Inge to Audrey. Also, he thought that Inge wrote better dialogue than he did, that Inge had a true ear for American regional speech. He proudly said in public one day that 'Inge may be Audrey's gentleman playwright, but I prefer to remain her degenerate playwright.' " It may well have been this jealous attitude of which Williams was thinking when he told the press in 1958 that fame was agreeable, but that "it has poisoned my life."

From Rome that spring he heard of Cheryl Crawford's negotiation to produce *Sweet Bird of Youth;* this was facilitated by an advance sale of film rights to M-G-M, which amused Williams for years, since his former employer was buying the rights to his play even before it was played on Broadway. The letters to Cheryl continued throughout the summer, ending on September 14 with his reminder to her that he needed Kazan for director since this was certainly his last play. She must have smiled: *Cat on a Hot Tin Roof* and *Orpheus Descending* and *Suddenly Last Summer* were his "last plays" too.

During a brief stop in New York on his way to work in Key West, Williams was told how solid his financial condition was. The film of *Cat* had opened in August and was already the fifth largest grossing film in M-G-M's history. *Suddenly Last Summer* was a success in New York and London and a lucrative deal was struck with film producer Sam Spiegel. *Sweet Bird of Youth* had been sold in advance to M-G-M, and work was proceeding on a film of *Orpheus.* Williams was at the peak of his income and his fame. In the four-year period beginning in August 1958, Hollywood would buy seven of his plays, thus adding over four million dollars to his income. (Of the fifteen films based on plays by Tennessee Williams, he involved himself in the adaptation and script revisions of only seven — *The Glass Menagerie, A Streetcar Named Desire, The Rose Tattoo, Baby Doll, The Fugitive Kind, Suddenly Last Summer,* and *Boom!* He repeated, over the years, his keen dislike of all the films based on his work — with one exception, *The Roman Spring of Mrs. Stone.*)

The task that was to occupy him for at least the next several months of 1958 was the screenplay for one of them, *Orpheus Descending,* on which the collaborator was to be the young playwright Meade Roberts. Lilla van Saher, who had been introduced to Roberts through Gore Vidal, had brought Williams to a preview of Roberts's play *A Palm Tree in a Rose Garden* late in 1957. By June, Roberts had been hired to write the film treatment of *Orpheus,* and after working on this in Hollywood while Williams was in Europe, it was decided that they should collaborate in Miami that autumn.

Roberts returned briefly to New York before their reunion in Florida and by chance met Frank Merlo at a party given by mutual friends. "Tennessee doesn't believe how much I love him," Merlo said sadly. "He goes around saying I want him to die, that I only want his money." To this Roberts replied, "Frank, you know that's only Tenn's paranoia." Merlo repeated, "But he'll never believe I love him, never again."

During October, Roberts and Williams worked and the two kept Williams's coterie entertained.

"We didn't really discuss the collaboration very much," Roberts recalled. "I had written part of it in Hollywood and part in New York, and Tennessee wrote some scenes which we exchanged in the mail. Finally in October, because he did not want to go to Key West while Frank was there, he told me to meet him at the Towers Hotel in Miami, near his friend Marion Black Vaccaro.

"The Towers was the only hotel in southern Florida without air-conditioning," Roberts continued, "without a pool and without an address, which made it interesting for people to find us. The hotel simply listed itself as 'The Towers Hotel, Facing the Miami River.' But there is no Miami River — it was just a dried-up creek. There we were, in this huge establishment, which was quite empty. I had one wing all to myself, and Tennessee had another. When I asked why we were alone in this sprawling hotel when we could have stayed at the Robert Clay Hotel next door, where they had a pool and air-conditioning and an address, he said, 'Because the management is never astonished. . . .' "

The two worked separately each morning and then met at the Robert Clay pool, had lunch, and planned the afternoon and evening. "Late in the day or in the evening after dinner we read aloud to one another what we had written or rewritten. But we were not alone. The scenes were also heard by an audience of what can only be called extraordinary people — Lilla, Marion, a body-builder we knew only as Jack the Judo, and a mysterious, silent girl no one knew but who always joined us. We called her The Catatonic."

Often in the afternoons there would be excursions with this crew of admirers, to the Florida Seaquarium, to the Parrot Jungle — "and to the movies," as Roberts vividly remembered. "Tennessee loved the movies. Not only serious film artists Antonioni and Fellini and Visconti [whose work he had seen in Italy]. He loved old movies like *Hollywood Canteen* and *The Maltese Falcon*. One evening we all trotted off to see *Gigi* at Loew's Coral Gables. Fortunately, I had seen the movie earlier, because with Tennessee it was something of a riotous scene. First, he supplied himself and everyone else with popcorn, Goober's candy, Good-and-Plenty — whatever anyone wanted. He was in great humor. Then we'd settle into our balcony seats, and as soon as the film began Tennessee began a running satirical commentary. When [Louis] Jourdan made his first appearance in the film, Tennessee jumped up and shouted, 'I met you last year in Paris with Charles Boyer!' Then later, he decided that the movie was going on too long. He stopped munching popcorn, stood up and shook his fist at the screen — 'Actors! Actors! Pick up your cues!' We got hysterical of course, although the other patrons weren't so thrilled with our hysteria. And once, when he heard that the film of *Cat on a Hot Tin Roof* was playing — which he hated — he went downtown and said to the people on line for tickets, 'This movie will set the industry back fifty years! Go home!'

"We had many good times during those weeks," according to Roberts, "but Tennessee could be very paranoid too. He had just begun taking a combination of amphetamines and barbiturates [which produced alternating shifts in mood], and during the last days of our work together he had a strange attitude about himself, which was very divided. On the one hand he knew how important he and his work were, and he was angry and hurt that he had never received the Nobel Prize. And then within hours he would be convinced he was a terrible writer and a poor craftsman, and he was very insecure. At times like this, he would tell me that of course Inge was the better dialogue-writer, an opinion not widely shared."

In late November, Roberts returned to Hollywood to complete the script. (Eventually, after arguments with the producers, Williams settled on the title for this screen version of *Battle of Angels/Orpheus Descending:* he went back to his 1937 play and called it *The Fugitive Kind.*)

At the same time, in a rush of activity partly induced by drugs, he completed another draft of *Sweet Bird of Youth,* with greater emphasis in the opening scenes on the actress's use of hashish, marijuana, vodka, pills and sex; he also drafted the first version of a strangely ambiguous marital comedy, *Period of Adjustment.* By the end of December he was assisting with rehearsals on the latter at the Coconut Grove Theatre. In a letter to Cheryl Crawford, he wrote that it was not his best work by any standard, but that it was an honest appraisal of how he saw intimate relations; he added that his motive was to earn money for Rose's care.* He may also have had his mother in mind, for at Christmas he brought her to Miami, where he noticed a sudden deterioration in her mental state that sug-

---

* Once again — and beyond any link with reality — Williams gave the impression that his financial situation was precarious. Meade Roberts recalled that once, in a Miami bookshop, Williams had decided to purchase a limited edition of Van Gogh's letters to his brother. But when he was told that the book cost fifty dollars, Williams reneged, saying, "I can't afford it."

gested incipient senility, and that would demand her transfer to a senior citizen center where she could receive care and attention. She complained to him that season that a rocket from Cape Canaveral had fallen in the yard, and that she had to comb radioactive fallout from her hair. This first amused, then annoyed, finally upset him. For the most part, Edwina was lucid — and as sweetly tyrannical as ever — but there were occasional lapses into unreality. In St. Louis, Dakin continued to be devoted and attentive to her.

Barbara Baxley, who rejoined Williams to play in *Period of Adjustment,* remembered that during the opening night celebration on December 29, Edwina "couldn't stop telling Tennessee to stand up to greet a lady, to straighten his tie, to fix his coat, to use his napkin — as if he were five years old. She was, you might say, a very strong lady."

During the one-week run of the play (billed, like *Sweet Bird of Youth* in 1956, as "a work in progress"), Baxley recalled that Williams was a great help to actors. "In talking about [her character] Isabel, he could say a small thing that would illuminate the whole woman for me — and because he was a great actor as well as writer, he could play a bit of business for me, or for any of us, and any problem was solved. He and Bill Inge were the only playwrights I ever knew who could do that. They could act out the line for an actor, and then the whole sense of it became clear. But as solid as he was in this, he could be terribly insecure. Bill Inge visited us during that week, and he said to me, 'Barbara, Tenn is so insecure about his work and about actors. If he volunteers something, fine. But if you have a question, don't ask him outright — ask his assistant [i.e., the assistant director, Owen Phillips].'" But in spite of this counsel, Williams — who was directing the play himself for the early part of rehearsals — dealt smoothly with his cast.

With the new year 1959, Elia Kazan sent Williams a letter detailing those elements of the script of *Sweet Bird of Youth* which he thought needed special attention. "The relationship between Kazan and Williams," said Joseph L. Mankiewicz, who knew them both, "was a rare symbiotic relationship in the theatre. Williams's drafts were so rough as submitted, they had to be turned into workable, playable dramas for the stage. They had to be adjusted to specific dramatic requirements. Kazan did this. Tennessee gave him the softness, the malleable material of the work, and Kazan, like a truffle-dog, sniffed out the violence and brought it into the open. He peppered the work — sometimes, I think, over Tennessee's objections."

By early February, a cast had been selected. Kazan had recently seen

Geraldine Page perform the role of the faded model in *Separate Tables,* and he recommended her for the role of Alexandra del Lago (the "Princess Kosmonopolis," as she calls herself when traveling incognito); for her gigolo, the aptly named Chance Wayne, they chose Paul Newman, who had first appeared in *Picnic* and later in *The Desperate Hours.*

Rehearsals were full of strain and tension, as Williams wrote to Donald Windham. Williams was again convinced that this was his last play, that he was now — for certain — a dying man. "But he was always going to die the following week," Kazan remembered. "He was always very fair to me during rehearsals, however, whatever his personal complaints. He was as fine to work with as he had been on the other plays. He was never difficult, never falsely critical, always generous. He worked every day, he brought in new material for rehearsals every afternoon. He was really an adorable man to work with, and I loved and respected him enormously." The cast recognized that the respect was mutual: "Kazan was a wonderful influence on Williams," according to Geradine Page. "He worked so hard with him."

After a preview-run in Philadelphia, the play opened on March 10, 1959 at the Martin Beck Theatre in New York. (Williams was paid $400,000 for the film rights, plus a percentage of profits to come, and at once the box office drew almost $15,000 daily in ticket sales — of which he received ten percent.) Audiences found that the play contained Williams's strongest material: drug addiction, alcoholism and male prostitution, venereal disease, racism and castration.

A few critics responded favorably. Atkinson called the material "acrid," but felt that Williams was "in a relaxed mood as a writer." But the majority unleashed a storm of negative comments. Robert Brustein called it "disturbingly bad — aimless, dishonest and crudely melodramatic, [full of] hazy notions about Sex, Youth, Time, Corruption. . . . [It] contains the author's most disappointing writing since *Battle of Angels.*" Contrasting him with Strindberg, Brustein added that the Williams nightmare "does not penetrate to a deeper subjective reality [and is full of] fraudulent conflict." And Harold Clurman felt that Williams had "become immobilized in his ideology." He was joined by John Chapman, who emphasized Williams's strength but feared that he was essentially a "dirty minded dramatist who has been losing hope for the human race [and] has written of moral and physical decadence as shockingly as he can." *Time* magazine damned it and the few favorable reviews, calling the play "very close to parody," and three Williams partisans issued alarms:

Walter Kerr felt that Williams was capable of writing real tragic drama "but [was] not yet ready to reach for it"; Kenneth Tynan said everything about *Sweet Bird* "dismayed and alarmed" him; and even John Gassner lamented the sense of tragic isolation and a "sensational expression of his most nihilistic mood. . . . Williams ought to become more serious about the convention of tragedy itself." But audiences responded to its boldness in portraying the fading movie queen Alexandra del Lago; her young gigolo Chance Wayne; his former sweetheart Heavenly Finley; and her father, the hypocrite Boss Finley — all caught in a sordid net of corruption. The play ran almost a year, for 383 performances.

Considered later, as part of Williams's complex late development, *Sweet Bird of Youth* might be regarded as the best example of an earnestness of continued confession (drug-abuse, paying for sex, the fear of professional decline) unharnessed by a sufficiency of esthetic control. Kazan and Williams admitted that the play is essentially two separate works: out of the original Florida production came acts one and three, with the insertion of the Chance Wayne episodes in act two. Too often the characters are the author's mouthpieces, speaking not from their own inner logic and wholeness, but out of the author's own anger and frustration, with an inappropriately poetic reflectiveness. The Heckler, for example, present in one scene only to cause a political stir, suddenly says: "I believe that the silence of God, the absolute speechlessness of Him, is a long, long and awful thing that the whole world is lost because of. I think it's yet to be broken to any man. . . ."

This intrusion of the authorial voice into a character continues right through to the awkward curtain line, in which Chance Wayne addresses the audience: "I don't ask for your pity, but just for your understanding — not even that, no. Just for your recognition of me in you, and the enemy, time, in us all."* This is surely the single most jarring interruption of dramatic structure in Williams's work. As a rather presumptuous coda (permissible in a Mozart opera, but difficult to sustain in a modern-dress play), it suggests that in fact Williams may well have had in mind Billy Wilder's classic story of Hollywood madness, *Sunset Boulevard*. *Sweet Bird* has astonishing parallels with that motion picture, which Williams had seen in a preview screening in 1950, later telling friends like Meade Roberts that he found it shattering and "wonderfully awful."

---

* Cf. *The Roman Spring of Mrs. Stone:* "The opposite force had been time, time the imponderable, not moving amicably with her but treacherously against her, and finally meeting her and arresting her in mid-flight with a shattering crash."

Within the year, even the academic critics were joining the reviewers in a growing weariness against what they considered his shock tactics. In an important essay published in the *Tulane Drama Review,* Henry Popkin wrote: "Williams now seems to be in a sort of race with himself, surpassing homosexuality with cannibalism, cannibalism with castration, devising new and greater shocks in each succeeding play. It is as if he is trying to see how far he can push the Gothic mode of playwriting."

On opening night, the audience cheered wildly, there were many curtain calls, and Williams went to the stage. Clearly the public was fascinated by the latest of Williams's fading, fierce women and her dangerously appealing man. Alexandra del Lago and Chance Wayne joined their dramatic antecedents — Blanche and Stanley; Myra/Lady and Val; Serafina and Alvaro; Mrs. Stone and Paolo.

Later in the evening, however, Williams was terribly depressed. "He was wretchedly nervous and much changed," Kazan remembered, "and after the opening he wouldn't let John Steinbeck or me into his house. Despite the wonderful performances and some important good notices, he felt he and the play were a failure, and so he went into hiding — he didn't want any social intercourse. He wouldn't see Steinbeck, who had been a real admirer for years and wanted to let Tennessee know that."

Williams left at once for Miami and the Towers Hotel, and took Marion Vaccaro with him to Key West. From there, they went to Havana, for since Fidel Castro had come down from his retreat in the Sierra Maestre Mountains and had taken power on January 1, 1959, Tennessee had wanted to meet him. "He told me during several telephone conversations we had, from Miami to Hollywood, that he had a great crush on Castro," Meade Roberts remembered. "He invited me to come along with him, but I said, '*You* go! If *you're* kidnapped, MCA [the agency with which Audrey Wood was then associated] will ransom you — you're Tennessee Williams. *I'm* Meade Roberts: Ashley-Steiner [his agents] won't ransom *me!*" Williams's desire to meet Castro was more than fervent, Roberts remembered: "In fact he wanted to be *kidnapped* by Castro and Ché Guevara even while the two were still outlawed and hiding in the Sierra Maestre, kidnapping Americans for ransom. Tennessee thought very seriously about getting himself into a situation like that — *anything* to meet Castro."

And so Williams and Marion Vaccaro, whom Roberts remembered as a "wonderfully warm, supportive and tragic woman, the prototype of

Cora in his story 'Two on a Party' " — made their second trip to Havana; they had gone briefly for Marion's fifty-third birthday on January 17, just after Castro's victory. Castro, as it turned out, had once entertained theatrical ambitions, and even took a nonspeaking part in a Mexican film; he was pleased to meet the playwright he called "that cat" (presumably identifying author and play). There is no record of his reaction to Marion Vaccaro, and it is likely that neither she nor Williams informed Castro about her husband: Regis Vaccaro had been a major executive with an American fruit company long accused of monopolozing the Latin American banana industry.

Williams and Castro — an intelligent, well-read, reflective host — talked of the theatre and movies, and Williams mentioned that Jerry Wald, the independent producer for Twentieth Century–Fox, was considering a film about Castro's life that would star Marlon Brando. "I was in Jerry Wald's office some time later," according to Meade Roberts, "and he phoned Castro, who was on a brief American tour. 'I'm here with the fella who's written Marlon's next movie,' Jerry said to Castro about me, 'and we can get Brando right after that to play *you!*' Politics intervened, however, and of course the project never got very far."

For years Williams praised Castro's gentlemanliness and charm, though he seems to have known about the capture and execution of political enemies. According to several friends, Williams even attended public political executions in Havana during one of his visits that year. To no one's surprise, Williams never admitted this publicly. For such a gentle soul to have endured this spectacle, he would perhaps have had to be in an atypical condition — under the influence of drugs, for example. Since pills were a regular part of his life at this time, it would explain conduct at variance with his normally gentle, nonviolent character. (He did, however, like bullfights and frequently dragged Marion Vaccaro to them in Spain, where he chided her for getting sick at the sight.)

But meetings with Castro were not the only activity of the Cuban excursion. Williams and Marion also went to a male brothel, where (Williams later told Roberts) they took adjoining rooms and later compared the avidity of their exploits.

By the end of May, Williams and Vaccaro had passed several weeks with Merlo in Key West; then they returned to Miami, flew to London for the British premiere of *Orpheus Descending,* and visited friends. By the time Williams returned to New York, in early June, Frank had reopened the apartment on East 65th Street, where he was needed — he was, after all, still on salary for practical duties — while Williams attended rehearsals of *The Fugitive Kind*.

"An odd situation prevailed by this time," according to Meade Roberts. "My play *Maidens and Mistresses* had opened off-Broadway, and Tennessee's attitude began to change. I think he thought of me as a competitor, the way he spoke of Bill Inge. One day he said to Sidney Lumet [the film's director], 'We can't have two writers sharing the limelight on this production.' He seemed to resent me being at the rehearsals, even though both he and Sidney had specifically wanted some on-the-spot rewrites."

But the rehearsals — held in the Palladium Ballroom on Broadway — were a tense time for everyone. During the first two weeks of June, Anna Magnani (who agreed to play in the film version of the play written for her), eager to work with Marlon Brando, now found herself in a strained relationship with him.

"There we were, in this dance hall," recalled Maureen Stapleton, who had played Magnani's role on the stage and had, with her typical breadth of spirit, agreed to take the lesser, supporting role of Vee Talbot in the film. "Marlon and Anna were there, and Joanne Woodward, Tennessee and Frankie, Sidney Lumet and Meade Roberts. The first week, Marlon and Anna and Joanne rehearsed alone. The second week, the rest of us were called in. Marlon sat there, mumbling his lines in a barely audible whisper. Anna refused to reply. Joanne was unsure what was going on. I had known Marlon ever since our days in the Drama Workshop at the New School, in 1945, so I wasn't afraid to say something to him.

"Finally, after we read our first scene and I couldn't hear anything being said, I said, 'I think I'm going deaf! You guys may be geniuses, but I have to hear what you're saying!' I was surprised Tenn didn't speak up and tell *them* to speak up. That night he and Frankie came over to my house, and I said, 'Tenn, you've got the muscle and the clout! Tell them what has to happen for this thing to work!' But he said, 'Oh, I'm just an old faggot to them.'"

This was, of course, far from the truth. Everyone on *The Fugitive Kind* had enormous respect for Williams and showed it, and Magnani, Brando, Woodward, Stapleton and Roberts were especially close to him and warmly supportive — and in spite of private differences, Merlo was ready to help Williams and certainly never wavered in his loyalty. But Williams had to hear what he wanted to hear — perhaps because of paranoia, but also to support his belief that he was an artistic and social outcast. He wrote of marginal people, after all — those with whom he could emotionally identify, whose pain and loneliness and spiritual isolation he had first known himself. Tennessee Williams had the energy, the vision, the pride and the tenacity that mark the life of every artist, and he perhaps unconsciously coveted the sense of being an outsider in order to see clearly what is the grotesquerie of so much on the inside.

"If artists are snobs," he wrote in the introduction to the second edition of Carson McCullers's *Reflections in a Golden Eye,* "it is much in the same humble way that lunatics are: not because they wish to be different and hope and believe that they are, but because they are forever painfully struck in the face with the inescapable fact of their difference which makes them hurt and lonely enough to want to undertake the vocation of artists . . . [with] a sense, an intuition, of an underlying dreadfulness in modern experience."

Rightly, he never believed in the enduring value of his wealth or of his celebrity or of a position as the controversial man of modern theatre over whom critics and academics argued. But he also realized that in the perverse nature of such things in our time, it was precisely his dramatic insistence on being different that made him newsworthy and that guaranteed him an audience for the deeper values his work sought to affirm. Like Sebastian Venable, "he dreaded, abhorred false values that come from being publicly known," but he always knew how to exploit the media, how and when to shock onstage and off. "He created his own dramatic world around him," as Meade Roberts said, "and he dealt with it when he could."

It was perhaps from this point in his life, when his importance as a dramatist was no longer unchallenged, when both he and America were on the verge of new, louder questions and a new violence, that Williams moved further into a distrust of colleagues, friends and self. And his concomitant reliance on drugs made him less appealing both to himself and others. What he might have meant was not "I'm just an old faggot to them," for in the matter of his sex life no one really cared very much; what was of truer consequence was that he might be, at forty-eight, so established in his visibility, so evident, so open and public about his art, his life, his loves and his antipathies, that his newsworthiness itself would soon be eclipsed by others. Less familiar, younger faces, and voices with new vocabularies would soon be heard — on television, most of all, but also in the theatre, where Harold Pinter and Edward Albee were about to be proclaimed prince regents.

Among those willing to take a longer view in 1959, there was no doubt that Tennessee Williams had given the world a collection of enduring and important stageworks — *The Glass Menagerie, A Streetcar Named Desire, Summer and Smoke, Cat on a Hot Tin Roof* and *Suddenly Last Summer.* But it was an age of anxiety eager for constant and instant diversion, a time of the sudden eruption of the cult of bigness as excellence. Spectacle and size were everything — in automobiles, in the size of television and movie screens, and in household and national budgets.

In such a culture, Williams had won his two Pulitzer Prizes. He worked at his craft, and often enough he jolted his audience. But he was a known presence — too well known — by 1959. Celebrity had made him a commodity, and the culture was entering a time of such worship of novelty that no one person could satisfy for long. He had been for fifteen years in the vanguard of his craft, and he was now considered by the arbiters of changing taste — a few critics, a few academics, a new generation of young, flashy producers — to have fallen behind, simply by virtue of having survived so long. "Not new, therefore not interesting" was becoming the standard. And perhaps most significant of all, there was an accumulation of alcohol and drugs in his mind and body that contributed to a physical, emotional and mental confusion and decline that would eventually take a dreadful toll, and that would forever deaden something rich and essential in his creative powers.

In early July, while the filming of *The Fugitive Kind* proceeded in a Bronx studio and in the town of Milton, New York, Williams attended the Chicago production of *Suddenly Last Summer.* The role of Catharine was taken by Diana Barrymore, then thirty-eight; she had, after a series of roles almost twenty years earlier, made six films, but then led a wandering, unhappy life controlled by alcohol. She had also desperately hoped, after a period in an asylum and after playing in a road-company production of *Cat on a Hot Tin Roof,* to make a Broadway comeback in *Sweet Bird of Youth.* Williams, however, correctly judged that her life was too close to the role, and that her fragile mental condition would not be right for the role of Alexandra. Why he approved the not less intense part of Catharine is not clear, but she was determined and he was sympathetic. Socially, they had spent a good deal of time together during the previous year in New York, and he arranged for her to meet the Chicago director. But unfortunately by this time Diana Barrymore had augmented her theatrical aspirations with the desire to become Mrs. Tennessee Williams.

"Poor, sad Diana," Paul Bigelow said. "She was another in Tenn's group of lost ladies. She saw in him a savior for herself, and she hoped to marry him. Like others, Diana imposed on him, but she was really invited to do so because Tenn saw her as a defeated soul in every way, very like himself [and in some ways like Rose]. And so he took her on, as a project. This of course turned out very badly, very savagely, with a good deal of mutual abuse."

The relationship between Williams and Barrymore was indeed unfortunate — "one of the oddest and sickest," according to the director George Keathley, who saw them together that summer. Barrymore not only kept pace with Williams's drinking and drug-taking; she also quietly procured for him, helped him to dress in drag for private parties and — as contrary as all these were to her stated hopes of marriage — she agreed with Dr. Kubie's earlier assertion that Williams might not be permanently homosexual, and to his conversion to heterosexuality she was passionately dedicated. How she thought she could effect this even as she played offstage Catharine Holly to his Sebastian Venable is difficult to understand.

For a week following the run of *Suddenly Last Summer,* she joined Williams and Marion Vaccaro for a trip to Havana, and shortly thereafter began a series of desperate telephone calls to Dakin Williams, telling him how she hoped to be his sister-in-law.

"She had become part of Tom's social life," Dakin recalled, "and had partied with him and Frank and Magnani and the others. She had followed him to Havana, and by late 1959 she was terribly unhappy over him. It was all very sad, for she was a warm and likable person." And Dakin's wife Joyce agreed: "She had a childlike appeal, and a real sweetness. But there had been so many disappointments in her life, and by this time she was ill and confused." Within a year, Diana Barrymore was found dead in her New York apartment at the age of thirty-nine, in strange and violent circumstances that were at the time reported as suicide.* (Whether she was in fact murdered is still an open question, however, among some who knew her and her friends, and who have studied the ambiguous police reports.)

On August 20, Williams and Merlo departed for a three-month vacation around the world. From Japan, Williams wrote a sad letter to

---

* At the time of Barrymore's death, Williams was in fact writing a new play especially for her. Called *Poem for Two,* its (undeveloped) narrative had a vaguely political thesis and was set in a penthouse suite at a Houston hotel. The manuscript probably does not exist; the material resurfaced, years later, in *The Red Devil Battery Sign.*

Brooks Atkinson, admitting that both *The Roman Spring of Mrs. Stone* and *Sweet Bird of Youth* dealt with his own artistic and moral dilemmas. He said his low creative energies during the last several years were due to a screaming cry for love and forgiveness, and that, far from being helped by either doctors or success, he was more deeply troubled than he had been when he wrote *A Streetcar Named Desire*. As he was writing, however, he was risking an international scandal by carrying with him illicit drugs, which, he wrongly hoped, would help him through the period of deep trouble. "I am," he said that year, "poisoned by success."

By Thanksgiving they were back in New York, where a preview of *The Fugitive Kind* was scheduled at the RKO 58th Street Theatre. The Sunday of the holiday weekend was, as Meade Roberts remembered, one of the more newsworthy days in Williams's life, and it had some of the flavor of Federico Fellini's 1959 film, *La Dolce Vita*.

"The production of dramatic television shows was beginning the move to Hollywood that year, and actors in the East were out of work in greater and greater numbers. The audience that night, and the crowds of bystanders outside the theatre, included organized numbers of unemployed actors, resentful of just about everyone who had anything to do with this film. There were harsh words for Sidney Lumet, who had been a television director, and for Anna Magnani, who was a foreigner working here. Finally, Tennessee arrived, very drunk, with an equally unsteady Diana Barrymore. There was an unfavorable response from the enemy camp at the end of the film, and a small gang of hoodlums recognized Williams leaving the theatre. They spat at him, he spat right back, and he went off with Diana to watch a first print of *Suddenly Last Summer* at [the film's producer] Sam Spiegel's apartment on Park Avenue." And there, as Speigel later told Joseph L. Mankiewicz, Williams covered his nervousness at the film's powerful rendering of his play by giggling into his drinks all evening. (It is worth mentioning that Williams was not giggling when *The Fugitive Kind* opened to the public in April 1960; Bosley Crowther, in the New York *Times,* expressed a typical reaction when he wrote that it was the best film rendering of a Williams work since *Streetcar.*)

At the beginning of 1960, Williams and Merlo were living quietly in Key West. Although he was exhausted from the long trip and the month in New York, there was a sudden resurgence of purpose and energy, rather as if he were fulfilling a New Year's resolution. With an

With Tallulah Bankhead and Herbert Machiz,
before 1956 revival of *A Streetcar Named Desire*

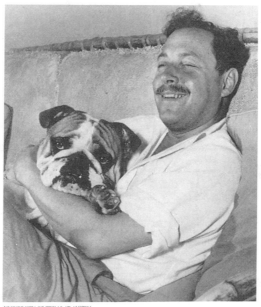

In Key West, about 1960

With Maureen Stapleton, after a revival
of *The Glass Menagerie*, 1965

With Bill Glavin, 1968

With Edwina, 1969

In Key West, 1972

Before appearing at the YMHA, New York, 1972

In *Small Craft Warnings*, 1972

During rehearsals for
Out Cry (The Two-Character Play), 1973

In New York, 1975

Cheryl Crawford

With Edwin Sherin, Bill Barnes and Anthony Quinn,
during rehearsals for *The Red Devil Battery Sign,* 1975

With Rose Williams, at the National Arts Club, 1975

With Mitch Douglas in Chicago, 1980

With Vassilis Voglis and Jane Smith
at Williams's seventieth birthday celebration in Chicago, 1981

Tennessee Williams

acute sense of self-criticism and an attitude that can reasonably be called valorous, he devoted himself to an expansion of what would, in the opinion of many, be his last great play — *The Night of the Iguana.*

Based only remotely on the short story of the same name he had written long before, *Iguana* was first performed as a one-act play at the Spoleto Festival in Italy, on July 2, 1959. For the director of this production Williams had great admiration — and well he could, for Frank Corsaro had staged *A Hatful of Rain* in New York, as well as the opera *Susannah.* Sensitive and imaginative, patient and energetic, Corsaro realized in 1959 that the manuscript of *Iguana* was (at a mere twenty-one pages) a full-length work in progress, and that the first production in Italy would have a successor.

"He was totally charming at first meeting," Corsaro remembered, "and he continued to work during that summer and winter until it was eighty-one pages, a kind of long one-act play. In the fall of 1959 we came to New York and I directed that longer version at the Actors Studio."

In Key West that winter, Williams continued work on the play. Inspired by his 1940 summer on the Mexican coast, it was becoming an important, poetic play about art and religion, about the nature of the poet's vocation (a subject introduced in *Suddenly Last Summer*), and about the necessity of self-forgiveness. The role of a wandering poet nearing one hundred years of age combined Williams and his grandfather; the grandfather's spinster granddaughter, the sketch artist Hannah, was a kind of half-achieved, half wish-fulfillment of what Williams would have liked to be; and the defrocked, alcoholic, sex-crazed minister "at the end of his rope" (like the captured iguana) was a self-portrait of the playwright. As it evolved into full-length form in 1960 and 1961, the personal models became more nuanced. For perhaps the first time since *Streetcar,* the lineaments of his inner life were transcended into something universal, and an overt concern for spiritual health gives this play at once a human warmth and a tragic serenity absent from his work in the previous several years.

Corsaro saw that depth emerging, however, and he joined Williams and Merlo in Key West in early 1960. "Frank [Merlo] was the best part of Tennessee's life. He took no nonsense from him — and Tennessee could ladle out nonsense — and he was a man of sense and good taste. He was a street kid who had grown up and become a real, literate gentleman. As Tennessee's general factotum, he was his right arm and I think the bright side of his life."

Merlo kept pace with Williams's daily work on *Iguana,* reading portions of the script as they came from the typewriter, realizing that a major work was in progress, and making their visitor Corsaro welcome. But Tennessee was unsure of the quality of the play. "He felt that his star was in decline by this time," Corsaro said, "and he wasn't at all sure he could pull off *Iguana.* He was always complaining about critics, and about the future, but on the level of daily work and conferences on the script he was extraordinary — just extraordinary. The problems with his life, and the interruptions in his production of first-rate work, were due to those who formed his social circle at the time — people like Marion Vaccaro and Lilla van Saher." Corsaro was right: for in 1960 it was clear to him, to Merlo, to Paul Bigelow, to Audrey Wood, and to a number of New York friends that Williams's creative life was in a period of sudden, mysterious enrichment, and that he required quiet encouragement, not distraction; as so often, he was not the best judge of who offered what.

"When he was working or reworking at this play," Corsaro continued, "he was a genius, and he was inspiring to be with. You could see his understanding of people's pain, his compassion, his gentleness, his modesty in the face of the universe. But outside the work, he was becoming a travesty of himself. Those he chose to be with were such a sorry crew. There was Carson McCullers, twitching her way through an alcoholic evening, and William Inge, who had such a bad problem with drink, too, and whom Tennessee did not like — he played on Inge's weakness for drink and was obviously jealous of his success in the 1950s. And Lilla van Saher — what a fantastic creature! — they were all like rejects from a road company of *Streetcar.*"

Occasionally, Williams interrupted work on *Iguana* to revise portions of *Period of Adjustment,* the bittersweet marital comedy Cheryl Crawford was producing for a fall Broadway premiere. There was considerable talk in the press that season about Tennessee Williams writing a comedy, and to the *New York Times* he replied to the objection that his tragic (and, some said, sordid) vision indeed needed correction. To the surprise of none of his friends, he chose the metaphor of illness and diagnosis:

"We [playwrights of darkness and violence] have done no worse a deed than the X-ray machine or the needle that makes the blood test. And, though these are clinical devices, I think we have tried our best to indicate which are the healthy blood cells and which is the normal tissue in the world of our time, through exposing clearly the dark spots and the viruses on the plates and in the blood cultures."

* * *

By late April, it was necessary to find a director for *Period of Adjust-ment,* and the offer finally went to George Roy Hill, whose first Broadway direction (for *Look Homeward, Angel*) won the Pulitzer and Drama Critics Circle Award for the play. Reporters eager for gossip ran from Williams to Kazan and back again, hoping to prey on Williams's para-noia by suggesting that Kazan had stormed away from the play in dis-appointment over its quality, had aligned himself instead with Inge's work, and had terminated the friendship. This made for imaginative writing, but an egregious lack of truth. The simple fact was that Kazan was scheduled to direct a film of Inge's original screenplay *Splendor in the Grass,* but that he was also developing other interests in his own career:

"After *Sweet Bird of Youth,* he offered me his plays all the time, but by then I was directing more films. It was hard for me to keep turning him down, to keep telling him that my interests were elsewhere. [Kazan directed only three plays in New York after 1959 — all in 1964, at the ANTA Washington Square theatre.] It was hard for him to understand why I wouldn't do any more plays, that I was increasingly involved in my own writing and filmmaking. The affection between us persisted, and he was always very interested and generous toward my novels and films. We didn't drift apart emotionally — that never happened — but we did drift apart professionally."

In early June, Williams invited his mother and his brother and sister-in-law to join him for a vacation in Los Angeles, where they took a bun-galow at the Beverly Hills Hotel. They visited William Inge, film stars and directors, and industry people Williams had known over the years — Miss Edwina took a particular delight in meeting Elvis Pres-ley — and at one party they were introduced to the legendary Mae West. Williams volunteered — with the hyperbole he reserved for ladies of stage and screen — that she was one of the three great movie talents in history, the other two being W. C. Fields and Charlie Chaplin. "Well," she replied slowly, "I don't know about Fields."

As usual, especially when he could not work on manuscripts, he kept up a lively correspondence from California. To Brooks Atkinson he wrote from the hotel that he had that spring supervised the construction of a patio at the poolside of his Key West house, and that life there was his only refreshment. He then outlined the contours of his life for At-kinson. The ugliness, blackness and violence of his late work, he wrote, as if still defending himself before the press, was not an expression of cynicism or nihilism. He dealt with evil obsessively because he hated it. Sensationalism was never, the letter concluded, his true aim: in spite of compromises and lapses of taste he now regretted, his purposes had always been humanistic.

By the end of June he had returned alone to Key West, where Merlo awaited with a copy of *Newsweek,* in which Williams had admitted that he took barbiturates regularly. As for drugs, it seemed to the playwright that Merlo himself needed some — but not for psychological or diversionary reasons. He looked pale and nervous, and he was smoking excessively. Silence prevailed between them, visitors detected an emotional vacuum, and Williams spent more time with other men (at bars and on the beach) and with his adoring women. There seemed to be a quiet *diminuendo* to what had once been the lively, tender duet of Tennessee Williams and Frank Merlo.

"The years in which Tenn was willing to have the scheme of order placed on his life by another, especially a lover," according to Paul Bigelow, "were coming to an end. Now there was enough money for hotels and servants and cooks. A great deal of what Frank had offered over the years became available with Tenn's fame and wealth, which had grown enormously, and which — his protests aside — he was entirely aware of. He knew just what he was worth, and what his considerable wealth was. As his material life changed so dramatically, Frank could not adjust to it. He grew more and more bitter as his usefulness diminished. He had put up, all those years, with Tenn's promiscuity and with certain of his acquaintances who were less than helpful and in fact contemptuous. There was never a dramatic, final break, or a grand scene, packing the bags and so forth. It just ended gradually, and more or less calmly.

"But there was another element in this, and it had to do with Williams's increasing distrust of others, and his essential inability to accept the fact that he was the object of someone's commitment. Friendship he could accept; but sex he distrusted, in spite of all the celebration of it in his plays — perhaps because he ordinarily disconnected it from affection in his own life. He never accepted that he was sexually loved — it wasn't that he didn't accept love itself. Physical intimacy he tended to distrust, even as he needed it constantly."

Not long after 1960, Williams himself admitted this in even broader terms: "I have an unfortunate inability to believe in people's admiration," he told a reporter, "or even their acceptance . . . that's awful. I know it is." Meade Roberts saw this, too: "I don't think he could accept deep commitments, and I think that after a dozen years that's what really made Frankie so unhappy, for he too realized that Tennessee would never believe how much he *could* be loved, and not just in spite of any human failings, but because he had so much to offer."

In the years to follow, in some ways he had less to offer because he believed less in himself. The potential for great feeling would always be there and would occasionally manifest itself from his breadth of human understanding. But the ability for emotional commitment (apart, of course, from his devotion to Rose) began to be foreclosed as his belief in himself, as artist, friend and lover, diminished.

In August 1960 the evolution of *The Night of the Iguana* continued, as the Actors Studio cast came to Coconut Grove for another production. Williams arrived, unstable but full of praise for his cast and director, and sensitive toward a crew-member whose family was in trouble. Fragile and dependent himself, he was still in touch with others' pain and able to respond, warmly and directly, in word and, if necessary, with cash.

Ironically, his comedy *Period of Adjustment,* when it opened in November in New York, was what everyone had been demanding — a gentle, funny-sad treatment of heterosexual domestic life. (Two couples confront a time of psychological, sexual and social crisis — and all ends happily.) The reviews, however, emphasized its conversations about sexual performance and technique, although some correctly deduced that the play could be considered a comedy only because it was not clearly a tragedy.

"The real problem with *Period of Adjustment,*" according to Cheryl Crawford, "was not in the play, which I still think is delightful and has never been properly appreciated. The problem was, to put it bluntly, that the original cast was too old. The audience didn't really care very much about the problems and the arguments of couples who, because they weren't young onstage, couldn't make credible the cries and complaints and nervousness natural for young married couples." The play closed in March, after 132 performances; only a film sale made it profitable, and this did not help Williams's recessive confidence.

At the beginning of 1961, Williams was in virtual seclusion in Key West, working with sullen intensity on *The Night of the Iguana* — which, he assured Cheryl Crawford in a letter dated January 8, would be his last play; he understood (incorrectly) that she did not want to produce it, and this saddened him since the play was, he said, a dramatic poem of great personal value and one of his clearest autobiographical statements. (The play was produced by Charles Bowden.) What he did not say was that he had recently been rereading the poems of Rainer Maria Rilke, and whether he was aware of it or not, this new play drew on the poet who had so deeply affected him three decades before. *Iguana* was becoming a journal of Williams's soul, passed through the prism of his poetic-dramatic art. With Rilke the play shares an idolization and idealization of women: Hannah Jelkes is described as "a Gothic cathedral image of a medieval saint," and she is certainly the most spiritual woman in the Williams canon, the clearest exponent of Wisdom. But he was also writing *Iguana* in highly religious, not merely archetypal terms: the God sought by Williams, as by Rilke, was not the God of organized religion, but "an incomplete sentence," a tendency of the heart.

Cheryl Crawford — who held the record as producer of a quartet of Williams's plays — was disappointed in his unexplained decision to move to another producer, but she accepted this with her customary good grace. She was among the first whom he gradually separated from his life.

"After *Period of Adjustment* I saw very little of him, and when I did he was very cool and distant. I found this hard to accept at first, since we were so close for ten years [and considering how intimately he had disclosed himself in letters]. It had been a period during which I had produced four of his plays and spent so much time with him. But later I found that he was changing a good deal in his life, and that a number of other people were treated somewhat differently too." And according to Jane Smith, "He was unsure about who liked him for what reasons, and even his oldest friends were suddenly suspect. It was a difficult thing for him to be in the limelight. He dropped everybody at some point, and then he'd come back again into one's life — in and out — with everyone it was the same way."

But while there were changes in his professional associations, Williams preferred to keep the same comfortable traveling companions; they did not challenge him, they simply accompanied him uncritically. In late January he left for Europe with Marion Vaccaro, and from London he wrote a final letter to Cheryl in which he expressed concern for Frank's health. At this time, Williams believed that Merlo was taking drugs, and that this was responsible for his withdrawal from their Key West social life; in fact, Merlo took no drug more potent than an occasional bit of marijuana. But he was smoking several packs of cigarettes daily, and with Williams absent and no Reverend Dakin to cook for, he was eating irregularly and poorly.

In April, Williams and Marion were in Rome, where they met Donald Windham and Sandy Campbell. "We sat together on Via Veneto," Windham recalled; "it was fun to see him surrounded by the paparazzi; but it was a little unreal, as though we were on the set of a Fellini movie." Within days, however, Williams and Vaccaro had departed for Taormina, Sicily, where they took rooms at the splendid San Domenico Palace Hotel, a sprawling Renaissance monastery more luxurious in its refurbished state than it had ever been in the days of Sicilian friars. On the terrace of his suite he set up his typewriter, and when he and Marion were not at the bar or strolling the beach in Taormina or Giardini di Naxos, he continued to write mostly disconnected scenes for *Iguana*. The Reverend Shannon of the play, by early that summer when Williams had returned to New York, had become a surrogate for the author himself — a man haunted by "blue devils" (as he called them in the play and in letters to Donald Windham) who takes refuge in the oblivion of drink and the quick affirmations of sex with young people. Audrey Wood, a champion of this difficult play from the start, saw the connections at once between the aged Nonno (the Italian word for grandfather, and the term Frank Merlo had used for Reverend Dakin) and Hannah (the sketch artist who insists that "Nothing human disgusts me unless it's unkind, violent") and Shannon (the sensual renegade).*

Enthusiastic as Audrey was, she soon joined Cheryl in the discovery of a subtle transformation in Williams's attitude. *Esquire* magazine had asked him to compose an article detailing the client-agent relationship. This took a year, and when it was at last ready it was full of praise for her — but in a coolly professional tone, and with a subtext of resentment that she was his "mother-image . . . and this is bound to create an ambivalent relationship when the filial image has arrived, as I have, at an age in his life and profession as an artist when he feels humiliated by the acceptance of what he thinks is too much domination, too many decisions for him not made by himself."

With characteristic dignified calm, Audrey confided her reactions to

---

* Up to this point, all the full-length plays of Tennessee Williams (except *Camino Real*) were set in the South — including *The Glass Menagerie*, for its St. Louis, Missouri, was very much an extension of the urban South; and he would return to that setting for three full-length plays later. The action in most of the one-act plays is similarly located.

no one (at least not publicly); she might have thought that if she had not indeed assumed responsiblities, his life would have been more chaotic, less artistically fertile. Also, nowhere in the piece does Williams address the strange situation of an internationally famous writer of mature years who has supposedly allowed himself to be "humiliated by . . . domination." Strange words, an ungrateful tone and an imaginative transference of his feelings about Edwina to Audrey: if his agent had felt this, she would not have been sharing his paranoia. In any case, she must have been surprised to read the final sentence: "I know that if someday our professional relationship should come to a close, it is she who would close it, not I. . . ." That closure would occur in time, but even then, in 1961, Williams was putting distance between himself and a woman who had devoted her energies to his career for over twenty years.

By early autumn he had returned to Key West where, as he wrote to Donald Windham, Merlo's presence at least saved him from the results of his inability to function alone. Merlo found him more than ever addicted to liquor and pills. "That's the only thing [that keeps me going]: liquor and swimming — Miltowns [a popular tranquilizer then widely prescribed], liquor, swimming," he told an interviewer at the time. At least part of his unhappiness was due to the growing conviction that his creative life had desiccated: "My kind of literary or pseudo-literary style of writing for the theatre is on its way out," he said. Harold Pinter was the writer of the future, and Pinter "drives me crazy with jealousy." With that admission, Pinter joined Inge; soon, Edward Albee would join Pinter. The list would grow in the 1960s. His insistence that each long play was his last, or that his best work was behind him, eventually became a self-fulfilling prophecy.

The out-of-town previews for *The Night of the Iguana* were as violent, as tense and as suspenseful as the first uneven drafts of the play itself. In October, after cordial introductions of the cast (Bette Davis, Margaret Leighton, Patrick O'Neal, Alan Webb), rehearsals began.

"It was a very difficult time," according to Frank Corsaro, "for him, for me, for the performers. He was rewriting furiously and delivering new script every day, which was hard on the actors, and he had a strange lack of perspective about how the play might gather focus and momentum. His working habits were not helped by his reliance on pills and shots from a quack doctor, and his resulting nervousness didn't help the cast."

The last week of rehearsals in New York City, before the company's departure for a week in Rochester, Williams told an interviewer, "I create imaginary worlds into which I can retreat from the real world because I've never made any kind of adjustment to the real world." But the retreat was given a harder edge and an urgency by his increasing reliance on drugs. For an artist seeking deeper contact with reality through the forms of art and fiction and drama, a lack of adjustment to much of what passes for social intercourse can be helpful, and is in fact necessary. But if the inner realm where reflection occurs is influenced by chemicals, it becomes hard for an artist to gauge the depth or truth of his feeling, and harder still for him to evaluate the results realistically.

From Rochester, they moved to a two-week engagement in Detroit. Revisions descended from Williams's hotel room daily — brought to director and cast by Frank Merlo, who usually reported that the playwright had been awake most of the night and so was sleeping until afternoon. It was in Detroit that an unfortunate accident severed any hope of a reconciliation with Merlo.

"As if it weren't bad enough that the cast was hardly on speaking terms," Corsaro recalled, "we were told that Williams's dog had bit him on the ankle, and that an infection had set in. He had to be hospitalized." He also had to be calmed with increased sedation, for he was not only in acute pain from the wound but he was virtually irrational with rage and fear. The dog, given to him by Anna Magnani (and aptly named Satan), had been set on him by Merlo, he raved: Frank wanted him dead, all Frank wanted was his money, the dog always loved Frank more — it was a first major explosion of unreason. Only Merlo knew what was responsible, and he was powerless now to prevent Williams's pattern of self-destruction.

But somehow, with his remarkable recuperative and resilient powers, Williams returned to work on the production, bandaged ankles and unstable nerves notwithstanding. For the five-week run in Chicago he lived quite soberly and sensibly — but without Merlo, who took the dreaded dog and returned to Key West. Merlo was himself strangely weak and livid from a constant hacking cough; and neither he nor Williams had the emotional or physical energy for dialogue. This was the major moment of rupture in the declining relationship.

"I was shocked when I heard that they had really split," Maureen Stapleton said. "And it was Tennessee who brought it on. He was paranoid about everything — his health, the opinion others had of him, Frankie's intentions. And it was one of the things Frankie had dealt with so well, that paranoia. I was stunned by their separation, and although I never stopped loving Tenn — who could? — I think it was the craziest thing he ever did. And the craziness began with those awful crazy pills he was getting."

Finally, on December 28, *The Night of the Iguana* arrived at the Royale Theatre in New York. In the first night audience were Edwina, Dakin, Joyce and her father, but the author made no appearance inside the theatre: he paced outside before, during and after the performance. A bracelet of celebrities surrounded Edwina, who chatted gaily with Donald Windham, Judy Garland, Helen Hayes, Lillian Gish and Eleanor Roosevelt. The only one to speak with Williams that night was Carson McCullers. The two writers tried to cheer one another, but without success: he was convinced of his total decline, she of hers. He had remained attentive to Carson, visiting her on her birthday whenever he could make the trip to Nyack, recommending her for Guggenheim Foundation grants, reading manuscripts of her stories and of her new novel, *Clock Without Hands* (whose considerable flaws he saw at once, and which he urged her to withhold from publication — a counsel, unfortunately, that she did not follow).

The second night, Edwina dined with her son and Frank Corsaro at Sardi's. "There was Edwina," Corsaro said, "looking and acting like a grand duchess — and suddenly, to her son's dismay, she asked if she and I could exchange plates. She said my food looked better. When Tennessee scolded her, she just said, 'Well, honey, we do it down home.' This was certainly inconsistent with her famous manners. She was the archetypically mad Southern woman by this time."

The response to *The Night of the Iguana* was uneven; its overt yearning and discussion of matters transcendent seemed to confuse reviewers ready for a sequel to *Sweet Bird of Youth,* or expecting an addition to Williams's range of shocking topics. *Time* magazine was perhaps closest to the truth when the reviewer suggested that it was "the wisest play he has ever written."

The Night of the Iguana is set on the verandah of a rustic hotel on the coast of Mexico, in the summer of 1940. To this torrid, primitive way station come the Reverend T. Lawrence Shannon, a defrocked Episcopal priest leading a group of American women on a tour; Hannah Jelkes, a Nantucket spinster and artist; her aged grandfather, Jonathan Coffin (Nonno), "the world's oldest living and practicing poet"; a group of Germans, exultant over Hitler's early war victories — all of them guests of the hotel's proprietor, the formidably crude Maxine Faulk. Over one steamy day and a stormy night, Shannon confronts the demons of frantic sexuality, religious guilt and emotional confusion, and he learns from both the earthy simplicity of Maxine and the cool serenity of Hannah. At the end of the play, the old poet dies after completing a poem about the quiet acceptance of life's cycles of death and rebirth, and Shannon — with the help of the wise Hannah — accepts the possibility of a changed, healed life with Maxine.

No one could have foreseen then — although several may have suspected — that this would be considered Williams's last great work for the theatre. Certainly it has a poetic depth of compassion, and it allows hope even while it proclaims the author's love for Nonno and for the natural saintliness of Hannah and for the tortured but still searching Shannon. These three characters were closest to the playwright's heart, and they had the greatest value for him as poet, as artist, as struggling believer. Their names were changed late in his revisions, very likely to show — in the similarity of Shannon-Hannah-Nonno — how spiritually linked they are.

In an important way, this is the work that corrects the morbidity of *Sweet Bird of Youth*. In these two plays, Williams dealt with the attraction to youth and beauty (Alexandra's for Chance; Shannon's for Charlotte and other nymphets) — not only for the satisfaction of the flesh, but because each character identified with the ambitions of the young, whose energy was dramatized in terms of erotic power. And because the two characters identify with those young, they also (as Williams well knew) could overidentify with the less appealing aspects of that energy — with youth's unawareness of the passage of time, of the value of sacrifice; with its preoccupation with self and with the demon of fashion. In *Sweet Bird of Youth*, the refuge is the accident of a temporary restoration to work; but in *Iguana*, Williams suggested, there may not even be refuge anywhere in this world (although on this the play is indecisive). What is very clear, however, is that to be redeemed for meaning is to find a way through the jungle, and this we can do only in the company of one another. The terrifying, tangled, primitive garden of *Suddenly Last Summer* has become in *Iguana* full of promise for the future.

His compassion never wavered in this play, as it never did for his family and for his friends — and even as he knew the break with Frank Merlo was irreversible, he could not accept it with cold equanimity. "He was one of the few people I ever knew," according to Paul Bigelow, "who felt he had no basis for making judgments in human affairs. The power of his work is testament to that. There is no character anywhere for whom he expressed contempt. It's the breadth of his compassion and his understanding that gives his plays such power. At the same time, it's not that he offers approval to some of the worst excesses of a character — it's just quite simply the most unselfish compassion. And it was the same in life — he never expressed a severe judgment about anyone. A momentary remark, a sarcastic comment, certainly. But never a moral judgment."

Colleagues recognized the connection between the work and the man too. "His theme," Arthur Miller reflected years later, "is perhaps the most pervasive in American literature, where people lose greatly in the very shadow of the mountain from whose peak they might have had a clear view of God. It is the romance of the lost yet sacred misfits, who exist in order to remind us of our trampled instincts, our forsaken tenderness, the holiness of the spirit of man."

On March 9, 1962, *Time* magazine put Tennessee Williams on its cover and devoted six pages to an appreciative survey of his life's struggles and achievements. *"The Night of the Iguana* . . . is a box-office sellout and much the best new American play of the season. The fact is that Tennessee Williams . . . is a consummate master of theatre." The New York Drama Critics Circle agreed: on April 10 the play was chosen best of the year, a week after Bette Davis, unhappy with the production and her role, was succeeded by Shelley Winters as the boisterous hotel proprietor. To his surprise (but not his agent's) Williams received another accolade that season, a lifetime fellowship in the American Academy of Arts and Letters.

Immediately after the *Time* story, an editor at G. P. Putnam's in New York saw the possibility for an interesting book: the life and career of Tennessee Williams as seen from the viewpoint of the legendary Edwina. Author Lucy Freeman was sent to St. Louis, Edwina liked her at once, and a contract was prepared for her story to be told with Freeman's collaboration. "She simply *was* Amanda," Lucy Freeman said, "there in her cozy house full of Tennessee's awards and photos. She was a perky little lady, a nonstop talker, with a great veil of privacy she could lower whenever she wanted." To the author's credit, however, it must be said that she sustained Edwina's rambling memory, corrected several important lapses in accuracy, and produced a readable memoir, selective because of Edwina's own limitations.

While Edwina opened her scrapbooks and ransacked her memory for anecdotes, her famous son was once again in Europe, fleeing, like Shannon and Hannah, his "spooks and blue devils." Since 1958 he had worked intermittently on a series of reflective dialogues based on "Man Bring This Up Road," the 1953 story about the selfish Flora Goforth and the hapless young man who wanders quickly in and out of her villa.

In July 1962 a short version of *The Milk Train Doesn't Stop Here Anymore* (as he uneconomically called it) was presented — appropriately, in Spoleto, Italy, at the Festival of Two Worlds. Hermione Baddeley and Paul Roebling played Flora and Chris, and Mildred Dunnock the enigmatic Witch of Capri. Unfocused and undramatic, it was like a page of diary jottings, and it is in fact on her notebooks that Flora works (even in the earliest version of this much-transformed play): "I'm more interested in producing literature this summer than in having it read to me," Flora reflects. Like her, Williams had gone away to escape — in his case, the crowds then flocking into Key West: "they're pleasure-seekers, frantic choosers of silly little distractions."

The Spoleto audience was polite, the cast earnest, but the roles lacked what Kazan elsewhere called "spines" — controlling images, characteristics or centers from which the actors could develop and with which an audience could associate.

For the trip to Spoleto, Williams brought as companion (as he did for several other journeys in 1961 and 1962) the young poet Frederick Nicklaus. A graduate of Ohio State University who had moved to New York in the 1950s, Nicklaus had met Williams casually several years before the playwright invited the poet to live with him — and Frank — in Key West. At first, Nicklaus's relationship with Williams was pleasant and positive; their intimacy was sustained by a mutual professional respect. Then, as Nicklaus recalled years later, the domestic situation of a trio became intolerable — especially because of Tennessee's increased consumption of alcohol.

But there was, of course, something deeply hurtful to Merlo about this arrangement. And by tragic circumstance everything in the lives of all three men was very soon altered. In London, where Williams stopped to visit, a telegram arrived from Audrey Wood. Friends of Frank in Key West had called her with the news that he was desperately ill. For once, it was Frank who needed attention and care. Williams was in Key West the next afternoon.

Chapter Eight

DANGEROUS
ELEMENTS
(1963–1969)

I feel this chapter ought to begin with a serious comment on the meaning of life, because
... sooner or later, a person's obliged to
face it.

— Flora Goforth, in
The Milk Train Doesn't Stop Here Anymore

THE CALL to London, informing him of Merlo's illness, frightened Tennessee Williams. "There were a few people close to Tennessee who loved him over the years," said his old friend David Greggory, "not because he was a great and famous writer, not on a professional basis, but on a human level. Frank Merlo was certainly at the top of the list."

In agreement was Paul Bigelow, another who had known Williams long before, during and after the years with Merlo: "Tenn behaved with a great deal of generosity toward many people, and when Frank needed him he was there."

During the autumn of 1962, a situation had arisen that called for Tennessee Williams's generosity, and his response to almost fifteen years of companionship. In Key West, the tentative diagnosis was at first encouraging: Frank probably had bronchial pneumonia; or he was suffering from mononucleosis, or anemia; or — more alarming — he was to be tested for tuberculosis. All they could be sure of, as late as October, was that he was constantly exhausted, he had a hacking cough, he ate very little, and he and Williams found conversation difficult. Audrey Wood, at the same time, had arranged for Roger L. Stevens to produce *The Milk Train Doesn't Stop Here Anymore* on Broadway in January, and Williams and Merlo parted for a time. Frank would in any case be more comfortable in the warmth of Key West, where his physician could monitor him. Williams, meantime, would work on the script and attend rehearsals with the Spoleto cast in New York.

In January 1963, Frank came north to see Williams and a New York doctor. He stayed several evenings with friends like Johnny Nicholson, visited relatives in New Jersey, and then moved briefly to a hotel. A week later he called and asked to see Williams, and they met at an East Side bar. Frank, with astonishing calmness, told what he had just learned. His illness was inoperable lung cancer.

In fact, Williams had surmised as much: he had remembered his grandmother's appearance and symptoms from twenty years earlier, and his suspicions were confirmed by a call to Frank's doctor before they met. At once, he offered every practical and emotional support, but both of them suspected there was little to be done.

The cast of *Milk Train* had noticed Williams's anxiety during the last rehearsals in December and early January. "When he complained about anything," according to Mildred Dunnock, "it seemed to us that he was suffering over something other than the play, and one was fearful of intruding on a man who was living such an intense level of creativity as well as enduring some personal anguish at the same time. I thought then that the character I was playing, Vera Ridgeway Condotti, was meant to bring out something in [the Hermione Baddeley character] Mrs. Goforth — she represented the nastiness people thought was in Mrs. Goforth but was not. And I sometimes thought that in this way the two women represented something about the public and the private Williams, too."

The new year thus began unhappily for both the public and the private Williams. *Milk Train* opened in January during a newspaper strike, but even before the critics could publish their mostly negative opinions, audiences were making their decisions. "The opening night crowd," according to David Greggory, who attended with Cheryl Crawford, "was composed of those who wanted a great success for him, and those who didn't want it to be a big thing at all — it was a very uncomfortable feeling for those of us who really cared. At Sardi's afterward it was like being on a roller-coaster, and people who were expecting *Menagerie* or *Streetcar* were totally confused."

When the professional opinions were added to the public's, the roller-coaster ride was over, but only after an upsetting finale: Stevens kept the play running as long as he could, but business was so poor that the closing notice was posted after sixty-nine performances. By that time critics like Richard Gilman had been in the vanguard of a new sourness in the business of reviewing. He wrote in *Commonweal* of Williams's "creative suicide," in an article superciliously and cruelly titled "Mistuh Williams, He Dead," and he expanded his anger for the *Tulane Drama Review* later that year: "The American drama is itself almost mindless; we weep for the intellectual deficiencies of [Arthur] Miller and Williams." A lacerating tone was beginning to infect the writing of a few critics — a callous indifference not only to an artist's past achievements, but also to his present feelings. Apparently Miller and Williams were not acceptable to some academics; that they were intellectual deficients creating "mindless drama" was itself a mindless exaggeration.

"He just didn't have an armor for the criticism offered to his plays in the 1960s," according to Maureen Stapleton. "There was no life for him but his writing, and when he thought his writing failed, he thought it was the beginning of the end."

But not only his writing failed him that season. Very quickly, it became clear that Frank Merlo was not responding to any therapies. To his credit, Williams at once insisted on taking Frank to the warmth of Key West, which Merlo always preferred to New York in any season. Frederick Nicklaus was still in residence there.

"As Frank became more and more ill," Meade Roberts remembered, "Tennessee certainly realized how wrong he'd been about his life with Frank, how unfair and how selfish and ungiving to Frank he'd been in the last few years." He tried to devote equal time daily to his writing and to caring for Frank, who was not yet bedridden nor in need of hospital attention. But Frank felt himself an intruder in Williams's life, and kept to his room.

"It was so depressing to visit," according to Frank Corsaro, whom Williams invited to read new scenes of *Milk Train* he was preparing for a revival out of town that autumn and, it was hoped, a Broadway restaging later. "With Frank ill, Tennessee just couldn't cope for himself with the details of real life. Of course he told me, 'Baby, it's my last play,' and then he told me long, mournful stories about Frank's illness. I felt very badly for both of them, and when I sat with Frank he gave me vague hints about Tennessee's tendency to suicide. By this time, Tennessee had come to believe in his failures even more than his successes. The failures, after all, were tangible and provable, and the successes he tended to think of as unreal or accidents that could never be repeated. He was incapable of relying on himself or his own strengths, and I think this is why he turned to those bereft souls who provided him with easy distractions and no challenges."

In April, Merlo came to New York with Williams and Nicklaus and tried to keep a semblance of social life in New York, and although weakened by simple daily tasks, he insisted on going to see their friend Barbara Baxley in the new Broadway show *She Loves Me*.

"They took me out for a drink afterward," she recalled, "and when Tennessee left us alone for a moment Frank turned to me and said, 'I have cancer and I'll be dead in less than a year.' Just like that. No emotion, nothing. He said it with complete coldness, and from that evening I saw him gradually withdraw. I've always thought he did that to make his dying easier — for himself and for me as his friend, but most of all for Tennessee. Frank was a strong, good man, and I think his illness made him feel ashamed of being so useless to Tenn and so helpless for himself."

The revisions for the planned revival of *Milk Train* were becoming more and more clearly a dialogue with Death, approaching inexorably as the inevitable reality of a woman's age. The reality that had obsessed the playwright since before his fortieth birthday, since the months in Rome that had inspired Karen Stone, had now come into the parlor. "I think Tenn felt a strange guilt about Frank's final illness," Paul Bigelow said, "as if, just like with Rose, there was something he could have done to prevent it from happening."

But there was nothing to do except wait — and try to work, which is what Williams did. He also tried to invent distractions and comforts for Frank, at least one of which was imprudent. He took Merlo and Nicklaus to a rented house in Nantucket for several weeks in July — a period that Nicklaus remembered as emotionally trying for all three, especially since Frank's condition was deteriorating rapidly. By early August, it was clear to everyone that Frank would have to be hospitalized. His roommate at Memorial Hospital, in New York, was a man named Samuel Posnock, who was also from Elizabeth, New Jersey; Frank was at first quite talkative and outgoing with Posnock and with his family.

"Tennessee Williams came to visit Frank Merlo every day during August," according to Sheldon Posnock, who was also there daily, visiting his ill father. "Both Williams and Merlo were very friendly to us, but as the weeks passed and Frank's status deteriorated, it was clear that Williams was very upset, very drained by the ordeal. His attention to Merlo and his caring were certainly very intense and affectionate, and he was clearly upset by his friend's pain." Of those last weeks, Williams later said, "Frankie had an honest dignity. He gave his life to me, arranged everything and never lost a fraction of his pride in the face of the most awful death a person can have."

Cheryl Crawford was an attentive friend at this difficult time. "The breakup with Frankie, which Tenn really brought about, was a crazy thing. Frankie was the only one who really understood him, really knew how to deal with him and help him. When Frankie was dying, there was a new form of grief, and maybe a new form of guilt, for Tennessee to deal with, and I think it just broke him."

As so often in the last weeks of a lingering illness, the doctors could not predict the length of the final agony, and Williams was advised to proceed with his own professional plans. In this case, he was to attend a production of *Milk Train* in Abingdon, Virginia, before the new Broadway staging that coming winter. In early September, Williams went to the Carter Theatre, returning the third week of that month, the night after a dubious premiere.

Next afternoon, Williams went to Memorial Hospital.

Merlo removed his oxygen mask, and with a sudden rush of energy climbed from his bed to a nearby chair. Then he needed oxygen again, and had to be helped back to bed. Williams urged him to conserve his strength, saying that he already looked better — which they both knew was a pathetic lie. The two sat in silence, and when Williams offered to leave so that his friend could sleep, Frank asked him to remain, and not to admit other visitors: "I'm used to you," he said quietly.

Finally Merlo slept, and visiting hours ended. Williams was met downstairs by friends, who took him for drinks at a local pub. When he arrived back at his apartment after midnight, there was a message that Frank had died at eleven o'clock.

There had already been keen losses in his life, and for the first two days a haze of confusion blunted his grief. His beloved grandparents had died in 1944 and 1955, and even the death of his father in 1957 affected him in a deeper way than he had anticipated. Margo Jones had died suddenly in 1955, and before that people whose talents had been so important — Laurette Taylor first among them. But with the death of Frank, there was a wound in his life that never healed, and whose pain was comparable to what he felt about Rose.

Merlo had loved everything in Williams's work except what he considered the occasional lapses of sentimentality, and when he died Williams knew that anything he wrote would perhaps betray that quality. Risking it to deal openly with his sorrow, he wrote a letter to Frank in death, telling him how grateful he was that Frankie had never lied while he — Williams himself — was a person too sick to know the truth. The rooms of Key West, the rooms of East 65th Street, he wrote, seemed roofless and without walls; places no longer had names, and his sleep was now full of dreams of suffocation. He could go nowhere they had been together, he wrote, and nowhere they had never been, for Frank had always been the first to go with him to the new — and therefore terrifying — places, and to make them warm with memories.

As he resumed work on *Milk Train,* he wrote new words for the angel of death to speak to the agonizing widow Flora Goforth, words that described Williams when Frank was buried that September: like her, he would "go from room to room for no reason, and then go back from room to room for no reason, and then go *out* for no reason and come back *in* for no reason." Like Mrs. Goforth, he was mourning for having left a beloved "alone with his death."

Within a week of Frank's funeral, Williams and Frederick Nicklaus flew to Mexico, where John Huston was directing the film of *The Night of the Iguana.* By the end of October they were back in New York, where Williams pitched himself into meetings with the new director for the revised *Milk Train,* Tony Richardson, and with his new leading lady, Tallulah Bankhead. But the results were disastrous, for when the play finally opened she was in bad health and bad voice and could not be heard beyond the fourth row.

"I draw every character out of my very multiple split personality," Williams said later. "My heroines always express the climate of my interior world at the time in which those characters were created."

Just so, for Flora Goforth, whose name combines both his beloved flower-image and his cry — "En avant!" — "Go forth!" or, more fashionably, "Right on!" She expresses his "interior world" more directly than any character in his work, and the play, rewritten for the 1964 production after the death of Frank, became a conversation between himself and Death. Not a mystical or religious tract, as some have claimed, the last version of *The Milk Train Doesn't Stop Here Anymore* is an attempt by Tennessee Williams to come to terms with his relationship to Merlo, to articulate in death what was unspoken in life.

The identification between himself and Mrs. Goforth exists in every scene of the play, a work so intimate that it was virtually impossible for it to reach an anonymous public:

> MRS. GOFORTH: My outside is public, but my insides are private. . . .
> Blackie [the secretary-companion], the boss is sorry she took her
> nerves out on you. It's those night injections I take for my neural-
> gia, neuritis, bursitis. The pick-up pills and the quiet-down pills:

nerves shot ... I'm scared! You know what I'm scared of? Possibly, maybe, dying this summer!

BLACKIE (later): She eats nothing but pills: around the clock. And at night she has nightmares in spite of morphine injections. ... Insists she's only suffering from neuralgia, neuritis, allergies and bursitis. ... Morning doesn't begin on Mrs. Goforth's mountain till she sleeps off her drugs ... when people are very ill and taking drugs for it, they get confused, their memories are confused, they get delusions.

MRS. GOFORTH (later still): Why is it considered ridiculous ... to seriously consider and discuss the possible meaning of life? ... I've often wondered, but I've wondered more lately. ... Sometimes I think that everything that we do is a way of not thinking about it. Meaning of life, and meaning of death, too ... *What in hell are we doing?* Just going from one goddam frantic distraction to another, till finally one too many goddam frantic distractions lead to disaster and blackout?

More painful than *Suddenly Last Summer* because it derived from an actual death (and because it refers to all the antecedent deaths in Williams's experience, including that of Kip Kiernan), *The Milk Train Doesn't Stop Here Anymore* left Williams dry and breathless, naked and wounded. Revised — but as formless as before — it opened the first day of 1964 and closed three nights later. By January 13 the Brooks Atkinson Theatre was dark, the sets were dismantled and he had flown to Jamaica to recover (as he wrote to Donald Windham) from the latest professional disaster of his life — one made even more poignant because it was really a long poem of regret, of tribute, of gratitude and of guilt, for fifteen years with Frank Philip Merlo.

"When he died," Williams said later, "I went to pieces. I retreated into a shell. For nine months, I wouldn't speak to a living soul. I just clammed up. I wouldn't answer the telephone and I wouldn't leave the house." By March, even Williams's visits to Key West were so withdrawn, and frighteningly sunk in drink and drugs, that Frederick Nicklaus moved out. Soon after that, Williams flew back to New York, moved from East 65th Street and subleased a penthouse at 145 West 55th Street. In the spring and summer of 1964 he was virtually a recluse, although he did resume daily visits with a new psychoanalyst with whom he felt more comfortable. "I like [the new one] very much. The old one [Kubie] scared me. He reminded me too much of my father who scared me all my life."

Helpful as he found the new doctor to be, there was such complete withdrawal from people that in fact the writing began to suffer too; there were no longer springs from which to draw, no sources in which his feelings were nourished. At the same time, his fame reached its greatest peak. By 1964, twelve films based on his works had been made, to his great fortune. Three more would follow, in 1966, 1968 and 1969; for screen rights alone, he was paid in excess of five million dollars for these. But beginning in 1964, the celebrity which surrounded him for twenty years was no longer welcome; it became a terrible threat with a terrible toll. He was withdrawing from work to the solace of drugs, and from people to the darkness of solitude. And with this unfortunate shift in the personal and professional bases of his life, a cycle of misery and despair and decreativity enveloped him through the end of the decade.

"I had suffered a great loss in my life," he told an interviewer later, "and I sought oblivion through drugs. I lived from 1963 to 1969 under various drugs, and while I continued to write every morning, through the use of 'speed' injections, amphetamines intramuscularly, I was not in a very real world and unconsciously I might have been seeking death. . . . I went on speed, and my mind started going too fast for the typewriter."

The drugs were then easily obtained through the notorious Dr. Max Jacobson, who became widely known in artistic, political and social circles in the 1960s as "Dr. Feel Good," a provider of substances that were in those days neither strictly controlled nor difficult to obtain. Williams was first taken to Jacobson (so he claimed in a 1981 interview) by Robert MacGregor, his editor at New Directions: "He'd been a patient of Dr. Max Jacobson. He took only little pills that Jacobson gave him. I was in a state of such profound depression that he thought anything was worth trying, so he took me to Jacobson. . . . I had those three years of Jacobson shots that he mailed to me in the various parts of the country." According to Williams (who was in Jacobson's care considerably longer than three years), his error was not only in uncritically accepting the regimen of pills and injections, amphetamines and vitamins and barbiturates ("Nembutal, Doriden, Luminal, Seconal, phenobarbital — the same drugs we all took right through the 1960s"), but he continued to drink alcohol as well.

It must be remembered, however, apart from the grief and the creative pressures that may have motivated his initial visits to this doctor, that Tennessee Williams already had a well-established hypochondriacal personality. Since he was always, as he believed, suffering from cardiac arrhythmia, chronic indigestion, headaches and a wide variety of muscular, ocular and joint aches and pains and disabilities, he had for years been seeking from physicians all over the world treatments for ailments real and imagined. Many of these medications interacted badly, and most should have been taken only under specified conditions. Williams, however, used them liberally — not only for whatever pleasure or comfort they might induce, but because he felt he could not function as a writer if he were at all physically ill. "I have a sort of witch doctor," he said, "a very benign one. How I manage to stay alive I don't know. . . . It's not very comfortable to be a hypochondriac."

It was this unfortunate but fairly common trait that made him easy prey to the more dangerous results of drugs that added psychological to physical dependency. He never pursued the shabby-chic ritual of drug-taking as a bogus mysticism. For him, hypochondria, an obsession for constant work and his essentially Dionysian personality made alcohol and drugs perhaps inevitable. It was the ultimate phase of a frenzied pursuit both to celebrate and to deaden the senses.

By September 1964 he was seeing his new analyst seven days a week, he wrote to Paul Bowles from the penthouse on West 55th Street. He was taking little yellow pills for depression and said they worked for him like magic; to those he added the injections he had been taught to self-administer. With Frank's death from lung cancer he had stopped smoking cigarettes. "I now rely mainly," he said, "on drink and pills. My intake of liquor is about a fifth a day — half Bourbon, half vodka. . . . To pep up, I take half a Dexamyl, and when I find it's necessary to smooth things over I take one and a half Seconals. And when I suffer from acute insomnia, which is also often, I take up to four sleeping pills."

Energized and sedated by drugs, he simultaneously entered a fevered new inner world. The first writing to come from this was a pair of one-act plays which were, to no one's surprise, of violent and uneven quality — *The Gnädiges Fräulein* and *The Mutilated,* which were to be produced in early 1965, but for which sufficient funds could not be procured, and the performance dates were canceled. When this production failed to materialize, he wrote to Donald Windham that he was on the verge of collapse. At this point he realized that it was increasingly dangerous for him to be alone.

"I can't bear to be alone," he told a London critic. "I've got to have someone near me." And so he invited as a paid companion a man he had met through a mutual friend. William Glavin — tall, handsome, alert and long an admirer of Williams's art — moved into the penthouse within weeks of their meeting.

"He never saw much of his friends in the 1960s," Glavin recalled. "He always called it his falling-down period, his 'Stoned Age,' and he knew it was hard for people to be with him."* When a group of friends wanted to attend his reception of a Brandeis University award that season, he decided not to go rather than risk embarrassing others because of his unsteadiness and slurred speech. Even at the worst of times, he never lost a sense of manners or a respect for the feelings of others. At the same time, however, he had begun to classify those he knew: " 'Bigelow is on my side, he always was,' Tennessee told me one day," said David Greggory, "and that made me feel that he was dividing people into camps, those in favor and those against him. It was understood that those who were on his side were very few, a gallant band. And he became very suspicious."

Nothing offered him comfort in early 1965, neither awards nor a twentieth-anniversary production of *The Glass Menagerie,* starring his friend Maureen Stapleton as Amanda, nor yet another revival of *Milk Train* (in San Francisco; ironically, it ran over a month and was well received). "By this time," Stapleton recalled, "the pill situation was so bad that we'd enter a restaurant and before Tenn had had even one drink, he'd fall down. After a while he was always falling down, and it wasn't alcohol — it was the pills and the shots. I wasn't the only one who tried to convince him that Max Jacobson was an exploitive quack, but Tennessee defended Jacobson and insisted that he was doing just fine by him."

Very soon Bill Glavin learned about Williams's gypsy life: before the end of July 1965 they had moved to a thirty-third-floor apartment at 15 West 72nd Street. "I don't remember three mornings that summer that he didn't work," Glavin said. "He might tear it all up and say it was rotten, but he worked every day. Behind all the nonsense and all the sickness there was the courage of the writer. He really wanted to go on writing."

His misery was not helped by the news that his mother, too, was frequently disoriented; in her case, however, the reason was age. She turned eighty-one that summer.

* "I'm a built-in definition of hysteria," Williams told a reporter on his fifty-fourth birthday. "I hate myself. I feel I bore people — and that I'm too physically repulsive."

He went to St. Louis to see what could be done to help her, and he found his mother obsessed with the nation's space program, which she confused with the effects of the atomic bomb. He came back with the tragicomic tale of finding her in the yard, "combing radioactive fallout from her hair and crouching under a tree, like some ancient Ophelia in a mad world of her own." This somewhat grotesque visit found its way into an equally grotesque novella he was then completing. *The Knightly Quest* — with its double-edged title referring also to the protagonist's obsessive sexual searching for nighttime partners — begins as political antiwar satire in the style of *Dr. Strangelove,* but is blurred by muddled characterization and an incoherent narrative whose tone contradicts its theme.

In January 1966, *Slapstick Tragedy* — the combination of the one-act plays *The Mutilated* and *The Gnädiges Fräulein* — was at last in rehearsal with Margaret Leighton, Kate Reid and Zoe Caldwell. Although he was for much of the time unstable and in need of Glavin's constant attention, he had moments of sudden clarity and even of social concern. In a statement prepared for insertion in the play's program, he termed the Vietnam war "incomprehensible evil ... incredibly cruel, and believe me, nothing that will be won out of this war will be worth the life of a single man that died in it." To counteract the fear of the war's extension and also a growing fear of madness, he kept a Russian icon by his bedside, a gift from a friend. "I don't suppose I would keep it there if I did not have some religious feeling.... It isn't associated with any particular church. It is just a general feeling of one's dependence upon [a] superior being."

At rehearsals, Williams tried to encourage his valiant cast. "He laughed so hard at the rehearsals," Glavin recalled. "He loved giving actresses great moments on the stage — giving them fun so the audience could have fun. That cast really loved him, and it wasn't just pity." And to a woman who warned him that even his last-minute rewrites would not save *Slapstick Tragedy* from a critical attack, he replied, "I must continue to dare to fail. That is my life."

The cast was uncertain about the plays' contents, but audiences and critics were even more perturbed, and the double bill closed four nights after it opened at the end of February. Seen as a series of fantastic autobiographical vignettes from his "stoned age," the plays continue the author's anguished self-appraisal.

The Mutilated contrasts one woman's mastectomy with another's ample bosom, and the theme of the play is expressed in the claim that "we all have our mutilations, some from birth, some from long before birth, and some from later in life, and some stay with us forever." A funny-sad crew of outcasts is assembled, around the central figure of the tortured, maimed artist trying to persevere — an image of himself Williams would amplify in the later play *In the Bar of a Tokyo Hotel.*

In *The Gnädiges Fräulein,* a one-eyed performer past her prime has fallen into a wretched state and has become a demented resident of a fantastically rearranged Key West; the cottage-porch setting is his own house on Duncan Street. Written, as he admitted, under amphetamines, this play is unlike any other he wrote. But it has a strangely touching quality as the playwright identified with the battered, forlorn performer, and there is something heroic about the woman who gives everything for a vague chance to be loved. Her dignity, Williams perhaps tried to say, derives precisely from the fact of her endurance in the face of a hopeless situation. In February 1966 Tennessee Williams considered his own artistic, physical and emotional condition hopeless; his plays acknowledged that, even as their creation was a brave bid to prevent his total collapse.*

"Mr. Williams," wrote a critic in a typical reaction to these plays, "is turning old ground and re-working old characters [and] stealing from himself." But apart from any consideration of the merit of the double bill, the charge of self-plagiarism is not sufficient to demerit the plays.

"When critics accused Williams of repeating certain themes in his plays," Robert Anderson said, "they were being unfair. Artists are allowed to go back over the same material. Think of how many variations of water lilies Monet gave us! But perhaps because of the time and attention span demanded by a play, there has been the idea that playwrights especially cannot return to previously covered dramatic ground; they have to provide constantly new ideas. This is an unfair demand."

Perhaps the strangest aspect of the critical charge of repetition that was sounded against Williams in 1966 is how inconsistent it was with the prevailing state of theatre: that season, more than one-third of the sixty-nine new productions on Broadway were revivals, and to considerable critical acclaim.

Audrey Wood, meanwhile, was still working constantly on her client's behalf, placing short stories and poems and negotiating with film studios

---

* Edwina, who had been brought to New York for the premiere, suggested to her son after the abrupt closing, "Well, Tom, you can always teach!" He was not amused.

and book publishers. As for his private life and dangerous habits, he kept evidence of these from her — which was easy to do by simply avoiding personal contact. She was not unaware of his crises, but because he did not ask for help she rightly refused to interfere.

By spring 1966 Williams had completed a sprawling treatment for a film of *Milk Train,* and Audrey arranged for a contract by which he would be paid $50,000 for film rights, an additional $100,000 to write the screenplay, $20,000 as coproducer's fee, and a percent of any profit.

"I wanted to make a visually lyrical film about the welcome and the terror a person can give to death," said Joseph Losey, who was to be the film's director. "This is what I felt Tennessee's major feeling was in *Milk Train.*" In March and again in November 1966, Williams and producer Lester Persky and Glavin flew to London to meet with Losey. The remainder of the spring and summer Williams and Glavin went to a hotel high above the sea at Positano, where Williams's cousin visited; from there they went to Barcelona and Taormina. Somehow, even after late nights and continued chemical intake, Williams managed to work on the script of *Milk Train* — then called *Goforth!* — as well as on a dramatic treatment of his short story "Kingdom of Earth," and on a strange dialogue for two characters that suggested to his friends an imitation of Pirandello or Pinter.

"When he lost contact with his roots, he turned to others' roots and to their work for inspiration," as Vassilis Voglis put it. "He turned to Beckett's *Godot* for his *Two-Character Play,* and to other plays by other writers later." Humorless and lacking both focus and coherence, that title described this new play — *The Two-Character Play.* It was written, Williams wrote on the first-draft title page, "from the state of lunacy.... It is the story of the last six to seven years of the 1960s. The play is about disorientation — these people are lost as I am. They are two sides of one person."

The remainder of 1966 was crucial in the life of Tennessee Williams; it established a pattern of tragic drug dependence that would lead to a nearly fatal collapse almost three years later, and it marred his psychological and physical health for the rest of his life. That it began innocently — with nothing like an overt death wish or a desire to act either irresponsibly or rebelliously — made the results even more heartbreaking.

The central nervous system stimulants that he was obtaining from the misguided and finally criminal generosity of Max Jacobson were beginning, first of all, to have toxic effects. Intravenous amphetamines, commonly known as "speed," caused typical reactions in him: a sense of markedly enhanced mental capacity with little need for sleep, and frequent states of euphoria. But by 1966, tolerance had developed, and he had to have higher doses for similar results — with the concomitant side-effects: compulsive grinding of the teeth, extreme suspiciousness and a feeling of being watched (what his friends and associates called his "paranoia") and the alternation of periods of deep and prolonged sleep.

But in addition to the multiple daily doses of amphetamines, which he injected into his own veins, Williams had over the last ten years been taking, more and more often and in greater and greater doses, a drug called glutethimide, under the brand name Doriden. Introduced in 1954, Doriden was within a year the sixth most prescribed hypnotic drug in America. It was recommended for sedation or insomnia by many physicians, who naïvely believed that, because it was not a barbiturate, it would not be abused and could even be widely beneficial. By 1964 it was clear to pharmacologists that the potential for addiction and the severity of withdrawal symptoms were as dangerous as those of the barbiturates. In addition, treatment for overdose was found to be even more difficult.

Ordinarily taken for only a week before careful monitoring or substitution, glutethimide is usually taken in doses of 250 milligrams (a quarter-gram), no more than once or twice daily. If a person takes two and a half grams daily over a prolonged period of time he is certainly addicted; by 1966, Williams was taking four to five grams daily. (Lethal overdoses have occurred at five grams.) Passersby and acquaintances judged him drunk from this drug, since the effects of glutethimide intoxication resemble those of alcohol: a sluggishness, unsteady gait, slurred speech, hallucinations and a conviction of being plotted against or watched, faulty judgment, sudden and unprovoked laughter or crying, irritability, quarrelsomeness, moroseness, frequent tremors and a chronically dry mouth which the sufferer seeks to remedy by lip- and tongue-smacking and licking.

By 1966, Williams had unfortunately built up resistance to this drug which he regularly took to sleep well at night so he could work refreshed in the morning; or, alternately, to calm himself after a period of intense work. But simultaneous with his need for sleep and relaxation was the desire to be alert and energetic for daily work at the trying task of writing plays, which caused the vicious cycle of amphetamines, and then sedatives. These prescriptions were much easier to obtain and to have limitlessly refilled in the 1960s. Besides Jacobson, Williams knew doctors in Key West, New Orleans, San Francisco and New York, and few house doctors at hotels would refuse a request from Tennessee Williams for a sleeping tablet. The round of "highs" and "lows" continued, as well as the chemically caused alertness and sedation — artificial stimulation and a state sometimes mimicking coma.

It is important to emphasize that the tyranny of both the amphetamines and the hypnotics was almost accidental. In the 1950s and 1960s, the chemical and medical dangers of regular drug ingestions were not considered with the alarm that such abuse has since caused through expanded medical knowledge and sad public experience. Just as it was for a long time believed that prolonged psychotherapy was indicated for every small confusion and minor crisis in the life of the average American, so the taking of tranquilizers such as Miltowns was a sign of sensitivity, of a busy and demanding (and therefore glamorous) life in the 1950s and 1960s. (A popular song called "Tranquillizers" lightly and amusingly described the chemical becalming available to anyone in the slightest distress; in 1960, people were urged to reach for pills the way their grandmothers had urged fresh vegetables.)

With the widespread demand for counseling and for various prescriptions to deal with modern living, it was perhaps inevitable that there would be a few exploitative therapists and unscrupulous physicians, ready to keep a crowded list of regular patients by catering to their demands and even creating dependencies. Max Jacobson's name became synonymous with this abuse; as "Dr. Feel Good," he was the open secret of New York.

In early 1967, Williams and Glavin were in the Virgin Islands, where work continued on both *Goforth!* and *Kingdom of Earth* — without vials of amphetamines when he could, but ordinarily with them in ready supply. In New York, friends became more and more concerned, and when they expressed this to Williams he insisted that there was no danger, that he was simply tired, or that he was going to have a complete neurological examination because he thought there might be a nervous disease. About this time, Audrey Wood and her husband Bill Liebling pleaded with Williams to break with Dr. Jacobson. "No, Bill," Audrey reported Williams replying with slurred speech. "He is a *lovely* man . . . a *lovely* man." This, as Audrey wrote, "was all he would say, over and over again, until the repetition made it obvious he was far from rational."

"I visited him occasionally at West 72nd Street," Elia Kazan remembered, "and he seemed to me less well than he'd ever been in his life — less in control of himself." By midyear even Williams could not avoid acknowledging that his mind was very confused after he had taken (or not taken) his now increased doses. To Oliver Evans in Florida he wrote in early summer that he was going on with his work although he felt wretched. Shortly thereafter, he was told by Audrey that David Merrick would produce *Kingdom of Earth* as a full-length play early the following year; it was based on the earlier short story and a one-act play published in *Esquire* in February 1967. Instead of taking encouragement from this news, however, Williams panicked. It was sure to be his last play, but he was unsure he had the strength to complete it.

In July, he and Glavin were in Spain, and then, because Williams wrongly suspected that Glavin was either hiding or stealing his drugs, they returned hurriedly to New York to have the supplies refilled and the hypodermic needles replaced. By this time, the chemical and psychological effects of the drugs greatly alarmed Glavin. He knew nothing about them and, because he suffered a series of illnesses which in fact required gastrointestinal surgery, never even considered sharing this part of Williams's life. At the end of July, they went to Rome and then to Sardinia, where the filming of *Goforth!* — now unhappily called *Boom!* — would proceed, with Richard Burton, Elizabeth Taylor and Noël Coward in leading roles.

"Swimming, drinking and sleeping — that's all he was capable of in Rome," according to Joseph Losey. "Williams was not much help to us there or in Sardinia. He stayed only three days on the island, and he was clearly in no condition to do any rewriting for us. He left me to cut the script as best I could."

In late August and early September they were back in New York, but then Glavin's need for surgery and a recurrence of Williams's hemorrhoids and his depression over the massive stroke and imminent death of Carson McCullers conspired to bring them South. From Key West they heard of the death of McCullers on September 29. He also heard from Lilla van Saher, and at first he thought he got a wrong message. No, she insisted, it was true: although she was over sixty years of age, she was pregnant! The crib and the infant clothes had been purchased, and he must come to visit her in New York. When he returned North later that year, he learned that poor Lilla had abdominal cancer, the news of which had deranged her.

In early December, "totally addicted and very depressed," as Audrey Wood described him, he went to London for the premiere of *The Two-Character Play*. She accompanied him and later wrote: "When we got to his hotel, he began to say, over and over again, 'I want to die. I want to die. . . .' Nothing but this, over and over." To this Audrey replied: "Well, I'm terribly sorry, you may want to die, my friend, but God is not ready for you. God is not strong enough to take you, it's impossible. You cannot die yet." And with this, she "broke through the spell of his self-pity. Miraculously, he began to laugh. The litany, at least for the moment, was ended." So was the brief run of the play, which the London critics found at best confusing, and at worst pretentious.

Kingdom of Earth opened in Philadelphia in February 1968, with Harry Guardino, Estelle Parsons and Brian Bedford. José Quintero, who directed, recalled that Williams was "very nervous, and his nerves would provoke this laugh that was like a hyena's — sometimes at the worst possible moments. He would be riding the action of the play, and would become more and more nervous as it developed. When the action neared the crisis he would let out one of his laughs, and, of course, it was most disconcerting." The sudden, unmotivated laughter was symptomatic of glutethimide intoxication.

Kingdom of Earth shows Tennessee Williams at a desperate time in his life and career, reaching back to a story and a simple one-act, three-character play in an attempt to wrest a full-length play from it. In spite of its obvious homage to D. H. Lawrence, with the connection between repressed sexuality, an imminent flood and the nature of proprietorship (all contained in Lawrence's *Virgin and the Gypsy*), and despite flashes of humor and poetry, the play never developed into a compelling drama. The characters — the dying Lot, his wife Myrtle and his brother Chicken — are ciphers in an incomplete parable of religious inversion (which was in fact clearer in the story). A static, spiritless work of terror written at a time of spiritual dissolution, it italicizes the playwright's suspicion that he might soon die, and that his estate would pass to unworthy others. The final scene, with a grotesque self-parody in a moment of gratuitous "drag show" as a last crazy joke, crudely parodies everything preceding.

Before the New York opening on March 27, everyone was almost as nervous as Williams. He suggested a change of title to help the play's commercial appeal, and soon the marquee announced the premiere of *The*

Seven Descents of Myrtle, but in spite of that and other last-minute changes the play opened and closed within a month. (At once, Williams blamed David Merrick for the change of title and the subsequent failure of the play. That account unfortunately became taken as fact but the reality — as Audrey Wood, her contracts and those in the Merrick office attest — is that the second title was ordered by the playwright.)

"The cast came over to Sardi's after the final curtain," according to David Greggory, "and they were as marvelous offstage as on. But nobody knew what to expect, because the play itself was far from marvelous. Tennessee finally came in, assisted by several people, but he was stumbling so badly and was so unhappy that the bad reviews didn't seem to touch him at all." His withdrawal continued into May, and although the notices on the release of *Boom!* were as disappointing, Williams sent a letter to Joseph Losey thanking him for his efforts. Once again, his illness and his apparent indifference had not deadened his thoughtfulness. Losey had seen to the final version of his beloved *Milk Train,* and Williams was quick to acknowledge that whatever failures it offered were not the fault of the director, but that its merits were to his credit.

Abruptly, Williams announced to Glavin that in June they must move from West 72nd Street. Quickly and quietly, Glavin did as he was bidden, moving their luggage to the St. Moritz Hotel on Central Park South. Days of city wandering followed — of half-eaten restaurant meals, of half-viewed movies at local theatres, of Williams's long blackouts in his separate suite. Then, in an outburst of irrational, suspicious rage directed at Glavin in public — at a Third Avenue restaurant on June 22 — he accused his companion of indifference, disloyalty and theft. Glavin, hurt and embarrassed, simply left the table, to wait outside. What he did not know for several days was that while he waited Williams summoned a waiter, asked for a piece of paper and scrawled a letter:

> Dear Dakin:
>
> If anything of a violent nature happens to me, ending my life abruptly, it will not be a case of suicide, as it would be made to appear. I am not happy, it is true, in a net of con men, but I am hard at work, which is my love, you know.
>
> Devotedly,
Tom

The effect of the glutethimide was becoming more and more bizarre.

*　*　*

The following week, Dakin received the letter at his home in Collinsville, Illinois. Unable to locate his brother at West 72nd Street and fearing for his life, he notified the police. Four days later, Tennessee (in virtual seclusion at the St. Moritz) had not yet been traced, and when Glavin read this in the *New York Times,* he all but ordered Williams to call Dakin at once, to reassure his family. On Sunday, June 30, the *Times* reported that Williams had indeed been depressed over the failure of *Seven Descents* and of the recent film, but that he was "alive and well."

That was only half true, and when several days later he learned of the death of Lilla van Saher after three more operations for cancer, he said that he, too, was near death.

During the summer of 1968 two deliberately autobiographical plays occupied his uneven attention — revisions on *The Two-Character Play* and the first draft of *In the Bar of a Tokyo Hotel.* In spite of Audrey's suggestion that he consider revising the former for an experimental production in an off-Broadway house, he insisted that it was his masterpiece. To the end of his life it remained so important to him that he personally supervised several productions; invariably they were more highly regarded by him and his friends than by critics or public.

The Two-Character Play (later sometimes called *Out Cry*) has a brother and sister, Felice and Clare, trapped in a theatre during the run of something called *The Two-Character Play.* In the "performance" part of this play-within-a-play, autobiographical elements from the childhoods of Rose and Tom Williams are introduced (parental fights, the Southern setting, the name-callings, the accusations that they are both insane). But in his now fragile state — as he was writing this play — Williams used those elements to establish most plainly the psychospiritual kinship with his sister that had been his obsession in *The Purification, The Glass Menagerie, The Rose Tattoo, Suddenly Last Summer* and elsewhere. Although the two characters are parts of Williams himself (as he always insisted), he had always seen Rose as part of himself, and the lost and confined characters-as-single-character in this play is as much Rose as her brother. Obsessed throughout his life with her illness and operation, and with his own life of (he thought) abused freedom, he was aware that from 1966 he too was destined for breakdown. The part of himself that he felt he had lost was the part of himself that was Rose — the virginal, the untainted, the Lady of the Roses. The play was a method of establishing integration.

His precarious sense of sanity that year in fact strengthened the identification with his sister even more closely. Imprisoned in the theatre, Clare and Felice are surrogates for Rose and Tom, enclosed within the refuge of a shared asylum. They can neither escape from this nor, as they try, can they kill one another. They are doomed to a cold and endless grief, and to an inarticulate, misperceived love. *The Two-Character Play* represents what for Tennessee Williams was the greatest damnation — the possibility that he had lost, and perhaps never had, even the solace of spiritual intimacy with his own sister. The revisions and restagings of the play were not a repeated antiphon of therapy over the next several years; it was the constantly echoed cry of despair. And it was then, as Bill Glavin recalled, that Williams began to speak of admitting himself to Stony Lodge, to live with his sister forever in the asylum.

At the same time, he created two variants on these characters — the failed, dying artist Mark and his shrewish wife Miriam of *In the Bar of a Tokyo Hotel.* More brother and sister than spouses, this demonic inversion of Felice and Clare admit in the alternating, spastic dialogue that concludes part one:

MIRIAM: Are we two people, Mark, or are we
MARK: Stop there!
MIRIAM: Two sides of
MARK: Stop!
MIRIAM: One! An artist inhabiting the body of a compulsive
MARK: Bitch!
MIRIAM: Call me that, but remember that you're denouncing a side of yourself denied by you!

By the end of 1968, Williams and Glavin had returned to Key West, since there was no point in his remaining at a New York hotel: the walk along the corridor to an elevator, or from an elevator to a restaurant, was becoming a dangerous and embarrassing ordeal: "I was writing my plays under speed," he said later, "and I was falling down a lot." Those who spent time with him — Bill Glavin, Maureen Stapleton, Audrey Wood, actors, producers — could not recall a day that was not filled with the fear that he would suffer a fatal fall in public, or alone in his room.

Dakin arrived in Key West with the new year, after a call from Audrey that his brother was in a dangerous state. He found the man unable to complete a coherent sentence, unable to negotiate five steps without stumbling. His eyes were unfocused (and usually hidden behind dark glasses), he alternated long periods of erratic activity wih periods of twenty-four hours of nearly comatose sleep.

A convert to Roman Catholicism when he was in the military service, and a religious man ever since, Dakin Williams asked his brother if he did not think a visit from a local priest might be helpful, or at least comforting and encouraging as a first step toward health. Williams at once agreed, and during the first days of January, Father Joseph LeRoy, a Jesuit priest stationed at the Church of St. Mary Star of the Sea in Key West, visited Duncan Street regularly. From the time Dakin suggested his brother consider entrance into the Roman Church, very little of what transpired was clear to the drugged Tennessee: "My conversion was rather a joke. I couldn't learn anything."

"This is how it happened," according to Father LeRoy. "On Sunday, January 5, I was approached after Mass at the church by a gentleman who asked if he could speak with me. In my office, he introduced himself as Dakin Williams, brother of the famous playwright. He had come to tell me that Tennessee wished to be received into the Catholic Church as soon as possible." Later that afternoon, the priest accompanied Dakin to Duncan Street, where Tennessee provided a cordial if numbed welcome and in reply to Father LeRoy's questions said that he was indeed in despair, that he wanted to have his goodness restored, that he wanted to find God. "He wished to have now what as a child he said he had missed," Father Leroy said, "an understanding of the meaning of his baptism. I found Tenn an eager listener."

And so he remained for the next several days — an eager listener who unfortunately heard very little. Of the goodwill and concern of both Dakin and the priest there can be no doubt: since Tennessee refused to acknowledge that he needed hospitalization, or that chemicals were responsible for his deterioration, he submited with the casual carelessness of the drugged to the spiritual ministrations offered to him. Neither his brother nor the clergyman could assume anything other than his willingness to find consolation and challenge from the life of faith; they later learned, along with everyone else, that for Tennessee it was simply something of the moment. He was never, by even the widest of definitions, a churchgoer; much less did he subscribe to the creed or doctrines of organized Christianity. "I loved the beauty of the ritual," he said later, "but the tenets of the Church are ridiculous." He never had sufficient interest to consider the connection between the two.

On Friday, January 10, Margaret Foresman (managing editor of the

Key West Citizen) and Leoncia McGee (Williams's housekeeper) met with them in the small white church. "It had concerned him terribly that he'd had no success with his plays since Frank's death," Foresman recalled. "Frank's Catholicism was often a topic of discussion with him, and that might have had an influence on his decision to become a Catholic — and of course the guilt preyed on him too. That afternoon he told me that he thought a change might occur in his life because of his baptism."

The event, alas, ignited a minor ecumenical controversy; in the life of Tennessee Williams, not even a quiet religious ceremony could, it seems, pass without drama. It is irregular to rebaptize a Christian: the Roman Church has always recognized the validity of Christian baptism within a non-Catholic (Protestant) denomination, and after Vatican Council II (1962–1965) strict guidelines were issued on the matter to prevent offense to other Christian communions. If one of their members wished to enter the Roman Church, a simple rite of acceptance — without a repetition of baptism — was prescribed. Father LeRoy, not quite sure of those guidelines and wishing to accede to the Williams brothers' requests for a fully ritualized afternoon, was the unfortunate object of an ecclesiastical scandal. "It was [Tennessee Williams's] wish that the rite be repeated," Father LeRoy said later. "Neither he nor I intended to convey the appearance of any doubt regarding the validity of his baptism in the Episcopalian communion. Nor did we intend any other offense." As it happened, the event of Williams's baptism made worldwide headlines — as did every later, irreverent remark that he never took any of it seriously, or that it was done to please his brother.

Before the end of January, Williams had flown to Rome, where he met with Father LeRoy's superior general, the Reverend Pedro Arrupe, the Spaniard who headed the Society of Jesus at that time, an office commonly thought to be so powerful that the holder is called "the black pope" — i.e., he wears not white but black. On his return to Key West, Williams told Leoncia that he had met the black pope. She was delighted and replied that it marked a great step forward when one of her people headed the Catholic Church.

Never hypocritical with Father Leroy, Williams took his "religious period" as an extension of what he called his "stoned age." Rather like the bored Catholic convert in Evelyn Waugh's *Brideshead Revisited,* for whom religion is unimportant if not downright boring, Williams accepted the occasional practices of that winter as unharmful and perhaps even beneficial. But in a number of interviews later, he was inclined to refer to the whole event as "boring."

Exhausted after his visit to Rome, and with almost no resistance to infection, Williams was easy prey to the unpleasant strain of Hong Kong influenza that year, and for almost a week in February he was confined to Mercy Hospital in Miami. On his release, because rehearsals would soon begin for *In the Bar of a Tokyo Hotel,* he insisted that Glavin arrange for them to depart.

After meetings with Herbert Machiz (who had directed *Suddenly Last Summer*), Anne Meacham (who had starred in it) and Donald Madden (who would play opposite Meacham, as the dying artist Mark), Williams managed to accept an invitation to an evening at the home of Maureen Stapleton.

"It was a birthday party for Robert Whitehead [who had produced *Orpheus Descending*]," she recalled. "When Tenn arrived I met him at the door and he just stared at me and said, 'Maw, I've just overdosed.' So I pushed him into the bathroom and gave him two large beakers of warm water laced with mustard, to force him to throw up the overdose. Well, it took me quite a while to clean up — he was violently sick with all those pills. He rejoined the party, however, and he thought that everybody *else* was crazy."

What cannot be explained is how Williams in fact survived 1969, or how he saw to the revisions and rehearsals of his new play. "He stumbled a lot that April during rehearsals," Anne Meacham said, "even when he took over after Herbert Machiz was dismissed. But somehow he was mostly lucid with us."

Daily, Glavin walked him to the theatre, the Eastside Playhouse on 74th Street, "and if he could barely walk on the way, something miraculous happened when he arrived. He sat in the orchestra and directed Anne and Donald, and he was so sensitive and beautiful and encouraging with them. We were all amazed at how he could do this."

After several postponements, the doomed play opened on May 11, after an extended series of twenty-two previews. Critics and audiences were angry and disappointed, although there were almost universal expressions of hope and respect. "One must never forget that, despite his present esthetic humiliation, Tennessee Williams is a thoroughbred," *Time* magazine reminded. "I hope," Harold Clurman wrote plaintively, "that it's not Williams's last testament." Clive Barnes, in the *New York Times,* considered the play "almost too personal, and as a result too painful"; and Henry Hewes and Richard Watts, Jr., who for so long had been among the playwright's most fervent supporters, wrote essays expressing personal concern for him, affirming their affection and respect and their hope (as Watts put it) "that he will soon return to the high estate that has made him the foremost of our playwrights."

The play, as Williams told his cast, was about the humiliation of the artist who, when he loses confidence in himself, his body and his lovers, "hasn't the comfort of feeling with any conviction that any of his work has had any essential value." The eventual fate of the play neither surprised nor shocked him, it seemed; his generally detached state was a kind of emotional bulletproof vest.

But on May 21 there was some redress: he received the gold medal for drama from the National Institute of Arts and Letters, and his acceptance speech has probably not yet been equaled for brevity, wit and boldness:

"I think I'm essentially a humorist, you know, so I'm going to try to tell you something that will make you laugh," he said after Lillian Hellman had presented the award. "One time, Maureen Stapleton received a phone call from a friend who said that so-and-so was getting married, and the caller said, 'Why she is marrying that man, you know he is a homosexual,' and Maureen said, 'Well, what about the bride?' And the caller said, 'Well, of course we know she's a lesbian. And you know they're not even being married by a real minister, but by one who's been defrocked!' And Maureen said, 'Will you do me one favor? Will you please invite Tennessee Williams? Because he'll say "Oh, they're just plain folks!" ' "

Another award was to be presented to him that spring, and unenthusiastic as he was by this time, he had earlier agreed to visit the University of Missouri at Columbia to accept an honorary doctorate from his alma mater. On May 31, he and Glavin flew to St. Louis, where Dakin took them to Edwina's home on Wydown Boulevard. Then in her eighties and still an incessant chatterer, she seemed overwhelming to her visiting son, who withdrew to the basement with a portable typewriter. It was, Glavin felt, perhaps not so different from the situation at home forty years earlier. For three days, Williams was hardly seen except at meals. Glavin cared for Gigi, the bulldog Williams had insisted on bringing with them, and he sustained with good humor the role of substitute son Edwina imposed on him. On the third day of their visit, she suddenly burst into tears, telling him that Tom always blamed her for what had been done to Rose, but that a team of doctors had advised her about the lobotomy — two in favor and one opposed — and that she had been given six weeks to make a decision in which her husband took no part.

On Tuesday, June 3, the Williams brothers, Glavin and the dog went out to Columbia, where the playwright was given the honorary degree and escorted to the Alpha Tau Omega fraternity house where he had lived from 1929 to 1932.

"He was not in good shape at all," according to their host, Dr. Larry D. Clark of the university faculty. "Dakin had to be by his side constantly, and it was clear to us that he was ill when he announced that the journalism department should be shut down: 'You can't teach people to write!' he told us." Moody, withdrawn, uncongenial and suspicious of everyone around him, Williams had never been unhappier.

Before their departure from New York, Williams had told Glavin that they might proceed to Taos from St. Louis — or to San Francisco, and then on to Japan, where the famed Bungakuza Theatre was preparing *A Streetcar Named Desire*. "Poor Tom," Glavin remembered thinking to himself, "he has no idea where to go, or what to do now." One fact was clear, however: he could not much longer remain in St. Louis, for his mother was a torture to him, and her openly anti-Semitic and anti-black sentiments were an embarrassment. "You know," she confided to Glavin with complete seriousness, "the Negro parents don't feed their children so they can all get right thin and their parents can slip them through the mail chute and rob your home!"

On Saturday, June 7, Williams had finally made a decision. Glavin was to reserve seats for a flight to San Francisco. At the Fairmont Hotel there, he joined Williams in his room at odd hours for a meal or a drink — whenever he was summoned — or Williams would suddenly decide to leave the hotel for dinner across the bay, in Sausalito. With his amphetamine injections, he managed to sit at his typewriter a few hours each morning; the rest of the day and night he withdrew into a drugged sleep. The staff at the Fairmont catered to his requests, but within a week they were as nervous as Glavin.

As if Williams were not miserable enough, he had the ill fortune to read *Life* magazine's review of *In the Bar of a Tokyo Hotel,* which appeared that week. Not content with detailing his negative comments on the play, critic Stefan Kanfer also indulged in a vicious *ad hominem* attack against Williams, calling him a "White Dwarf," the label given by astronomers to stars that shrink and fade in space: "Tennessee Williams appears to be a White Dwarf. We are still receiving his messages, but it is now obvious that they come from a cinder. . . . Gone are his sustained flights of rhetoric — which always bordered on hysteria. Gone, too, are his poetic tendencies, which always risked ridicule. . . . Other playwrights have progressed: Williams has suffered an infantile regression from which there seems no exit."

Even in his emotional isolation, Williams was devastated by Kanfer's article. He wept — just once — and then kept to his hotel room, refusing to leave the floor for three days; his pain and his terror were mirrored yet again in manuscript pages, this time of a short play he called *The Frosted Glass Coffin,* with its references to heart failure, the problems of old age, the horror of senility and breakdown.

But he was not the only one ill, although he could not recognize that another might require care too. Glavin, who had already required several intestinal operations, needed still another. When Williams insisted that Japan was to be his next stop but that Glavin should return to New York for surgery if he preferred, it was then necessary to find a replacement companion. Anne Meacham, who had stood by Williams during the difficult experiences surrounding the play, agreed to fly to San Francisco and then attend him in Japan. She was to arrive June 19.

During the several days before this, Glavin tried to discourage Williams from a voyage that could only be disastrous. Unable to walk or to perform the simple task of feeding himself, Williams was close to toxic coma; when he knocked over a liquor glass, he accused others of doing it to embarrass him; a plate of pancakes required more than an hour to be eaten; Seconal tablets were still washed down with gin. Equally unfamiliar with the intricacies of drug protocols, and equally concerned, Dakin flew to San Francisco on June 16 and found his brother in a desperate condition. Two days later, Glavin — relieved to depart to the relative comfort of a hospital room — flew to New York; the next day, Dakin, unable to convince his brother to enter a hospital, returned to St. Louis. Meacham arrived at the same time, and the final arrangements were completed for their departure for Japan.

"We arrived in Tokyo on Saturday, June 21," she recalled, "and from the start it was exhausting and difficult. First, the necessary papers had not been cleared for the admission to Japan of his dog Gigi, so the animal had to be quarantined at Haneda Airport, which upset Tennessee terribly. Then, when we arrived at the Hotel New Otani, he was so weak and tired that he just wanted to sit in the lounge for a while. He didn't want a drink, but he hadn't the strength to go to his room." And there, in a bizarre congruence of art and life, the drained, sick artist and his leading lady sat in the bar of a Tokyo hotel. This did not escape the attention of the press, who reported a drunk and disorderly Williams.

The next day, novelist and playwright Yukio Mishima came to pay his respects, and he took them to — of all places — a local Italian restaurant where Mishima's quiet, gentle manner temporarily soothed Williams. But just as Glavin had predicted, the situation was soon too burdensome even for Anne Meacham's patience. Williams's regimen was unchanged — self-injected amphetamines by day, along with Seconal and Doriden — and she was anxious not only for his health but also for his freedom: Japanese drug laws (especially regarding drugs imported by foreigners) were known to be much more severe at the time than America's. She sought help from Mishima, and from Raymond Purls and Walter Nichols.

Purls was an executive of Union Carbide, and he and his wife were living in a Tokyo suburb; Nichols was on the staff of the American embassy. By June 28 they had moved Williams from the hotel to a rented house, the better to insure freedom from public scrutiny. Within days, however, Williams was accusing Meacham the way he had accused Glavin and others: she was stealing his pills and syringes. She telephoned her friend and co-star Donald Madden in New York, asking him to call Audrey Wood and Dakin Williams. She knew the limits of her ability, and Tennessee would have to return to America for treatment — that would be the best thing she could do for him.

At once Dakin made a reservation for Tokyo, but then a call came that Williams had insisted on flying alone from there to San Francisco, and his brother need come only that far. Meacham remained to close the house and settle final details with friends, officials and the solicitous people at the Bungakuza. Williams, as it turned out, had seen only the first act of *Streetcar;* illness forced him to leave.

By July 13 he was in New York and Glavin, released after surgery, resumed the attentive care he, too, might have appreciated. Unable for several days to decide on their next destination, Williams at last chose Key West. For ten days there, Williams slept, ate little, rarely left the house, and wrote the draft of an absurdist political nightmare-drama, *The Demolition Downtown.* One evening, obviously aware of the trouble he was causing others, he apologized to Glavin and offered to read aloud to him — an evening pastime they had once enjoyed together. In a strained and touching effort, he opened a biography of Hart Crane and read the account of the poet's suicide.

Since they had left West 72nd Street in June 1968, Tennessee Williams and Bill Glavin had never been a month in any one place. The restlessness was symptomatic of the sedative's overdosage; for Glavin the constant moving was simply exhausting. On Monday, July 28, they were back in San Francisco at the Fairmont, where Williams continued his self-imposed isolation. In one of his rare conversations with Glavin during a dreadful three-week stay, he again told his companion that he would move to Stony Lodge to live with his sister Rose — after all, he said, he wrote only for her.

He added that the cause of his unsteadiness was a brain tumor, and that the people in the room adjacent to his were plotting his death. Glavin, trying to ignore these irrational suspicions, was keeping account of the Doriden tablets: Williams was then taking more than five grams daily, and it was entirely possible, if not likely, that he might not awaken one morning. Once again, Dakin received an emergency call, and once again he responded by coming to San Francisco, only to be dismissed by his brother five days later. When Williams badgered the hotel staff with constant complaints that the people in the hotel were shouting at him, laughing at him, planning to kill him, Williams and Glavin were politely but firmly asked to quit the hotel.

On August 17 they flew to New York, Williams obtained a bottle of one hundred Doriden tablets, and another black week passed. (Audrey Wood, in spite of her efforts, could not locate him, and he never contacted her.) The following Saturday, they were driven to Stony Lodge, where Williams visited his sister and took her for dinner at a local restaurant. "Rose never took her eyes off her brother," Glavin remembered. A sad, inarticulate connection existed between them; it was a scene from *The Two-Character Play* poignantly sprung to life.

For the first week of September, Glavin attended Williams in New Orleans, where the playwright wanted to visit with Pancho Rodriguez. They met for dinner, and with an irony worthy of the character-reversals in *Summer and Smoke,* Pancho was now leading a professionally stable, quiet life radically different from the one he had known with Williams more than twenty years before. And it was the older man who now seemed childish and unpredictable and destined for grief.

On September 7 they returned to Key West, where Margaret Foresman met them. "I was ready to help my genius friend," she recalled, "but he was in a paranoid state. He insisted someone was going to break in the house and kill him. After he sent Glavin away for a week, he'd call me to come over and check around the house — he was convinced there were prowlers and murderers. He wouldn't call the police himself, he had me do it — he was used to having people do things like this — and when the deputy sheriff arrived, Williams insisted that someone guard the house all night. All that week he became worse and worse."

Foresman called Audrey Wood, who recommended calling Dakin. But he was understandably hesitant to respond when his help was never accepted.

Finally the inevitable crisis occurred. In mid-September, Williams was preparing a pot of coffee in his newly rebuilt kitchen and, as Margaret Foresman remembered, "he fell and spilled some, burning his shoulder. It was not such a terrible burn, but since he dramatized everything he was convinced he was dying. He told me to call Dakin, who came at once. Dakin took advantage of the situation to convince his brother that he had to go to a hospital. And thank God, Tennessee was willing. I think he knew he needed to get off the drugs. This was the most painful moment for all of us. A lot of eccentricity went along with his genius, but now he was really dangerously ill. And because of what happened in the next week, he cut me and Dakin dead for the rest of his life."

What happened saved the life of Tennessee Williams. When Dakin arrived in Key West, he urged his brother to come back with him to St. Louis, where he could enter Barnes Hospital, a first-rate medical center near the family. When Williams agreed, it was the first indication that a seed of life-affirming energy still lay beneath the self-destruction of the last years. There was a brief hesitation, when he stopped to see his mother and gather personal items: he had changed his mind, he said, and would recuperate nicely at her home. Rightly, Dakin forced the issue and drove his brother to Barnes where, the record shows, he admitted himself voluntarily. Physicians determined that his violent, destructive and possibly suicidal behavior warranted the constant supervision and confinement in the psychiatric division, and he was placed (as "Thomas L. Williams") in Room 9126 of the Renard Psychiatric Division; he was denied telephone, mail or visitors for the first several days, and immediately evaluated for total withdrawal from all drugs.

"I was so demented," he admitted later, "that even the television programs in the psychiatric ward seemed to be personally directed at me. Even Shirley Booth's little program, *Hazel*. I thought Shirley was making veiled innuendoes about me."

And then it happened. The total withdrawal of all drugs — especially the strong doses of Doriden — took a toll on the third day, in a way that could not have been foreseen in 1969. He had three *grand mal* seizures in one morning, suffered a violent upset of normal body chemistries, and had two heart attacks within the next two days. These reactions, it is now known, are typical of sudden withdrawal from prolonged megadoses of glutethimide; why Williams was in fact put on the "cold turkey" treatment is unclear, but it is important to stress that the effects of such withdrawal were not always foreseen. As of October 1, no one was quite certain he would survive.

Gradually, however, he responded to treatment; slowly, awareness, lucidity and normal speech returned. His mother and brother were at last permitted brief visits, but the greetings were not what they expected. With his remarkable resiliency there was a new articulateness, and it was neither quiet, humble nor grateful. He had always been terrified of hospitals and confinement, he told his brother: Dakin knew what a terrible thing it was to put him there, and that was just why he did it; Dakin hated him, he wanted him dead, he wanted only his money. Shortly afterward, Dakin Williams was permanently excised from any mention in his brother's will.

For the rest of his life, Tennessee Williams could never admit that he needed in 1969 the sort of drastic treatment for an illness that afflicted celebrities from Judy Garland (that same year) to, later, his friend Elizabeth Taylor, the singer Johnny Cash, even a First Lady, Betty Ford. These people admitted their problems, sought help, and (except for the doomed Garland) recovered and have tried to help others similarly afflicted. Perhaps it was only guilt that led him to consider the experience as reprehensible; his open admission of it later should not be mistaken for anything other than shame.

But there is another element too. All his life, Williams had been somehow able to avoid the extreme to which Rose (and Blanche DuBois, Catharine Holly and others in his plays) had been subjected — unwilling confinement in an asylum. Now what he had always feared had become a reality, and, unable to see how his life had been saved, he instead accused his brother of making real the terrible event which hitherto had been dealt with, as if by sympathetic magic, in his art. What must never happen, happened. "It's true," Elia Kazan said later, "he was absolutely terrified of confinement and of breakdown. And of course there was the example of Rose."

As Maureen Stapleton reflected, "Tennessee could never accept that what Dakin did for him saved his life. He would have been dead in no time. Dakin stepped right in and saved his life. It's that plain. I called Tennessee later and told him he should be grateful to his brother, but he never forgave him for what he did, and when I said that, he turned on me for a time, too. He made up his mind that Dakin was the enemy, that Dakin had done this awful thing to him. A blind goat could see that Dakin acted unselfishly, but Tennessee could never see that point. And he remained unconvinced for the rest of his life."

His return to health, the doctors had to admit, was nothing less than astonishing. By early December he was back in Key West, playing with Gigi, telling Bill Glavin the horrors of institutional life, inviting friends for drinks and inspecting the completed patio garden and new kitchen appliances.

"He looked better than I had ever seen him," according to Father LeRoy. "He said he was limiting himself to one drink a day, and only limited pills."

Chapter Nine

ENDURANCE

(1970–1976)

Sometimes you work on a play by inventing situations in life that correspond to those in the play. . . .

— Clare, in *The Two-Character Play*

F ROM 1970 to the end of his life, Tennessee Williams continued to work at his craft with his habitual, insistent energy — daily, and sometimes on more than one play, story and poem simultaneously. Only rarely, however, was the result satisfactory to him, to audiences or to critics. Tennessee Williams was mentioned as the great American playwright whose creative powers went into decline after 1969, and in an important way that much was true. The extreme partisans — friends and colleagues with varying accuracy of judgment — were indeed more enthusiastic than he about his writing. But no artist's powers remain at the most fervent creative peak, none of the gifts retain their sharpness and brightness undimmed. In fact, few artists in our time worked so long and with such brilliantly fruitful results as he: from 1944 to 1960, there was no doubt that he was the most consistently serious, the most poetic (and not merely the most controversial) playwright in America.

As cultural fashions shifted, so did his own fortunes, however, and he endured inner exhaustion and outer confusion, the effects of physical dependencies and psychological depletion. His body was wounded, his mind was ravaged, his spirit had been shattered — by the death of Frank Merlo, to be sure, but just as violently by chemicals. It would be naïve to pretend that this confluence did not affect his art. With great courage and simplicity and hope he kept on, and he was always grateful — sometimes even desperate — for the interests of producers and actors and directors.

But as the writer Louis Auchincloss suggested in a perceptive tribute, Williams after 1969 "never recaptured his old stature. Why? [There was] a lack of coherent thinking that wrought havoc with Williams's later theatre, [and a] sentimentality that ultimately broke through walls unsupported by any basic moral fabric."

That may seem a harsh assessment, but in fact it defines the enduring value of Williams's great early achievements as much as it laments what came after; it describes the contours of the works in which Tennessee Williams gave an accurate diagnosis on the condition of an era, and of what Rilke called a tendency of the heart. What happened in American culture in the 1960s and after has eluded the understanding of very many statesmen, teachers and parents — as well as men and women, young and old, everywhere. To expect that the upheavals in contemporary life would not also leave behind some great artists like Tennessee Williams would also be naïve — especially if, as was the case with him, there were the concomitant problems of poor health, emotional instability and psychological frailty.

Somehow, Williams summoned the old Dionysus in himself, to go on working, to go on seeking for a resting-place with someone, somewhere; the romantic voyager continued to travel, even if he often seemed as doomed as the Flying Dutchman. Somehow, for the unaccountably long period of thirteen years after his worst collapse, he found the courage to go on going.

But as Auchincloss added, "Dionysianism, undiluted, is, in the last analysis, only chaos," and chaos was always the predominant motif of Tennessee Williams's life.

In his golden period, however, his gift shone as a spectacular blessing on the development of art, and his late decline cannot diminish the splendor of those early accomplishments. *The Glass Menagerie, Summer and Smoke, A Streetcar Named Desire, Cat on a Hot Tin Roof, Suddenly Last Summer, The Night of the Iguana* — these remain among the great literary and dramatic works of our time, and at least a few of the short stories ("One Arm," "Three Players of a Summer Game") will perhaps be recognized as masterpieces of that genre.

"I hope I can continue," he told a reporter from the *New York Times* at the beginning of January 1970. "I hope I can escape. I think I can. I've been through a great catharsis . . . I've been abusing myself for at least seven years. Although I continued to work, God knows I didn't work well."

There was a great hope of newness with the new year, and clearly a desire for change. The press, which had not missed a nod of his head during the last two years, reappeared, pens and cameras and tape recorders at the ready, as soon as he emerged into public view. He wanted to give the impression that much had altered; indeed, he no longer seemed dependent on drugs and alcohol, and he had a new companion. But there was an

uncharacteristic bitterness in his voice. His brother Dakin was mentioned in angry phrases, and the staff at Barnes Hospital was denounced.
He was glad to be returning to work, but his judgment was at least
questionable.

"The young men who attended him in the early 1970s," David Gregory believed, "were very pretty and not very bright, but I don't think he
really cared very much one way or the other. Merlo had been the one
person for whom he felt a really deep personal attachment. Unfortunately, the feeling that replaced deep attachment, the situation with later
companions, had the tone of employer-employee. Still later, when he was
drinking heavily again, I think he accepted people into his life that he
would not have accepted earlier. Some of them seemed to me like people
who were in it for what they could get out of it."

With this new era, Williams paradoxically lost another type of steadi-
ness in his life, that of companionship. In the last months together with
Glavin, during 1970, the suspiciousness caused by drug intoxication had
become ingrained. He left a two-page note for Glavin one day, requiring
them both to read what he said was one of his three favorite modern
plays, Strindberg's *Dance of Death.* He was living, he reminded Glavin,
for his work — and since he believed that Glavin was destroying him, he
accused him of the worse sin of destroying that work.

The choice of *The Dance of Death* for required reading is indicative of
how Williams saw his life in 1970, for Strindberg in that play depicted a
long-term marriage as a strange symbiosis of love and hatred. The story
of Alice and Edgar is that of a dying man who attempts to continue his
dominance of his wife after years of emotional imprisonment. Finally she
attempts to retaliate, and their relationship becomes like the medieval
Totentanz, in which Death personified triumphs over all mortals. But
Williams also knew that the couple in Strindberg were self-parodies; they
dispense with maniacal delight a mixture of cruelty and pain. That this
grotesque black comedy should occur to Williams as he considered the
end of his companionship with Glavin tells us how consistently theatrical he saw his own life. But it also tells us that he was capable of a self-
fulfilling prophecy. The drama of his illness required an epilogue if not a
sequel; the dismissal of Glavin would do nicely.

When he spoke to the reporter from the *Times,* Williams had come to
New York to promote the revival at Lincoln Center of *Camino Real.* He
appeared on David Frost's live television program, and before Maureen
Stapleton, Jessica Tandy and Eli Wallach joined him onstage, he submitted to the usual inquiries about his family and his past life. Guarded in

most of his replies, he then answered Frost's question about homosexuality in his work with the first public statement on the matter as it related to himself: "I don't want to be involved in some sort of a scandal, but I've covered the waterfront."

In this and other interviews that winter, his ingenuousness about his collapse and his hospitalization was remarkable; for the present, however, he chose not to elaborate on what had slipped out to Frost before a commercial interruption. His willingness to discuss his "stoned age," however, was to his advantage as a celebrity, for in the late 1960s began a time when the public fed on "sincerity" and "honesty" and "letting it all hang out," especially if the news was sordid or at least intimate. Williams at fifty-nine was taking all the laundry from the baggage, hanging it out for public scrutiny. But in the curious nature of such things, the more horrific his admissions were, the more people gasped in admiration. It was consistent with a new pattern: murderers, assassins, terrorists, irresponsible celebrities and cheap crooks in government office were being paid enormous sums, and appearing on television talk shows, to describe their stories to a public famished for trash. Tennessee Williams was not at all like them, but for a while many were confused about his attitude to himself.

It is odd, therefore, that when reporter Tom Buckley spent several days with Williams in Key West with a tape recorder that spring, Williams later resented the appearance in print of the details of his home life and social intercourse, which he had offered with casual abandon. Perhaps he wanted to be controversial — the hard-drinking, openly homosexual writer with nothing to hide — and at the same time, a man of *his own time,* a Southern gentleman from a politer era who would never abandon propriety and privacy. In any case, he was not always so alert or so guarded that he was able to pre-edit his own remarks.

The day after the television appearance, he flew back to Key West. Other reporters and some university students wanted to discuss a strange story published that month in *Esquire,* "A Recluse and His Guest." His sudden retreat was in fact a clue: *he* had been the recluse in his own period of confusion. He had not much interest in the story, however, and he preferred to resume work on what he thought would be the greatest plays of his career. He could not admit to himself that he was barely strong enough or disciplined enough yet to produce any serious piece of work.

"I work so hard," he told David Greggory at that time, "because I know it [success] will happen again."

Greggory was not so sure: "I wasn't at all convinced it would happen again, however. If you live at the top of fame and material success, of course, it's hard to live anywhere else. At this time he began to group people in terms of those who believed it would happen again and those who didn't. There were times when he felt he might prefer becoming the unofficial dean of American theatre, and the mentor to younger play-wrights, or a much sought-after writer in residence at a prestigious uni-versity, but that feeling didn't last. He had to feel he could do it again — hit the jackpot."

But during the last dozen years of his life, Tennessee Williams was clearly of divided heart about this matter. He would sustain with good grace the changing patterns of Broadway, and the changing taste of the theatregoing public; he would often agree to the first productions of new plays in modest circumstances, and he would be grateful for these pro-ductions. What mattered was that he continued to work in the theatre.

If serious work was indeed his major goal in 1970, he apparently ap-proached it with some diffidence, for in Key West he celebrated his re-turn by hosting a number of parties, often for as many as forty guests. Liquor flowed, guests brought uninvited friends, and factions and cliques quickly formed round him: *This* one must not be trusted, since he tells everything to Tennessee.... *That* one is a friend of so-and-so, and he passes information on to such-and-such a crowd, so be careful of *him*.... *This* one is an aspiring actor and wants to be Tennessee's houseboy but he also wants money for drugs.... *That* one sleeps with *this* one in order to ingratiate himself with *those over there* ... And so it went, with all the charm of typical social carnivores. Key West, once a quiet retreat where he could work well, live a reasonably ordered life with Frank and Grand-father, was now really no longer suitable for him.

"The crowd there really did not help him to live well or to work well at all in the last years," according to Edwin Sherin, a director who collaborated with Williams in the 1970s. "They gave him nothing but a phoney admiration, and took whatever they could get."

The social life he had known changed, too, as his friends died. There were no longer women like Lilla van Saher to shield him with her warm, crazy humor, and to hold forth with a crowd nearer his own age. Then, in April 1970, his loyal, tortured friend Marion Black Vaccaro died. "He took care of everything," according to Father LeRoy, who looked in reg-ularly on Williams. "He made the funeral arrangements at St. Paul's, he invited their friends, he gave a reception."

At the same time, Williams was trying to improve his image in the community. For the benefit of the local library's expansion fund, he agreed to read from his own work at the Waterfront Playhouse on May 2. A vision in white — he was, after all, a risen soul — he arrived in a white suit, a white lace shirt, and white buckskin loafers. With a decanter of red wine at his elbow, he stood in a pale blue light, rather like a movie ghost, and read from *The Frosted Glass Coffin* and *A Perfect Analysis Given by a Parrot.* The two hundred guests attended politely, but there was some shuffling when he read certain sexually explicit paragraphs from *The Knightly Quest,* and then some coughing when he read the text of an angry dialogue he had had with a Barnes Hospital doctor, and then a series of homosexual love poems, most of which were later published in his collection *Androgyne, Mon Amour.* Williams was back, and Key West — like it or not — had him.

In the audience was Audrey Wood, who had come to visit. Her husband had died the previous December, just as Williams was returning to Key West, and she had looked forward to the trip south. She helped in the preparations for the evening, obtaining the rose design he wanted for the program leaflet, meeting with local press people, and generally straightening difficult turns in the social road. For her arrival, Williams arranged a pleasant ceremony, a public ground-breaking for the small garden and gazebo to be added to his property. Just to the left front of the yard, he had planned the Jane Bowles Summer House, named for his friend and Audrey's client, and for her 1953 play (*In the Summer House*) about a tyrannical mother. The earth was turned by Williams and Wood on Saturday afternoon of that same weekend, and by June the little wooden structure was complete. The Monroe County Library Association, grateful for his public reading in May, presented him with what he had requested — Key West rock roses that were at once planted by his gardener, Frank Fontis.

When Audrey returned to New York, she took a sheaf of poems, short plays and one short story she placed immediately, called "Happy August the Tenth," the story of two lesbian lovers who live in an East 61st Street brownstone. The two are plainly modeled on Tennessee Williams and Frank Merlo, and the story is a gentle tribute to what was and what might have been. Elphinstone (as in "elf in stone") is the variant stand-in for the author himself: she has become hard and somewhat bitter, is in psychoanalysis, was born under the sign of Aries at the end of March, and regularly visits her aged and confined mother in an upstate institution called Shadow Glade. Her mate, Horne, has a different group of friends and has grown emotionally distant.

His real-life August was followed by a three-month cruise to Asia, on which he was accompanied by his old friend, the poet and teacher Oliver Evans. After a brief visit to the retired streetcar named Desire in New Orleans, they departed from Los Angeles for Honolulu, where they visited Christine Jorgensen (one of the first to undergo sex-change surgery), and then they continued to Yokohama. There, on October 1, Yukio Mishima dined with them and warned Williams about his drinking. After Hong Kong, they finally arrived at their destination — Bangkok — and there Williams learned that Mishima, before a great crowd, had committed ritual hara-kiri and was then beheaded, a death that did not surprise Williams: the suicide, he later wrote, was "because [Mishima] felt that . . . he had completed his major work as an artist." Oliver Evans's interpretation of the death was even more curious than Williams's, however: in an article for *Esquire* he maintained that Mishima's death was an inevitable decision resulting from his having achieved a perfect physique — there was no bodily ideal left to pursue.

In Bangkok, Williams submitted to minor surgery to remove a fatty tumor from his breast, a simple procedure he was told could be treated in any large city. In California and Yokohama, however, he told the press he was dying of breast cancer; that report was spread around the world at once, and Williams was able, when he finally returned to America at year's end, to hold forth on his brave insouciance in the face of what might have been terminal disease.

By early 1971 he had revised and retitled *The Two-Character Play* as *Out Cry;* its second production, later that year, caused an event of such emotional and professional significance that there are almost as many versions about it as there were productions and versions of *The Two-Character Play/Out Cry.*

Responding to a request for a play, Williams gave George Keathley, the director of the first version of *Sweet Bird of Youth,* the revised manuscript called *Out Cry.* By this time, Keathley was manager of the Ivanhoe Theatre in Chicago, and he at once saw fascinating possibilities in the play. He suggested a summer revival, with Donald Madden and Eileen Herlie as players. "I knew it bore the stamp of illness and confusion," Keathley said, "but he was very devoted to it and I thought we could make it work."

From the start, however, the project was doomed. Instead of working with Keathley and the cast, Williams withdrew to a Chicago hotel room where — perhaps because the bases and resonance of that play were simply too frightening and depressing — he resumed a round-the-clock dependence on drugs. He no longer self-injected amphetamines, but he was able to find a doctor who agreed to supply him with shots of methylphenidate hydrochloride, sold under the brand name Ritalin, which was then available by injection. A nonamphetamine stimulant, Ritalin must be given cautiously to unstable patients — especially those with a history of drug dependence or alcoholism. At the same time, Williams needed something to counteract the effects of the Ritalin, and to sleep, and since he was afraid of returning to Doriden, he requested a generous supply of Nembutal, a barbiturate brand of pentobarbital sodium he always called "yellow jackets." These he obtained in the highest dosage, one hundred milligrams. A short-acting sedative, Nembutal takes effect in ten to fifteen minutes and lasts for about four hours — enough for him to sleep between long bouts of revising the play.

Pre-production for *Out Cry* was, therefore, difficult for the players and director. By the time of the preview performances in early July, Williams's anxiety had been caught by everyone else. The entire time in Chicago was frantic, as he wrote to producer William Hunt, who at the same time was staging his short play *Confessional* at a Maine summer theatre.

Audrey Wood had sprung to Williams's defense by firing an indignant publicized letter to *Life* magazine when the devastating attack by Stefan Kanfer appeared, and when the *New York Times* republished it as an advertisement for *Life*. Now, she knew that this play — with its intimate importance for Williams — would encounter difficulties even if Williams were in the best health. At once she went to Chicago for the last rehearsals and previews, intending to remain through the opening and assist in any way possible; her presence alone, she might have suspected, could benefit her client in dealing with the press.

"Audrey wanted to protect him until the play was ready," according to Anne Meacham, who was in Chicago at the time. "Tennessee was terrified about *Out Cry* and he never should have asked for a fully staged production of it. When it encountered troubles he had to blame them on someone. Audrey was closest. She was a mother to him in the way his own mother had never been, and he turned on her the way one can turn on a parent."

In *Memoirs,* Williams told his account. In one of his hysterical mad scenes, he turned on her after the second preview performance and quietly said, "You must have been pleased by the [cool] audience reaction tonight. You've wanted me dead for ten years. But I'm not going to die." He admitted that this was a terrible thing to say, but that he was convinced she had neglected him for a decade — especially during his years of drug abuse — and that he felt like a lost child.

But Audrey offered a somewhat different account: after the preview, she was met backstage by Williams, who — in the cast's presence — "swiveled about to stare at me, and with the vigor only he possessed, shouted at me, 'And as for you, you have wished I was dead for the last ten years!' . . . As I exited, I heard him say, 'That bitch! I'm glad I'm through with her!' "

George Keathley, who was present, confirmed Audrey's version, with this nuance: "We were all in Eileen Herlie's dressing room after the performance, and I suggested to Tennessee an idea about altering a line of dialogue. This set him off in a rage — 'How dare you make such a suggestion to me,' and so forth. Audrey, trying to smooth the situation, said quietly, 'Tenn, it may be a good idea — just listen to George for a moment.' And with that he turned on her and shouted, 'And you! You've wanted me finished and dead for years!' Audrey was devasted, Tennessee remained furious, and that was the end of their relationship. Still in a very bad state, he left Chicago immediately after opening night, July 8."

This unfortunate incident — over which both Williams and Audrey grieved for the rest of their lives — could never be healed. Because he felt she no longer gave him total dedication and because, as he told his next agent, he felt she was simply too old, he had even before that night decided to seek another representative: "I want my work in younger hands and she is seven years my senior."

"This was another shocking episode in Tennessee's late life," Cheryl Crawford said, "and none of us could make much sense of it. He had turned Frankie away, he had turned against his brother after the breakdown, and now he turned against Audrey."

Unfortunately, the final severance of the relationship was, ironically, due to Audrey's near-sightedness. At a New York hotel restaurant later that year, Williams went to greet her, but when she reached out she was momentarily unsure it was he, and she withdrew her hand. Misunderstanding her and just as vulnerable, he walked away, angry and (he thought) rejected again.

"Audrey was a great lady," according to Robert Anderson, her client for over thirty years, "and she could act very much the grande dame.

Whether the split between her and Tennessee was precipitated by his rudeness or by his earlier decision to leave her, we'll never know for sure. But Audrey had a way of speaking somewhat imperiously to men by beginning, 'Now, young man —' and this may have, at one bad moment, rubbed Tennessee the wrong way. As for his statement that he wanted a younger agent, well, that's the remark of an aging writer who's afraid that his powers may be declining and who hopes that a change of agent may bring about a change of his fortunes or a deepening of his talent."

Wisely, however, Audrey — who never lost her concern or devotion for the writer she had represented since 1939 — saw to it that he remained within the agency of which she was then a senior member. By the autumn of 1971, she had effected a meeting between Williams and Bill Barnes, and for the next seven years Barnes gave his new client as much loyal devotion and attention and personal sacrifice as any agent could. At their first luncheon, Williams announced, "I want my name back up in bright lights, Bill!" And to that end Barnes devoted himself, as Anne Meacham and others said, "twenty-five hours a day." In time, he, too, would be followed by a thoroughly dedicated professional.

In October, Williams was back in Key West. He kept an active correspondence with Barnes, asking that he not be dismissed as a working playwright. He added that he lived to write, to swim, to love. By November, Barnes, inspired by the Maine production of *Confessional,* had interested a trio of New York producers in the play, and he wrote to Williams about expanding it for off-Broadway as a full-length drama. Williams in turn wrote to Hunt in the poignant tone of a man unsure of his current worth, claiming that he felt only half-alive when he was not at work in the theatre.

By November's end, Williams had determined once again that a change of locale would improve his spirits, and he and his companion had moved to a New Orleans hotel while he sought an apartment. Almost immediately, they went on to Houston, where Nina Vance was reviving *Camino Real* at her Alley Theatre. Actor Ray Stricklyn, who had met Williams in New York twenty years earlier, was cast as Lord Byron, and he recalled Williams's presence on opening night in November 1971 as "a very sad occasion. . . . Tennessee's condition had degenerated — he was on pills and arrived intoxicated. He was completely out of it. He was practically carried backstage, presumably to pay his respects to the cast. But he could have been in any city in the world that night."

It seems clear that the situations which triggered Williams's return to drug dependence were invariably connected with the theatre, or with theatre people. In many social situations, when he entertained a few neighbors, or when engaged in other important activities, he could be quite sober and alert. One of those occasions was his attendance, in December, at an anti–Vietnam war rally at the Cathedral of St. John the Divine in New York. He spoke against the war and was greeted with some bewilderment by young activists who were not quite sure what era he represented.

While in New York, he met often with Bill Barnes: he intended to be involved in every aspect of the forthcoming production of the extended *Confessional,* now called *Small Craft Warnings.* He reminded Barnes that when his play was staged, the playwright himself would be the real subject of the reviews; too much was at stake for a risk, and he intended a major revival not of a play, but of himself.

Until rehearsals brought him to New York in the spring of 1972, Williams shuttled uneasily between New Orleans, Key West and New York, anxious, as he wrote in notes for the published version of the play later, that a "remnant of life . . . redeem and save me . . . from a sinking into shadow and eclipse of so much of everything that has made my life meaningful to me." He wrote to William Hunt, who agreed to direct the play in New York, that he hoped desperately for the restoration of his destroyed reputation. His last play (as he said it would be) had a humanistic purpose that the corrupt press and public of New York must be made to appreciate.

In 1972 Williams made his second house purchase, this time in New Orleans, at 1014 Dumaine Street. He lived in modest quarters on the second floor and rented out several smaller units, which were managed by a resident housekeeper-superintendent. Later, he added a landscaped patio and a small kidney-shaped pool — so small, in fact, that he often walked to the nearby New Orleans Athletic Club, where he had retained membership over the years. At the same time, he continued revisions on *Small Craft Warnings,* for which Hunt and the new producers had set an April 2 opening date at the Truck and Warehouse Theatre on East 4th Street.

The final weeks of rehearsal for that play, however, were a stormy period. Personal differences between Williams, Hunt and the cast led to Hunt's withdrawal from direction, and for several days Williams himself led the cast; Richard Altman was then engaged to undertake that task. In vain, the playwright sought to have the April opening postponed. He felt the play was "inviting disaster" with the cast "groping after lines [and] mugging.... [We] have been warned by two [preview] audiences that the sea is very rough."

But his anxiety about the critics' reactions was not entirely warranted. Although most thought that the evening was more a series of character revelations in the tradition of Eugene O'Neill's *The Iceman Cometh* (with which it shared the barroom setting), there were none of the personal attacks that he expected. The collection of reviews was mixed, but there was no personal vituperation, nor even the veiled attacks that had hurt him before. His frailty that season was well known in New York, and there was apparently an unspoken agreement not to discourage a man who told everyone he had been broken by the theatre to which he had given his life.

With the play open (and, as it happened, showing a profit quite soon), Williams departed for Purdue University, in Lafayette, Indiana, where he accepted an honorary degree and introduced the actors Olive Deering and her brother Alfred Ryder, who performed *The Two-Character Play.*

"In spite of a certain timidity and uncertainty that he'd had all his life," recalled Ryder, "he showed a compulsion to charm everyone." Olive Deering was an especially welcome guest at Purdue, for she had been a good friend to Williams for years, and she had succeeded Anne Meacham in *Suddenly Last Summer* in New York; she played the same role to equally great acclaim in Los Angeles later, and would appear in *Vieux Carré* in 1977. "Tennessee was very gracious," according to Deering, "but it was getting harder and harder for him to camouflage his tragic life, his deeply tormented life." Williams loved their readings at Purdue, and several years later he asked them to act in the same play off-Broadway in New York.

He returned to New York at the request of the publicist for *Small Craft Warnings,* and submitted to dozens of interviews and promotional ideas that became embarrassing and sometimes bizarre. Williams himself was turning into the attraction, the barker who would perhaps be more interesting than the play, but he would bring them in. When the play moved uptown in June, he went into it in the role of the alcoholic doctor. But there was too close a resemblance between art and life, as he had once said of Diana Barrymore's desire to play Alexandra del Lago. Onstage frequently that summer — only to improve business off-season — he stumbled over his lines and others' and ad-libbed outrageously, addressing the audience (and thus disorienting the cast) and generally advertising the very condition for which he dreaded condemnation. "It's a successful little play," he said later, "but it's not a major work. It's badly constructed, with one monologue after another. I enjoyed acting in it very much, but the other actors hated it because they didn't know what I was going to say — I ad-libbed so much!"

Bill Barnes, always ready with professional support, had advised Williams against this kind of showmanship, but to no avail. Williams went on with this, and with an appearance on a television newscast in which he warned small crafts about an impending summer storm. His manner for these increasingly hammy tactics was that of a man under the influence of Ritalin injections, which, as he openly admitted, he was obtaining all that year.

"He liked people to pay a lot of attention to him, even when it was somewhat embarrassing," according to Paul Morrissey. A member of Andy Warhol's film production crew, Morrissey had become a director, and had met Williams at this time through the curious Candy Darling, a transvestite actor who (as Cherry Davis) was appearing in *Small Craft Warnings* as the indomitable, oversexed Violet.

In his suite at the Elysée Hotel — the very one formerly leased by Tallulah Bankhead — Williams drafted in July the short story "The Inventory at Fontana Bella."* This grotesque tale concerns a century-old Italian principessa who lives in a wild, hallucinatory world of memories of past lovers. She forces her household of servants and a doctor to take her to Fontana Bella, her estate across the Bay of Naples. En route, her entourage exchange (*à la* Boccaccio's *Decameron*) tales of sexual exploits, and they engage in appropriate illustrative actions; after one such, the principessa dies. The story is noteworthy insofar as it fuses images of uncontrollable sexual urges with the fact of death: Williams was exploring sex from its first to last experiences in this (as in all the stories he wrote that year and the vast majority thereafter). There is a link between the habit of insatiable sexual arousal, guilt and death. And the need for penance is regarded wistfully, but it is invariably overwhelmed with a lunatic lewdness.

That autumn, he also completed "Miss Coynte of Greene," in which the same theme is emphasized: the erotic life of a thirty-year-old spinster

---

* The story seems based on Mrs. Goforth's remark in *The Milk Train Doesn't Stop Here Anymore:* "I had an intuition that things were disappearing ... fabulous china, my Sèvres, Limoges, Lowestoff. . . . Half of it gone, decimated! And my Medici silver . . . gone! That's what the inventory disclosed!"

(like Alma Winemiller) is awakened after the death of her mother, and she leads a life of frenzied promiscuity. Years later, visiting the grave of her first lover, Miss Coynte — now sixty-one (as Williams was when he wrote the story) — is on the verge of a new, interior revelation. But Williams draws back, afraid: "In her prone position among the roses . . . the clouds divided above her and, oh, my God, what she saw. . . . Knowledge of . . . Well, the first man or woman to know anything finally has yet to be born. . . . It's time to let it go, now, with this burning inscription: *En avant!* or 'Right on!' "

And onward he moved. He was invited to be an honorary juror at the Venice Film Festival in August, and he gladly attended with Barnes, Morrissey, Warhol and actors Sylvia Miles and Joe Dallesandro. At the Cipriani Hotel, Venice, activities took on an atmosphere vaguely reminiscent of the glamorous literary-social set popularly connected with the Riviera in the 1920s — fashionable, attractive, monumentally self-indulgent. Williams was disappointed by all the films screened except Morrissey's *Heat,* which starred Miles and Dallesandro; he spent an entire night talking about his story "Two on a Party," which he thought would be the perfect vehicle for them. For years, his friend the producer Lester Persky hoped to realize that project.

But at the end of August, Williams returned alone to New York while the others remained in Italy: he had been notified by the company of *Small Craft Warnings* that box-office business had decreased, and he resumed acting in it. He also resumed an inchoate companionship with a young Vietnam war veteran named Robert Carroll, whose writing and person he very much admired. This relationship deepened intensely over the years, and even after they eventually lived apart, Williams maintained a profound affection for Carroll, and an unshakable belief in his talent. Only Carroll and Rose Williams were mentioned as personal beneficiaries in the last will and testament of Tennessee Williams.

When Morrissey returned to New York in September, he invited Williams to rest in Montauk after the closing of *Small Craft Warnings.* There Williams stayed in a sparsely furnished cabin at Deep Hollow Ranch, where he revised *Out Cry* for a projected Broadway revival the following year. A picture of English actor Michael York was set up over the typewriter — "my inspiration," Williams told Morrissey, who recalled Williams's "enormous vitality, in spite of about thirty bottles of pills and several bottles of liquor that were strewn around his rooms." His work, his swimming, his medications — these provided buffers against loneliness for several weeks that autumn, his companion having for the time traveled elsewhere. In *The Night of the Iguana,* the defrocked Reverend Shannon observes that "people need human contact." Just so with Williams: "I need to be touched and held and embraced," he said that year. "I need human contact. . . . Age bothers me only in this area; at my age, one never knows whether one is being used as an easy mark or if there is a true response."

"He had a sometimes disastrous need for companionship," according to Paul Morrissey. "He simply could not be left alone for any period of time that summer or in the fall, back in New York. He depended entirely on others for advice — not only about his plays, but about all the practical details of everyday life."

The desire to see *Out Cry* succeed on Broadway became an obsession in 1972, and on revisions of this play he worked with an almost manic frenzy in Key West, New York and New Orleans throughout the rest of the year. But when it finally opened on March 1, 1973, at the Lyceum Theatre, *Out Cry* disappointed and confused both audiences and critics. About this time, speaking of this play, Williams described more and more openly the link between himself and his sister:

"I've had a great deal of experience with madness; I have been locked up. My sister was institutionalized for most of her adult life. Both my sister and I need a lot of taking care of. . . . I'm a lonely person, lonelier than most people. I have a touch of schizophrenia in me and in order to avoid madness I have to work."

As he worked and reworked the elliptical dialogue between Clare and Felice ("This is me," he told Bill Barnes that year, "and it's my most personal work"), Williams inserted stage and character descriptions: the exterior setting, he insisted, "must not only suggest the disordered images of a mind approaching collapse but also, correspondingly, the phantasmagoria of the nightmarish world that all of us live in at present. . . . [Felice] is a playwright, as well as player, but you would be likely to take him for a poet with sensibilities perhaps a little deranged."

It is in the work patterns and the comparisons of manuscript revisions of this tortured play that the inner world of Tennessee Williams is most clearly revealed, for *Out Cry* was not merely the revised text of a play that documented an earlier breakdown: it was also a description of a continuing state of decline. At every stage of reentering this play, of re-presenting it, it became the artistic canvas on which he drew the harsh and disjointed lines of his own illness. "I consider myself scattered," he said at the time of another revival of this play. "Very scattered. Psychoanalysis didn't put me together at all. I'm about as together as Humpty Dumpty after the fall."

Audiences, critics and admirers of Tennessee Williams's art could not have been expected to know that the image he tried so valiantly to offer in the 1970s — that of a healed survivor — was simply that, an image. On closer examination it could be seen, however, to have shattered, as he said. The public, whom he continued to address in his work and in interviews and all the glittery tawdriness that publicity and celebrity demanded, could not have known that he was only apparently a well man — and often enough he did not even seem very well.

Whenever he said he was ill and confused and frightened, friends and colleagues too often contradicted him: he looked fine, they said; he was working hard; all was well. But he was more honest. As an artist of the first rank, Tennessee Williams felt the tragedy of the modern world — of its alienation, of its loneliness, of its loss of a sense of the transcendent. He heard its echoes of pain and despair earlier and louder, within himself, and in his great plays he told us what was wrong. But at the same time, he lived — by his own ready admission — on an alarmingly grim course of self-destruction.

Out Cry closed on March 10, after twelve performances. The critics were as disappointed as the New York public, sensing the energies Williams had put into it but feeling left outside of it. Each of the critical reactions lamented the burial of authentic feeling in a morass of verbal and dramatic confusion, and it was Harold Clurman who came closest to the mark when he expressed a hope that Williams would abandon his confessional, turn his attention away from himself, and reach out to an affective, dramatic consideration of others — for that, after all, was his great strength. Williams needed to change the topic of his personal and professional meditation, but no one was willing to suggest this to him.

Within days, he was in Los Angeles, where he introduced the film of *A Streetcar Named Desire* at the Los Angeles County Museum and, on Sunday, March 18, spoke to a luncheon gathering at the University of Southern California, where he accepted praise from its president, the local press and several actors. He also went to Grauman's famous movie palace, looking for Vivien Leigh's footprints, and he visited William Inge, who was even more ill and withdrawn than Williams had been in the last year. Williams's birthday was celebrated after he attended a new production of *Streetcar,* with Faye Dunaway and Jon Voight.

"His companion called me and invited me to the party," David Gregory recalled, "and most of the cast was there. To be frank, I don't think Tennessee really cared about this or any other revival. The great performances were past, the play was finished, and no one was really going to add very much. He retained cast approval over the years, but I heard him say many times that if the actor was nice enough, what the hell, it didn't make any difference." (For the next three years, there was every month, somewhere, an important American revival of a Tennessee Williams play: *The Glass Menagerie, Summer and Smoke, A Streetcar Named Desire, Cat on a Hot Tin Roof, Sweet Bird of Youth, The Night of the Iguana* — even *Kingdom of Earth* — were staged by major companies with star casts.)

During his Los Angeles visit, Williams welcomed Harry Rasky, the Canadian filmmaker who had had his cooperation in producing a filmed documentary celebrating Williams's life and career. Rasky brought a completed print of it for a birthday celebration. At the same time, Williams's magazine and television interviews altered significantly once again. Perhaps because his plays were no longer shocking people, he was trying to do just that with his life (in April 1973 *Playboy,* for example). Now he was speaking more intimately, more crudely in fact, about his sexual history. This new bluntness, of course, was just what journalists and interviewers wanted, and just what "sold" in the 1970s, as was described above; the more personal, even the more imprudent a public figure became, the more the statements were valued as newsworthy. When Tennessee Williams himself replaced his characters, detailing the private corners of his life, it was the new showmanship replacing art.

That spring he was working on an original play (for televison, he said, since his theatrical experience had recently been so unhappy). Titled *A Second Epiphany* (and later, less felicitously, *Stopped Rocking*), it was a story of madness and confinement, of breakdown, of infidelity, despair and self-destruction. Written for and dedicated to his friend Maureen Stapleton, it was presented to her that year. Later, as she recalled, "a number of meetings were held with producers and network people and public broadcasting executives. Then they asked for more revisions, so he rewrote. Then we had more meetings, but we just couldn't arouse sufficient interest, and it was abandoned."

Also in progress that spring was a short story he called "Sabbatha and

Solitude," about a writer full of sexual energy who keeps her Italian lover in a Maine cottage and tries to sort out her failing professional life and her fierce sex drive. "I detest confinement, you know," Sabbatha says, and the omniscient narrator comments: "Going mad can have a certain elation to it if you don't fight it, if you just pull out all the stops, heedless of consequence . . . there is slight difference between the noun 'decade' and the adjective 'decayed,' just an accent." The story stops abruptly with a further link between profligacy and death; even her crippled state does not deter Sabbatha from paying for sex.

The story was completed during a sea voyage that brought him the news of two deaths. On May 4, Jane Bowles died; then, in Rome, he read of the death (on June 10) of William Inge, who had also been for some time in the grip of alcohol and drug dependence.

"Near the end of Bill's life," according to his close friend Barbara Baxley, "when he was in great trouble, I turned to Tennessee. He gave detailed instructions on what to do. He said, 'Don't let them put Bill where they put me,' and he asked hard questions so I could try to help Bill's sister decide what to do. 'What has he taken?' he asked. 'How much of this and how much of that?' He advised me how to go about getting Bill the proper help."

But nothing availed, for all their concerted efforts, and on June 10, Inge succeeded in a last suicide attempt. Although his feelings about Inge had passed from romantic attachment to mentorship, then from collegial support to a deep resentment and jealousy, Williams had recently felt a real concern for Inge's suffering, which in so many ways was like his own. He was deeply upset by Inge's death, and soon after he said quietly to the grieving Barbara Baxley, "Don't you think that our whole lives, yours and mine and Bill's, have been one long nervous breakdown?"

He wanted also to be with Paul Bowles, and now, on his journey, that was possible. For two weeks in July he visited Tangier where, according to a companion, "he was not at his most buoyant. . . . He was preoccupied with finishing a play, *The Red Devil Battery Sign*. He was exceptionally restless, having cut short a stay in Italy, as he would cut short the stay in Tangier."

The visit was difficult for everyone, not least of all because Williams's restlessness was exacerbated by drugs: "I take Nembutal myself," he said. "But only one, to fall alseep." The other drugs were taken at other times, along with alcohol.

From Tangier he proceeded to London — before returning to New York and the Elysée Hotel. Once again in a scattered state, he visited several physicians and obtained, as he wrote in a letter to Sylvia Miles in August, medications for high blood pressure, high cholesterol, for heart palpitations, for anxiety. He was also revising *The Milk Train Doesn't Stop Here Anymore,* and he thought it would be a good vehicle for her and for Michael York, perhaps in London. But he was in no condition to make any serious decisions until he had rested in Key West. There, in September, he was deeply affected by the death of Anna Magnani, who succumbed to cancer, in Rome, at the age of sixty-five. For her coffin he sent twenty dozen roses.

The return to Key West resulted in another story in the "Rose cycle," written at exactly the time he was considering bringing his sister to live with him. Titled "Completed," it was about twenty-year-old Rosemary who endures a painful social debut. She has a grandfather named Cornelius and, because of her mother's selfish manipulation, takes refuge with her Aunt Ella in a timeless world of confinement and seclusion. Her life is "completed" before it begins.

The story threw him, for several days, into a blank depression from which he emerged to return to New York in December to receive the first centennial medal — as "the foremost dramatist of our day" — from the Cathedral of St. John the Divine. He also met with Kate Medina, the editor at Doubleday with whom Bill Barnes had contracted the previous year for Williams to write his memoirs. Tennessee had originally hoped to call this project *Flee, Flee This Sad Hotel,* from a poem by Anne Sexton, who had also documented her mental breakdowns in her writing. But when she took her life the following year he settled on the simpler *Memoirs.*

This collection of random thoughts and impressions of his life (a first, 650-page draft was completed in October 1972) could not have come at a less auspicious time for Williams, and to her credit his editor worked bravely for two years to give shape to the palette of impressions. In the revised version of *Milk Train* he was writing at the same time, Williams inserted extended comments about the enterprise of publishing these reminiscences: "My memoirs, my memoirs, night and day," says Mrs. Goforth. "The pressure has brought on a sort of nervous breakdown, and I'm enjoying every minute of it because it has taken the form of making me absolutely frank and honest with people."

Although the original intention of his own memoirs was to attempt a new form for the autobiographical genre — images and impressions floating to the surface of his mind while he was performing in *Small Craft Warnings* — *Memoirs* suffered from the chaos, inner and outer, that marked his life ever more acutely in the 1970s. As in his interviews and press appearances, he wrote frankly about sex — more frankly, in fact than he could in any other medium. But such frankness must not be confused with real psychological intimacy or spiritual self-disclosure, and in fact *Memoirs* conceals more than it shares, misrepresents more than it documents, omits major events, confuses dates and, as every critic lamented, tells virtually nothing about the playwright's career. For a writer who insisted that his life was his writing and that to write was the core of his being, this was a curious treatment of the life indeed: the craft is mentioned casually here and there as if it were an avocation. This is not beguiling humility, it was partly deliberate obfuscation and partly the incoherence of the 1970s. Kate Medina stitched and rearranged, and Barnes encouraged them both. The book that resulted was often spicy, sometimes witty, never self-approving and always maddeningly disorganized. Near the conclusion of the first draft, Williams had written — on October 1, 1972 — that he had just completed a task for which he had been duly engaged but which he was incompetent to discharge.

For his friend Anne Meacham, Williams created in early 1974 another role, actually a revision of *The Gnädiges Fräulein*. But after various problems before and during production, the play — into which both director and star had put considerable emotional energy — fared even less well than in 1966. As *The Latter Days of a Celebrated Soubrette,* it was seen for only one performance in the spring at a church hall in New York. Another revival — of *Out Cry,* in Greenwich Village that June — contained excessive cuts, as would the numerous productions to follow across the country in the next several years. Few found it more coherent.

Interviews continued throughout the year, and work on three new full-length plays in which he made valiant attempts to inject an easier, gentler style and a more traditional structure. But he took advantage of opportunities offered to travel to Puerto Rico and California, in addition to the normal, sudden jaunts to New York and New Orleans to approve revival casts, to meet with his agent or editor, to accept an award, to grant an interview, to do a campus reading. Restless travel was the single constant characteristic of his life, then as always.

But he also paid regular visits to Rose in Ossining. No matter the weather, his mood or his level of energy, his sister was never neglected. Often he brought her to New York for a few days, and they strolled, shopped for clothes, saw a movie, lunched at the Plaza. Rose chain-smoked in private and public — which, because of Frank Merlo's death from lung cancer, disturbed Tennessee more than Rose. But she was in all respects a lady of great dignity, and she very often greeted passersby with a Windsor wave of her right hand, whispering that it was her duty as queen of England to greet all her children. At dinner, she invariably ordered a soft drink, but when it was served she would not touch it until her brother had sipped it first and assured her it contained no gin. At such moments, he was convinced there were vague memories of Edwina's tirades against liquor. Harry Rasky recalled watching his film about Williams in New York with Rose and her brother present. "The entire time she listened to the voice on the television set, but she stared at her brother in the room."

About the same time, Williams seemed to be considering the place of religion in his life. "I never defined it precisely to myself. In times of great distress I pray ... the act of prayer is consoling. And back of existence there has to be a creative force ... otherwise we wouldn't exist!" His spiritual life was indistinguishable from his artistic quest, however, and the formalities of Christianity did not interest him; it would be difficult to imagine him feeling at ease in a crowded church. If asked by a prodding interviewer to detail his pattern of worship, he parried: "I love to receive Communion, but I'm usually working on Sunday morning, so I take Communion at funerals."

But back of the humor and the vagueness, it was clear there was also concern. Working on *The Red Devil Battery Sign* in late 1974, he inserted a telling line beginning with a prayer: "God, in whom my heart fervently believes ..." — and the play describes, among other less clear concerns, the crisis of faith in both God and man.

In early 1975 he moved freely between cities and manuscripts, interrupting work on *Red Devil* to polish a scene on a seriocomic fantasy titled selfconsciously *This Is (An Entertainment)*. In New York, the National Arts Club presented him with a gold medal for literature on February 20, and the dinner was attended by Elia Kazan and Maureen Stapleton, among others whose confidence was dear to him. "My obligation is for me to endure," he said, and often repeated this over the next several years.

The endurance was manifest that spring in his work in Key West, mostly on *The Red Devil Battery Sign*. To direct, Edwin Sherin was engaged; he had in 1974 staged a revival of *A Streetcar Named Desire* in London with Claire Bloom as Blanche, and Williams had very much admired it.

"In Key West that spring, I found Tennessee lonely and worried about his health, but pushing on," Sherin remembered. "A typical day began with his rising at five in the morning, and setting to work at once in his small studio. He finished by eight or nine, and then we had breakfast by his pool. Scene by scene, we went through the typescript, making changes. Then he swam, and after lunch he'd sleep. In the evenings we always went into town."

But by this time there was a group in Key West who took advantage of Williams, according to Sherin: "There was a loud and boisterous crew who weren't really worthy of him, and when he was in his cups he was especially vulnerable. At times like this he seemed helpless. He was very protective of me, since he knew I wasn't quite at home with them — and I thought, well, he wasn't either. He had so much more to offer. With those hangers-on, he lost some of his focus and identity."

Also that spring, Edwina arrived for a visit. Now in her ninetieth year and sometimes disoriented, "She was a hard lady to reach," Sherin said. "But Tennessee catered to her every whim, although it was clear — and he said it — that he neither liked her nor felt comfortable with her. I don't think he was very clear really what he felt about his family deeply. But when it came to the play, and why and how he wrote what he wrote, he had enormously keen perceptions. Apart from the writing, I found him terribly shy and rejected, as if hesitant about reaching out to any director. Alone with his work, he had more confidence."

In May, Williams returned to New York, to congratulate others and to promote his own work. Paul Newman and Joanne Woodward were honored by the Lincoln Center Film Society, and Williams, in a bright red dinner jacket, came onstage to introduce a selection of film clips. "This country has served its time with moral decay," he said somewhat enigmatically, in tones of doubtful sobriety, "and the redemptive power is in the country's culture."

The promotion and publicity that month surrounded the publication of his second novel, *Moise and the World of Reason*. What the editors at Simon and Schuster had hoped would be a major literary event turned into a major disaster; readers agreed with critics that the incoherence and lack of sustained tone or theme destroyed the work.

Essentially a partial autobiography linking his Greenwich Village life in the early 1940s with his difficult time during *Small Craft Warnings,* the novel is a lightly veiled counterpart to *Memoirs,* without which it can scarcely be comprehended. The narrator is a failed, thirty-year-old writer with an unconventional, sex-crazed friend named Moise who shares her art the way she shares her bed — prodigally. Interwoven are Williams's real-life and openly named friends, Christopher Isherwood and Don Bachardy, Jane and Tony Smith and a host of others; these private connections did not help the general reader through a tangle of times and feelings and cross-purposes.

There, too, were Frank Merlo's hospitalization and death, travels with Marion Vaccaro, childhood scenes, constant journeys — all bearing the veil of fiction. The novel is a conversation piece among three aspects of its author: the young man he remembers being — talented and idealistic but expert only at sexual athletics; the mature playwright he has become, now in decline, "a has-been attempting a comeback at the Truck and Warehouse [where *Small Craft Warnings* opened]"; and the alter ego Moise (based on his artist-friend Olive Leonard), the sexually voracious artist in whom the Smiths — most loyal of all friends — persistently believed. (Among his fraternity brothers pictured in the 1932 yearbook for the University of Missouri was the handsome Matt H. Moise, whose name was borrowed for the title character.)

A grimy novel about the terror of failing powers in sex, art and faith, *Moise and the World of Reason* depends for its effect on many incomplete sentences (which even the characters wonderingly appraise). It is Williams's most overt homosexual statement (before *Memoirs,* published later that year), but it celebrates no self-understanding, no liberation to adult living — only a gray accommodation to the ravages of time. The novel was dedicated to Robert Carroll.

The unpleasant reaction to this unpleasant book could be diluted only with the hasty business of the next production, for as *The Red Devil Battery Sign* approached a June opening in Boston, there were script revisions and design problems; producer David Merrick still hoped, however, to bring the play to New York later that year.

Anthony Quinn and Katy Jurado joined Claire Bloom in the cast, but their energy and dedication, with Sherin's, could not save the play, a disjointed, unclear story of political terrorism and social enmity. With a pervasive fear as its major emotion — fear of being followed, of being drugged, beaten, overheard, misjudged, confined — *Red Devil* is not at all a political manifesto, as some have claimed, in spite of its allusions to the assassination of President Kennedy. In fact it is a treatment of Williams's drug-induced paranoia, which he believed was mirrored by a national paranoia. The title itself is the clue, for a "red devil" is the popular jargon for secobarbital, a short-acting barbiturate which, under the brand name Seconal, he used liberally right up to the time of his death. That drug, like all others, was dangerous for him, and that it warned like the flashing neon sign advertising an identically named brand of battery appealed to him all the more; thus it reinforced desire with danger, the personal with the public. But again, as with *Out Cry,* his personal anguish was related to the "cutting through the skull" that was performed on his sister, and which is mentioned here along with the second act's numerous other references to the details of Rose's earlier years.

Confessional and private or not, the response from audiences was at first polite, then impatient; the critics, however, were furious: "Dreadful," wrote Kevin Kelly in the *Boston Globe.* He found a "lurking pomposity in [Williams's] ever-darkening vision.... It is all utterly raucous." And Elliot Norton, who had for more than thirty-five years admired Williams's plays, found it "unfocused.... It needs to be rewritten." And so it was, but subsequent European and British productions managed only minimally to improve its wild admixtures of sense and nonsense.

"Part of what made him really sick," according to David Greggory, "was the realization that his level of creativity didn't remain the same. Nothing else remains, why should that? But Tennessee didn't want to acknowledge that. The realization that just working hard and constantly doesn't necessarily 'do it' was hard for him to see. After the failure of *The Red Devil Battery Sign,* I thought, 'What will happen to Tennessee?' He always bounced back, and publicly at least he said he had ideas for reworking failures. But by the mid-1970s, he was unable to accept that he wasn't going to do what he once did."

Before the play closed after ten days in Boston, on June 28, Williams fled to Rome; before his departure, however, he approved Sherin as director of a planned revival of *Sweet Bird of Youth,* which would star Irene Worth and Christopher Walken. It opened in Washington that autumn, and continued a healthy run in New York through early 1976; if anything, it showed that even the lesser but earlier works by Tennessee Williams could be successfully revived. These productions brought money and attention and a new generation of admirers; they also revealed the sharp decline in his ability to structure a drama, or even, apparently, to select a consistently sustained narrative idea.

Throughout the autumn, he was back in New York: for a revival of *Summer and Smoke,* for multiple interviews and media appearances surrounding the publication of *Memoirs,* and for rehearsals for another revival of *The Glass Menagerie,* again with Maureen Stapleton as Amanda. (Her performance as Serafina in a New York revival of *The Rose Tattoo* in 1966 had been also greatly praised.)

"By this time he was a *cause célèbre* of the season," she said. "A lot of *Memoirs* seemed designed to shock for its own sake, and Tennessee was becoming that way in some social situations too. He would talk of various details of his sex life to embarrass or to shock, or for whatever reasons I couldn't figure out. At the same time he was a wonderful person to be with most of the time. He saw everything with a blinding clarity."

Theodore Mann, whose association with Williams went back to *Summer and Smoke* in 1952, produced and directed *Menagerie* for Circle in the Square's new uptown theatre. "Tennessee came to the first rehearsal in November and he frequently interrupted to say, 'Let's change that word or phrase,' which made the time very exciting for all of us — it made *Managerie* like a new play. He told us quite openly how it was based on his family — himself, his mother, and especially his sister. He was totally devoted to her."

Before that revival opened in December, Williams had already begun work — and play — for several weeks in and around San Francisco. The American Conservatory Theatre there, under William Ball, had engaged Gene Persson as producer-in-residence; through Bill Barnes, negotiations had been concluded for ACT to stage the work in progress, *This Is (An Entertainment).*

"There was a lot of talk about Tennessee when he arrived in San Francisco, because of the recent publication of *Memoirs,*" according to Persson. "He was offered a suite free of charge at the Clift Hotel, but he preferred the less formal El Cortez nearby, and there he settled in for rewrites and rehearsals."

The form and tone of *This Is* resembled *Camino Real:* the play is a dreamlike, hallucinatory, kaleidoscopic jumble of scenes in which a Count and Countess try to withstand the attack of an alien, unseen enemy from their base in a European hotel. Crude and disjointed, it lacks the poetry of the fantastic *Camino Real,* and even as a work in progress its subordinate theme — the same as *Red Devil,* that American society is on the brink of collapse — is lost in fragmented diction, unclear characterization and dizzy narrative. Little was clarified by rapid-fire alternation of slapstick, farce, songs, multiple scene changes, the apparently gratuitous introduction and disappearance of half-understood characters, and the interruption of dialogue by coy asides to the audience. One of them allows a rare mention of the playwright's brother, alluding to Dakin's current political aspirations: "Go Dake! He carried Peoria, too, in the last primary. Who needs Chicago?"

This is demanded extraordinary energies from cast, crew, technical staff and director Alan Fletcher. While they plotted the action, costume and set changes and timings of music and special effects, Williams and Robert Carroll drove daily to Kentfield, in Marin County, to swim. Back in San Francisco, his life was very active in the evenings. He was also very generous to several young writers: Williams read their work, offered criticism and financial assistance, and sometimes retired with them to their hotel rooms or his. He frequently came to the ACT offices, where he met with students and apprentice actors. "During rehearsals in December and January," Persson recalled, "he rewrote vast amounts of material and was in quite good spirits. Some of the dialogue, however, was very blunt sexually, and that eventually cost us some subscriptions."

During rehearsals, Williams rushed off to Vienna, for an end-of-the-year revival of *The Red Devil Battery Sign* at the English Theatre. That city was not, however, appropriate for a play of such pessimism and sordidness with its bestial gangs and multiple onstage deaths, its barbarous language and muddled pieties. Like so much in his late work (and so little in his masterworks) sexual motifs were prominent, and psychological aberrations were gratuitous rather than markers of deeper turmoils. Accidents of life masqueraded as its deepest level. It is difficult to say whether this continued decline infected the revised version because he thought it was what the audience wanted, or because he thought it was all an audience would be capable of receiving. In any case, he returned to San Francisco full of unrealistic expectations that *Red Devil* could be further reworked and presented, perhaps in London, the following year.

Prior to the opening of *This Is,* friends of the ACT presented, at the Geary Theatre, "An Evening with Tennessee Williams," at which he read poems, scenes from plays and a short story. Because of his easy humor and unassuming attitude with his audience, the evening was in fact more warmly received than the play two nights later. One San Francisco critic found *This Is* "a sadly, even sorely deficient work"; the visitor from *Variety* thought it "terribly depressing." Even after the dust had settled backstage, a Williams scholar had to admit that the fault was not in Williams's desire to experiment, but in the uncritical acceptance of an unformed, sloppy work: Ruby Cohn wrote in the *Educational Theatre Journal,* "He is such a grand old man that I suppose no one will tell him when a play simply stinks." Crude but true (and a quote from the play), her bluntness might indeed have been appreciated by Williams, to whom everyone deferred, but to whom criticisms were rarely offered.

If anyone in the cast needed encouragement after the reviews appeared, they had only to approach Williams himself. Grateful for their efforts, he appeared the morning after opening — even as the unhappy reviews were being circulated — and distributed twenty-one pages of rewrites.

Before the mid-February closing, however, at least one San Francisco theatregoer was sufficiently impressed to contact Williams's agent. Lyle Leverich, leaseholder and managing producer of the 99-seat Showcase Theatre, asked Bill Barnes if there might be a new play to offer later that year. Barnes, knowing how close *The Two-Character Play/Out Cry* was to Williams's heart, and how much he wanted a production of the latest version, suggested that playwright and producer meet. They did, and thus began a friendship that lasted until Williams's death.

Then Williams was off to New York and Key West, working still — on scenes for unlikely plays and screenplays, on revisions of works current and past, and on first drafts of a series of plays that would cast the net of his memory back over his entire history. "At my age," he told an interviewer, "you know you're approaching death and air becomes very clear, very refined. . . . You cease to feel the little things that weren't worthy of such big things as life and death. Although I feel well physically, I know that I am approaching the end of my life and thank God I'm not scared."

This remark, spoken while en route to the Cannes Film Festival that May — where he was an honorary jury president — was the first recorded example of a shift in his discussions about mortality. Up to this time, his tune had been the standard one of hypochondria, "my last play . . . I'm a dying man," and so forth, as usual. But there was a difference now, an acceptance and a quiet conviction of approaching death. There was, several interviewers recalled, a lightness about it, as if their replies did not much matter. They wondered, years later, if his survival to 1983 did not in some way disappoint him.

In August of that same year, 1976, he returned to San Francisco for conferences with Leverich and with the director of *The Two-Character Play,* Jay Leo Colt. (After 1974, subsequent stagings of *Out Cry* were always billed with the original title.) Colt recalled Williams as endlessly patient with the two actors, polishing their Southern accents and cutting and rearranging lines until he felt it was as good a play as he could make it.

Concomitant with his concern for the play, however, was a new strain of loneliness in his life. A protracted separation from Robert Carroll evoked a cry from him, which he poured into a poem about the last solitary moments of a typical day and evening:

> Turning out the bedside lamp ...
> taking an extra wine-glass of Dry Sack sherry, placing
> the sleeping capsule where I can locate it easily
> in the dark, should the preliminary tablet of Valium not suffice,
> Because you see, at sixty-five
> abdicating your consciousness to sleep
> involves, usually, a touch of nervous apprehension
> that it may not ever revive. However
> I suspect that there's
> a certain luxury submerged in this: a touch of
> concealed fascination in the surrender as well.

His fascination with the possible effects of his dependence, as well as an endless loneliness — with or without company — plagued him from this time forward. To most people he showed a thoughtful cheerfulness (he knew that nothing alienates so quickly as gloom). But there were some who knew he was whistling in the dark.

"Tennessee knew so much about loneliness," José Quintero recalled later. "He learned the pain of loneliness, [but he] was probably one of the funniest men I've ever known. I adored his wit. It was like a needle that pierces bubbles — goes right through the masquerade. ... And he was a very kind man."

One of the objects of his kindness was a young aspiring playwright Williams engaged as secretary-companion for several months in 1976. "My first assignment," Dan Turner remembered, "was to walk Madame Sophia, [his] asthmatic English bulldog. My last effort was to type the first draft of *A Lovely Sunday for Creve Coeur.*" From San Francisco, Williams and Turner departed later that summer for New Orleans.

"It was there that I was introduced to his routine of rising every day before dawn to write. I prepared a thermos of coffee the night before. . . . He took a nap before we went out for brunch. After an afternoon walk or nap, he took me to the Athletic Club, where we swam."

At this time, Williams's old friend Oliver Evans was suffering a long, gradually paralyzing battle with a malignant brain tumor. Williams not only stopped in a local church to pray for his friend; he also offered Evans the use of his Dumaine Street apartment, since the nursing home seemed so uncongenial; he would, in addition, pay for a nurse-companion if Evans wanted to make the move. But more care was needed, and to insure that, he sent checks — channeled through Muriel Bultman Francis — for Evans's nursing home maintenance.

By early October he was back in San Francisco at the El Cortez Hotel. But not for long: the management, he wrote to Gene Persson, would not allow his dog. But the hotel staff recalled another reason for his transfer to another residence:

"We simply couldn't have Mr. Williams as a guest in our hotel a second time," according to Chuck Ingebritsen, the assistant manager. "He made a most unpleasant scene in the lobby, and it was clear to everybody that he was drugged — not just drunk and a little disorderly, but worse. And there was a dreadful commotion, because even though he was a Pulitzer Prize playwright, we just couldn't allow him to remain. It was very embarrassing for us, and he was very upset."

Immediately after the opening of *The Two-Character Play* at the Showcase Theatre, he returned alone to Key West, and then he left almost at once for New York with Robert Carroll. The reason for the sudden travel was that finally, after years of effort, *The Eccentricities of a Nightingale* (a reworking of *Summer and Smoke**) was finally to be staged. For the opening at the Arena Theatre, Buffalo, Edwin Shcrin had assembled a cast headed by Betsy Palmer as a more aggressive, determined character than the Alma of the earlier play. Bill Barnes arranged to have a New York producer, Gloria Hope Sher, attend a performance in Buffalo and then meet Williams in New York.

---

* After the 1948 Broadway failure of *Summer and Smoke,* Williams revised the play drastically. The new version lay unproduced for years — and no wonder, for it is a vastly inferior work in which the protagonists lack subtlety and sensitivity, and the writing lacks coherence. Alma Winemiller, for example, is merely an aggressive flirt intent on the seduction of John Buchanan. Donald Windham has put forth the fascinating hypothesis that in fact *Eccentricities of a Nightingale* may not, as Williams said, be a revision — rather, it may be a first draft of *Summer and Smoke.*

"At our first meeting," she recalled, "Tennessee was quite charming and during rehearsals in New York at the end of November he was wonderful. He loved everyone in the play and everything connected with it, and his laugh filled the theatre. I remembered that he got to the stage to speak to the cast only once. He simply said, 'Look, *I'm* Alma,' and he acted out a long scene for Betsy Palmer. He then added that Alma was his favorite character."

Williams was well tended at this time: Gloria Hope Sher and her colleagues, Edwin Sherin (again the director) and the entire cast brought him an alert respect and attention to every detail they knew he wanted for the play. "But he didn't seem to be eating much," according to Sher. "He only picked at food. The wine saw him through any social occasion. And the minute he had one sip of red wine, his personality changed completely. He became very aggressive, caustic to waiters, unpleasant to be with. A maître d' once had to ask him to calm down." What Sher perhaps did not know was that wine interacted badly with the pills he had taken for sedation or alertness.

The play fared poorly. *Summer and Smoke* did not benefit from wholesale revisions that made its sensibilities broader, duller and cruder. "When the bad reviews came out after our opening on November 23, Tennessee was shocked," according to the producer. "The night before our closing in December, we held an onstage symposium after final curtain. Henry Hewes [a critic and admirer of Williams for many years] was moderator, and Tennessee and I and the cast were onstage. He charmed everyone until someone asked about the critics, and then he really lashed out. He went on for two hours about the rotten critics, how serious work wasn't appreciated anymore, and how playwrights were at the mercy of a few reviewers and one newspaper. And he didn't mince words."

One event during the run of the play, however, escaped Williams's notice. To a performance at the Morosco Theatre came Audrey Wood, who went quietly to Sher, with tears in her eyes, and thanked her for the production.

Because the play opened at Thanksgiving, the producer invited the cast and crew to a festive dinner at Sardi's after the holiday matinee. Williams, to her surprise, arrived too. "He was so lonely, so forlorn. People drained him. He was so vulnerable at this time in his life. He was frightened to be alone, and anyone who extended a helping hand would be confided in. He seemed such a lost soul, so alone, that anyone could touch him and get a warm response. In my playbill for our show, he wrote, 'Stay in my life, Gloria, to keep me alive.' So many people were taking advantage of him — in the theatre and in his personal life — everyone wanted his life and his blood. He was responsive even to the crazy autograph hounds on the street. He never denied anyone, even with that custom. He always stopped to smile and to sign. But what I remember most of all is that he really thought he was Alma Winemiller — he was writing himself, playing himself in the rehearsal. He was enchanted with Alma, and with her density and her dilemma. That much was clear to me, and I think to everyone in the cast too."

That same season, Williams taped an interview for publication in *Gay Sunshine,* a review dedicated to serious exploration of issues of special relevance to the homosexual population and its more open and active participation in the cultural and political mainstream of American life. Williams spoke with playwright-novelist George Whitmore at the Elysée Hotel.

"We met at two in the afternoon," Whitmore said, "and without any difficulty Mr. Williams drank a full bottle of red wine, ate a large roast beef sandwich and took several cups of strong coffee. He looked perfectly dreadful, ruddy and puffy-faced and incoherent. But when I played back the tapes and then read the transcript, much of what he said was articulate. It was the long pauses that had confused me."

It was the playwright himself who requested the interview with this publication, to counter the statements issued by some activists in gay circles who claimed he could never deal openly with the theme of homosexuality in his plays. After admitting that the politics of gay liberation did not much interest him, he continued: "People so wish to latch onto something didactic; I do not deal with the didactic, ever. . . . You still want to know why I don't write a gay play? I don't find it necessary. I could express what I wanted to express through other means. . . . I would be narrowing my audience a great deal [if I wrote for a gay audience alone]. I wish to have a broad audience because the major thrust of my work is not sexual orientation, it's social. I'm not about to limit myself to writing about gay people."

Williams also revealed that day that he was at work on a play called *The Wild Horses of the Camargue,* which had "a great deal to do with a relationship between a tyrannical older man and a very beautiful younger man who's not really a homosexual but who is enslaved by the older man." It is not likely that his remark, or the projected play, would have found favor with those in the gay political movement, nor with many homosexuals in general — like much in his plays (and in this Whitmore was on the mark) there was a negative quality, and an underlying resentment, to Williams's attitude to homosexuality in his work. And Christopher Isherwood, Paul Bigelow and Meade Roberts are among many who had the distinct feeling that Tennessee Williams in fact hated homosexuality, hated being homosexual, and could never accept those who could come to peaceful terms with being one of a sexual minority. (To Gene Persson, Williams had written on July 1 of that year that *The Wild Horses of the Camargue* was shaping up as an obscene and decadent play, with a simple and terrifying narrative line. The play remained incomplete at the time of Williams's death.)

Meantime, Persson had gone ahead to London to prepare for the third production of *The Red Devil Battery Sign,* which was to open in the middle of 1977. "Tennessee kept saying he'd never be alive when the time came," according to Persson. "He complained constantly toward the end of 1976 about his health, but that's one of the things you put up with in genius."

Before Williams left to join the company in London, he attended rehearsals for the revival of *The Night of the Iguana,* which had been imported from Los Angeles to the Circle in the Square. "He made extensive comments for us about the lighting and the backdrop," Theodore Mann said, "and he was very precise in his feelings about the production." But his good cheer was an effort to hide a return of a deep depression as 1976 ended. He wanted *Iguana* to succeed; his friend Sylvia Miles was playing Maxine in it, and he still hoped to rewrite for her the dying Flora Goforth, now closer than ever to his heart (and in his correspondence) as an alter ego. Before departing for London he accepted life membership in the American Academy of Arts and Letters.

When he arrived in London, however, he gave Gene Persson cause for alarm. "He was staggering, he was unable to arrange the practical details of everyday life, money appeared and disappeared strangely. There was a lot of vagueness at this time."

Chapter Ten

THE KINDNESS
OF STRANGERS
(1977–1983)

Whoever you are — I have always depended
on the kindness of strangers.

— Blanche DuBois, in
A Streetcar Named Desire

THE LAST six years of Tennessee Williams's life were a restless quadrille into which he drew various professional and personal partners. Scenes from old plays were revised, restructured, updated and shuffled with odd bits of new material written in hotel rooms or on the Concorde. Acts of new plays were rewritten late at night in Key West, or after dinner with a new producer. Major changes were incorporated at dizzy rehearsals. Always on the jump, eager to have his remarkable survival extend to his art, Williams at sixty-five was in one way as energetic as he had been at twenty-five. That was the year of *The Magic Tower* and of the constant flow of lyric poetry. He had the same zeal at thirty-five, when he completed *Summer and Smoke* and drafted short stories and scenes for what would very soon be *A Streetcar Named Desire*. At forty-five, he divided his time between *Sweet Bird of Youth* and *Orpheus Descending,* and new stories and poems. And now, in 1976, he demonstrated a vigor that exhausted some who worked with him and astonished all who knew him. At this time, he began to call his studio "the Madhouse."

"He seemed to have no great personal needs except to write," Gene Persson said, referring to the time Williams spent in London in late 1976 and early 1977. "He made a number of trips back and forth from Key West — someone said he held the record number of trips on the Concorde."

In mid-January 1977, he wrote to Persson in London that he was en route to New Orleans; he was at work on a new play that would be set there, and which joined parts of earlier plays and short stories and finally became *Vieux Carré.* He added that his traveling companion was a young, handsome Frenchman he had met in a New York restaurant, whose only asset was that he was trying to teach Williams French, and whom he intended to discard in New Orleans.

Once the young man was paid and dismissed, Williams settled for several weeks into the Dumaine Street apartment, where his resident manager saw to practical details. Since Robert Carroll was off on a Mexican holiday, Williams often ate alone at the Quarter Scene, at the corner of Dauphine and Dumaine, or took his laundry, alone, to the machines at Dumaine and Burgundy. Neighbors found him at Marti's Restaurant and at the Café Lafitte in Exile, a famous bar that never locks its doors. *"Garden District* is about one side of Canal Street, which is the fashionable world of New Orleans," Williams explained, "and *Vieux Carré* is about the Bohemian world, which is much more interesting."

After shuttling a half-dozen times in ten weeks between Key West and New Orleans, he was back in New York at the end of winter for rehearsals with director Arthur Alan Seidelman on *Vieux Carré*. Some of the problems with it were foreseen by actress Sylvia Sidney, but having worked with Seidelman when she played Amanda Wingfield in *The Glass Menagerie,* she was eager and hopeful about a new play by Tennessee Williams.

"When I first read the play," she said, "I was very enthusiastic but disappointed. I said I'd love to do it if it were a *play,* but as it was there were terrific problems. That was late in 1976. Several months later, Seidelman called me and said, 'Now it's a play, we're ready to go.' "

At the rehearsals, however, the cast and director were left very much on their own; promised rewrites were delivered by Williams's friends, who made notes, reported decisions, conveyed requests to and from the playwright. "None of us saw Tennessee for a long time," according to Sylvia Sidney, "until we had major problems with several scenes. When he finally arrived, his excuse was, 'I need to see it on its feet!' By then it was almost too late." But when she insisted on a rewrite for a certain phrase, or on a good exit line or a revision of some action, he could accommodate himself magnificently — "almost on demand," she recalled.

But she and others also noticed that the reasons for Williams's absences at this crucial time were a way of avoiding one disaster by courting another: Williams was wandering around New York, mostly at night and often in unsavory quarters, and at rehearsals he was too often incoherent. And there was a coterie of young men, of dubious value to him, who clung to him constantly.

"We were nervous, and he was sad," Sidney said. "He was frightened of getting old, terrified that he was no longer attractive, that his figure wasn't good anymore, that he couldn't attract young men except with his money. Meanwhile, we were in trouble. The set was impossible, clumsily built, and the production was misconceived. . . . After the last preview [in early May], he came backstage, and he was crying with gratitude. I don't know what I'd done, but it must have been good, because he said he was going to rewrite the whole play and no one would ever play Mrs. Wire [the New Orleans landlady] but me. Of course the following year it reopened in London with Sylvia Miles, but I knew that he gave dozens of actresses this line about 'You're the greatest actress who's ever done my plays.' "

At this time, it seemed as if Williams himself was beginning to sabotage his name and reputation before columnists or critics could. Richard Alfieri, who played the young writer in *Vieux Carré*, recalled that a few weeks before opening, Williams sat for a newspaper interview and "individually attacked all the major theatre critics in New York, charging them with everything from incompetence to hypocrisy. . . . The cast groaned almost in unison upon reading the interview. We knew it would jeopardize the play's chances — and perhaps Tennessee did, too."

As for the public self, his conduct often did not help in that regard, either. On March 10, he appeared onstage at the Winter Garden Theatre to address over eight hundred New York high school students. But he brought a bottle of vermouth along, and the event, to the dismay of everyone present, turned into a "hard-to-hear question and answer session, with the students trying to outshout each other for Mr. Williams's attention," as one eyewitness reported.

As opening night approached, Williams affected an unjustified if generous optimism, dancing late into the night at the opening of a new discothèque and laughing for society photographers — but he was, as Alfieri recalled, "very nervous about what the critics would have to say." His nervousness was unfortunately manifest with his cast, just before the opening, as Alfieri and Sidney remembered; he stormed away after delivering an angry tirade about what a disservice he had done to himself by being too kind with them all. "We knew he didn't mean all of it, and we loved him when he came backstage after the first performance," according to Alfieri, but the damage had been done.

"He was so passionate about everything going well with regard to his work," as Bill Barnes said of that time, "that he was in absolute despair when there was not a successful outcome. His life was full of trauma, turmoil and pain — and this paradoxically made his life and work possible."

Just before opening night, Williams fled New York in panic. "I don't think I chose the right place. It's so desolate here," he said of Atlantic City in early May. "But I simply have to travel, even if it's to Atlantic City. I have a fear of confinement, of claustrophobia."

"The day after opening," Sylvia Sidney added, "a small group of us lunched at the Stanhope. He had made a surprise return to New York just before opening night, and at the Stanhope he told me that he knew he had to be surrounded by a few respectable-looking people in order to be accepted for luncheon at better places. He had a bad reputation in New York by this time — or so he said. I don't think he was helped much by the group of hangers-on and sycophants that surrounded him then, either." At a reception in his suite at the Elysée Hotel, a few days after the opening of *Vieux Carré,* that group begged him to read his poetry; he complied, and then said everyone had to read Shakespeare aloud. Most of the cast, embarrassed and angry at the coterie who seemed to be taking advantage of Williams, quietly departed.

The poetry reading was prompted by the publication that spring of a second collection by Williams, *Androgyne, Mon Amour.* The book did not demonstrate anything even his greatest admirers did not already know: that Williams's poetic genius was invariably passed through the prism of dialogue into prose, and that on the contrary the selfconsciousness, the coyness of most of his poems — unmoored by character or conflict — were hollow and inauthentic. His best plays were characterized by an astonishing inevitability of narrative line, by a fluid and poetic diction that belied countless revisions; the poems, on the other hand, sounded artificial — or, like the worst moments of his last plays, designed to shock rather than to illuminate.

Vieux Carré was a crashing failure. But those who had followed his career felt that he was entitled to minor exercises at this point. "Tennessee Williams's voice," Walter Kerr wrote in a warm appreciation that week, "is the most distinctively poetic, the most idiosyncratically moving, and at the same time the most firmly dramatic to have come the American theatre's way — ever. No point in calling the man our best living playwright. He is our best playwright, and let qualifications go hang. In fact, he has already given us such a substantial body of successful work that there is really no need to continue demanding that he live up to himself, that he produce more, more, more, and all masterpieces. We could take some casuals and just tuck them into the portfolio, gratefully, as small dividends."

That generous comment, however, was part of a longer piece in which Kerr — like all the critics — regretted that *Vieux Carré* was simply a pastiche, not a play; a series of dream-images, not a coherent and focused drama. Box-office business was poor, and the play closed after five performances. Pointed and cogent remarks like Kerr's did not encourage Williams; he needed critical approval, reinforcement, constant commendation.

Vieux Carré is, however, remarkable in retrospect for what it reveals about the mood and temperament of the playwright at the time of writing, for it is as much a play of *tableaux vivants* as *The Glass Menagerie,* and the first in a series of late plays in which he created scenes that were really leaves from a personal album, without the transmutation found in earlier plays of the great period, 1944 to 1961. Narrated by a young writer who is clearly the young Williams, the play animates real-life events at 722 Toulouse Street in the winter of 1938–1939, between his graduation from Iowa and the trip with Jim Parrott — the season when he lived in penury but as a practicing poet and writer, the season in which he became actively homosexual.

But the other characters incarnate aspects of Williams, too: the older sick and haunted artist, desperate for sexual intimacy and even more desperate for friendship, and the young couple, Jane and Tye, caught in a brutal duel for sexual and emotional dominance. Offstage voices call "Edwina, Edwina, come see this dream of a little courtyard," as the young writer speaks of a home where "the storm of my father's blood obliterated the tenderness of Grand's," whose spirit comes to comfort him in the alcove of his cramped room. Scene images tumble haphazardly in *Vieux Carré;* it is a series of free-associations, drawn on a poeticized past, and its deepest value was for its author, as he reentered in memory the closed house on Toulouse Street, and as he forgave and dismissed some of its ghosts and begged an embrace from others.

Before the end of May, Williams had jetted to London for more work with Gene Persson and the new director of *Red Devil,* Keith Hack. In an effort to raise needed funds, Persson invited an English publisher to meet with Williams for luncheon at the Berkeley Hotel, the playwright's preferred stopping-place because of its swimming pool. "But Tennessee put the man through such a relentless grilling — 'Are you going to kick in some money or aren't you?' — that the man of course backed out." Exhausted, nervous and unwilling to rest, Williams had resumed taking megadoses of Ritalin tablets, alternating them with Nembutal for sedation. The producer and his staff had to be alert to prevent him from stumbling and falling in offices, on the street, and in the theatre.

After preliminary performances in June, the third version of *Red Devil* opened at London's Phoenix Theatre at an hour they thought might bring them luck: seven o'clock on the seventh day of the seventh month of 1977. But no occult force guided the critics' reactions or the audience's response. Another closing quickly followed.

Back in Key West, Williams revised the teleplay *A Second Epiphany,* now called *Stopped Rocking,* for his friends Maureen Stapleton and Anne Meacham, in hopes of a television sale. A story of despair, lunacy and attempted suicide in and around an asylum, it carries to an extreme the dual personalities trapped in the theatre in *The Two-Character Play/Out Cry.* The teleplay also dramatized the association between playwright and sister, as the man who in this case visits his demented wife feels that his affair with another woman has been a selfish betrayal. Fraternal and conjugal feelings meld in a series of ever more violent scenes, and the specifications of St. Louis, of St. Vincent's asylum, of the needlework done by both wife and sister reveal a concern for the linked lives. ("I have been punished by her punishment," Williams said of his sister, "and by difficulties of my own.")

As he wrote each day, Williams was also erecting a little shrine to Rose at his Key West home — a crude altar modeled on Serafina's shrine to her late husband in *The Rose Tattoo.* Here, he set pictures of his sister and of St. Jude, patron of hopeless cases — which, as he said in private and in this teleplay, he considered her and himself: "Such cases exist; we know that, so what can we do but pray?"

The failure of *The Two-Character Play,* after numerous reproductions, may have necessitated *Stopped Rocking.* Its brutality, its confession of guilt and its longing for forgiveness recall the earlier play, and it advances the motif of a man's freedom and a woman's confinement. His work was becoming more and more a folio of memories, indistinguishable from what private journals might have been. But since his private heart was often worn on a public sleeve, he described the feelings, the guilt and the longings in plays that were by this time of his life perhaps never really meant to be staged, in images he never really wanted to share much of the time. And this may explain why his producers and casts and directors felt, from 1977 to the end of his life, that Tennessee Williams himself wanted to sabotage and subvert the work — and his own name — before anyone else could. *The Glass Menagerie* had, long ago, been as personal. But it had been gentler, devoid of the overt madness, the grotesque breakdown, the storm of sexual confusion; it was, as Tom said in the opening scene, "truth in the pleasant disguise of illusion." There were few pleasant disguises in 1977.

During the last weeks of that year, Williams accepted an offer from the Alliance Theatre in Atlanta to present a new play. What he gave them was a rescaled version of the film *Baby Doll*, adapted to the limitations of the stage and called *Tiger Tail*. In appreciation for the documentary film, he arranged for Harry Rasky to direct. At the same time, a new twist of pain entered his life. The circle of attractive young men ever in attendance now more than ever, and more boldly than ever, sought the glamour of association, some too willing to exchange sexual for professional favors, and a number who simply filled idle hours drinking his liquor and draining his energies. They had manuscripts for him to read, stories for him to hear. If they were at all talented, he listened and supported and helped financially. If they were at all attractive to him, they were guaranteed even more attention. He was, unfortunately, an easy prey for the unscrupulous, and his best instincts — a generous concern for fledgling writers, a desire to protect and to embrace — often clashed with an acute vulnerability.

Meantime, another project was being developed. A year earlier, José Quintero had told theatrical producer Elliot Martin that Williams was at work on a long play, called *Clothes for a Summer Hotel*, about Scott and Zelda Fitzgerald. From the start, Quintero and Williams thought of Geraldine Page for Zelda. Now, Quintero again contacted Martin (who had produced *More Stately Mansions* and *A Moon for the Misbegotten* as well as a revival of *Camino Real* and a series of major Broadway successes). The three met in Key West, Martin recommended some cuts, Tennessee agreed. "He was bright and articulate and cheerful in January 1978," according to the producer, who also remembered Quintero's belief that the play had all the ingredients of a hit. If Williams could be surrounded with the loving support he needed, they could all repeat the miracle of 1952 (when Quintero, Williams and Page made history with *Summer and Smoke*).

Tiger Tail was staged, and *Clothes for a Summer Hotel* now received daily cutting. Williams met with Bill Barnes and Maureen Stapleton about still another project, a one-act play he had written in San Francisco in 1976. Titled *Creve Coeur,* after a park not far from central St. Louis, it was a simple play, set in the 1930s, about lonely women seeking love and security. A key role, they thought, was tailor-made for Stapleton. They read the play for Craig Anderson, founding director of the Hudson Theatre Guild in Manhattan, who would produce the play; Keith Hack was brought from London to direct.

"Tennessee was cool and somewhat distant at our first meeting," Anderson recalled. "But we were deeply interested in a new play by him, of course, and he seemed to need the public life the play would give him. He needed to have something in the works, something that could guarantee him a production and soon." Anderson's wife, Elena Azuola, found Williams in March 1978 "a fairly fragile man, but with an ability to lash out suddenly if a tender spot were touched."

The reworking and expansion of *Creve Coeur* (literally, "heartbreak") continued through the spring of 1978, when they all moved to Charleston, South Carolina, where the play was to be in the Spoleto Festival scheduled for late May and early June. (By this time, there had been inaugurated an American counterpart to this Italian gala.) Barnes attended Williams, and frequently the playwright withdrew to Kiawah Island, twenty miles offshore, to enjoy its secluded beaches and ten thousand acres of maritime forest.

For the first week in Charleston, the Andersons recalled, Williams rose each morning and was at his typewriter by five o'clock (this Elena knew since his motel room adjoined hers). He swam midmorning, before the sun was at its zenith, then worked again until lunch.

But before the preview performance on June 1, "the pills and the drinking really played havoc with him," as Anderson said. "We didn't know how to take care of all the needs he had, but we felt that as producers we had to demand better writing. We knew one thing clearly: he had to be protected from the press, and from the nagging of those around him who wanted to pick at him and bother him. As it was, he had an adoring entourage entirely too much and too close." On June 2, there was some uneasiness when he read from his work and fielded questions for students at a local college in Charleston; the pills he was taking, in injudicious combinations, reacted badly with wine. Three nights later, at the play's formal opening, as Anderson recalled, "He became something of an amusing outrage. He arrived at a formal reception in a safari suit with short trousers, sneakers and a Panama hat. He got away with playing the eccentric — after all, he was Tennessee Williams, the playwright."

To everyone's relief and surprise, visiting critics from New York newspapers joined local reviewers in praising the play, expressing the hope that it would move to New York. At once, the Andersons met with Bill Barnes and offered to do everything to bring about that move.

In Charleston, some of Williams's paintings were exhibited, and this greatly pleased him. What had begun as a hobby in the 1950s was now a public curiosity, and his celebrity guaranteed fancy prices for the essentially simple, unsubtle work he could sell.

"He made us feel very welcome when we came to discuss *Clothes for a Summer Hotel* that June," Elliot Martin said. "He invited us to a party, and we discussed casting. I felt by this time that we had what we were going to get from him. The play was still much too long, but I felt he had reached his limits. 'I want to warn you, Elliot,' he said to me, 'the critics are out to get me. You'll see how vicious they are. They make comparisons with my earlier work, but I'm writing differently now.'" This was especially curious in light of the recent favor toward *Creve Coeur*.

The enterprise of raising money for a Broadway production of *Creve Coeur,* however, was a difficult one. "After the unfortunate reception of *Vieux Carré* in 1977," Anderson said, "everybody distrusted his abilities. No one would come across with money for a production. During this period, death was very much on his mind — he spoke of it frequently — as he spoke of his sister Rose, even more than usually. We strolled around Charleston and he remarked that a lace gown or a parasol or this or that item would please his sister. It was very touching and a little sad."

During the summer, Williams flew to London for the revival of *Vieux Carré*. Generous and supportive with his cast, he especially appreciated the robust humor and enthusiastic attitude of his leading lady, Sylvia Miles, with whom he still talked about Flora Goforth. "We spent a lot of time together," she said, "and he was full of ideas for plays and stories. His humor seemed quicker than ever. One day we were walking through Piccadilly and I saw a terribly thin young girl. I whispered to him, 'Oh, Tennessee, look — anorexia nervosa,' and without the slightest hesitation he shot back, 'Oh, Sylvia, you know everybody!'" (He appreciated his own joke, for it found its way later into the final version of *Clothes for a Summer Hotel*.)

Vieux Carré opened in London in August — to poor reviews for everything about it except Sylvia Miles, whose performance as the crusty Mrs. Wire was edged with humor, brittleness and an unsentimental poignancy of madness at the end.

In September there were at least two more trips to and from London from New York and Key West — necessary, it seems, only as distractions from the pressures of *Clothes for a Summer Hotel,* which he did not want to refine further, and *Creve Coeur,* which he did. Just after Labor Day he wrote to Craig Anderson that he had substantial revisions and expansions for what they now called *A Lovely Sunday for Creve Coeur;* he added, however, that he felt that sustained praise would elude him as long as he was alive. This play, he hoped, would mark the return to his rightful place during his lifetime: he did not believe, he added, that there was any reward coming in the hereafter.

He also mentioned, in the same letter (dated September 7) that it was now clear that Bill Barnes would sever his ties with International Creative Management to pursue an independent career, and that there would be a new agent representing him by winter. The tone of the letter has more than a hint of desperation: Williams also hoped that Anderson would consider reopening *Vieux Carré* on Broadway, and that together they could show an anonymous "them" that Tennessee Williams could inject real power into the theatre.

The carousel of activity continued to revolve, and he continued to reach for an elusive gold ring. "He seemed more fragile than ever when he returned from another trip to London," Elena Azuola said. "He needed constant encouragement and protection. But for all the care he needed, he was also seeing to the needs of others. He was supporting a number of actresses who had fallen on hard times." Her husband agreed: "He was very generous as well to a number of young writers who needed cash. There was a generous streak in him, and he seemed to want to protect as much as he asked for protection."

After quick journeys to San Francisco, New Orleans and Key West that autumn — travel again for its own sake — he returned to New York and signed a lease for an apartment at Manhattan Plaza, a complex on West 42nd and 43rd Streets especially designated for those in the arts. Although he took the residence for the privacy and the swimming pool and at first spent a good deal of time there, the noise and crowded atmosphere finally displeased him and he relinquished the lease after three years, having spent most of the time at the Elysée Hotel in any case. "He hated the sheer size of Manhattan Plaza," according to Vassilis Voglis, "and the fact that everyone there recognized him. He much preferred to live at the Elysée, and even sometimes to stay with me and John Cromwell [the writer] at our apartment on East 72nd Street."

From San Francisco Williams invited Jay Leo Colt, who had directed *The Two-Character Play,* to become a temporary secretary and assistant throughout that autumn and winter. "I helped him furnish the Manhattan Plaza apartment and helped him keep the script of *Creve Coeur* up-to-date, which wasn't easy with all his rewrites. Tennessee didn't like to give orders, so I had to be very persistent with him to determine just what he wanted me to do." Eventually, Tennessee's irrational suspicions, certainly exacerbated by his mixed regimen of tablets and capsules, were turned on Colt, whom he accused of stealing the manuscript of *The Wild Horses of the Camargue;* it later turned up in the Key West studio, where Williams had forgotten it in a hurried departure.

In the thick of professional and personal problems for the playwright, he accepted as his new agent Mitch Douglas, a literary agent at ICM whom their actors' agent, Williams's old friend Milton Goldman, recommended. "The real trouble, I remember thinking in 1978, was the people around him," Douglas said. "Everyone wanted a piece of him, and sometimes he seemed to thrive on those who were the worst for him. He was forever getting himself in some sort of entanglement or other, either with his professional or his intimate life, and after a while he really seemed to trust nobody. He believed he was constantly being cheated, and no convincing changed his mind." The paranoia, as his friends called it, had a strange basis in truth at that time (as Douglas and a few others realized), for Williams was surrounded by a pack of glamour-hungry jackals who used sex like a fly-swatter. But his suspicions were diffuse, and eventually he turned against those like Jay Leo Colt and Mitch Douglas.

"As the rehearsals for *A Lovely Sunday for Creve Coeur* began in New York," Craig Anderson remembered, "we had the impression that Tennessee would have preferred not to have it presented. He enjoyed working on it, but once he realized that audiences and critics would be there in January, with their possible disapproval, he began to withdraw."

The holiday season Williams spent with his sister, whom he brought from Stony Lodge to New York. "So much love passed between them," Anderson said. "He brought her to dinner, and there she sat, this quiet little lady, almost seventy years old, and Tennessee gently mothered her — he cut her meat, responded to her every whim and need. She seemed in all innocence to bring out something very sweet in him."

As the reopening of the play drew near, Williams tried to defuse his anxiety by writing an open letter to the cast. As never before, he begged plainly for their attention to every word of the script, every nuance of every line, each cadence of the language; he asked them to review the play with intensest care. Creating a play, he concluded, was an act of love. He added that he was writing to them at four in the morning, before his coffee and even before his first glass of wine. He begged for their attention and their love and their patience.

"By the time we opened [in January 1979]," Anderson said, "he was in a terrified, suspicious state. The failure of the play [which closed after thirty-six performances] he seemed to blame on me, and that was the end of our relationship."

The reviews, however mixed (and less favorable by far than what had been written about the Charleston premiere), were nowhere near the disaster Williams believed; several critics in fact praised the gentleness and humor of the play, and welcomed his return, after other wilder experiments, to the traditional form of *A Lovely Sunday for Creve Coeur*. Like *Vieux Carré*, it has a desperate tone, and the lonely women are very like the confused quartet of *The Glass Menagerie*. *A Lovely Sunday for Creve Coeur* presents four emotionally unfulfilled women, each terrified of being abandoned: one (Sophie) cannot go back to her apartment alone after the death of her mother, and so remains with neighbors; another (Bodey) fears losing her brother to marriage, and fears losing her roommate (Dorothea) to anyone at all, so she encourages a match between them in order to keep them in her life. Another (Helena) desires a companionship that may be spinsterish, but may be something else. This is a play of heartbreak indeed, and of a sad accommodation to the realities of adult life. With the character of Dotty, Williams felt at the time that "we must pull ourselves together and go on. Go on, we must just go on, that's all that life seems to offer and demand." Spiced with literally two dozen references to his own life in St. Louis in the 1920s and 1930s, *A Lovely Sunday for Creve Coeur* is another page in Williams's personal album, for the four driven, lonely women each speak from a part of the author's life in the days of his attendance at the Ben Blewett school and University High, the days at International Shoe, the front porch in Memphis, and the final acceptance of life's compromises. But Williams offered only the accidents of his past, without the shape of emotionally compelling characters or dramatic structure.

Before the play had completed a brief run, Williams had left the New York winter for the warmth of New Orleans and Key West, meeting before his departure with Elliot Martin and José Quintero about *Clothes for a Summer Hotel.* In New Orleans he was told that his Key West home had been burglarized — twice, in fact, on January 8 and 14 — and he was furious and puzzled that the reports on this should have taken more than three weeks to reach him. But the second burglary was accompanied by a crime even more bizarre. Williams's forty-nine-year-old gardener, Frank Fontis, who also tended the house during Williams's absences, was found murdered in his own home. When police searched Fontis's house for clues, a pile of manuscripts was discovered — all by Tennessee Williams.

Williams affected detachment when he returned to Key West at the end of the month. "Fontis was a very eccentric but harmless man, I thought, but it now appears he really wasn't my friend, and it took his murder to reveal this to me. The things he confiscated over the years, found in his safe, included personal letters, pictures, one of my earliest journals, written when I was very young, and an only copy of a manuscript, which I value very much. I don't know how many times I'll have to be taught the lesson that even friends aren't always what they seem."

Until the end of February, Williams remained in Key West, coping once or twice with a sudden burst of antihomosexual prejudice in the neighborhood. Once he was involved in late-night street scuffles, although the altercation was caused by a sailor's angry rebuff of Williams's gentle proposition — not, as was claimed, by a gratituitous attack on Williams and a companion. Strollers on Duval Street at two in the morning in 1979 were not surprised by this incident: young wanderers, sailors or not, heterosexual or not, had long been amused, tolerant or even flattered by an occasional invitation from Williams. But in this case, a fight broke out. Within days, at least two groups of young drifters had stopped their cars in front of Williams's house, tossed empty beer cans and dirty names, and roared off in a cloud of smug vulgarity. "Maybe," Williams told guests, "they weren't punks at all, but New York critics." But he told a visitor, with sudden ominous anger several weeks later, "I suspect I'll live only another two years. I've been working like a son of a bitch since 1969 to make an artistic comeback ... there's no release short of death."

For a revival of *The Eccentricities of a Nightingale,* Williams flew to Long Beach, California, in late March. He was welcomed by Gloria Hope Sher, who introduced him to Sandy Dennis and the rest of the cast, but according to Sher "he became very abusive and insulted a lot of people after he'd had a few sips of red wine. That was all it took to change his attitude for the evening. He was very polite up to that point." Mitch

Douglas agreed: "Unfortunately, by this time he had no tolerance for alcohol at all — one glass of red wine went straight to him." And the reason was that he had preceded the wine with pills.

In April Williams was back in Key West, working with Keith Hack on yet a further revision of *Goforth,* but delaying further toil on *Clothes,* which he insisted must be staged before he would make any further cuts. To Sylvia Miles he wrote on April 11 that he was negotiating the purchase price of a second house in Key West, fully furnished and suitable for several guests, complete with sun deck, swimming pool, television. He invited her to join them for work on *Goforth,* which he hoped to stage in Vienna and London. He also mentioned that a screenplay was almost finished, and that he hoped she would play in it under Paul Morrissey's direction. (Morrissey thought later that this must be the film of "Two on a Party," which Lester Persky had so long hoped to produce.)

Miles did visit Williams several times from that summer through the following year, and the planned production of *Goforth* went as far as meetings in Vienna with the managers of the English Theatre, Franz Schafranek and his wife Ruth Brinkman. Williams, however, thought the facilities there not lavish enough, and he at last withdrew, in September 1980, what he had so long developed. This was perhaps another act of fear, although one more reasonably founded: no version of *The Milk Train Doesn't Stop Here Anymore* had ever pleased more than a small San Francisco audience.

In May, Williams accepted invitations from two universities to address their students; neither appearance did much to increase the respect of a younger generation for an older playwright. At New York University's Loeb Student Center, on May 10, he read several poems and two grotesque pieces — the one-act play *Lifeboat Drill* and the short story "Tent Worms."

Throughout the 1970s, Williams's stories and short plays were invariably about sexual exploitation, madness, disease, death and the ultimate triumph of catastrophe. So much was true of the play he read that day, and of stories like "Mother Yaws" (which *Esquire* published in 1977) and "The Killer Chicken and the Closet Queen" (which appeared in *Christopher Street* the following year). His writings, except for two long plays in progress, were replete with images of disfigurement and addiction and with a merciless absence of any human warmth. The reaction of New York University students that day was neither serious nor respectful, since unfortunately they had difficulty understanding his slurred speech. At the University of Pennsylvania commencement the following week, the situation was scarcely improved.

When he was in the company of old and trusted friends, however, he fared better. With several he attended the opening production of a festival at the Williamstown Theatre; opening night, June 28, was a production of *Camino Real* devised by Nikos Psacharopoulos, a staging highly praised and much appreciated by audiences, critics and playwright. He remained through a long weekend at Williams College, meeting visitors and students, giving readings of poems, and enjoying himself more than he had in months.

The Williamstown journey was sufficiently heartening to send him back to New Orleans in a rush of optimism. He ransacked the files of old manuscripts kept there, and found, among other neglected items, a teleplay that had later been used as the basis for *Creve Coeur*. It was titled *All Gaul Is Divided,* and he submitted it to Mitch Douglas with a note that it, like *The Loss of a Teardrop Diamond* (a screenplay inspired by his sister's social debut), were his offerings to a theatre which had given him life despite what he called his transgressions.

But in addition to scripts devised for television, there was one short play that could never be offered to anything but an experimental, intimate theatre company that thrived on risk as much as talent. A bizarre mixture of softcore pornography, hallucinatory comedy and poorly considered social comment, it was titled *Kirche, Kutchen und Kinder: An Outrage for the Stage.** In the summer of 1979 he tried to find a home for this "doodle of a play," as the director eventually described it.

Because Williams was so eager to see it in production, Mitch Douglas suggested one of New York's off-off-Broadway companies, one with an intelligent appreciation of American theatre and the requisite willingness to take a risk. A German television company had once come to the Jean Cocteau Repertory Theatre on the Bowery to film Williams reading. In addition, the Cocteau's artistic director Eve Adamson had presented *In the Bar of a Tokyo Hotel,* and because Williams still had an affection for that failed work, Douglas asked Adamson to stage it for Williams's especial benefit.

"Mitch cared deeply about Tennessee's work and wanted the best for him every time," Adamson said. "They came to a revival of *Bar,* and I found poor Tennessee so besieged by people that we were functioning as

---

* On all versions of the script, Williams mistakenly wrote "Kutchen" for what should have been "Küchen." His title will be used here.

much like bodyguards as producer and agent. He seemed like such a bewildered little man, as if he always needed to be headed in the right direction, which is probably why there was always someone living with him who saw to the practical details of his life.

"The summer of 1979, Mitch said only that it [*Kirche, Kutchen und Kinder*] was an eccentric play about a male hustler who finally returns to work after retirement. I read it, and we agreed to present it as a work in progress in repertory during the 1979–1980 season."

During late summer and autumn of 1979, Williams divided his time between the Elysée Hotel, his apartment at Manhattan Plaza, meetings with Elliot Martin and José Quintero about the increasing difficulties of *Clothes for a Summer Hotel,* and irregular work on *Kirche, Kutchen und Kinder.*

"Tennessee had great faith in how Eve Adamson was handling his material," Douglas said, "and although his first choice for *Clothes* was certainly José, he wanted Eve to stand by as second choice. Because he was having trouble in his personal life at the time, and because he couldn't keep a secretary very long in such chaos, he wanted me to assume various personal and domestic duties. I insisted I could serve him best as his literary agent, period, and to that he replied, 'I like you, Mitch, you're funny.' I never quite figured out what he meant by that."

Attempts to make theatrical sense out of the bizarre *Kirche* continued, however. "He revised it on little scraps of paper that were always turning up," Adamson recalled. "As a play it was as badly structured as a later full-length play we did was much better structured [Williams's *Something Cloudy Something Clear*]. He was full of paranoia about both plays, about the productions and everyone in his life at the time, but there was a certain nobility and courage in him. And I do feel that the paranoia was partly caused by and was capitalized on by the coterie around him."

Kirche, Kutchen und Kinder is nevertheless remarkable for two diametrically opposed elements: it reveals, on the one hand, Williams (as Mitch Douglas put it) "trying to shock an unshockable society and an unshockable audience. There was a strong masochistic streak in Tennessee which sometimes made him want to undermine a work before the critics or audience disliked it. This was not a good play, but he insisted it be done. And Eve and her company gave it the best they had."

The best was in fact extremely ingenious for a play about a male hustler in New York's SoHo. "We designed it like a Fellini movie, and Tennessee loved the concept," Adamson said. "When we ran it in repertory during our ninth season, beginning in September, we found it was smart to bill it as a work in progress. We all knew the press would roast him on this, so we had a way of keeping them out."*

But beneath the vulgarity and a text resulting from unstable health, there is a character named Miss Rose who wanders through the lunacy, offering gentle encouragement and calming the craziness by playing hymns at the organ. "Miss Rose," says the retired hustler whose voice is Williams's own as both try for a comeback, "you've given me all the poetry that's in my soul."

His sister was not only in his mind and on paper, as it turned out. The second house in Key West was at last his, and he decided that it was time to move Rose from Stony Lodge to a more private residence, and one near himself. Late that autumn he brought her to 915 Van Phister Street, a two-story gray clapboard where he arranged for their cousin, Stell Adams, to be a companion. The arrangement lasted just over a year, when it became clear that more specialized care was still indicated. Rose returned to Ossining at New Year's 1980, far less disappointed than her brother.

As the plans to bring Rose to Key West were realized, he completed a bitter satire on the famous painting idealizing the American dream; *This Is the Peaceable Kingdom* describes total personal and social breakdown, and is set in a nursing home during the 1978 New York strike against those facilities. The play presents images of war, senility, disease, hatred and death, and ends in a staged battle between blacks and whites, Jews and Christians, patients and families.

Also by autumn 1979, Elliot Martin and José Quintero were ready to complete casting for *Clothes for a Summer Hotel,* a play which, in its first three extended drafts, reveals its clear purpose: the visits by Scott to Zelda Fitzgerald in the mental asylum are representations of the visits by Tom to Rose Williams. For the leading man, Williams was eager to sign Donald Madden, and when Madden declined the role, "Tennessee just backed off," as Elliot Martin recalled. "He didn't concern himself with casting after that." Kenneth Haigh played Scott Fitzgerald.

With that, Williams and Mitch Douglas left, at the end of October, for Gainesville, Florida, where a revival of *Tiger Tail* was to be staged at the University of Florida, in the Hippodrome Theatre. From his arrival

---

* Ironically, a review did appear in, of all publications, *The Tennessee Williams Newsletter* (which later became *The Tennessee Williams Review*). "Call it 'The Katzenjammer Kids Meet the Boys in the Band,' " wrote Richard Wray Hornak.

on October 31 to his departure November 3, there was a crowded schedule of theatrical, academic and social events that left him drained and irri-
table. At a reading of his poems he took his revenge for what he
considered wretched personal exploitation by reading several of his more
blatantly sexual poems and "chuckling wickedly throughout," as an eyewitness noted. Then, at the performance of *Tiger Tail*, as director Marshall New observed, Williams was in "the worst case of opening night
paranoia known to man," which was not alleviated by "three bottles of
white wine [drunk] during the day since breakfast ... the formal dinner
that evening ended with only a brief stop-in by the playwright, who had
coffee and carried away three doggie-bags full of beef Wellington." And a
professor from the University of Florida, Winifred Frazer, sadly reported — in the *Tennessee Williams Review* — "his paranoia, his irritability,
his fear of death, his frustration at not producing any new successes."

On December 2, Williams, Henry Fonda, Martha Graham, Ella Fitzgerald and Aaron Copland were honored at the Kennedy Center, Washington, for their contributions to the arts. No one appreciated his best
work better than Elia Kazan, who that evening reminded the audience
that "One comes out of his plays feeling that particular mixture: sadness
transmuted into joy, the two together or the one unexpectedly following
the other. Also this: that despite ourselves we may have a chance after all.
One feels — gratitude.... His concern is humanity and what can be
found there to sing about and respect. Still he is anything but bland: his
words have sharp teeth."

The White House dinner and the Kennedy Center honors buoyed him
for a time. Close friends accompanied him, the press observed the
formalities and asked no intimate questions, and with his medal in his
pocket he returned to New York determined to apply his "sharp teeth"
to the problems brewing over *Clothes for a Summer Hotel*. As trying as
those problems would be, however, they were equaled by the ugly sexual
sparring that now intensified around him, and that would become even
more brutal until his death. A number of those in Williams's social entourage — several of whom tried to remain as "personal assistants" —
were interested only in the social and sexual contacts that can always be
made through a celebrity; and several were all too willing to offer themselves in the hope of some sort of compensation. Terrified as he was of
being abandoned, of being thought unattractive, of aging and death, he
was just as fearful of the loss of all creative instincts and powers. And

since he was already aware of the severe diminution of those powers with the dependence on pills, he did not intend to complicate his life with risk of venereal disease — a condition familiar to him from several earlier escapades. In early 1980, he pitched himself out of a sexual frenzy that had plagued him since the early years. He announced that he would live a chaste and celibate life. As he and others may have suspected, however, this would not be long sustained.

"He was absolutely terrified of going back to Broadway for *Clothes for a Summer Hotel,*" Eve Adamson remembered. "At the same time as his minor doodle of a play, *Kirche, Kutchen und Kinder,* was in our repertory season, he was getting ready to confront the hassle again. He was as full of fear and insecurity as he was of dramatic insight, but those of us who cared for him seemed more often to be catching him from falling."

Work with the cast on *Clothes* began in early January 1980 with a mood of high expectations, deriving mostly from a deep nostalgia: the team of Williams–Quintero–Page was thought unbeatable, after all.

But at once things were, as Quintero said, "very, very painful. The play touched on his own terrifying experience in the hospital. There were still some vestiges of his paranoia that clung to his psyche in that play. He knew that there were lapses in the play, parts that didn't quite connect, and he didn't know how to make them connect. He didn't blame anybody, but he wouldn't come out of his [hotel] room. I would have to go and say, 'Come on, Tom. It's alright.' There were sad moments, very sad moments."

The New York rehearsal period was, as Elliot Martin remembered, a nightmare for everyone. There were personal problems among director and cast, there were winter illness and budget problems. And the script was at least an hour too long. "We got to the point that Williams was so defensive that I couldn't even mention the possibility of a cut to him, and there was very little editing, although some rearranging. When we opened in Washington at the end of January, I begged him, saying that we could have a fine show by Chicago or New York if he would just cut the play. But we never really got very far on this."

As first rehearsals began, in fact, Williams absented himself from the Cort Theatre in New York. He not only withdrew from rehearsals, he also failed to keep publicity appointments, failed to meet the press to publicize or discuss the play.

"Williams refused," according to journalist Stephen Silverman, "to show up for a press conference. The press agent told the barrage of photographers and newsmen we could catch up with him at his Manhattan Plaza apartment. I led the parade. Williams answered the door half-naked and very coquettish. 'I didn't think there'd be any ladies,' he told the woman from one magazine. The apartment was a pigpen. Unflushed toilets. Broken glass on the kitchen floor. The photographer had to fix a coffee machine so Williams could stop and have a cup — even though he was obviously enjoying the chase and leading everyone on. The one time he snapped was when the young lady asked if his plays were autobiographical.

" 'Where did *you* come from?' he replied, dismissing her. My only personal question was, 'Are you going to leave your apartment in this condition?' — 'When I arrive in Key West,' he drawled, 'I'll call back here and get an actor to come in and clean it up. For twenty-five dollars, you can get an actor to do anything.' "

The very next morning, in fact, Williams quit New York for Key West — with an excuse more legitimate than nervousness over Broadway. Florida Keys Community College was about to open its new Tennessee Williams Performing Arts Center with a production of his 1969 play *Will Mr. Merriwether Return from Memphis?* Written when he was on the verge of collapse, it was then packed away with no hope of production. When the administrators of the college and the social leaders of Key West asked him in 1979 for a play with which to christen the center, he offered them the yellowing manuscript.

"He came to rehearsals and to campus several times [in January]," according to William Seeker, the college president. "He was complaining of insomnia and bursitis, and we all knew his health, like his local friendships, blew hot and cold. At the same time, his beard was growing one week, shaved off the next, back and forth. There were constant changes in his appearance: he was healthy and cheerful, then sickly and depressed. The alternate moods were startling. All the same, he could not have been more cordial to the campus community. He signed a notarized document giving the college the right to use his name at the Fine Arts Center. On the second night of the play [January 25] a number of private gala parties had been planned for him, but when he heard that the students and campus employees were to see his play that night, he showed up — in tennis shoes and an informal shirt — to meet them. He signed programs, chatted with people and did everything his normally shy nature shrank from. He took time to walk around with me and meet the audience. This was the other side of the man, the gentler soul who was so much the reverse of the paranoid man of tantrums and unpredictability."

The events of that week in late January were a success for the college and for the town. The play, however, was dismal, obviously the product of a confused mind. Apparitions of historic characters (Rimbaud, van Gogh) appear to a woman and her neighbor, lonely souls each, one of them awaiting the return of the romantic Mr. Merriwether. The daughter of one initiates a young man to the mysteries of sex. Finally, Merriwether returns — in terms and dialogue recalling Williams's return from Memphis to St. Louis in 1934, and the apparition of the other woman's late, drunkard husband Cornelius returns to admit his infidelity.

There was a desperation in his trying, in an earlier drugged state, to come to terms with the ghosts of what he and his father were in the 1930s. And the event of his 1969 entrance into the Catholic Church — however briefly before he made an exit — was reflected in the character's seriocomic confessions. Nightmare rather than dream, distortion rather than clear memory, *Mr. Merriwether* is a virtually unperformable play. It does, however, anticipate the same stream of memories with which he would deal somewhat more successfully in 1981 and 1982.

Williams prolonged his Key West interval for a long weekend — not only for the round of social events, but also to draft scenes for an idea suggested to him when he saw this play staged. The history of his own family life was foremost in his mind, and he began a strange household melodrama, *Some Problems for the Moose Lodge;* the title referred to his father's attempts to be accepted by the Elks in St. Louis.

At the end of January, *Clothes for a Summer Hotel* opened at the Eisenhower Theatre, Washington. The response was so loudly negative that Williams rushed at last to make cuts and meet with his director. He then returned to Key West, locked the door of his room (telling a new young companion that he feared burglars and muggers), slept for two days, and emerged to work in his studio.

Calls continued to come from his agent in New York and from his producer in Washington, but as messages accumulated he departed again, for a festival of his plays in Atlanta, at the Alliance Theatre. His next association with *Clothes* was in Chicago, where the company moved in February. "He seemed in better form there," Martin recalled. "His brother Dakin came to opening night with a big crowd of well-wishers, and Tennessee agreed to make more cuts. He worked closely with the cast, we had a good notice from Claudia Cassidy, and by the time we were ready to move to Broadway we all had a false sense of security."

Quintero recalled a poignant moment in Chicago. "The morning after the [press] notices, which in general were not very good, it was windy, cold and snowing. I saw Tennessee leave the hotel, so I put on my coat and caught up with him in front of the Art Institute. He was sitting on the steps, in the snow, like some half-demented creature. I said, 'What are you doing, Tom?' He said, 'I'm waiting for them to open because I know they will have a swimming pool, because this is a place for artists where I can catch my breath to go on living.' " It was apparently an episode of complete withdrawal from reality. After a day's rest, he was more lucid.

Back in New York, Williams met with Elliot Martin. "We discussed the fate of the show," Martin said, "and of course I said we still had a fighting chance. But then the blizzard of 1980 came, and on top of that a transit strike. The play had been budgeted at $400,000 — one-fourth came from Columbia Pictures, one-fourth from the Shubert Organization, and I raised the remainder privately." (Mitch Douglas added that in fact Elliot Martin gave substantially and generously of his own funds to try to keep the show running when funds were depleted.)

"Tennessee also agreed readily to defer his monies until some of our costs could be made up," Martin continued. "We opened on March 26 — his sixty-ninth birthday — and the audience was really ecstatic about the play. But the critics were not, and the weather and the transit strike finalized the decision. We had to close the show on April 16. All plays did badly that season, but especially plays like ours, which had every problem well documented in the press during rehearsals and the out-of-town run. Tennessee was eager to keep it going, but when that was impossible, he said, 'What did I tell you? They were all out to get me.' The *Times* had asked him for the usual Sunday prior-to-opening essay, but he gave them a bitter, anti-press piece, which of course wasn't published."*

---

* Some who attended opening night and performances afterward were not quite as ecstatic as Martin recalled. Part of the problem was that some of the players simply could not be heard, even in the first rows.

With the failure of *Clothes for a Summer Hotel,* Tennessee Williams never returned to the Broadway theatre, although he did bring a play back to the Jean Cocteau the following year. He harbored a deep bitterness toward the New York critics, an attitude more justified by what had happened a decade earlier than by the tone of the press in 1980. When Walter Kerr was asked about Williams's allegation later that year, that the critics all hated him and wanted his work to fail, Kerr replied, "That's so silly, of course. If anything, we were overeager to see the play do well. . . . I think he's the finest American playwright. But the talent isn't always there every time you turn on the faucet."

Producer Martin was convinced that almost everyone, however, misread and misheard the play — an easy thing to do, one might add. "It's not about the Fitzgeralds, it's about a brother and sister, about Tennessee and his sister, with the image of the asylum looming over all. And it's a play with a certain transferred paranoia — from the situation of Rose to that of Williams himself who [exactly like the tortured and alcoholic F. Scott Fitzgerald] was blaming the critics and the media for his own failures."

As a studied text, the play indeed has that sensibility, and it continues the personal meditation he began with *The Two-Character Play.* From the 1960s, his sister had been the source and inspiration of everything he wrote, either directly — with a surrogate character representing her — or indirectly, in the situation of romanticized mental illness or angrily unvarnished verisimilitude. Fitzgerald was clearly modeled, in this play, on Williams's experience, and the claims of heart trouble and heavy drinking linked them: "At one point I went through a deep depression and heavy drinking," Williams said. "And I, too, have gone through a period of eclipse in public favor. . . . [The Fitzgeralds] embody concerns of my own, the tortures of the creative artist in a materialist society. . . . They were so close to the edge. I understood the schizophrenia and the thwarted ambition."

He could perhaps most of all understand those experiences because he had spent many years confronting the fate of his sister, who is the real character behind Zelda Fitzgerald in this play. As a reminder of their shared covenant with the past, Scott gives her a ring — just as Williams had given a ring to Rose (which, after its return to him, he had given to Carson McCullers). "Between the first wail of an infant and the last gasp of the dying," Zelda says, "it's all an arranged pattern of submission to what's been prescribed for us unless we escape into madness or acts of creation. . . . I'm not your book anymore! I can't be your book anymore! Write yourself a new book!" After this play, he would.

A final cry about lunacy and institutionalization, about alcoholism and the fear of waning creative power, about the confusion that had always linked Williams to his sister, *Clothes for a Summer Hotel* could, as Martin rightly suggested, be easily misperceived. That it was not a dramatically compelling work made it even more disappointing for Williams. The confession to and about Rose in this play pleased almost no one. His last two works, yet to come, would be confessions to others.

With this fresh disappointment, friends in New York gave him refuge whenever he was willing to stop shuttling from city to city, from apartment to apartment, hotel to hotel.

In the last years his visits to his mother had been infrequent; his own instability was the main reason for this, but his mother's condition was another. From the early 1970s, she had grown increasingly disoriented, and finally Edwina Dakin Williams had to be removed from a condominium apartment to a nursing home. She failed distressingly in mind and body from 1975, and on June 1, 1980, at the age of ninety-five, she died.

"Tennessee was a guest at my summer home on Long Island," Vassilis Voglis said. "At three in the morning a call came for him. I awakened him and said his brother was on the telephone, but he simply said, 'It's probably the news that my mother has died,' and rolled over in his bed. 'Tell them to call me in the morning.' "

This reaction should not be regarded as merely callous.

"I was spending as much time with Tennessee as anyone," Mitch Douglas said, "and I can say that he was very upset about his mother's death — more deeply than he wanted people to know."

There was no question, however, that his feelings, as expressed and recorded, were mixed. "I can stand my mother for only fifteen minutes at a time," he said once to Lucy Freeman. "Then I have to flee." And Freeman understood why: "Edwina infantilized everyone. It was clear that there was a terrible rage in Tennessee against her and what she had done to turn her children against their father, and what she had done to Rose. Edwina was a great woman and a courageous woman and a terrifying woman, and every woman she saw was in competition for her in the lives of her children. She was ever the dominant Southern belle."

Shortly before his mother's death, the playwright admitted: "I cannot feel anything about my mother. I dream about her, but I can't feel anything.... She was always on the verge of hysteria. She was called a nightingale. She had nice legs and kicked up her legs very high for a minister's daughter."

He had remembered her telling him, years earlier, that she had been so impressed at learning that the violets she had so admired in the state of Tennessee were imported by English settlers. For the funeral in St. Louis, he imported a blanket of two thousand English violets which covered her coffin with a simple lettered ribbon — "Love from Tom."

"I think there was a great relief and a great release for him when his mother died," Maureen Stapleton said. "He was attentive and supportive and generous with her — and the portrait of her in *The Glass Menagerie* is extremely generous — but how much deep love there was, or how much resentment, is hard to gauge."

Within a week of the funeral, Williams was at the White House again, this time receiving from President Carter the Medal of Freedom. (More than a dozen others were similarly honored at the same time.) Friends accompanied him; he was glad there were no critics. "When he wanted to," according to Mitch Douglas, who was present, "he could be the gentleman of the world, as he was at the White House. He behaved very well there."

From mid-June to late July, Williams and the Southern artist Henry Faulkner, then fifty-six, traveled in Europe. In Taormina, Carlo and Mirella Panarello welcomed them to their home for luncheon, as they had often welcomed Williams in the past. They recalled that he was relaxed and in good spirits that June, but when the reporter arrived from *La Sicilia,* Williams was outspoken about his resentment of critics, the academic establishment and the theatregoing public. "They gave me the Medal of Freedom, sure," he told journalist Giuseppe Di Bernardo. "It's as if they wanted to say to me, 'Here's your award, now take it and get out!' " His anger was short-lived, however, and by early August he had returned to Key West, gathered various manuscript drafts and departed for Chicago to meet with Gregory Mosher, artistic director of the Goodman Theatre.

Williams was eager to give them three one-act plays, as Mosher had requested. At first he offered *The Chalky White Substance, The Traveling Companion* and *Some Problems for the Moose Lodge.* These were to be directed by Gary Tucker, who had directed a Williams one-act play, *The Frosted Glass Coffin,* in Atlanta.

"Gary introduced me to Tennessee at the Ambassador Hotel," Mosher recalled. "He said he was working on a new one-act play, *Some Problems for the Moose Lodge,* a comedy about insanity and a release from an asylum, and death — serious in its concerns, but definitely comic in treatment." At the same time, Williams was writing to Anne Meacham that he felt utterly rudderless, without direction for his future. All the more reason, Mosher thought, to give Williams the opportunity to have professional activity.

In spite of the Goodman's interest, Williams's personal insecurities were unalleviated. Quite simply, his life had no basis of really adult emotional reinforcement. He was traveling so obsessively that he was unable to spend sufficient time with his older friends; the only constant companionship was provided by men young enough to be his children, which is how most of them acted.

Nevertheless, personal anguish notwithstanding, Williams spent the first part of autumn in Chicago, supervising rehearsals of *A Perfect Analysis Given by a Parrot, The Frosted Glass Coffin* and *Some Problems for the Moose Lodge,* the trilogy on which they had finally agreed to compose an evening called *Tennessee Laughs.* "He was staying in an apartment hotel," Mosher said, "working very hard and very seriously on the new short play, and we were all very impressed."

But Williams was also anxious about other markets for his work — especially for the full-length plays of the 1970s. "By this time," Mitch Douglas said, "he was out of vogue and he knew it. His plays had lost money and he was hard to sell. There was no new market for him, and naturally this upset him." There seemed, however, to be a cheerful answer when an offer came from Vancouver, where the University of British Columbia offered him the post of Distinguished Writer in Residence. "But I wanted also to make things happen for his plays," Douglas added, "which I knew he wanted. So I suggested to Vancouver that they do one he liked — *The Red Devil Battery Sign.*" And so he went to Canada that autumn.

Life in British Columbia began very well, and Williams was at ease in the social life. "The theatre people there called a press conference with the local Gay Activists League," Douglas said, "and they threw him a party with a band of worshipful admirers. Tennessee was in his element.

"But when rehearsals were underway for *Red Devil,* Tennessee got very nervous, and suddenly he mysteriously vanished! Finally he turned up, in San Francisco, some time later, living quietly. He was soon on his way back to New York, and then to Chicago. It was, frankly, getting harder and harder to deal with his professional life at this time. Since he wouldn't open his mail, you couldn't send him checks, and everything was forwarded from here to there. Finally, mail had to be sent to his accountant. And Tennessee forgot so many practical details that more and more often he would accuse someone else of stealing money from him, forging his checks, not sending statements of his account, and so on. If he had only opened his mail, every problem would have been solved."

Some Problems for the Moose Lodge, the only play of the evening trilogy to be a world premiere, raised sufficient interest at the Goodman Theatre, meanwhile, that Mosher and Tucker approached Williams to suggest that it be expanded to a full-length play for spring 1981. He promised to work on it in Key West, in New York and back in Vancouver. Almost at once, the name of the play was changed — at the suggestion of an assistant on the production — to *A House Not Meant to Stand.*

For the Christmas–New Year holiday, he returned to Key West, where it was now necessary to arrange for Rose's return to Ossining. Then, ignoring his own dismay at her departure, he pushed forward on the new play, which suddenly took quite a different turn. He wrote on the new title page that it was his kind of "Southern Gothic spook sonata," pointing literally and deliberately to Strindberg's play *The Spook Sonata* (sometimes also called in translation *The Ghost Sonata*).

The dilapidation of the house of Cornelius McCorkle in *A House Not Meant to Stand,* he wrote to Mosher, was a metaphor for the state of society; the characters of the play, however, were obviously emblematic of the Williams family — especially with the alienating, heavy drinker Cornelius, his aging and confused wife Bella (named for Cornelius Williams's sister, their Aunt Belle) and the vague dreams of political stardom that refer to both Williams's paternal grandfather and to his brother, Dakin. There is also a pointed reference to his own use of drugs: "When a man's got to live off pills in the quantity and at the price, with only temporary relief at best, why I say it's time to quit hangin' on, it's time for a man to let go." *Clothes for a Summer Hotel* had been a last cry of pain and apology for Rose; *A House Not Meant to Stand* was an attempt at another exorcism of family ghosts, and each page of the new and expanded script contained references to him and to his bitterness about his family.

The action concerns the McCorkles, whose advanced age, selfishness and illusions about the past conspire to estrange them from one another, their children and their neighbors. A struggle for a hidden family fortune is complicated by the visit of their negligent son and his pregnant fiancée. At the end, Bella sinks into irreversible madness.

But the writing did not have a cathartic effect on Williams. Instead, he lost confidence as he spread out his personal pains, and this frightened him. He wrote again, early in 1981, to the patient and supporting Mosher, reflecting that it might be nice to be dead without having to endure the business of dying. And in another letter shortly after, he referred to a speech in his one-act play *I Can't Imagine Tomorrow* which, he said, perfectly described his life since the death of Frank Merlo almost twenty years earlier:

"A small man came to the house of Death and the uniformed guard at the gate asked him what he wanted. He said that he wanted Death. The guard said that's a very large order for a small man like you. The small man said yes, he knew it was a large order, but that's what he wanted. The guard asked him for his documents. The only document he had was his birth certificate. The guard looked at the date on the birth certificate and said: Too early, you've come too early, go back down the mountain and don't come up here again for twenty years. The small man started to cry. He said: If you won't let me in for twenty years, I'll wait twenty years at the gate, I can't go back down the mountain. I have no place down there. I have no one to visit in the evening, I have no one to talk to, no one to play cards with, I have no one, no one. But the guard walked away, and the small man, who was afraid to talk, began to shout. For a small man he shouted loudly, and Death heard him and came out himself to see what the disturbance was all about. The guard said the small man at the gates had come twenty years too early, and wouldn't go back down the mountain, and Death said: Yes, I understand, but under some circumstances, especially when they shout their heads off at the gates, they can be let in early, so let him in, anything to stop the disturbance."

Mosher at once set in motion, in early February 1981, plans for a gala celebration of Williams's seventieth birthday. Invitations were sent to dozens of friends and colleagues. This was also, Mosher thought, an excellent way of getting Williams back to Chicago, for he feared that the playwright's spirits had fallen so low that he might not arrive with the revisions for production. A turnout of friends, a display of loving support, might enable him to go forward with his work.

Williams did indeed return to Chicago, but his mood was erratic, his health fragile. "After Tennessee emerged from his breakdown," Mosher said, "theatre had changed so much, had altered so radically. Nonprofit theatres had proliferated, old-fashioned producers were no longer producing, long and expensive road tryouts were no longer possible, and not-for-profit productions were numerous: 15 of them quickly became 250. Tennessee never really understood the changes in American theatre, yet in a way he may have felt responsible for them. He often spoke of his agony at not being taken seriously, of being old and washed-up. His expectations weren't unreasonable. He expected serious writing to be attended seriously. He was also a man coming to grips in his plays with what he was coming to grips with in his life — the price of fame, the value of true relationships, the approach of death."

Rehearsals proceeded with considerable delicacy, for it was clear to everyone that feelings all around were vulnerable — not only Williams's, but those of his friends, and those of Gary Tucker. "It was hard to know who to please," recalled Bonnie Sue Arp, a member of the 1981 cast; another, Marji Bank, remembered that Williams could be "a blessed man when we needed him during rehearsal, but he was unpredictable. I remember him coming to lunch with us at the Art Institute cafeteria, in his fur coat, his arms loaded with manuscript pages and all his paraphernalia. Most of the time he seemed a little vague — it was as if there were a wall around him. But he wrote me a dear note when my husband died, and suddenly he could clarify a line of dialogue with a single rewritten line. When we were ready to open, there was still much to be reworked, but it just seemed to elude him."

Other problems were even more sensitive. "When [Gary] Tucker [the director] had me wear jockey shorts for one scene," according to Scott Jaeck, who played the indolent son Charlie, "Tennessee heard about it, came to the rehearsal and was furious — he didn't want his play to be a burlesque." Instead, as another player, Rachel Stephens, recalled, Williams wanted the emphasis on the fact of aging and death — not the attraction of youth: "He became enamored of what the character Jessie could tell us all, and he made revisions to stress that. He gave a character profile to each of us for the role we played, and he often gently evaluated our performances — in fact he rewrote the role for me as we went along. This was not always diplomatic as far as the director was concerned, and there was some tension." And Les Podewell recalled that Williams was always involved with his cast, "and he never showed whatever unhappiness was plaguing his private life. His only concern was, would he be remembered?"

Because of his concern for them, the 1981 cast of *A House Not Meant to*

Stand had great affection for Williams in spite of the bumpy road of rehearsals. "From what we saw of his rewriting," Scott Jaeck said, "he was obviously concentrating on his own family and its destruction. But he simply couldn't solve the creative problems of the play. He worked hard, but his energies faded quickly, and he came to rehearsals only in the morning."

The seventieth-birthday dinner at the Goodman was attended by none of the invited theatre luminaries and actors (who sent various excuses with their messages of congratulations) and only a few close friends of Williams — Vassilis Voglis and Jane Smith, whose husband Tony had recently died.

"His mood changed sharply," Mosher recalled. "The night before the party, Tennessee ordered to his hotel room a print of [Alfred] Hitchcock's movie *Lifeboat,* and a group of us sat and watched while he provided a hilarious running commentary about the star, Tallulah Bankhead. But hours before the party next day, he was so upset about the revisions of the play that he said, 'Let's cancel!' Well, he wasn't the first playwright to feel that way when it comes down to the wire, but in his case it took some hard convincing. By that evening, he was in good form, and he danced the night away with just about every woman among the two hundred guests."

After the toasts at dinner, Williams took the microphone. "Chicago was the first place I had a success, and perhaps it will be the last." As it would happen, he was correct — but it was not the last in 1981; that would happen in 1982. *A House Not Meant to Stand* opened in previews the following evening, and Williams remained to make several textual emendations. Again, his manner changed sharply, and again it was an imprudent mixing of mood-altering pills that was the cause.

"There was a short period of time during which he made no sense at all," said Mitch Douglas, who may have guessed the reason but never mentioned it to anyone then or later. "He came up with the notion that I had been dealing with the airlines to put him on a depressurized airplane to cause him to die of a heart attack. His paranoia was becoming more and more bizarre. And he threatened to make this publicly known. He said we'd have to get a hit-man to silence him, he was going to publicize everyone's crimes.* Finally, I said, 'Tennessee, I'll do anything for

---

* This imagined murder-method suggests that Williams was living out the fear of the deranged Mark (*In the Bar of a Tokyo Hotel*), who "kept complaining that the plane cabins were not pressurized enough, and they were pressurized perfectly."

you, but *I* won't have a heart attack.' I always insisted that he deliver his work on time, that he show up for appointments. He owed that to himself. Whenever he failed to keep appointments with the press, I knew he'd be criticized for it. But he just said he didn't want to be an Olympic high jumper for the press."

Then, even more irrationally, Williams began to accuse Douglas of stealing mail and money again, and claimed that his agent was diverting cash due to him. Even when the records and canceled checks were produced, he would never take the proof.

"He listened to everyone but those he should have," Douglas added, "and many of the people around him were concerned only for themselves. When he accused those who didn't deserve the accusation, he could have a nasty side, and a few like myself found that we were always defending ourselves. I, for one, was more and more unwilling to be a doormat for him."*

On April 30, 1981, Audrey Wood suffered a massive stroke that kept her comatose for years. Williams said nothing, but he was then at work on a gruesome one-act play called *Now the Cats with Jewelled Claws*. Set in hell (or its anteroom), it is a tale of madness, depravity and death, and a single revision paid tribute to what must have been his sorrow at the news of Audrey's incapacitation: "What dreadful news about Susie," one woman says, "a massive brain hemorrhage but may linger indefinitely in a coma." Six weeks later, when asked to make a formal statement on her behalf, he admitted: "I was a difficult client for Audrey Wood from the beginning."

For the summer, he divided his time between New York, Key West and Vancouver, where he worked on an adaptation of *The Sea Gull* in which he hoped to star Anne Meacham and Donald Madden, and perhaps Kate Reid. He also drafted scenes for a bizzare tale of venality and seduction which he then called *Gideon's Point*.

In August he was in New York discussing a third memory play he had written, and one with the same evident intention of reconciliation, apology and healing that he had attempted in *Clothes for a Summer Hotel* and

---

* Williams was still convinced that people were becoming rich at his expense. Years before, he had sent Audrey Wood to Bergdorf Goodman to buy a fur coat for his mother. When it arrived at the hotel where he was entertaining Edwina, he ordered the coat returned, since he suddenly had the idea that Audrey was receiving a percentage of the store's profit. Audrey loved to tell this account of his absurd suspicion. By 1980, his fears included not only agents, but attorneys, actors and accountants as well, and a good number of loyal old friends.

A House Not Meant to Stand. It was from the start titled *Something Cloudy Something Clear,* and it was, he said, "one of the most personal plays I've ever written — it released for me some of the emotional content of my life during the pivotal summer when I took a sort of crash course in growing up. . . . It's wrecked my nerves, but I felt I had to complete certain things because I felt time was limited. . . . I'm very conscious of my decline in popularity, but I don't permit it to stop me because I have the strength of so many playwrights before me. I know the dreadful notices Ibsen got. And O'Neill — he had to die to make *A Moon for the Misbegotten* successful. And to me it has been providential to be an artist, a great act of providence that I was able to turn my psychosis into creativity — my sister Rose did not manage this. So I keep on writing."

For what would be his last New York play, he once again turned to Eve Adamson. There was a professionalism she could offer, a sympathetic hearing and a sensitive interpretation of his play. She was no sycophantic yea-sayer; instead, she combined a sharp eye and a clear voice with her respect. She became, at the end, the last woman who offered the support other women had earlier: Margaret Webster, who surely could have given more had she herself been given a better play to work with; Margo Jones, who adored him and his work, but had limited gifts; Irene Selznick, who had given him all the support and creative freedom he needed to write a masterwork in 1947; the patient, generous and understanding Cheryl Crawford, who had produced a quartet of his plays; and of course the great Audrey Wood, who perhaps gave him more attentive devotion, certainly for a longer time, than any woman in his life.

Something Cloudy Something Clear was a remarkable play late in Williams's creative life. He had spoken of it to virtually no one. This in itself would not have been unusual, except that it was possibly the best work of his last twenty years, and he must have known it. Set on the Provincetown dunes late in the summer of 1940, it is a memory play in which the writer August (the only name changed from real life, and the play's surrogate Tennessee Williams — possibly from his spiritual association with August Strindberg) meets Kip, Frank Merlo and Tallulah Bankhead — to sift and sort the memories, the long buried feelings of love and friendship, and to say farewell. Blatantly autobiographical, the play interweaves the beginning of Williams's affair with Kip with the refractions of later time, granting August the ability to interject latter-day observations from the perspective of Williams's later life. Frank, dying of cancer, makes a brief entrance, and Bankhead is brought out for a brief dialogue. More than any play in his life, it was a simple, tender elegy to three he had loved and lost; it is a poetic and apologetic farewell, an act of forgiveness of himself for the love he had not had the time to acknowledge. His life, as he then felt, was an alternating perception of "something cloudy and something clear," and the condition of his eyes, which those words described, fit his inner perceptions perfectly. Most of all, however, the play is an acceptance of the death which had already embraced them all, and that he knew must soon come to him — thus the final dance to the music of Ravel's funereal "Pavane."

It was indeed so personal a play that Williams considered withdrawing it during rehearsal. "Tennessee was so frightened," Eve Adamson said, "that the closer we came to opening the more convinced he was that we shouldn't. He could be very difficult at times like this, when his fears overwhelmed him, and as much as he rewrote, it never seemed to bolster his confidence. At one point he was really trying to sabotage his own play, to harm himself before the critics got a chance to harm him. This was a very sad part of his nature, and I must say I went through absolute hell on this production. But even when the worst did happen, and the critics savaged what I and the audiences knew was a very fine play, he called to ask if I was feeling all right. As depressed as he was, he was concerned for me."

In September, Williams returned from the distant retreat of Vancouver and attended, with friends, several performances of his last New York production. All who saw it loved it, and the Jean Cocteau Repertory sold out its performances then and again the following February and March. The play was an unexpected surprise, a minor miracle.

"I saw Tennessee for the last time at a performance of *Something Cloudy Something Clear*," Meade Roberts remembered. "I felt that the play — had it been prepared away from New York in a 'lab' kind of atmosphere — would have had the time to be improved. Even as it was, it was very, very fine, both beautifully written and played. Tenn looked wonderful that night. He was very warm, and we embraced, and he wanted to know all about my life, what I'd been writing and so forth. He talked about his adaptation of Chekhov, and ideas he had for new work. He seemed so young, as if the whole world lay before him that night.

"After that evening's performance, a symposium was held, and he was articulate and witty. Ruth Gordon and Garson Kanin were in the audience — God bless them, they were the only members of the uptown,

Broadway crowd who cared enough to come. Kanin rose from his seat and said he wished it to be made clear that Tennessee Williams was unquestionably the greatest dramatist America had brought forth and he wished the audience to acknowledge that fact. Everyone cheered, and it was all very genuine. Tennessee beamed, with tears in his eyes, and then he went out into the night, his shoulders squared, with a look on his face that seemed to say 'En avant!' "

That autumn, he was told about the deaths of the painter Henry Faulkner and the poet and teacher Oliver Evans, and this pitched him for days into despondency. Then he and Harold Pinter were selected as recipients of the third annual Common Wealth Award, a grant of $11,000 to each "for excellence and outstanding achievements in various fields of human endeavor." In his acceptance remarks at the Shubert Theatre, a withdrawn and unclear Williams said of the award money, "I'll have to think about using this for a tombstone," but then he recovered better manners and said he would like to dedicate the award "to my sister, Rose Isabel Williams," who was in fact in the audience that November day, celebrating her birthday with her brother.

Backstage, Pinter, who had just told the audience of his long admiration for "the greatest American playwright," was approached by him. "Harold," he said, "take care of your health. I could have done a lot more if I had taken care of my health." That day, according to Larry D. Clark, who was visiting from the University of Missouri at Columbia, "Tennessee was very ill, very frail."

The fact was that Williams had unfortunately resumed regular megadoses of pills for both sedation and alertness — mostly Nembutal and Ritalin and Seconal, although he was often able, with the help of those who called themselves friends, to obtain more potent, less legal substances. "He behaved very badly that day," as Eve Adamson recalled, "and he treated Mitch Douglas abominably."

Indeed, Douglas's days as Williams's agent were over: "The last time we really met for any period of time was the day of the award. Later I heard he was working and that he was sometimes even happy, and I was glad for him. And several times before the end of our relationship, he told people that I had had a real interest in his career and had kept him going — which I had, and which I was pleased to do — and that gratified me. He could be a terribly sweet man, childlike and grateful and the soul of sincerity. At the White House, for example, he was chipper and courtly. He pinned a flower in my lapel when I was wearing a dark suit.

At times like that his real gift for friendship shone out, and those are the times I like to remember."*

But those times were too rare, as Audrey Wood and Bill Barnes had known, too. Williams remained in New York until the end of the year, attending small dinner parties with friends like Vassilis Voglis and Jane Smith. "He was extremely reserved and quiet unless he had a drink," Voglis recalled, "but when I commissioned a portrait of him he gladly sat for it. That autumn we were at other gatherings — Milton Goldman honored Virgil Thomson, and Patricia Kennedy Lawford gave a party for him also. It was a pleasant enough season for him." (The party Mrs. Lawford offered was a polite and generous substitute for what was to have been a gala in Williams's honor at Lincoln Center on December 2. It had been canceled when virtually no tickets were sold.)

In January he was back in Key West, still revising *A House Not Meant to Stand,* which Mosher had promised to present at the larger main stage of the Goodman, after two productions in the smaller studio. New York friends, however, were concerned for Williams's health; Voglis flew down for a visit, but the coterie that still attended Williams annoyed the visitor — as it had a number of others, like Edwin Sherin — and a few days later, content that at least Williams was looked after and fed, he returned to New York.

By February 8, Williams, too, returned to New York. The mayor presented the city's medallion of honor on February 10, and the next evening there was a fashionable party for Williams, at which his former friend and sometime nemesis Truman Capote was present. Quietly, Williams asked when he thought they would meet again. "In Paradise," was Capote's response. For the moment, Williams was content with Key West.

On February 13, from Duncan Street, he telephoned a young filmmaker named Peter Hoffman, who had been eager to transform two of Williams's short stories — "The Resemblance Between a Violin Case and a Coffin" and "Completed," both based on Rose's youth — into a full-length screenplay. Two days later, Hoffman was at the Pier House restaurant in Key West, dining with Williams and discussing a collaboration.

No work on this project was possible until June, however, for Williams was still hopeful about the Goodman Theatre. The play was now over one hundred pages, and he took it to Chicago for meetings with

---

* From the end of 1981, executives at ICM assigned Luis Sanjurjo to represent Tennessee Williams's literary interests.

Mosher and the new director who had been engaged after personal and creative differences led to the dismissal of Gary Tucker.

Of his meetings with Williams, director André Ernotte recalled that the playwright was "afflicted with self-doubt, [eager to] say something bad about himself so that he can say it first before anyone else ... he's often hard to deal with." Mosher agreed that at this time Williams was riddled with vulnerability and pain, and that still he kept on revising and rewriting, even when that work produced no substantial improvements.

"Tennessee confronted his weaknesses and faults for years in a way that few others ever did," Elia Kazan said later. "We all try to appear tougher and stronger than we are, but there was something in him that reached out and touched everyone who saw his plays or who knew him. You felt that your own faults and sins were understood and that he had compassion for them. He accepted his own weakness and sinfulness, and he went on courageously and bravely — always writing. He never backed off."

The insistence on writing even in the midst of depression, even when exhaustion nearly pitched him into total collapse, was certainly a courageous part of Williams's character. The habit of work was an ingrained one for decades, not simply the automatic response to boredom or the autonomic response to drugs. "A playwright writes," as Kazan added, "even if he is in decline. Gallant is the word to describe Tennessee at the end. He went on writing, even when he was told his plays weren't very good by comparison with what had preceded. On he went, always working at the craft, never ashamed. All people in the arts have special weaknesses, but all we can be judged on is what's been worthwhile. If people are judged for their failures, the balance is upset, and the successes are themselves diminished."

But there is, after all, a limit to human genius, as there is a limit to the genius's lifetime; it is only a truism, only a cliché to say that everything human is finite. No one must have been more aware of this than Tennessee Williams, who had so long admitted that his masterpieces were things of the past.

On another level, of course, he continued because that is precisely the way struggle is endured by writers: the gift is exercised, not short-circuited or dulled by neglect. The only way he could maintain some affirmation of value, the only route he knew to attempt meaning in his life was to write. It was his way of healing, of thanking, of forgiving, of making a final attempt at inner order out of the external muddle that he knew had marked so much of his life.

He must have known, contrary to his sometimes cantankerous attitude about critics, his reputation, his place in history, that over the last forty years — the longest and the most public and most highly compensated career in the history of American theatre — he had been neither unappreciated nor underappreciated. Because he was a true artist, this never left him merely content; that it did not, however, give him a greater inner calm, a quietness and an inner gathering in the final years, must have been his keenest penance. It would have been natural for him to think in penitential terms, for that is very much the tone of the last plays and the last stories.

In late April 1982, after a stormy rehearsal period of frayed nerves, raised voices and hurt feelings, *A House Not Meant to Stand* finally opened and did a respectable business until the end of May. "There was a strong impression all around," recalled Scott Jaeck, "that this was his last play, and that he just didn't have the strength to deal with it. He came to the opening night, and he came back to thank us all, but he was a weary man." A month later, *Time* magazine called the play the best Williams had written in a decade, a work "inhabited by a rich collection of scarred characters."

But by this time Williams was beyond encouragement. He wrote to his friend, the actors' agent Milton Goldman, whose professional counsel he so valued, that he had endured an agonizing solitude for twenty years, since Frank Merlo's death; he knew not how much longer he could endure. Small dinner parties by New York friends did not cheer him, nor did the acceptance of an honorary doctorate at Harvard University's June commencement. Weary and distracted, he appeared disheveled in an open sportshirt at the Cambridge ceremonies. Then, with his loyal and concerned friend Jane Smith, he went to a festival of his plays at Williamstown, where he said plaintively, "Give my goodbye to Broadway, my many, many goodbyes, for there is a rock there, and it is not one from which water nor violets nor roses spring."

At Williamstown, however, on the suggestion of friends, he agreed to meet with Peter Hoffman, who presented a prose treatment of the projected screenplay. Until the end of July, they worked erratically in Key West. The major interruption was provided by the goodwill and concern of Gregory Mosher, who agreed to hear Williams's idea for another series of one-act plays to be called *Williams's Guignol*. There were also two un-finished longer plays, *In Masks Outrageous and Austere* (the new title for *Gideon's Point*) and *The Lingering Hour*. Williams, however, never re-sumed the contact.

Toward the end of July, he was again eager to travel, and he took Jane Smith and Peter Hoffman with him first to London, and then, on July 24, they checked into suites at the San Domenico Palace Hotel, Taor-mina. He was glad to return to the quiet, sprawling monastery that had become a regular hotel for kings and princes, for artists and writers and actors and the less celebrated who appreciated its cloister of plants and palm trees, and the clear, warm waters of the Ionian Sea below.

He continued to write every morning. And what he wrote was not the screenplay for a collaboration with Hoffman, but *The Lingering Hour*, a violent apocalypse of devastation and universal death.

"All the volcanoes of the world explode at more or less the same time," he told a visiting reporter, "and there are earthquakes and destruc-tion everywhere. Here [i.e., in Sicily], there is Etna and the action is set in the main square at a cafe, with people talking. . . . The first earthquake happens in California. Hollywood first disappears into the sea." The title of his play is the usual translation of the Italian *prima sera* — the first dusk he had described in *The Roman Spring of Mrs. Stone* as the moment "before the lamps go on, when the atmosphere has that exciting blue clarity of the noctural scenes in old silent films, a color of water that holds a few drops of ink . . . the amethyst light of prima sera."

The three visitors to Taormina were welcomed to the home of the Panarello family, who found their old friend, as Carlo said, "gentle and quiet — he listened a lot rather than speaking as much as he usually did with us. His family seemed to be the great sorrow in his life, and he un-derstood them with great warmth and humanity. When he spoke of them, his eyes would often fill with tears. This is perhaps why he under-stood so quickly and so deeply the family troubles of others, and people's anguish in general."

After a week, however, Williams grew restless again. "He found trav-eling difficult," Jane Smith said, "so we did not go on to Russia, as he had hoped.* And once the film people who had gathered in Sicily for a

* The plays of Tennessee Williams (invariably with some cutting and alterations) have been perenially popular in Russia. He had by this time amassed more than one million dollars in Russian royalties, which could not be taken from that country but would have had to be spent there.

festival found that he was there, he was plagued constantly. Finally we fled because some people at the hotel complained that his typewriter made noise at odd hours of the night."

On August 13, after stopping in Rome, they arrived in New York, where he met a last time with Gregory Mosher, who remembered being present after Williams had brought Rose to New York for a day. "He had bought a ring for her, and he was worried that she might not like it. But she loved it, and he was very relieved." *Clothes for a Summer Hotel* had reached its final closure. Rose (like Zelda in the play) again had a ring; this time it would not be removed, not given to any other.

During the first week in September, Williams ate little, slept much, and wandered around the house in Key West. His housekeeper, Leoncia McGee, was alarmed, and very nearly panicked when he vanished from the house early one morning and did not reappear all day.

There was an explanation. Williams had boarded a bus, heading north for an unknown destination. He got as far as Key Largo, where he waved the driver on and sat alone in a bar that rarely hosted more than drifters or desperate tourists who had stopped at the filling station outside.

A young couple were seated nearby. "As we were having coffee," the man recalled, "we noticed a man seated alone at another table." After a few moments of casual conversation across the aisle, they invited the man to join them. "We figured he was just a local hanging out by himself, but an intelligent man, because he was impressed with the fact that I said I am a writer." The conversation continued, and the strangers introduced themselves as Mr. and Mrs. Steven Kunes; their companion said he was Tennessee Williams, but that they should call him Tom.

"He was waiting for a bus, God only knows why, but soon we were driving him back toward Key West." They took him to Duncan Street, talking en route about writers and writing. Something in the young couple's optimism had opened him up, and made him for a while more expansive. They had just moved from New York, were taking a short holiday, and planned to move to California. Williams invited them into his house, and over coffee and a table piled with scattered manuscript pages, he asked about Kunes's novel in progress.

"And that's when it happened," he said. "Williams went into another room and emerged with a square black case, telling me to look inside. It was an Underwood typewriter from the 1940s. 'I write very rarely on this anymore,' he said. 'But I used it for *Summer and Smoke* and *Cat on a Hot Tin Roof.* It needs a new ribbon, and perhaps some oil. I didn't know I'd be finding a place for it so soon.' " He looked at Steven Kunes. "Write a play, Steven," he said. "Just write a play. I know you can hit the core. I know it like I know a good wine. Don't be flattered when I say this. You can flatter me by using this old machine here to do the job." They thanked one another for the kindnesses they shared that evening, and the couple left. Four months later, as a courtesy, Kunes sent Williams the first draft of the novel he wrote on the typewriter, but there was no reply.

In mid-September, Williams flew for a week to New York, went four days to Vassilis Voglis's summer house on Long Island, then returned to Key West. He was beyond encouragement. At Duncan Street, the petty sexual intrigues of a small group depressed him further; when his house should have been serene, he opened it to acquaintances who could not have been less helpful. At the end of the month, he invited Peter Hoffman for a few days' work on the screenplay, but he was so morose and withdrawn, living now only on wine and Seconal and coffee, that no work was possible. He was losing weight and also all interest in continuing with anything. By 1982 the life of travel that had been both diversion and search took him nowhere but to a deeper point of loneliness, and his Key West social circle enclosed nothing. On October 1, he told Hoffman that they would leave at once for New York, and then proceed to Asia, but once in Manhattan he abandoned further travel for the moment, and Hoffman was dismissed.

He then returned to Key West, only to find that his dog and cat had abandoned the house in his absence. Soon he was back in New Jersey, where he visited briefly with Jane Smith at her suburban home; he selected from her library the letters of Chekhov for them to read over the next several days.

In November, Williams was invited to read from his work at the 92nd Street YMHA. The reading at Kaufman Hall turned out to be his last public appearance. Richard Kennedy, an English teacher who regularly attended the readings by writers and dramatists, recalled that Williams received a most enthusiastic welcome from the audience. "His speech was occasionally slurred," according to Kennedy, "and his opening remark was that he almost forgot to show up. He seemed very uncomfortable." Williams read excerpts from unpublished poems and from a short story-in-progress, and after only a half-hour with his audience "abruptly stood up and said, 'That's the end of the performance.' " And according to Jane Smith, "When he came out onstage, I was shocked — I thought something was missing, I was so used to that vigorous man, and the energy seemed to have left him. Later, I learned from another friend that he became depressed in New Orleans and Key West."

In December, back again in Key West, he added a codicil to his will, transferring the joint administration of one special trust fund to the sole custody of Harvard University, which would also in time become for writers the repository of certain remaining papers. Within days, neighbors who were alerted to his frail condition were alarmed when they received no reply to persistent calls. Finally, on Christmas Eve, two of them found him comatose and rushed him to a hospital. Next day, Leoncia McGee telephoned Dakin: "She called to tell me that Kate Moldawer [a neighbor in Key West] and Gary Tucker had taken him to the hospital the night before, that he hadn't been eating and had locked himself in his room for three days. He was found totally dehydrated, and they had to flush the drugs out of his system."

Jane Smith went to Key West at once, suggesting that he come back north to rest, to stay with her and to see several New York physicians she knew.

After a week's recuperation at Jane Smith's home, however, Williams insisted on resuming his travels. He went south, to visit Robert Carroll, then he was in Key West again, then back in New Orleans, where he concluded the sale of the Dumaine Street house, and then he returned to Key West. It was as if he were animating the last lines of *The Glass Menagerie,* when Tom described how he had "followed, from then on, in my father's footsteps, attempting to find in motion what was lost in space. I traveled around a great deal. The cities swept about me like dead leaves, leaves that were brightly colored but torn away from the branches. I would have stopped, but I was pursued by something."

On Friday, January 21, 1983, Anne Meacham telephoned to report that their friend Donald Madden was desperately ill. At once Williams wrote to him that he, too, had recently been confined to a hospital. He praised Madden's decision to remain at home, among loved ones, rather than submit to the care of strangers; his own complaint, he added, was a serious one — he had had a sufficiency of life, and was in irreversible depression. The letter concluded with the hope that when he came to New York he hoped to find Madden restored; if he was not, Williams wrote, then life was surely the black joke he had mostly accused it of being.

In New York in early February, he announced to Jane Smith, and to his occasional secretary and companion John Uecker, that he would soon leave for Taormina — alone. When Uecker, who had a professional commitment that month, suggested engaging another traveling companion, Williams said simply, "It's too late for a stranger."

And so he made his way to Taormina; it was the first time he had traveled alone in years. The staff at the San Domenico Palace Hotel welcomed him on February 11, but as the concierge noted, "He was so sad and exhausted and withdrawn, and we could not encourage him to eat at all." Carlo and Mirella Panarello were surprised to learn, months later, that he had been to Sicily in February; it was the first time in more than thirty years that he had neither visited nor telephoned from the few blocks' distance.

Instead, he went alone and for the last time to the piazza where he and Frank Merlo had so often sipped wine or coffee, had dined together, watched the crowds go by, and walked arm in arm for the evening *passeggiata,* the traditional stroll, along the Corso Umberto. But there was no one in the empty piazza that February; there was only what he once called "a cold wind around my heart that wraps me in despair."

After five nights he returned to New York, where he secluded himself in his suite at the Elysée, refusing food and almost all company.

"I don't want to wind up in an intensive care unit with all kinds of tubes stuck in me," he said earlier. "I wouldn't allow that, and I don't think that's going to happen. . . . But I go mad at night. I can't be alone, because I have this fear of dying alone." He asked John Uecker to remain nearby, although he neither requested nor would accept much contact or conversation.

For the last five years, he invariably included in public readings his poem "Old Men Go Mad at Night," which, he felt, conveyed himself directly to his audience:

> What's left is keeping hold of breath
> and for cover never now a lover
> rests them warm . . .
> Was that a board that creaked
> as he took leave of us,
> or did he speak —
> "I'm going to sleep, good night."

On the evening of February 24, 1983, he withdrew quietly to his bedroom with a bottle of wine. On his bedside table was the traditional array of prescriptions—capsules, tablets, eyedrops, nosedrops, narcotics, hypnotics, barbiturates and all the paraphernalia associated with decades of hypochondria and chemical dependence. It was later reported by the New York medical examiner that during the night Tennessee Williams had ingested lethal quantities of a variety of drugs—cocaine among them.

In the morning, when he could not be aroused, friends entered the room. At last there was stillness.

Notes

Preface

p. xvii "Tennessee's life is" Elia Kazan to DS, Feb. 1, 1984.

xvii "a drama" TW, "If the Writing is Honest," *Where I Live* (New York: New Directions, 1978), p. 104. Originally published as a preface to William Inge, *The Dark at the Top of the Stairs* (New York: Random House, 1958).

xviii "I hope" TW, in a taped interview with Stephen Banker (1974) preserved in the *Tapes for Readers* series (Washington, D.C.).

Chapter One

5 "I was rarely" Edwina Dakin Williams, p. 162.

6 "I danced" Diary of Edwina Estelle Dakin, entry under year 1900–1901.

6 "Mr. Frederick" *Ibid.,* Oct. 8, 1901.

6 "secret ambition" Edwina Dakin Williams, p. 183.

6 "I remember" Melissa S. Whyte to TW, Dec. 7, 1948.

6–7 "Mr. Lide" Diary of Edwina Estelle Dakin, Aug. 18, 1905.

10 "She was" "The Life and Ideas of Tennessee Williams," *P.M.,* May 6, 1945, p. 7.

10 "I was" Washburn, p. 6-E.

10 "Other children" Edwina Dakin Williams, p. 15.

11 "diggin' to" *Ibid.,* pp. 13–14.

11 "It was" Rice, Apr. 24, 1958, p. M-2.

11 "She never" Lucy Freeman to DS, Sept. 1, 1983.

12 "I got" Davis, p. 12.

12 "Grandfather was" Dakin Williams to DS, Oct. 23, 1983.

13–14 "The changes" David Loth to DS, Oct. 9, 1983.

14–15 "At the boardinghouse" Dakin Williams to DS, Oct. 23, 1983.

15 "I preferred" Rice, Apr. 24, 1958, p. M-2.

15 "Her coming" "Grand," *The Knightly Quest: A Novella and Four Short Stories* (New York: New Directions, 1966), p. 172.

15–16 "Grand cared" Dakin Williams to DS, Oct. 23, 1983.

17 "The many moves" *Ibid.*

18 "He took no" Edwina Dakin Williams, pp. 35 and 39.

18 "I hated him" Rice, Apr. 24, 1958, p. M-2.

18–19 "Life at home" Dakin Williams to DS, Oct. 23, 1983.

19 "In her transition," Keith, sec. 3, p. 6.

19 "Rose was caught" Dakin Williams to DS, Oct. 23, 1983.

20 "She was doing" *Ibid.*

20 "It was just" *Ibid.*

20 "It immediately became" Rice, Apr. 24, 1958, p. M-2.

21 "Old Things" and "Nature's Thanksgiving" *The Ben Blewett* (junior high school newspaper), Oct. 1925.

22 "Mother became" Dakin Williams to DS, Oct. 23, 1983.

23 "Tommy Williams" Margaret Cowen, English teacher at University City High School, in Rice, Apr. 27, 1958, p. M-2.

23 "drinking, smoking" "Can a Good Wife Be a Good Sport?" *Smart Set,* vol. 80, no. 3 (May 1927), pp. 9, 13.

23 "Tom and Hazel" Dakin Williams to DS, Oct. 23, 1983.

23 "My mother did not" TW, *Memoirs* (New York: Doubleday, 1975), p. 15.

24 "She married another" Jennings, p. 74.

24 "Hushed were the" Thomas L. Williams, "The Vengeance of Nitocris," *Weird Tales,* vol. 12, no. 2 (Aug. 1928), p. 253.

24 "set the keynote" Rice, Apr. 24, 1958, p. M-2.

25 "His great affection" Paul Bigelow to DS, Feb. 3, 1984.

25 "the hospitalities were" *Clarksdale Daily Register,* July 6, 1928.

Chapter Two

31 "One had to go" David Loth to DS, Oct. 9, 1983.

31 "There were no" *Ibid.*

32 "Campus life was" *Ibid.*

33 "We went through" Donovan Rhynsburger to DS, Nov. 11, 1983.

33 "a play with" Unsigned review of *Beauty Is the Word,* in the *Daily Missourian* (student newspaper of University of Missouri at Columbia) 188 (Apr. 12, 1930): 2.

33 "I thought, when" Donovan Rhynsburger to DS, Nov. 11, 1983.

34 "The fact is" Lucy Freeman to DS, Sept. 1, 1983.

34–35 "There were forty" Elmer Lower to DS, Dec. 6, 1983.

36 "It's true that" Maxwell, p. 24.

36 "We used to drive" Brown, p. 276.

36–37 "one of the most amazing" Elmer Lower to DS, Dec. 6, 1983.

37 "I attacked my" Rice, Apr. 27, 1958, p. M-2.

37 "I was deeply" Jennings, p. 74.

37 "None of us" *Ibid.*

37–38 "It was so moving" *New York Post,* Dec. 12, 1947 (magazine), p. 1.

39 "those bound by" Sheaffer, p. 253.

40 "Father used the" Dakin Williams to DS, Oct. 23, 1983.

40 "There was absolutely" Elmer Lower to DS, Dec. 6, 1983.

40 "He had been" Donovan Rhynsburger to DS, Nov. 11, 1983.

42 "Mother was an" Dakin Williams to DS, Oct. 23, 1983.

43 "the very handsome" *Ibid.*

43 "Rose became" *Ibid.*

44–45 "It was a terrible" *Ibid.*

46 "the most moving" TW, in Harry Rasky's film, *Tennessee Williams's South.*

47 "By this time" Dakin Williams to DS, Oct. 23, 1983.

49 "Tom had fanatical" Clark Mills McBurney, in Rice, Apr. 28, 1958, p. M-2.

49 "the worship of" H. D. F. Kitto, "Dionysus," in Phyllis Hartnoll, ed., *The Oxford Companion to the Theatre,* 3rd. ed. (London: Oxford University Press, 1967), p. 242.

50 "She then became" Dakin Williams to DS, Oct. 23, 1983.

50 "[She] was rarely" William Jay Smith, p. 191.

51 "The amount of" DLB, p. 25.

51 "Even at parties" DLB, p. 26.

51 "We have been" Arleen Thyson, in *Washington University,* vol. 53, no. 3 (Summer 1983), p. 24.

51 "the model contributor" John M. Pickering, *ibid.*

51–52 "the shyest" William Jay Smith, p. 193.

52 "She never stopped" *Ibid.,* p. 190.

52 "I don't know" Thomas L. Williams, "27 Wagons Full of Cotton," *Manuscript,* vol. 3, no. 4 (Aug. 1936), p. 28.

52 "but Mother and" Edwina Dakin Williams, p. 83; see also DLB, p. 26.

53 "There was not" DLB, p. 26.

54 "a poignant little" Anne H. Jennings, "Review of Theatre Guild's Plays Presented Oct. 13," *Webster Groves Missouri Star-Times,* Oct. 16, 1936, pp. 1–2.

54 "I needed" Rice, Apr. 28, 1958, p. M-2.

55 "They were the" "Something Wild . . . ," *Where I Live: Selected Essays* (New York: New Directions, 1978), pp. 9–10.

55 "showed much more" Rice, Apr. 28, 1958, p. M-2.

55 "It was a" *Ibid.*

55 "very jealous of" Dakin Williams to DS, Oct. 23, 1983.

55–56 "He wore conservative" *Ibid.*

56 "very pitiful" Edwina Dakin Williams to Rose O. Dakin, letters dated Nov. 17 and 26, 1936

56 "She still says" *Ibid.,* letter dated Dec. 6, 1936.

56 "I can't take her" *Ibid.,* letter dated Jan. 26, 1937.

57 "It wasn't only" Dakin Williams to DS, Oct. 23, 1983.

57 "For all the" Davis, p. 13.

57 "that dreaded city" *Memoirs,* p. 28.

57 "It was a great" At Univ. of Southern California, Mar. 18, 1973.

58 "Well, I guess" Tischler, p. 56., e.g.

58 "Mr. Williams has" A report of the reading committee of the Mummers of St. Louis (HRC/Univ. of Texas, Austin).

58 "a vital and" Reed Hynds, "Mummers' Play Brilliantly Done, Though Unconclusive [*sic*]," *St. Louis Star-Times,* Dec. 1, 1937, p. 17.

58–59 "I was a terrible" Calendo, p. 31

59–60 "I was a freshman" Dakin Williams to DS, Oct. 23, 1983.

60 "She gave permission" Buckley, p. 98.

60 "My sister was" Berkvist, sec. 2, pp. 4–5.

60 "I don't think" Brown, p. 278.

60 "She was the" Maxwell, p. 256.

Chapter Three

65 "He had" Anthony Dexter to DS, Aug. 28, 1983.

65 "I have only" Elsworth P. Conkle to his wife Virginia, recalled in a letter to DS, Jan. 24, 1984.

65 "Tom Williams" Virginia Conkle, quoted in a letter from Ellis Conkle to DS, Jan. 24, 1984.

65 "The course also required" Elsworth P. Conkle to DS, Jan. 24, 1984.

67 "sounds like it" Press release, Liebeling-Wood Agency, 1948.

67 "the fellows in" *Memphis Commercial Appeal*, Nov. 24, 1940, p. 14.

68 "It was a period" *Tennessee Williams: Theater in Process*, an Encyclopedia Britannica Educational Corp. film, 1976.

68 "I found the" Rice, Apr. 39, 1958, p. M-2.

71 "I was desperately" Davis, p. 13.

72-73 "There's a wonderful" Elia Kazan to DS, Feb. 1, 1984.

74 "After all" Wood, p. 130.

74 "Tom's great god" William Jay Smith, p. 191.

76 "His primary need" Wood, p. 133.

76 "These plays were" Hume Cronyn to DS, Aug. 19, 1983.

76 "I was just" Steen, pp. 159-160; DLB, p. 80.

76 "That was truly" Wood, p. 133.

77 "Audrey came to" Robert Anderson to DS, Dec. 16, 1983.

78 "He put writing" Windham (a), p. 110.

78-79 "I had an" Paul Bigelow to DS, Feb. 3, 1984.

79 "He was a charming" Langner, p. 331.

79 "And so I put" Paul Bigelow to DS, Feb. 3, 1984.

81 "one of the irascibles" Fritz Bultman to DS, May 30, 1984.

81 "just like" Ruth Hiebert to DS, Oct. 15, 1983.

81 "My left eye" *Paris Review*, p. 169.

81 "Kip was" Fritz Bultman to DS, May 30, 1984.

81n "It was an intense" Paul Bigelow to DS, Feb. 3, 1984.

82 "a desperate period" "A Summer of Discovery," *New York Herald-Tribune*, Dec. 24, 1961.

82-83 "he had been" Webster, p. 66.

83 "Why they should" *Ibid.*, p. 66.

83-84 "a short, sturdy" *Ibid.*, p. 69.

84 "a mixture of" *Memoirs*, p. 62.

85 "astonishing" *The Boston Herald*, Dec. 31, 1940, p. 10.

85 "most interesting" Elliot Norton, " 'Battle of Angels' a Defeat, But No Disaster," *Boston Post*, Jan. 12, 1941, p. 25.

85 "sordid and amateurish" *Variety*, Jan. 1, 1941, p. 45.

85 "Then it was" "The History of a Play (With Parentheses," *Pharos* 1-2 (Spring 1945), p. 120.

85-86 "putrid. . . . This show" *Boston Post*, Jan. 7, 1941, p. 1.

86 "Tom asked me" Smith, in DLB, p. 29.

86 "Wherever he went" Wood, pp. 131, 138.

86 "although *Battle*" Windham (a), p. 110.

87 "just not being" Paul Bigelow to DS, Feb. 3, 1984.

87 "His eyesight" Webster, p. 71.

88 "I had a small" Fritz Bultman to DS, May 30, 1984.

90 "Then I must" "The Siege," *In the Winter of Cities* (New York: New Directions, 1964), p. 20.

91 "The Beggar's Bar" Fritz Bultman to DS, May 30, 1984.

91 "a pathetic lady" Paul Bigelow to DS, Feb. 3, 1984.

91 "our blood" "Iron is the Winter," *In the Winter of Cities*, p. 96.

92 "and just a few" Paul Bigelow to DS, Feb. 3, 1984.

92 "He was a real" *Ibid.*

93 "It was a" Anthony Dexter to DS, Aug. 28, 1983.

94 "He hated being" Paul Bigelow to DS, Feb. 3, 1984.

96 "I went to" David Greggory to DS, Aug. 12, 1983.

96 "We found" *Ibid.*

96 "I visited" *Ibid.*

97 "This is what" *Ibid.*

97 "This really hurt" *Ibid.*

97–98 "He just showed" Christopher Isherwood to DS, Oct. 7, 1983.

98 "sitting typing" Isherwood, pp. 135–136.

98 "It was wartime" David Greggory to DS, Aug. 12, 1983.

98 "In his private" Christopher Isherwood to DS, Oct. 7, 1983.

98 "He always had" Paul Bigelow to DS, Feb. 3, 1984.

100 "From the day" David Greggory to DS, Aug. 12, 1983.

101 "tidying up" *New York Times,* Oct. 17, 1943, sec. 2, p. 2.

101 "Tenn was in" Paul Bigelow to DS, Feb. 3, 1984.

101–102 "Son" Quoted by Dakin Williams to DS, Oct. 23, 1983.

102 "Tennessee was very" Burl Ives to DS, Aug. 26, 1983.

102 "a living poem" "Grand," pp. 169, 172.

Chapter Four

110 "Of course her" Eloise Sheldon Armen to DS, Sept. 1, 1983.

110 "a small flame" Courtney, p. 416.

110 "rather dull" Notation across the original ms. of *The Glass Menagerie,* deposited at Humanities Research Center, University of Texas/Austin.

111 "Mr. Dowling" Young, p. 33.

111 "the stamina" Claudia Cassidy, "Fragile Drama Holds Together in Tight Spell," *Chicago Daily Tribune,* Dec. 27, 1944, p. 11.

111 "has the courage" Ashton Stevens, "Great Actress Proves It In Fine Way," *Chicago Herald American,* Dec. 27, 1944, p. 11.

111 "Actually, she directed" Courtney, p. 396.

111 "It gripped players" Claudia Cassidy, "On the Aisle," *Chicago Sunday Tribune,* Jan. 7, 1945.

113 "the reluctant" Courtney, p. 411.

114 "The events of" Dakin Williams to DS, Oct. 23, 1983.

114 "We all knew" Randolph Echols to DS, Sept. 27, 1983.

114 "never understood" Blais, sec. 2, p. 2.

114 "All work is" Winakor, p. 4.

115 "It's human valor" "The Life and Ideas of Tennessee Williams," *P.M.* May 6, 1945, pp. 6–7.

115 "I may not" *New York Post,* Dec. 30, 1957.

116 "less a play" Nathan, pp. 326–327.

116 "pity for people" Nightingale, sec. 2, p. 3.

116–117 "It is usually" Miller, p. 30.

117 "and new problems" *Paris Review,* p. 154.

118 "During the" Randolph Echols to DS, Sept. 27, 1983.

119 "I never knew" Bosworth, p. 113.

120 "he was more" Steen, p. 151.

120 "a restless person" *Ibid.,* p. 101.

121 "If I can" Press release, Liebling-Wood Agency, 1948.

122 "Pancho was a" Fritz Bultman to DS, May 30, 1984.

122 "romantic pessimism" Joseph Wood Krutch, "Tennessee Williams," *The Nation* 162 (Mar. 2, 1946): 267–268.

123 "sentimental" Denham Sutcliffe, "Tennessee Williams," *New York Times Book Review,* Feb. 24, 1946, p. 8.

123 "Tennessee was such" Muriel Bultman Francis to DS, Dec. 17, 1983.

124 "Tennessee behaved very" Fritz Bultman to DS, May 30, 1984.

124 "It wasn't a" Ashley Pond, M.D. to DS, Oct. 10, 1983; see also *Albuquerque Tribune,* Feb. 29, 1983.

125 "hypochondriacal being" Maxwell, pp. 59–60.

125–126 "The meeting between" Paul Bigelow to DS, Feb. 3, 1984.

126 "a tall, slim" Carr, p. 272.

126 "Pancho was of course" Paul Bigelow to DS, Feb. 3, 1984.

126 "Carson went wild" *Ibid.,* p. 276.

127 "From that summer" Paul Bigelow to DS, Feb. 3, 1984.

129 "I live" Press release from Liebling-Wood (1947), e.g.

129 "She was neither" TW, "An Appreciation," *New York Times,* Dec. 15, 1946, sec. 2, p. 4.

130 "Whenever I'm disturbed" Maxwell, p. 132.

134 "Margo wanted desperately" Randolph Echols to DS, Sept. 27, 1983.

135 "I never saw" *Paris Review,* pp. 159–160.

136 "Tennessee was quite" Elia Kazan to DS, Feb. 1, 1984.

137 "At the end" Fritz Bultman to DS, May 30, 1984.

137 "This man has" TW at the University of Southern California, Mar. 18,1973.

137–138 "a quietly woven" Brooks Atkinson, "First Night at the Theatre," *New York Times,* Dec. 4, 1947, p. 42.

138 "heroic dimensions" Howard Barnes, "O'Neill Status Won by Author of 'Streetcar,' " *New York Herald-Tribune,* Dec. 14, 1947, sec. 5, p. 1.

138 "compassionate" John Chapman, " 'A Streetcar Named Desire' Sets Season's High in Acting, Writing," *New York Daily News,* Dec. 4, 1947, p. 83.

138 "a drama of" George Freedley, "Williams Writes a Brilliant, Moving Play in 'Streetcar,' " *New York Morning Telegraph,* Dec. 5, 1947, p. 2.

138 "deeply disturbing" Wolcott Gibbs, *The New Yorker* 23 (Dec. 13, 1947): 50.

139 "I write out" Davis, p. 14.

139 "I draw all" Whitmore, p. 322.

139 "Blanche DuBois" Ciment, p. 71.

139 "Kazan has always" David Susskind's MetroMedia network program *Open End,* Nov. 13, 1960.

140 "Tennessee liked Pancho" Elia Kazan to DS, Feb. 1, 1984.

Chapter Five

146 "His trip recalled" Paul Bigelow to DS, Feb. 3, 1984.

146 "In 1946" Vidal, p. 130.

146 "a bohemian annexe" Acton, p. 213.

147 "indifference to place" Vidal, p. 132.

149–150 "I came along" *Ibid.,* p. 143.

150–151 "I got tired" Paul Bigelow to DS, Feb. 3, 1984.

151 "a pretentious and" Howard Barnes, *New York Herald-Tribune,* Oct. 7, 1948, p. 16.

151 "a juvenile and" John Chapman, *New York Daily News,* Oct. 7, 1948, p. 81.

151 "almost unendurably" Wolcott Gibbs, *The New Yorker* 24 (Oct. 16, 1948): 51–52.

151 "the weaknesses" John Gassner, *Forum* 110 (Dec. 1948): 351–353.

151 "It's tremulous with" Brooks Atkinson, *New York Times,* Oct. 17, 1948, p. 33. See also the *Times* for Oct. 17, 1948, sec. 2, p. 1.

153 "Frank was" Dakin Williams to DS, Oct. 23, 1983.

153 "We were all" Paul Bigelow to DS, Feb. 3, 1984.

153 "Everyone who ever" Christopher Isherwood to DS, Oct. 20, 1983.

154 "In appearance" Jane Bowles, *Feminine Wiles* (Santa Barbara: Black Sparrow Press, 1976), pp. 7–8.

158 "I found him" Irving Rapper to DS, Aug. 11, 1983.

159 "By the time" *Ibid.*

160 "They stayed" Paul Bigelow to DS, Feb. 3, 1984.

163–164 "very detrimental remarks" Cornelius Wiliams to Audrey Wood, Feb. 8, 1950.

164 "Apart from Rose" David Greggory to DS, Aug. 12, 1983.

166 "I had been" Cheryl Crawford to DS, Jan. 18, 1984.

167 "first fictionalized" Windham, p. 262.

168 "Magnani first said" Cheryl Crawford to DS, Jan. 18, 1984.

168 "Tenn had written" Maureen Stapleton to DS, Jan. 16, 1984.

168–169 "something of a" John Pearson, *The Sitwells: A Family's Biography* (New York: Harcourt Brace Jovanovich, 1978), p. 401.

169 "We were performing" Maureen Stapleton to DS, Jan. 16, 1984.

169 "Tennessee was counting" Windham (a), pp. 59–60.

170 "Frankie gave his" Johnny Nicholson to DS, Mar. 2, 1984.

170 "Frank Merlo was" Maureen Stapleton to DS, Jan. 16, 1984.

170–171 *"The Rose Tattoo* is" "The Meaning of *The Rose Tattoo,*" *Vogue* 117 (Mar. 15, 1951): 96.

171 "He was quite" Cheryl Crawford to DS, Jan. 18, 1984.

171 "He was a" Maureen Stapleton to DS, Jan. 16, 1985.

172 "I made several" Cheryl Crawford to DS, Jan. 18, 1984.

172 "He found her" Johnny Nicholson to DS, Mar. 2, 1984.

173 "I spent several" Cheryl Crawford to DS, Jan. 18, 1984.

173 "Kiss me" quoted by Johnny Nicholson to DS, Mar. 2, 1984.

173 "praying for" Johnny Nicholson to DS, Mar. 2, 1984.

174 "He loved the" *Ibid.*

177 "When I saw" David Greggory to DS, Aug. 12, 1983.

177–178 "We were looking" Theodore Mann to DS, Aug. 3, 1983.

178 "When we finished" Geraldine Page at a seminar at the New School for Social Research, New York, Dec. 6, 1982.

179 "Merlo was a" Galligan, p. 46.

179 "Nothing has happened" Brooks Atkinson, "At the Theatre," *New York Times,* Apr. 25, 1952, p. 19. See also the *Times,* May 4, 1952, sec. 2, p. 1.

179 "Everything in his" Elia Kazan to DS, Feb. 1, 1984.

179–180 "I think the" *Saturday Review of Literature,* Apr. 29, 1972, p. 27. See also Jennings, p. 72.

180–181 "I met him" Quintero (b), p. 4.

181 "a talented" "Five Fiery Ladies," *Life* 50 (Feb. 3, 1961): 88.

Chapter Six

185 "my conception of" "Foreword to Camino Real," *Where I Live: Selected Essays,* p. 63.

185 "He was" Elia Kazan to DS, Feb. 1, 1984.

186 "Honey, you don't" Barbara Baxley to DS, Aug. 31, 1983.

186 "I was also" Quintero (b), p. 4.

186–187 "Frankie was" Barbara Baxley to DS, Aug. 31, 1983.

187 "Walter Winchell" *Ibid.*

188 "the worst play" Walter Kerr, "Camino Real," *New York Herald-Tribune,* Mar. 20, 1953, p. 12.

188 "but that people" Walter Kerr, in a letter to TW dated Apr. 13, 1953.

188 "It doesn't have" Elia Kazan to DS, Feb. 1, 1984.

189 "He wanted to" Paul Bigelow to DS, Feb. 3, 1984.

190 "I wouldn't be" *New York Post* magazine, Dec. 12, 1947, p. 1.

192 "But the real" Thomas Griffin to DS, Dec. 16, 1983.

192 "courageous and fearful" Crawford, p. 184.

193 "although illegal" Margaret Foresman to DS, Nov. 14, 1983.

196 "Audrey may well" Robert Anderson to DS, Dec. 14, 1983.

197 "I do think" Elia Kazan to DS, Feb. 1, 1984.

197 "Tennessee was very" Maureen Stapleton to DS, Jan. 16, 1984.

198 "My father had" In Harry Rasky's film *Tennessee Williams's South.*

198 "Tennessee told me" Burl Ives to DS, Aug. 26, 1983.

198 "Williams was a dreamer" Mildred Dunnock to DS, Aug. 24, 1983.

198 "Ben Gazzara and I" Burl Ives to DS, Aug. 26, 1983.

199 "I think Maggie" Elia Kazan to DS, Feb. 1, 1984.

199 "Maggie was the" Davis, p. 13.

199 "Kazan didn't want" Mildred Dunnock to DS, Aug. 24, 1983.

199 "The bird that" *Cat on a Hot Tin Roof,* in *The Theatre of Tennessee Williams,* vol. 3, p. 114.

200 "He left two" Paul Bigelow to DS, Feb. 3, 1984.

200 "The postwar theatre" Robert Anderson to DS, Dec. 14, 1983.

202 "She had all" *Paris Review,* p. 181.

202–203 "Then I began" Ciment, p. 74.

203 "Tenn is licking" Campbell, pp. 31–32.

203 "a sad, lost" Paul Bigelow to DS, Feb. 3, 1984.

203 "I don't know" Vidal, p. 140.

203–204 "He would allow" Jane Smith to DS, June 13, 1984.

204 "After the show" Campbell, p. 32.

204 "He had a dread" Ciment, p. 75.

205 "I found Tennessee" George Keathley to DS, Sept. 6, 1983.

205 "and Merlo held" Leavitt, p. 93.

205 "Oh, yes" "A Separate Poem," *In the Winter of Cities,* pp. 126–129.

206 "During rehearsals" George Keathley to DS, Sept. 6, 1983.

206 "work in progress" *New York Times,* Apr. 17, 1956, p. 27.

206 "She was a nonstop" George Keathley to DS, Sept. 6, 1983.

207 "Curtain rises" quoted by Meade Roberts to DS, June 3, 1983.

207 "Of course" *Time* (anniversary edition), Oct. 5, 1983, pp. 159–160.

207 "The Williamses have" Campbell, p. 15.

208 "I had heard" Maureen Stapleton to DS, Jan. 16, 1984.

209 "Although Mr. Williams" Brooks Atkinson, "Theatre: Early Williams," *New York Times,* Nov. 22, 1956, p. 50.

209 "Tennessee Williams's finest" John Chapman, "*Glass Menagerie* is Still Aglow," *New York Daily News,* Nov. 23, 1956, p. 60.

210 "revolting . . . a contemptuous" *New York Herald-Tribune,* Dec. 17, 1956, pp. 1, 15; *Newsweek* 48 (Dec. 31, 1956): 59.

210 "I disagree that" Elia Kazan in the *New York Times,* Dec. 17, 1956, p. 28.

210 "I can't believe" *New York Times,* Dec. 17, 1956, p. 28.

210n "possibly the dirtiest" *Time* 68 (Dec. 25, 1956): 61.

211 "There is a" Elia Kazan to DS, Feb. 1, 1984.

211 "I am increasingly" Davis, p. 14.

211 "I am an" Rose (a), sec. 4, pp. 1–2.

212 "a fallible minor" Harold Clurman, in *The Nation* 176 (Apr. 4, 1953), pp. 293–294.

212 "Tenn and Clurman" Maureen Stapleton to DS, Jan. 16, 1984.

212–213 "My writing has" Ross (b), sec. 4, pp. 1, 7.

213 "The people in it" Wolcott Gibbs, "Well, Descending, Anyway," *The New Yorker* 33 (Mar. 30, 1957), pp. 85–86.

213–214 "He always told" Paul Bigelow to DS, Feb. 3, 1984.

214 "and cut him out" "The Man in the Overstuffed Chair," *Antaeus* 45/46 (Spring-Summer 1982): 289.

214 "I have changed" Rice, May 4, 1958, p. M-2.

214 "In retrospect" Brown, p. 176.

215 "Aunt Ella" "The Man in the Overstuffed Chair," 291.

215 "Tenn became" Maureen Stapleton to DS, Jan. 16, 1984.
216 "At this point" Paul Bigelow to DS, Feb. 3, 1984.
216 "Tom, I know" Quoted by Lilla van Saher to Meade Roberts; Roberts to DS, June 3, 1983.

Chapter Seven

219 "I think if" Ross (b), sec. 4, p. 1.
219 "Sophocles, Euripides" Harold Clurman, "Theatre," *The Nation* 86 (Jan. 25, 1958): 87.
220 "Why don't you" Quoted by Anne Meacham to DS, Feb. 4, 1984.
221 "Tennessee was absolutely" Anne Meacham to DS, Feb. 4, 1984.
223 "The remarkable aspect" Robert Anderson to DS, Dec. 14, 1983.
223 "He was devoted" Vassilis Voglis to DS, Sept. 22, 1983.
223-224 *"Suddenly Last Summer"* Joseph L. Mankiewicz to DS, Feb. 24, 1984.
224 "ordinary words" Brooks Atkinson, *New York Times,* Jan. 9, 1958, sec. 2, p. 1.
224 "a serious and" Walter Kerr, *New York Herald-Tribune,* Jan. 8, 1958, p. 16.
224-225 "Audrey, it is" Quoted by Meade Roberts to DS, June 3, 1983.
225 "Bill's problem" *Memoirs,* p. 165.
225-226 "Williams was very" Meade Roberts to DS, June 3, 1983.
226 "it has poisoned" Rice, May 2, 1958, p. M-2.
226-228 "Tennessee doesn't believe" Quoted by Meade Roberts to DS, Apr. 15, 1983.
229 "couldn't stop telling" Barbara Baxley to DS, Sept. 1, 1983.
229 "The relationship between" Joseph L. Mankiewicz to DS, Feb. 24, 1984.
230 "But he was always" Elia Kazan to DS, Feb. 1, 1984.
230 "Kazan was a" Geraldine Page, at a seminar at the New School for Social Research, New York, Dec. 6, 1982.
230 "acrid" Brooks Atkinson, "The Theatre: Portrait of Corruption," *New York Times,* Mar. 11, 1959, p. 39.
230 "disturbingly bad" Robert Brustein, "Sweet Bird of Success," *Encounter* 12 (June 1959): 59-60. See also Brustein, "Williams' Nebulous Nightmare," *Hudson Review* 12 (Summer 1959): 255-260.
230 "become immobilized" Harold Clurman in *The Nation* 188 (Mar. 28, 1959): 281-283.
230 "dirty minded" John Chapman, *New York Daily News,* Mar. 11, 1959, p. 65.
230 "very close" *Time* 73 (Mar. 23, 1959): 58.
231 "but [was] not" Walter Kerr, in *New York Herald-Tribune,* May 17, 1959, sec. 4, p. 2.
231 "dismayed and alarmed" Kenneth Tynan, in *The New Yorker* 35 (Mar. 21, 1959): 98-100.
231 "a sensational expression" Gassner, pp. 228-231.
232 "Williams now seems" Popkin, p. 64.
232 "He was wretchedly" Elia Kazan to DS, Feb. 1, 1984.
232 "He told me" Meade Roberts to DS, July 29, 1983.
233 "I was in" *Ibid.*
234 "An odd situation" Meade Roberts to DS, Apr. 15, 1983.
234 "There we were" Maureen Stapleton to DS, Jan. 16, 1984.

235 "If artists are" Introd. to Carson McCullers, *Reflections in a Golden Eye* (New York: Bantam, 1950), pp. x–xi, ix.

235 "He created" Meade Roberts to DS, Mar. 15, 1983.

237 "Poor, sad Diana" Paul Bigelow to DS, Feb. 3, 1983.

237 "one of the oddest" George Keathley to DS, Sept. 6, 1983.

237 "She had become" Dakin Williams to DS, Oct. 23, 1983.

237 "She had a" Joyce Croft Williams to DS, Oct. 23, 1983.

238 "I am poisoned" Michelfelder, p. 17.

238 "The production of" Meade Roberts to DS, June 3, 1983.

239 "He was totally" Frank Corsaro to DS, Oct. 30, 1983.

239–240 "Frank [Merlo] was" *Ibid.*

240 "We [playwrights]" *New York Times Magazine,* June 12, 1960, p. 78.

241 "After *Sweet Bird*" Elia Kazan to DS, Feb. 1, 1984.

241 "Well, I don't" Jennings, p. 81.

242 "The years in" Paul Bigelow to DS, Feb. 3, 1984.

242–243 "I have an" Stang, sec. 2, pp. 1, 3.

243 "The real problem" Cheryl Crawford to DS, Jan. 18, 1984.

244 "After *Period*" *Ibid.*

244 "He was unsure" Jane Smith to DS, June 13, 1984.

245 "We sat together" Windham (b), p. 311.

245 "mother-image" TW, "The Agent as Catalyst," *Esquire* 58 (Dec. 1962): 216, 260.

246 "That's the only" Funke (b), pp. 72–73.

246 "My kind of" *Ibid.*

246 "It was a" Frank Corsaro to DS, Oct. 30, 1983.

246–247 "I create imaginary" Funke (b), p. 73.

247 "As if it" Frank Corsaro to DS, Oct. 30, 1983.

247–248 "I was shocked" Maureen Stapleton to DS, Jan. 16, 1984.

248 "There was Edwina" Frank Corsaro to DS, Oct. 30, 1983.

248 "the wisest play" *Time* 79 (Jan. 5, 1962): 53.

249–250 "He was one" Paul Bigelow to DS, Feb. 3, 1984.

250 "His theme" Miller, p. 30.

250 *"The Night of"* *Time* 79 (Mar. 9, 1962): 53.

250 "She simply *was*" Lucy Freeman to DS, Sept. 1, 1983

Chapter Eight

255 "There were a few" David Greggory to DS, Aug. 12, 1983.

255 "Tenn behaved" Paul Bigelow to DS, Feb. 3, 1984

256 "When he complained" Mildred Dunnock to DS, Aug. 24, 1983.

256 "The opening night" David Greggory to DS, Aug. 12, 1983.

256 "creative suicide" Richard Gilman, "Mistuh Williams, He Dead," *Commonweal* 77 (Feb. 8, 1963): 515–517.

257 "He just didn't" Maureen Stapleton to DS, Jan. 16, 1984.

257 "As Frank became" Meade Roberts to DS, June 3, 1983.

257 "It was so" Frank Corsaro to DS, Oct. 30, 1983.

257–258 "They took me" Barbara Baxley to DS, Sept. 1, 1983.

258 "I think Tenn" Paul Bigelow to DS, Feb. 3, 1984.
258 "Tennessee Williams came" Sheldon Posnock to DS, Feb. 23, 1984.
258 "Frankie had an" *People,* May 26, 1975, p. 37.
258–259 "The breakup with" Cheryl Crawford to DS, Jan. 18, 1984.
260 "I draw every" Calendo, p. 28.
261 "When he died" Hirshhorn, p. 22.
262 "I like" Margaret Laing, "T. L. Williams — All Play, Some Work," *Los Angeles Times,* Apr. 11, 1965.
262 "I had suffered" Taped interview with Stephen Banker in the *Tapes for Readers* series, 1974. *Cf.* also Kakutani, p. C17.
262 "He'd been a" *Paris Review,* p. 166.
262 "Nembutal, Doriden" Bosworth, p. 330.
263 "I have a sort" Laing.
263 "I now rely" Hirshhorn, p. 22.
263–264 "I can't bear" *Ibid.*
264 "He never saw" Bill Glavin to DS, Feb. 12, 1984.
264n "I'm a built-in" Hirshhorn, p. 22.
264 "Bigelow is on" David Greggory to DS, Aug. 12, 1983.
264 "By this time" Maureen Stapleton to DS, Jan. 16, 1984.
264 "I don't remember" Bill Glavin to DS, Feb. 12, 1984.
265 "incomprehensible evil" Wagner, p. 42.
265 "I don't suppose" *Ibid.,* p. 15.
265 "He laughed so" Bill Glavin to DS, Feb. 12, 1984.
265 "I must continue" Quoted by Lester Persky to DS, Feb. 12, 1983.
266n "Well, Tom" Quoted by Bill Glavin to DS, Feb. 12, 1984.
266 "Mr. Williams" Whitney Bolton, *New York Morning Telegraph,* Feb. 24, 1966, p. 3.
266 "When critics accused" Robert Anderson to DS, Dec. 14, 1983.
267 "I wanted to make" Joseph Losey to DS, Jan. 25, 1984.
267 "When he lost" Vassilis Voglis to DS, Sept. 22, 1983.
269 "No, Bill" Wood, p. 196.
270 "I visited him" Elia Kazan to DS, Feb. 1, 1984.
270 "Swimming, drinking" Joseph Losey to DS, Jan. 25, 1984.
271 "totally addicted" Wood, p. 192.
271 "very nervous" Quintero (a), p. 4.
272 "The cast came" David Greggory to DS, Aug. 12, 1983.
272 "Dear Dakin" Schumach, p. 19.
274 "I was writing" Christiansen (a), p. 41.
275 "My conversion was" *Paris Review,* p. 155.
275 "This is how" Rev. Joseph LeRoy, S.J. to DS, July 16, 1983.
275 "I loved the" *Paris Review,* p. 156.
276 "It had concerned" Margaret Foresman to DS, Nov. 12, 1983.
276 "It was" Rev. Joseph LeRoy, S. J. to DS, July 16, 1983.
277 "It was a birthday" Maureen Stapleton to DS, Jan. 16, 1984.
277 "He stumbled" Anne Meacham to DS, Feb. 4, 1984.
277 "and if he could" Bill Glavin to DS, Feb. 12, 1984.

277 "One must never" *Time* 93 (May 23, 1969), p. 75.

277 "I hope that" Harold Clurman, in *The Nation* 208 (June 2, 1969), p. 709.

278 "almost too personal" Clive Barnes, *New York Times,* May 12, 1969, p. 54.

278 "that he will" Richard Watts, Jr., *The New York Post,* May 31, 1969, p. 17.

278 "hasn't the comfort" TW, in a letter to the cast of *In the Bar of a Tokyo Motel,* in Leavitt, p. 146.

278 "I think I'm" Proceedings of the *National Institute of Arts and Letters and the American Academy of Arts and Letters,* second series, no. 20 (1970), pp. 27–28.

279 "He was not" Larry D. Clark to DS, Oct. 21, 1983.

279 "Poor Tom" Bill Glavin to DS, Feb. 12, 1984.

279 "You know" Quoted by Glavin to DS.

279–280 "Tennessee Williams appears" Stefan Kanfer, "White Dwarf's Tragic Fadeout," *Life* 66 (June 13, 1969), p. 10.,

280 "We arrived in" Anne Meacham to DS, Feb. 5, 1984.

282 "Rose never took" Bill Glavin to DS, Feb. 12, 1984.

282–283 "I was ready" Margaret Foresman to DS, Nov. 12, 1983.

283 "he fell" *Ibid.*

283 "I was so demented" Jennings, p. 78.

284 "It's true" Elia Kazan to DS, Feb. 1, 1984.

284–285 "Tennessee could never" Maureen Stapleton to DS, Jan. 16, 1984.

285 "He looked better" Rev. Joseph Leroy, S.J. to DS, July 1983.

Chapter Nine

289 "Never recaptured" Louis Auchincloss, "TW: The Last Puritan," *DLB,* p. 410.

290 "I hope I" Funke (a), p. 45.

291 "The young men" David Greggory to DS, Aug. 12, 1983.

292 "I don't want" TW, *The David Frost Show,* Jan. 21, 1970.

292 "I work so hard" Quoted by David Greggory to DS, Aug. 12, 1983.

293 "The crowd there" Edwin Sherin to DS, Sept. 17, 1983.

293 "He took care" Rev. Joseph LeRoy, S.J. to DS, July 16, 1983.

295 "because [Mishima]" *Memoirs,* p. 236.

295 "I knew it" George Keathley to DS, Sept. 6, 1983.

296 "Audrey wanted" Anne Meacham to DS, Feb. 4, 1984.

296–297 "You must have" *Memoirs,* p. 228.

297 "swiveled about" Wood, p. 200.

297 "We were all" George Keathley to DS, Sept. 6, 1983.

297 "This was another" Cheryl Crawford to DS, Jan. 18, 1984.

297–298 "Audrey was" Robert Anderson to DS, Dec. 14, 1983.

298 "I want my name" Quoted by Bill Barnes to DS, Nov. 4, 1983.

298 "a very sad" Ray Stricklyn, "Memories of Tennessee," *Drama-Logue,* June 9–15, 1983.

299 "remnant of life" *The Theatre of Tennessee Williams,* vol. 5, p. 228.

300 "inviting disaster" *Ibid.,* pp. 291–292.

300 "In spite of a" Alfred Ryder to DS, Apr. 17, 1984.

300 "Tennessee was very gracious" Olive Deering to DS, Apr. 17, 1984.

301 "He liked people" Paul Morrissey to DS, Sept. 20, 1983.

302–303 "my inspiration" Quoted by Paul Morrissey to DS, Sept. 20, 1983.

303 "I need to" Jennings, p. 74.

303 "He had a sometimes" Paul Morrissey to DS, Sept. 20, 1983.

303 "I've had a" Eugene B. Griesman, "Williams: A Rebellious Puritan," *Chicago Sun-Times,* Mar. 27, 1983, p. 4.

303 "This is me" Quoted by Bill Barnes to DS, Nov. 4, 1983.

303 "must not only" *The Theatre of Tennessee Williams,* vol. 5, pp. 308–309.

304 "I consider myself" Patrick O'Haire, "Tennessee's Dream," *New York Daily News,* June 3, 1975, p. 43.

305 "His companion called" David Greggory to DS, Aug. 12, 1983.

305 "a number of" Maureen Stapleton to DS, Jan. 16, 1984.

306 "Near the end" Barbara Baxley to DS, Sept. 1, 1983.

306 "Don't you think" Quoted by Barbara Baxley to DS, Sept. 1, 1983.

306 "he was not" Choukri, unpaged introd.

306 "I take Nembutal" *Ibid.,* p. 38.

309 "The entire time" Harry Rasky, *Nobody Swings on Sunday* (Don Mills, Ontario: Collier Macmillan, 1980), p. 211.

309 "I never defined" Harry Rasky's film *Tennessee Williams' South.*

309 "I love to" Jennings, p. 84.

309 "My obligation is" Encyclopedia Britannica film, *Theatre in Process.*

310 "In Key West" Edwin Sherin to DS, Sept. 17, 1983.

310 "This country has" *New York Times,* May 6, 1975, p. 48.

312 "Dreadful" Kevin Kelly, "New Williams Play Opens," *Boston Globe,* June 19, 1975, p. 25.

312 "unfocused" Elliot Norton, "Tennessee Williams's New 'Red Devil' Here," *Boston Herald American,* June 19, 1975, p. 14.

312 "Part of what" David Greggory to DS, Aug. 12, 1983.

313 "By this time" Maureen Stapleton to DS, Jan. 16, 1984.

313 "Tennessee came" Theodore Mann to DS, Oct. 3, 1983.

313 "There was a lot" Gene Persson to DS, Sept. 17, 1983.

314 "During rehearsals" *Ibid.*

315 "a sadly" Stanley Eichelbaum, *San Francisco Examiner,* Jan. 21, 1976; reprinted in *New York Times,* Jan. 25, 1976, sec. 2, p. 5.

315 "terribly depressing" *Variety,* Feb. 4, 1976.

315 "He is such" Ruby Cohn, *Educational Theatre Journal* 28 (Oct. 1976): 406–407.

315 "At my age" Robert Hayes and Christopher Makos, "Tennessee Sings for Madame Sophia," *Interview,* vol. 6, no. 6 (June 1976), p. 20.

316 "Turning out" "Turning out the Bedside Lamp," *Androgyne, Mon Amour,* p. 88.

316 "Tennessee knew so" Galligan, p. 45.

316–317 "My first assignment" Dan Turner, "A Tennessee Waltz," *The Advocate* 376 (Sept. 15, 1983), p. 47.

317 "We simply couldn't" Chuck Ingebritsen to DS, Sept. 2, 1983.

318–319 "At our first" Gloria Hope Sher to DS, Sept. 26, 1983.

319 "We met at" George Whitmore to DS, Sept. 16, 1983.

319 "People so wish" Whitmore, pp. 319, 320, 315.

319 "a great deal" *Ibid.,* p. 313.

320 "Tennessee kept saying" Gene Persson to DS, Sept. 17, 1983.

320 "He made extensive" Theodore Mann to DS, Oct. 3, 1983.

320 "He was staggering" Gene Persson to DS, Sept. 17, 1983.

Chapter Ten

323 "He seemed" Gene Persson to DS, Sept. 17, 1983.

324 *"Garden District* is" Arthur Alan Seidelman, "Tennessee Williams: Author and Director Discuss *Vieux Carré,"* *Interview,* vol. 7, no. 4 (April 1977), p. 14.

324-325 "When I first" Sylvia Sidney to DS, July 30, 1983.

325 "individually attacked" Richard Alfieri, "Tennessee Williams: A Remembrance," *Mandate,* Sept. 1983, p. 38.

325 "hard-to-hear" Klemsrud, p. 51.

325 "very nervous" Richard Alfieri to DS, Oct. 7, 1983.

325 "He was so" Bill Barnes to DS, Nov. 4, 1983.

326 "I don't think" Bernard Carragher, "Born-Again Playwright: Tennessee," *New York Sunday News,* May 8, 1977, pp. L3 and L14.

326 "The day after" Sylvia Sidney to DS, July 30, 1983.

326 "Tennessee Williams's voice" Walter Kerr, "A Touch of the Poet Isn't Enough to Sustain Williams's Latest Play," *New York Times,* May 22, 1977, sec. 2, p. D5.

327 "But Tennessee put" Gene Persson to DS, Sept. 17, 1983.

328 "I have been" Blais.

329 "He was bright" Elliot Martin to DS, Oct. 19, 1983.

330 "Tennessee was cool" Craig Anderson to DS, Sept. 14, 1983.

330 "a fairly fragile" Elena Azuola to DS, Sept. 14, 1983.

330 "the pills and" Craig Anderson to DS, Sept. 14, 1983.

330 "He became something" *Ibid.*

331 "He made us feel" Elliot Martin to DS, Oct. 19, 1983.

331 "After the unfortunate" Craig Anderson to DS, Sept. 14, 1983.

331 "We spent a" Sylvia Miles to DS, Aug. 23, 1983.

332 "He seemed more" Elena Azuola to DS, Sept. 14, 1983.

332 "He was very" Craig Anderson to DS, Sept. 14, 1983.

332 "He hated the" Vassilis Voglis to DS, Sept. 22, 1983.

333 "I helped him" Jay Leo Colt to DS, Nov. 8, 1983.

333 "The real trouble" Mitch Douglas to DS, Oct. 11, 1983.

333 "As the rehearsals" Craig Anderson to DS, Sept. 14, 1983.

335 "Fontis was a" Blais.

335 "Maybe they weren't" *Ibid.*

335 "I suspect I'll" *People,* May 7, 1979, p. 34.

335 "he became very" Gloria Hope Sher to DS, Sept. 26, 1983.

336 "Unfortunately" Mitch Douglas to DS, Oct. 11, 1983.

337-338 "Mitch cared deeply" Eve Adamson to DS, Oct. 3, 1983.

338 "Tennessee had great faith" Mitch Douglas to DS, Oct. 11, 1983.

338 "He revised it" Eve Adamson to DS, Oct. 3, 1983.

338 "trying to shock" Mitch Douglas to DS, Oct. 11, 1983.

338-339 "We designed it" Eve Adamson to DS, Oct. 3, 1983.

339n "Call it" Hornack, p. 33.

339 "Tennessee just backed" Elliot Martin to DS, Oct. 19, 1983.

340 "chuckling wickedly" Frazer, p. 32.

340 "the worst case" Quoted in Frazer, p. 34.

340 "his paranoia" Frazer, p. 37.

340 "One comes out" Elia Kazan at the John F. Kennedy Center, Dec. 2, 1979.

341 "He was absolutely" Eve Adamson to DS, Oct. 3, 1983.

341 "very, very painful" Quintero (b), p. 5.

341 "We got to" Elliot Martin to DS, Nov. 2, 1983.

341-342 "Williams refused" Stephen Silverman, in a letter to DS, Nov. 25, 1983.

342 "He came to" William Seeker to DS, Nov. 11, 1983.

344 "He seemed in" Elliot Martin to DS, Nov. 2, 1983.

344 "The morning after" Galligan, p. 46.

344 "We discussed" Elliot Martin to DS, Nov. 2, 1983.

345 "That's so silly" Blum, p. 29.

345 "It's not about" Elliot Martin to DS, Nov. 2, 1983.

345 "At one point" Weatherby, p. 38.

346 "Tennessee was a" Vassilis Voglis to DS, Sept. 22, 1983.

346 "I was spending" Mitch Douglas to DS, Oct. 11, 1983.

346 "I can stand" Quoted by Lucy Freeman, Sept. 1, 1983.

346-347 "I cannot feel" Blais. See also *New York Post,* Dec. 3, 1976, p. 31.

347 "I think there" Maureen Stapleton to DS, Jan. 16, 1984.

347 "When he wanted" Mitch Douglas to DS, Oct. 11, 1983.

347 "They gave me" Giuseppe Di Bernardo (tran. DS), "Desiderio a Taormina," *La Sicilia,* July 9, 1980.

347-348 "Gary introduced me" Gregory Mosher to DS, Oct. 10, 1983.

348 "He was staying" *Ibid.*

348-349 "By this time" Mitch Douglas to DS, Oct. 11, 1983.

350-351 "After Tennessee emerged" Gregory Mosher to DS, Oct. 10, 1983.

351 "It was hard" Bonnie Sue Arp to DS, Oct. 28, 1983.

351 "a blessed man" Marji Bank to DS, Oct. 28, 1983.

351 "When [Gary] Tucker" Scott Jaeck to DS, Oct. 28, 1983.

351 "He became enamored" Rachel Stephens to DS, Oct. 28, 1983.

351 "and he never" Les Podewell to DS, Oct. 28, 1983.

352 "From what we" Scott Jaeck to DS, Oct. 28, 1983.

352 "His mood changed" Gregory Mosher to DS, Oct. 10, 1983.

352 "Chicago was the" At the Goodman Theatre, March 1981.

352-353 "There was a short" Mitch Douglas to DS, Oct. 11, 1983.

353 "I was a" Wood, p. 325.

354 "one of the most" Kakutani, p. C17.

355 "Tennessee was so" Eve Adamson to DS, Oct. 3, 1983.

355-356 "I saw Tennessee" Meade Roberts to DS, July 1, 1984.

356 "I'll have to think" *New York Times,* Nov. 20, 1981, p. 84.

356 "Harold, take care" Quoted by Larry D. Clark to DS, Oct. 21, 1983.

356 "He behaved very" Eve Adamson to DS, Oct. 3, 1984.

356-357 "The last time" Mitch Douglas to DS, Oct. 11, 1983.

357 "He was extremely" Vassilis Voglis to DS, Sept. 22, 1983.

357 "In Paradise" Quoted by Lester Persky to DS, Oct. 20, 1983.

358 "afflicted with" Christiansen (b), p. 6.

358 "Tennessee confronted" Elia Kazan to DS, Feb. 1, 1984.

359 "There was a strong" Scott Jaeck to DS, Oct. 28, 1983.

359 "inhabited by a rich" *Time,* June 28, 1982, p. 69.

359 "Give my goodbye" Hughes, p. 232.

360 "All the volcanoes" Andrews, p. 12.

360 "gentle and quiet" Carlo Panarello to DS, Dec. 30, 1983.

360–361 "He found traveling" Jane Smith to DS, June 13, 1984.

361 "He had bought" Gregory Mosher to DS, Oct. 10, 1983.

361–362 "As we were having" Steven Kunes, in letters to DS, Nov. 17, 1983 and Jan. 18, 1984.

362 "His speech was" Richard L. Kennedy, in a letter to DS, Mar. 12, 1984.

362–363 "When he came out" Jane Smith to DS, June 13, 1984.

363 "She called" Dakin Williams to DS, Oct. 23, 1983.

364 "It's too late" Quoted by Jane Smith to DS, June 13, 1984.

364 "He was so sad" Antonio Savoca to DS, Dec. 30, 1983.

364 "a cold wind" Quoted by Bill Barnes to DS, Nov. 4, 1983.

364 "I don't want" Gaines, p. 28.

364 "But I go mad" Jennings, p. 74.

364 "Old men go mad" *Androgyne, Mon Amour,* pp. 9–10.

Selective Bibliography

EACH of the following entries is preceded by the abbreviated form used in the Notes. Many sources, particularly newspaper and magazine articles, are not listed below but are cited only in the Notes.

Acton. Acton, Harold. *Memoirs of an Aesthete 1939-1969,* vol. 2. New York: Viking, 1970.

Andrews. Andrews, Nigel. "The Key to Tennessee," *Financial Times* (London), Aug. 7, 1982.

Barnett. Barnett, Lincoln. "Tennessee Williams," *Life,* Feb. 16, 1948; reprinted in Lincoln Barnett, *Writings on Life: Sixteen Close-Ups.* New York: William Sloane, 1951.

Bentley (a). Bentley, Eric. *The Dramatic Event: An American Chronicle.* New York: Horizon, 1954.

Bentley (b). ———. *In Search of Theatre.* New York: Knopf, 1953.

Berkvist. Berkvist, Robert. "Broadway Discovers Tennessee Williams," *New York Times,* Dec. 21, 1975.

Blais. Blais, Madeleine H. "Tennessee Williams Gracefully Survives, in Violent Key West," *Chicago Tribune,* Apr. 9, 1979.

Blum. Blum, David J. "The Art and Anger of Tennessee Williams," *Wall Street Journal,* Nov. 21, 1980.

Bosworth. Bosworth, Patricia. *Montgomery Clift.* New York: Harcourt Brace Jovanovich, 1978.

Brown. Brown, Cecil. "Interview with Tennessee Williams," *Partisan Review,* 45 (1978).

Buckley. Buckley, Tom. "Tennessee Williams Survives," *Atlantic* 226 (Nov. 1970).

Calendo. Calendo, John. "Tennessee Talks to John Calendo," *Interview,* April 1973.

Campbell. Campbell, Sandy. *Twenty-nine Letters from Coconut Grove.* Verona: Stamperia Valdonega, 1974.

Carr. Carr, Virginia Spenser. *The Lonely Hunter: A Biography of Carson McCullers.* New York: Doubleday, 1975.

Choukri. Choukri, Mohamed. *Tennessee Williams in Tangier.* Santa Barbara: Cadmus Editions, 1979.

Christiansen (a). Christiansen, Richard. "At 70, Even Tennessee Williams is Impressed," *New York Daily News,* Apr. 23, 1981.

Christiansen (*b*). ———. "The Pain, Risk and Tumult of Staging Williams' New Play," *Chicago Tribune Arts and Books,* May 29, 1982.

Ciment. Ciment, Michel. *Kazan on Kazan.* London: Secker & Warburg, 1973.

Cogley. Cogley, John. "More on 'Baby Doll,' " *Commonweal* 65, Feb. 1, 1957.

Cole. Cole, Toby and Helen Krich Chinoy. *Directors on Directing* (rev. ed.). Indianapolis/New York: Bobbs-Merrill, 1963.

Courtney. Courtney, Marguerite. *Laurette.* New York: Rinehart, 1955.

Crawford. Crawford, Cheryl. *One Naked Individual: My Fifty Years in the Theatre.* Indianapolis/New York: Bobbs-Merrill, 1977.

Davis. Davis, Louise. "That Baby Doll Man," *Nashville Tennessean Magazine,* Mar. 3, 1957.

DLB. Dictionary of Literary Biography: Documentary Series, 4. Detroit: Gale Research, 1984.

Donahue. Donahue, Francis. *The Dramatic World of Tennessee Williams.* New York: Frederick Ungar, 1964.

Evans. Evans, Oliver. "A Pleasant Evening with Yukio Mishima," *Esquire* 77 (May 1972).

Falk. Falk, Signi. *Tennessee Williams.* Boston: Twayne/G. K. Hall, 1978.

Frazer. Frazer, Winifred L. "A Day in the Life of Tennessee Williams," *The Tennessee Williams Review,* vol. 3, no. 2 (1982).

Funke (*a*). Funke, Lewis. "Williams Revival? Ask the Playwright," *New York Times,* Jan. 8, 1970.

Funke (*b*). ———, and John E. Booth, "Williams on Williams," *Theatre Arts* 46 (Jan. 1962).

Gaines. Gaines, Jim. "A Talk about Life and Style with Tennessee Williams," *Saturday Review of Literature,* 44 (Apr. 29, 1972)

Galligan. Galligan, David. "Director José Quintero: Recollections of a Friendship," *The Advocate,* 376 (Sept. 15, 1983).

Gassner. Gassner, John. *Theatre at the Crossroads.* New York: Holt, Rinehart & Winston, 1960.

Gelb. Gelb, Arthur. "Williams and Kazan and the Big Walkout," *New York Times,* May 1, 1960.

Goodman. Goodman, L. S. and A. Gilman. *The Pharmacological Basis of Therapeutics.* New York: Macmillan, 1975.

Hewes. Hewes, Henry. "Broadway Postscript," *Saturday Review,* 35 (June 21, 1952).

Hirshhorn. Hirshhorn, Clive. "When I'm Alone It's Just Hell," *London Sunday Express,* Mar. 28, 1965.

Hornak. Hornak, Richard Wray. Review of *Kirche, Kutchen und Kinder, The Tennessee Williams Newsletter,* vol. 2, no. 1 (Spring 1980).

Hughes. Hughes, Catherine. "Tennessee Williams, Remembered." *America,* Mar. 26, 1983.

Ingersoll. Ingersoll, Louise. *Lanier: A Geneology of the family who came to Virginia and their French ancestors in London.* Springfield, Va.: Goetz Printing Co., 1981.

Isherwood. Isherwood, Christopher. *My Guru and His Disciple.* New York: Farrar, Straus & Giroux, 1980.

Jennings. Jennings, C. Robert. *"Playboy* Interview: Tennessee Williams," *Playboy* 20 (April 1973).

Kakutani. Kakutani, Michiko. "Tennessee Williams: 'I Keep Writing. Sometimes I Am Pleased,'" *New York Times,* Aug. 13, 1981.

Keith. Keith, Don Lee. "New Tennessee Williams Rises from 'Stoned Age,'" *New Orleans Times-Picayune,* Oct. 18, 1970.

Klemsrud. Klemsrud, Judy. "Tennessee Williams Is a Reluctant Performer for an Audience of High School Students," *New York Times,* Mar. 13, 1977.

Langner. Langner, Lawrence. *The Magic Curtain.* New York: Dutton, 1951.

Leavitt. Leavitt, Richard, ed. *The World of Tennessee Williams.* New York: G.P. Putnam's Sons, 1978.

Lewis. Lewis, R.C. "A Playwright Named Tennessee," *New York Times Magazine,* Dec. 7, 1947.

Londré. Londré, Felicia Hardison. *Tennessee Williams.* New York: Frederick Ungar, 1979.

Maxwell. Maxwell, Gilbert. *Tennessee Williams and Freinds.* Cleveland: World, 1965.

Michelfelder. Michelfelder, William F. "Tennessee Williams, Sensitive Poet, Still Searches for Serenity," *New York World-Telegram and Sun,* Mar. 11, 1959.

Miller. Miller, Arthur. "An Eloquence and Amplitude of Feeling," *TV Guide,* Mar. 3, 1984.

Nathan. Nathan, George Jean. *The Theatre Book of the Year 1944-1945.* New York: Knopf, 1945.

Nelson. Nelson, Benjamin. *Tennessee Williams: The Man and His Work.* New York: Obolensky, 1961.

Newlove. Newlove, Donald. "A Dream of Tennessee Williams," *Esquire* 72 (November 1969).

Nicklaus. Nicklaus, Frederick. *The Man Who Bit the Sun: Poems.* New York: New Directions, 1964.

Nightingale. Nightingale, Benedict. "This 'Menagerie' Is Much Too Cozy," *New York Times,* Dec. 11, 1983.

Popkin. Popkin, Henry. "The Plays of Tennessee Williams," *Tulane Drama Review,* 4 (Mar. 1960).

Quintero (a). Quintero, José. *If You Don't Dance They Beat You.* Boston: Little, Brown, 1974.

Quintero (b). ———. "The Imprint He Left," *Performing Arts,* vol. 17, no. 8 (Aug. 1983).

Reed. Reed, Rex. "Tennessee Williams Turns Sixty," *Esquire,* 76 (Sept. 1971).

Rice. Rice, Robert. "A Man Named Tennessee." *New York Post,* Apr. 21 through May 4, 1958.

Ross (a). Ross, Don. "Williams on Art and Morals," *New York Herald-Tribune,* Mar. 3, 1957.

Ross (b). ———. "Williams on a Hot Tin Roof," *New York Herald-Tribune,* Jan. 5, 1958.

Schumach. Schumach, Murray. "Tennessee Williams Expresses Fear for Life in Note to Brother," *New York Times,* June 29, 1969.

Selznick. Selznick, Irene Mayer. *A Private View.* New York: Knopf, 1983.

Sheaffer. Sheaffer, Louis. *O'Neill: Son and Playwright.* Boston: Little, Brown, 1968.

Smith, Helen C. Smith, Helen C. "Williams's Atlanta Visit Proof 'I'm Hanging In There, Baby,'" *Atlanta Constitution,* Feb. 12, 1980.

Smith, William Jay. Smith, William Jay. *Army Brat.* New York: Penguin, 1982.

Stang. Stang, Joanne. "Williams: 20 Years After 'Glass Managerie.' " *New York Times,* Mar. 28, 1965.

Stanton. Stanton, Stephen S., ed. *Tennessee Williams: A Collection of Critical Essays.* Englewood Cliffs: Prentice-Hall, 1977.

Steen. Steen, Mike. *A Look at Tennessee Williams.* New York: Hawthorn, 1969.

Stein. Stein, Harry. "A Day in the Life: Tennessee Williams," *Esquire,* 91 (June 5, 1979).

Tharpe. Tharpe, Jac, ed. *Tennessee Williams: 13 Essays.* Jackson: University Press of Mississippi, 1980.

Tischler. Tischler, Nancy M. *Rebellious Puritan.* New York: Citadel, 1961.

Vidal. Vidal, Gore. "Selected Memories of the Glorious Bird and an Earlier Self," *Matters of Fact and Fiction (Essays 1973-1976).* New York: Vintage, 1978.

Wagner. Wagner, Walter. "Playwright as Individual: A Conversation with Tennessee Williams," *Playbill,* 3 (Mar. 1966).

Wallace. Wallace, Mike *Mike Wallace Asks: Highlights from 46 Controversial Interviews* New York: Simon & Schuster, 1958.

Washburn. Washburn, Beatrice. "Tennessee Williams," *Miami Herald,* Jan. 22, 1956.

Weatherby. Weatherby, W.J. "Scott and Zelda Relive the Jazz Age," *London Sunday Times,* Mar. 29, 1980.

Webster. Webster, Margaret. *Don't Put Your Daughter on the Stage.* New York: Knopf, 1972.

Whitmore. Whitmore, George. "Interview: Tennessee Williams," *Gay Sunshine Interviews,* vol. 1. San Francisco: Gay Sunshine Press, 1978.

Williams, Dakin. Williams, Dakin, and Shepherd Mead. *Tennessee Williams: An Intimate Biography.* New York: Arbor House, 1983.

Williams, Edwina Dakin. Williams, Edwina Dakin, as told to Lucy Freeman. *Remember Me To Tom.* New York: G.P. Putnam's Sons, 1963.

Winakor. Winakor, Bess. "Tennessee's 'Out Cry,' " *Woman's Wear Daily,* June 28, 1971.

Windham (a). Windham, Donald. *Footnote to a Friendship.* Verona: Stamperia Valdonega, 1983.

Windham (b). ———, ed. *Tennessee Williams' Letters to Donald Windham 1940-1965.* New York: Holt, Rinehart and Winston, 1977.

Wood. Wood, Audrey, with Max Wilk. *Represented by Audrey Wood.* New York: Doubleday, 1981.

Young. Young, Michael C. "The Play of Memory," *The Tennessee Williams Newsletter,* vol. 2, no. 2 (Fall 1980).

Index

Other titles of interest

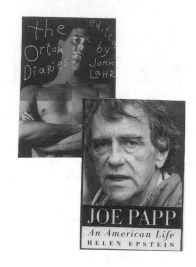